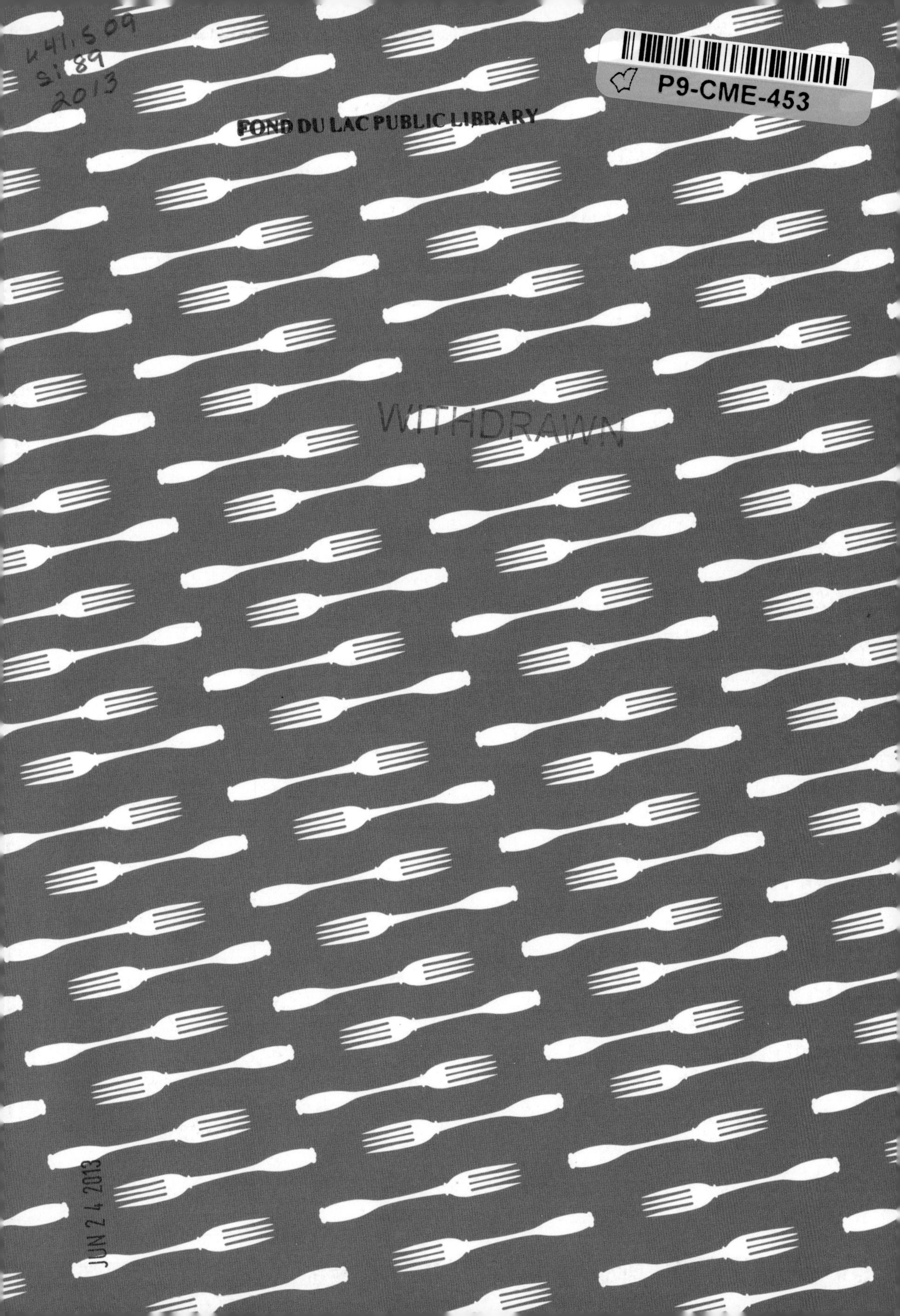

A HISTORY OF FOOD IN 100 RECIPES

WILLIAM SITWELL

LITTLE, BROWN AND COMPANY
New York Boston London

For Laura

Little, Brown and Company
Hachette Book Group
237 Park Avenue, New York, NY 10017
littlebrown.com

First Edition: June 2013

A version of this book was previously published in the UK by Collins, copyright © by William Sitwell, 2012.

Little, Brown and Company is a division of Hachette Book Group, Inc. The Little, Brown name and logo are trademarks of Hachette Book Group, Inc.

The publisher is not responsible for websites (or their content) that are not owned by the publisher.

ISBN 978-0-316-22997-5
LCCN 2013930038

10 9 8 7 6 5 4 3 2 1

Printed in China

Contents

About the Author

William Sitwell is the editor of *Waitrose Kitchen* magazine, can regularly be seen on TV programs such as BBC2's *Food & Drink* and *MasterChef: The Professionals,* and writes about food for a variety of newspapers and magazines. Following an early career in newspapers, he came to prominence in the food world after 1999 when he joined the then titled *Waitrose Food Illustrated,* of which he became editor in 2002. He subsequently won a string of awards, including "Editor of the Year" in 2005, for the magazine's writing, stories, design and photography. He spends his spare time growing vegetables, cooking, and making cider at his home in Northamptonshire, England, where he lives with his wife, Laura, and their children, Alice and Albert. This is his first book.

© Simon Brown

Introduction

After an auction at Sotheby's, London, in the summer of July 2010, I came away with an armful of nineteenth-century cookery books and a smattering of food-related paintings and cartoons. They had been a tiny part of a vast culinary collection owned by one Stanley J. Steeger, a collector from New York. Now, as I took them to my home in the English countryside, they would be a large part of a rather small collection of one William R. S. Sitwell.

There on a shelf in my study, a room filled with giant photographs of food—ripened figs in a bowl, peas in a pod and a Damien Hirst–style "shark in jelly"—the books added intellectual and historical weight to what I already had. There were cookery books sent to me by publishers and PRs over the years hoping for coverage in the food magazine I edit, autobiographies penned by famous chefs I know and the odd food tome that I had actually paid for.

I started leafing through the old books I had bought, slightly wondering if, while they certainly gave character to the shelf, they would be as dry to read as they looked from their tired bindings and browned paper. But I was quickly struck by the characterful writing that leapt from so many of the pages. Where I had expected placid cooking instruction I found verbose opinion. Entries in the nineteenth-century *Cassell's Dictionary of Cookery,* for instance, were filled with radical opinion and comment. "It is a shocking thought that many die annually of absolute starvation, whose lives might have been saved twenty times over," wrote the editor, A. G. Payne, in a long and ranting introduction.

That view sounded rather familiar, I thought. "Scraps of meat, fag ends of pieces of bacon, too often wasted, with a little judicious management, make a nice dish of rissoles," it continued, making the idea that using leftovers was "fashionable"—as promulgated in magazines such as mine—seem laughably prosaic.

I came across the writings of Dr. William Kitchiner in his hilarious 1817 *Cook's Oracle,* in which, aside from describing in every gory detail some of the cruelest cooking practices he had ever heard of (don't worry—I've also conveyed it with no stone left unturned, see p. 180), he lambasted those who had written cookbooks before him. Most, he wrote, were of no more use "than reading 'Robinson Crusoe' would enable a sailor to steer safely from England to India." He despaired of those who suggested of "a bit of this—a handful of that—a pinch of t'other—a dust of flour—a shake of pepper—a squeeze of lemon." Such recipes left him bewildered. By contrast, Kitchiner promised that he would give the reader "precision [that] has never before been attempted in cookery books." In a similar vein was Jules Gouffé—chef de cuisine of the Paris Jockey Club—in whose *Royal Cookery Book* of 1868 he attacked "the perfect uselessness of such cookery books as have hitherto been published."

This all sounded very familiar. Didn't every PR sending me a new cookbook from the latest culinary sensation claim that there hadn't been one quite like this one, that no previous book had been written with such clarity, that the recipes in this book really worked, that it was a new style of cooking guaranteed to capture the public's imagination?

Deciding to delve a little deeper, I soon came across Hannah Glasse, who had published *The Art of Cookery Made Plain and Easy* in 1747. It could have been 2011. Her book, she declared, "far exceeds anything of the kind ever yet published. I believe I have attempted a brand of cookery which nobody has yet thought worth their while to write upon."

Then back in 1500 there was *This Boke of Cokery* in which the anonymous author stated: "Here begynneth a noble boke of festes ryalle and cookery a boke for a princes household or any other estates and the makynge therof according as ye shall find more playnely with this boke." The inference is clear: this boke was plainer, simpler and clearer than any other boke.

As well as such bold claims of authenticity and brilliance, it struck me that across the centuries the characters making these claims were as strong as the sentiments they expressed. In other words, there is nothing new about chefs today being mad, bad, passionate, obsessive foodie fanatics. Furious rages echo out of kitchens throughout history, as does a passion for the best ingredients. Just as in the late 1980s Marco Pierre White was throwing the contents of a badly arranged cheese board at the wall of his restaurant, back in 350 BC the Sicilian Archestratus was losing his rag. If you wanted good honey, he said, it was only worth getting the stuff from Attica, otherwise you might as well "be buried measureless fathoms underground." And if you didn't cook simply and poured sauce over everything, you might as well be "preparing a tasty dish of dogfish."

Just as the passions of chefs, producers and consumers of food have brought the subject of food alive for me over the years, so this book is an investigation into, and a tribute to, the passionate people who have driven its story forward over the centuries. Were it not for a few rampant gourmands like the sauce-loving Apicius who in AD 10 wrote the only surviving cookbook from ancient Rome, or cheese-obsessed Pantaleone da Confienza sniffing his way around the dairies of Europe in the mid-fifteenth century, the dim and distant past would be a great deal dimmer and considerably less tasty.

Those figures throughout history who write about food tended to be as opinionated authors as they were rampant gourmands. I came across Eliza Leslie, for example, who was baking cakes in Philadelphia in the 1850s when she wasn't instructing young girls on how to behave, via *Miss Leslie's Behaviour Book.* Never, went one piece of advice, "play a piano in public unless invited." She also had a word or two to say about her cousins on the other side of the pond.

"There is no doubt that by the masses, better English is spoken in America than in England," she intoned. But her place is assured in food history thanks to her 1828 book, *Seventy-five Receipts for Pastry, Cakes and Sweetmeats,* containing the first-ever printed recipe for a cupcake.

And what of cookery teacher Fannie Farmer? America's answer to Britain's Mrs. Beeton? She was the woman behind the celebrated *Boston Cooking-School Cook Book* of 1896, containing not only the wonderfully alliterative recipe for "Fannie Farmer's Fudge" but firm advice on the dangers of drinking too much tea. "When taken to excess," she declared, it can "make a complete wreck of its victim."

Latterly there was Julia Child, who with her seminal *Mastering the Art of French Cooking* of 1961 taught a generation of American women to cook simple French food and once said of those who thought her obsessive about her subject: "I find that if people aren't interested in food, I'm not very much interested in them."

If I hadn't immersed myself in this subject, I'd never have come across some of the forgotten heroes of food history. There was Frenchman Denis Papin, for example, who invented the pressure cooker in the 1680s, but, ignored by everyone, died in poverty. It was others who, after Papin's death, discovered his "steam digester" or "Engine for Softening Bones," patented the plans and made a fortune.

Then there was Englishman Thomas Coryat, lampooned for championing the fork in 1611, and Clarence Saunders who created the format for the modern supermarket in Memphis in 1916 with his store Piggly Wiggly.

The history of food is colored by such individuals who enveloped themselves in their subject. The foodie exploits of some, the recipes of others help to tell this wonderful story. And this book is my partisan selection of what I reckon are the 100 best "chapters" in that story: the biggest characters, the occasional culinary villain and some of the most delicious food ever cooked, with recipes ranging from the dead simple ancient Egyptian bread (see p. 11) to the downright complicated "meat fruit" (see p. 348).

It's the story of constant stealing of recipes—from Platina's pilfering of the works of Martino de Rossi in 1475 to the theft of content from Epicurious.com in 2011. It charts the rise of British and American food and restaurant culture, and in following the rise of consumerism it considers the delights of supermarket convenience versus the well-being of the planet. And it's the account of the influences of kings, queens, conquistadors, cooks, restaurateurs and greedy pigs like me who live, breathe and talk food and are constantly on the lookout for as good a meal as we can lay our hands on.

William Sitwell
Plumpton, Northamptonshire

A note on the recipes

Unusually for a volume entitled *A History of Food in 100 Recipes* not every one of the ensuing chapters has an actual recipe and neither are they all eminently or indeed easily cookable. My ambition for the book is to take you on a journey where each stop gives you a colorful insight into the food scene of a particular period. Unfortunately in the early stages of this history not all the key players were as diligent in writing down their recipes as a cook might be today. As you'll discover, for example, there are no Viking recipes, so I've relied on evidence from an Icelandic saga, which details the various marauding shenanigans of Grettir the Strong and his rival Atli the Red, who might not have been foodies but surely ate a lot of dried fish. Neither, indeed, is there a recipe for bread in the early stages of English history—we have to wait until the fifteenth century for that. But of course people were eating bread centuries before then, which is why you'll have to forgive me for instead describing details of the Bayeux Tapestry to provide a glimpse into alfresco prebattle catering from the eleventh century.

In other words, rather than give a modern interpretation of what someone might have cooked at a particular moment in history, my aim has been to provide an exact contemporary reference. And where I have dug up some ancient method of roasting beef or poaching mussels I haven't updated it—except to "translate" some of the trickier terms and old spellings—or provided a modern version of the recipe in question. I want you to simply read and enjoy the recipes as they were written down. So, perhaps uniquely, this is not a book where every recipe has been triple-tested, where the ingredients have been tweaked, changed and replaced so you can knock them out after a quick trip to your local supermarket. Denis Papin's steam-digester-prepared mackerel from the seventeenth century (see p. 115) will, I freely admit, be hard to reproduce at home, but then again so will Heston Blumenthal and Ashley Palmer-Watts's bang up-to-date "meat fruit" (see p. 348). This may not be a recipe book that promises practical cookery, but I hope you nevertheless find it a delicious read...

1

Ancient Egyptian bread

AUTHOR: Unknown, FROM: The wall of Senet's tomb, Luxor, Egypt

Crush the grain with sticks in a wooden container. Pass the crushed grain through a sieve to remove the husks. Using a grindstone, crush the grain still finer until you have a heap of white flour. Mix the flour with enough water to form a soft dough. Knead the dough in large jars, either by hand or by treading on it gently. Tear off pieces of the kneaded dough and shape into rounds. Either cook directly on a bed of hot ashes or place in moulds and set on a copper griddle over the hearth. Be attentive while cooking: once the bottom of the bread starts to brown, turn over and cook the other side.

On the hot, dusty sides of the hill of Sheikh Abd el-Qurna, overlooking the Nile valley near the ancient city of Thebes—now Luxor—you'll find the discreet and humble entrance to the tomb of Senet. Carved into the limestone mountain, it is one of hundreds of burial chambers in the area. The tombs were the funerary resting places of the nobles, officials who wielded power under the pharoahs in ancient Egypt.

Painted onto the walls of their tombs are scenes from daily existence that they wished to be replicated in the afterlife. So everything that was pleasant—happy memories, experiences and rituals—is recorded in detail, giving us a clear picture of everyday life 4,000 years ago. There are scenes of hunting, fishing, the harvesting of crops and grapes, feasting and general rural life.

Almost all of the tombs were for men, but Theban tomb number TT60 is the resting place of Senet. Hers is both the only known tomb for a woman dating from the Egyptian Middle Kingdom period, between 2055 and 1650, and the oldest burial chamber whose decorated walls have survived in good order. In addition to images of hunting, plowing and sowing, there are depictions of bread-making. These are so detailed and colorful that those who have seen the wall paintings attest to their overwhelming power. "We are," wrote Egyptologist Thierry Benderitter on viewing them in the 1970s, "in the presence of the exceptional representations of actual cooking in the Middle Kingdom."

But who was Senet herself? It appears that she was either the wife or mother of Antefoqer, a vizier—the most senior of men who stood between the pharaoh and his subjects—who served both King Amenemhat I and then his son Sesostris I at the start of the Twelfth Dynasty, between 1958 and 1913 BC. That she was accorded her own hypogeum, or private underground tomb, attests to Antefoqer's importance. Yet the entrance today has no majesty. Less grand than others on the same hill, it now has a brick entrance with a simple wooden door added in 1914 by the English Egyptologist Norman Davies.

Only very few tombs are open to the public. This one is rarely visited—entry being highly restricted—and photography is banned to prevent light damage to the wall paintings. Those permitted access must first maneuver past the endless rubble that surrounds the entrance before removing a pile of stones that frequently blocks the actual door in a crude but effective form of security. Once opened, the door reveals a long, narrow and bleak passageway extending into the tomb, its roof descending in height and adding to a sense of compression. The passage leads to a dusty square chamber where there's a statue of Senet herself, seated; a reconstruction, the sculpture having been found completely fragmented.

Beyond the chamber is another long passageway, but this one is bright with paintings, in colors of ocher, yellow, red and blue. The eye is drawn first to an image of Antefoqer hunting, posing majestically in a simple loincloth, his bow fully extended. Around his neck is an elaborate necklace of blue, green and white, while his wrists are adorned with matching bracelets.

There are images of greyhounds, hippos and beautifully drawn birds: geese, ducks and flamingos in a bright, sky-blue background. Gazelles and hares are chased by dogs. Birds are netted and fish—so detailed you can tell their variety—are hauled in from a pond. And then halfway down the 20-meter passage, on the right, are scenes of cooking.

There is meat preparation, for instance. Under the cooling protection of an awning, men butcher an ox. They hang pieces of meat on ropes, while others out in the sun tenderize it, tapping it with stones. To their right a man adds a bone to a cauldron of soup with one hand while stirring it with a stick in the other. Another roasts poultry on a skewer over a raised grill, while encouraging the embers with a mezzaluna-shaped fan. It is a hive of activity.

As is a precisely drawn recipe for bread-making, summarized at the top of this chapter. The images were not of course intended to instruct the household cook, but to help the departed soul have some decent, freshly baked bread in the afterlife. Yet it is a foundation that has informed bread-making for thousands of years.

The images not only show how flour is prepared from grain, they also record some chatting (deciphered from hieroglyphs) between the characters, painted near some of their heads like speech bubbles. First, two men crush the grain in a wooden container. "Down!" one orders as another replies, "I do as you wish." Next a woman passes the grain through a sieve to remove the husks, while her female companion grinds the grain even finer using a grindstone. In another image a girl kneads small rolls of dough in her hands, while another adds thin lines of it to some tall conical molds. Behind the girl a man can be seen placing the conical containers into an oven. He pokes the embers with one hand while protecting his face from the heat with another. But he's not happy with the state of the logs. "This firewood is green," he moans.

Meanwhile, another woman can be seen kneading a much larger piece of dough. She leans over a table, pressing and stretching it out. The finished dough is presum-

Egyptian bread-making depicted in a painting on the wall of Senet's tomb in Luxor.

ably destined for the bakery in an adjacent picture. Here a foreman stands holding a threateningly pointy-ended staff while he encourages his workers. Below him a man on his knees kneads dough and meekly says: "I do as you wish, I am hard at work." His coworker carries some dough in a reddish-brown mold toward a hearth where another pokes at the flames. While others are kneading dough by both treading or mixing it by hand, a final character can be seen turning a partially cooked piece of bread, which has turned brown in the hot ashes.

Bread made in this way was a staple food of ancient Egypt. The world's earliest loaves show how people had progressed in agriculture and in the techniques of milling, leavening and baking, although we can't be sure when they learned to use yeast to help the dough rise and produce a lighter loaf.

It's likely that the products of this early baking were a little like modern-day pita bread. A set of beer-making scenes that exist in the same passageway suggests ancient Egyptians were using yeast. It's needed to turn the sugar to alcohol and even if it was incorporated in its natural state, from yeast spores in the air, it was used at some point in ancient Egypt. Other hieroglyphs in tombs near Luxor show bread being left to rise near ovens, although the detailed scenes of grain being turned to dough in Senet's tomb do not include this part of the process. Perhaps some dough that had been left for a day rose a little due to the presence of airborne yeast and the baker enjoyed the resulting, fluffier loaf. (Although it is safe to assume that at that time he would not have understood the science behind the process—fermentation expanding the gluten proteins in the flour and causing the dough to expand.)

As bread- and beer-making often occurred in tandem, it could be, whether by accident or experiment, that some fermented brewing liquor was added to the dough. However, it did occur and using starter doughs (a soft lump from the previous day added to the next morning's batch) became common practice. The regular use of yeast to make leavened bread is evident, at least, from the Bible—Exodus 12:34 and 39, to be precise. As the Israelites fled from captivity in Egypt, "the people took their dough before it was leavened, their kneading troughs being bound up in their clothes upon their shoulders." The bread they made subsequently, as Exodus goes on to recount, was not a nice, airy country-style loaf: "And they baked unleavened cakes of the dough which they brought forth out of Egypt, for it was not leavened; because they were thrust out of Egypt, and could not tarry, neither had they prepared for themselves any victual."

Records show that in addition to bread, the ancient Egyptians enjoyed a diet rich in fruit, vegetables and poultry. They used herbs, from cumin to fenugreek, and that scenes of domestic cooking were considered important for the afterlife confirms that it was as vital a part of everyday life then as it is now.

2

Kanasu broth

(Meat and vegetable stew)

AUTHOR: Unknown, FROM: The Babylonian Collection

Recipe 23, tablet A, 21 kinds of meat broth and four kinds of vegetable broth. Kanasu Broth. Leg of mutton is used. Prepare water add fat. Samidu; coriander; cumin; and kanasu. Assemble all the ingredients in the cooking vessel, and sprinkle with crushed garlic. Then blend into the pot suhutinnu and mint.

Does the average Iraqi wandering the banks of the Tigris, munching on a minced meat kubbah, realize that he or she is treading a patch of land that 4,000 years ago saw the birth of haute cuisine?

While the Middle Kingdom of ancient Egypt developed some of the rudiments of cooking (see p. 11), Mesopotamia, which occupied the patch between the Tigris and Euphrates rivers, became a gastronomically advanced civilization. The land was fertile, more fertile than today. Indeed, the people had an extraordinarily diverse diet that featured many kinds of vegetable, including leeks, shallots, garlic, rocket, chickpeas, lentils, lettuce, peas, figs, pomegranates and much more. They ate a huge diversity of cheese, up to 300 different kinds of bread and an amazing variety of soup. A Mesopotamian's supper of bread, soup and cheese might be more sophisticated than our own.

Recipe for Kanasu broth carved on a clay tablet.

We know all this from detailed records. But while today you might sketch out a recipe on a notepad, publish it in a book, put it online or on an iPhone app, in those days it was a rather more laborious process. Firstly, assuming you were a member of the rarefied and literate professional classes, you made a clay tablet, then, presumably while it was still wet, with a blunt reed stylus you slowly carved out your recipe in Akkadian cuneiform, an ancient pictorial precursor of alphabetic writing.

Many such stone tablets have lasted and survived more or less intact. At the New England university of Yale, a large number of tablets are stored as part of its Babylonian Collection, among some 40,000 artifacts acquired by the university in 1933. In an effort to preserve the tablets further, the curators had them baked and then had them copied. For many years it was assumed that the inscriptions were obscure pharmaceutical formulas but then French Assyriologist Jean Bottéro took a closer look, reporting his findings in 2004.

Focusing initially on three cracked, caramel-colored tablets, he managed to decipher the code and on reading them discovered that they weren't complicated equations, just recipes. The tablets revealed a rich variety of cuisine, moreover, a sophisticated mix of skill and artistry and a wonderful breadth of ingredients. Among the tablets, on a piece of clay measuring just 12 by 16 centimeters, is the recipe for kanasu broth.

Kanasu, ancient wheat—not dissimilar to durum—was mixed into a lamb stew as a thickener. Think of it as lamb casserole cooked with pearl barley. The recipe itself is brief, partly due to the time it would have taken to scratch it onto the clay and partly, as Bottéro believes, the recording of the dish constituted a kind of ritual. This wasn't a recipe for the beginner, either: with no quantities or cooking times, it assumes a fair degree of culinary know-how.

The lamb stew is just one of twenty-one meat- and vegetable-based dishes, but it sounds a little tastier than some of the other recipes, such as one for braised turnips that begins: "Meat is not needed. Boil water. Throw fat in." Because many of the ingredients need some deciphering—samidu, for instance, was either semolina or fine white flour used for thickening, while suhutinnu was probably a root vegetable like a carrot or a parsnip—they can be hard to replicate in the modern kitchen. Indeed, having spent years deciphering the recipes, Bottéro—himself an accomplished cook—declared: "I would not wish such meals on any save my worst enemies." He may have been thinking of grasshoppers in a fermented sauce, which turns up in one of the tablets. By constrast, an editorial in the *New Haven Register* gave the thumbs-up to Bottéro's decoded recipe for kanasu broth, stating: "You can almost smell the 4,000-year-old leg of lamb bubbling in a sauce thick with mysterious Mesopotamian herbs."

While the dishes may not all be to the modern taste, the ingredients listed in the tablets are impressively varied, as are the various cooking techniques, suggesting that—given the number of tools required—these were dishes cooked in temples or palaces, rather than in the average home, in a mud hut, or cave, where equipment would have been rudimentary, to say the least. Recipes variously call for slicing, squeezing, pounding, steeping, shredding, marinating and straining. So even way back in the days when countries had eleven letters to their name, when people were inventing the wheel, reading the livers of chickens and believing that when you died you went underground and ate dirt, cooks were doing pretty much what most still do today.

3

Tiger nut sweets

AUTHOR: Unknown, FROM: *The Bible, Genesis 43:11*

And their father Israel said unto them, If *it must be* so now, do this; take of the best fruits in the land in your vessels, and carry down the man a present, a little balm, and a little honey, spices and myrrh, nuts and almonds.

Don't think that food in prehistorical times was entirely savory—all roasted lamb, flatbreads and chickpeas. After all they were human, just like you and me. And while I might crave a HobNob come four o'clock, so the ancients would have needed to sate their cravings for sweet things.

If we are to believe the story of Joseph's rise to prominence in Egypt—and a large entertainment industry depends on it, or his colorful coat, to be precise—then archaeological evidence suggests he may have lived around 1700 BC.

According to the biblical account, after Joseph's jealous brothers had forced him into exile—selling him as a slave to people traveling into Egypt—he rose in prominence partly due to his gift for interpreting dreams in which he advised the Pharoah to store up food during the good years, in anticipation of lean years to come. Sure enough those lean years came and people flocked from neighboring countries to buy grain, including Joseph's estranged brothers, looking for food to take back to famine-ravaged Canaan.

Joseph, rewarded with king-like status for his dream-interpreting and so grand now that they don't recognize him as their long-lost brother, permits them to take food back to their family, saying that they can have more food but only if they return with their younger brother Benjamin. This they tell their father back home, who is suspicious at first but then relents. He then sends off his sons with advice and a few things in their pockets that unwittingly ensures him a place in *A History of Food in 100 Recipes*. For take a closer look at what he stuffs in those pockets: honey, spices, nuts and almonds. All the ingredients, in short, for tiger nuts.

No doubt he also popped a recipe for them in Benjamin's top pocket. It was an early example of the tradition of taking a sweet gift to someone as a sign of appreciation or affection. Fragments of such a recipe exist on scraps of parchment from the same era and they are called tiger nuts because they resemble the tuber root of the same name. They are thought to be the earliest sweets and, with their sticky mix of honey, dates, sesame seeds and almonds—blended together and rolled into balls—are pretty nutritious too. Try them after dinner with a dark, black cup of intense coffee. And make sure to don a dressing gown or cloak decorated with a patchwork of colors, for added authenticity.

A piece of fine parchment paper showing Genesis, the creation of the universe, from the magnificent Italian Renaissance Bible of Borso d'Este Vol 1.

4

Fish baked in fig leaves

AUTHOR: Archestratus, FROM: *Hedypatheia (Life of Luxury)*

You could not possibly spoil it even if you wanted to ... Wrap it [the fish] in fig leaves with a little marjoram. No cheese, no nonsense! Just place it gently in fig leaves and tie them up with a string, then put it under hot ashes.

Archestratus's mission in life was to visit as many lands as he could reach in search of good things to eat. A Sicilian, he ventured all over Greece, southern Italy, Asia Minor and areas around the Black Sea. He tasted his way to paradise and then recorded it in classical Greek hexameters. Not the way one might record recipes these days, but maybe he felt it added a lyrical nuance to his findings, as well as a playful parody of epic poetry.

The entire project was recorded in the form of a poem appropriately entitled *Hedypatheia* or "Life of Luxury." And while only fragments of it remain, there are enough of them for us to get a good idea of the food he ate, what he thought of it and, vitally, how it was cooked. Archestratus's writings on ingredients, dishes and his views on flavor combinations paint a picture of the well-to-do of ancient Greece in around 350 BC. Their tastes were cosmopolitan and they appear to fit the stereotypical image of them taught at school—lying languidly on couches, eating in a reclining position, grapes dangling from their fingers.

The poem shows Archestratus to be a man of strong likes and dislikes. He was not a great eater of meat, for instance, its link with religious sacrifice making it less appealing as a dish for feasting, but he loved sea and river food. Of the sixty-two fragments that remain of his poem, forty-eight concern fish. He divided these into two categories: tough fish that needed marinating and the finer type that could be cooked straight away. And his guiding principle in cooking it was simplicity. He believed that the better quality of the raw product, the fewer additional ingredients the cook needed to add. Cooking should be simple—preferably grilling with the lightest of seasoning and oil, such as in this recipe for cooking a variety of shark: "In the city of Torone you must buy belly steaks of the karkharias sprinkling them with cumin and not much salt. You will add nothing else, dear fellow, unless maybe green olive oil." The recipe for baked fish, at the top of this chapter, is prepared with a similar lack of fuss.

"All other methods are mere sidelines to my mind," he wrote. "Thick sauces poured over, cheese melted over, too much oil over—as if they were preparing a tasty dish of dogfish." Perhaps this was a rebellion against the meals he had endured as a child, which could be very rich as well as overabundant. As Plato wrote disparagingly: "[Sicily is] obsessed with food, a gluttonous place where men eat two banquets a day and never sleep alone at night."

As well as his disdain for sauces, Archestratus was insistent on what he considered worthy ingredients. "Eat what I recommend," he said. "All other delicacies are a sign of abject poverty—I mean boiled chickpeas, beans, apples and dried figs." And he was obsessed with where food came from and where the best ingredients were to be found. "Let it come from Byzantium if you want the best," he wrote, like the voiceover of an early product endorsement.

Of the few meats he liked—hare, deer, "sow's womb" and all sorts of birds, from geese to starlings and blackbirds (animals not used for sacrifice, that is)—he preferred the following method of serving: "[Bring] the roast meat in and serve to everyone while they are drinking, hot, simply sprinkled with salt, taking it from the spit while a little rare. Do not worry if you see ichor [blood—used normally with reference to the Greek gods] seeping from the meat, but eat greedily." As with cooking fish, the principles are of a dish simply prepared and served.

Highly opinionated Archestratus may have been, but he was also extremely knowledgeable. Indeed, he demonstrated a sophisticated appreciation of the various parts of a fish, writing of the subtle differences in texture between the flesh of the fin, belly, head or tail. Subsequent writers relied on his expertise. Athenaeus of Naucratis (see p. 30), author of the *Learned Banquet* in around AD 200 and a man without whom we would have little knowledge of the cultural pursuits of the ancient world, was much influenced by his predecessor. He wrote of Archestratus: "He diligently traveled all lands and sea in his desire . . . of tasting carefully the delights of the belly."

While his musings on food are appealingly vivacious, Archestratus's recipe writing is deliciously free and passion-fueled, such as when championing the finest-quality ingredients: "If you can't get hold of that [sugar], demand some Attic [Greek] honey, as that will set your cake off really well. This is the life of a freeman! Otherwise one might as well . . . be buried measureless fathoms underground." Probably the world's earliest cookbook, *Life of Luxury* has all the energy and color of a modern bestseller.

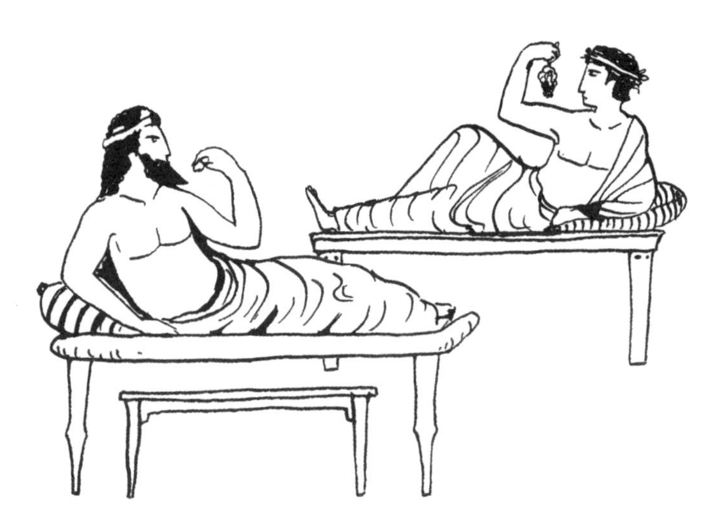

5

To salt ham

AUTHOR: Cato the Elder, FROM: *De agri cultura (On Farming)*

Salting of ham and *ofellae* [small chunks of pork] according to the Puteoli [a Roman colony in southern Italy] method. Hams should be salted as follows: in a vat, or in a big pot. After buying hams [legs of pork] cut off the hooves. Use half a *modius* [a dry measure equivalent to about 9 litres (2 gallons)] of ground Roman salt per each ham. Put some salt on the bottom of the vat or pot, and place the ham on it skin downwards and cover it with salt. Then, place the next ham on it skin downwards and cover it with salt in the same way. Take care that the meat does not touch … After all the hams are placed in this way, cover them with salt so that the meat cannot be seen; make the surface of the salt smooth. After the hams stay for five days in the salt, remove them all, each with its own salt. Those that were on top should be placed on the bottom and covered with salt as previously. After twelve days altogether take the hams out; remove the salt, hang them in a draught and cure them for two days. On the third day, take the hams down and clean them with a sponge, smear them with olive oil mixed with vinegar and hang them in the building where you keep the meat. No pest will attack them.

Roman politician Marcius Porcius Cato was brought up on a farm southeast of Rome near a city called Tusculum. He enlisted as a soldier at seventeen and later rose to high office as a statesman, known as a skillful orator who made use of his public-speaking prowess by chastising those in the Senate whom he felt were too liberal. This accorded with his latter role as censor, an official position that included supervising public morality and which he took to with enthusiasm. With his clamp-down on immoral officials and support of a law against luxury, he was identified with the job — known to posterity as Cato the Censor. He was censorious about those he thought were extravagant — he wouldn't have approved of the creamy sauces that came out of Apicius's kitchen 150 years later (see p. 26) — while the first-century historian Plutarch praised him not for any triumphs as military leader but that "by his discipline and temperance, [he] kept the Roman state from sinking into vice."

Perhaps it was his childhood on the farm that had instilled in the young Cato a Spartan frugality. His father apparently died while Cato was quite young and he inherited considerable responsibilities, learning the business of farming in his early teens. As an older man, he ate with his servants, was a strict parent, a harsh husband, an inflexible official and, by all accounts, a downright bore.

He was also a prolific author, although only fragments tend to remain of his writings. He wrote a history of Italy in Latin, published a collection of his speeches—including the deadly retrospective *On His Consulship* (he'd been a consul before discovering his métier as censor)—and a tome entitled *On Soldiery.* Not even fragments of the latter remain but one can imagine the sort of thing it might have included: dawn rises, cold showers, spotless uniforms and suicidal charging at the enemy.

But one volume that has survived completely intact is his *De agri cultura,* or "On Farming." A manual on good agricultural practice, it advises, for example, how many slaves to hire for the olive harvest and how—in one particularly charming note—a slave's ration might be reduced should he be so audacious as to fall ill. It also gives details on how to preserve food, including the earliest recorded description of how to salt pork—the recipe that heads this chapter. In addition Cato offers recipes for pickling and smoking, and his writings show that he had considerable expertise, employing methods that would be just as workable today.

Knowing how to preserve meat, fish or indeed fruit was vital in the centuries preceding the advent of the supermarket and the fridge (see pp. 212 and 222). Indeed Polish professor Maria Dembinska, writing in the late twentieth century, has described it as "the greatest worry of primitive man." In the days when finding food for everyday consumption was a trial, if not life-endangering, its preservation was all the more important. That ever-present fear of hunger challenged man's ingenuity to find methods to both preserve food and then store it effectively.

How much less meat we might waste today if we had to hunt it ourselves—if we had speared it while it was charging at us. Preserving food was necessary not just so that it would last beyond the weekend but because food might be sourced at quite a distance from where it would be consumed. So people buried food in situ. Excavations on the Irish and Norwegian coasts have uncovered bones, for example, from fish buried between 5000 and 2000 BC. That they were excavated shows a skill in burying fish, if not in retrieving it. Without a map to mark the spot, that fish remained buried for rather longer than was perhaps intended.

Herodotus, meanwhile, wrote 2400 years ago of the Babylonians and Egyptians drying fish in the wind and the sun. And meat was often hung in the roofs of houses. Perhaps that is how it came to be smoked—by mistake over a home fire, but resulting in another method of preserving food as well as enhancing the flavor. The Vikings may have developed this concept, although no records exist to confirm this (see p. 35). Once it was discovered that salt was a proficient preserver, that idea quickly spread too. By 1800 BC there were salt mines all over the place. Although many still preferred to bury their fish, particularly in the lands of the north.

A Swedish census from 1348 records the existence of a man called Olafuer Gravlax. He lived in Jamtland in central Sweden and as his surname means "buried fish" we can assume that that's what he did. Whoever first produced gravlax—cured salmon—in Scandinavia probably did it by mistake, his aim simply being to store fish for the winter season when freezing temperatures and ice-covered rivers and lakes would have made fishing almost impossible. Burying it also would have kept it away from thieves—from "those on two, as well as those on four legs," as the Norwegian author Astri Riddervold puts it.

So he buried his fish. Then when he dug it up months later, it would have stunk, horribly, having lain underground and then fermented. But, ignoring the smell, whoever dug it up then bravely tasted it and found it not just to be edible but to have a remarkable flavor, albeit very different from that of the fresh fish he had buried all those months before. It was a miracle. The following season, maybe he added salt to one fish, a little sugar to another and sugar and salt to another. Perhaps he then experimented to see what happened if he stored it for less time—a few months, weeks, then days.

Who knows quite how it happened and when it became an established practice. But people liked the tart taste and it became a culinary tradition, not to mention a commercial enterprise. Indeed, while Olafuer Gravlax buried fish he may not have run the entire business. This we can surmise from another record—this time in the 1509 annals of Stockholm—which lists one Martin Surlax, whose surname translates as "sour fish." So as sour fish is the result of burying fish, perhaps Mr. Gravlax buried it while Mr. Surlax dug it up.

Gravlax brings echoes of the 1980s, when it was all the rage in Britain, served at dinner parties with dill sauce. These days you don't of course need to bury it to make it as a trip to the supermarket makes its procurement rather easier. And with the addition of salt, sugar, dill and some spices (peppercorns and coriander seeds), you can even do your own burying—in the fridge for just two days. Back in the fourteenth century it wouldn't have been quite so straightforward, but those early fish buriers were clearly onto something. They may have been using their instincts when they added salt and sugar, but they were unknowingly engaging in a very complicated scientific process. The salt drew out the water but also refreshed the proteins and preserved the fish.

Be they medieval fish buriers who cured salmon for a living or a Roman disciplinarian who salted pork in his spare time, these early innovators used their ingenuity to keep hunger at bay. Meanwhile, the techniques that once staved off real hunger in former times now sate the greed of the modern snacker today. For where would we be without all those salty, sugary goodies to make us obese and thirsty?

6

Roast goat

AUTHOR: Virgil, FROM: *Georgics II:545*

Therefore to Bacchus duly will we sing,
Meet honour with ancestral hymns, and cakes
And dishes bear him; and the doomed goat
Led by the horn shall at the altar stand,
Whose entrails rich on hazel-spits we'll roast.

You may not consider Virgil to be a recipe writer, yet here is what amounts to a recipe for goat, roasted on an early version of a spit. And I'm not the only one who has cited this extract as a recipe. It was quoted back in the 1800s, to illustrate the simplicity of roasting as a cooking method. In a section entitled "The Ladies Department" in an 1825 edition of the U.S. publication the *American Farmer,* the poem is referred to with the comment that "Roasting is the most simple and direct application of heat in the preparation of food." While four years earlier, in 1821, Frederick Accum in his *Culinary Chemistry* also cites Virgil, going on to say: "Roasting on a spit appears to be the most ancient process of rendering animal food eatable by means of the action of heat."

Before metal spits were devised, meat would be skewered onto branches pulled from trees—often hazel wood, as in Virgil's poem. The sap in the wood, when heated, would make the branch turn (so long as the animal being cooked was light enough, such as a small bird like a lark; it wouldn't happen if you skewered a pig on it) and people who witnessed it thought it supernatural. Hazel was also used as a divining rod.

But quite how roasting came about can only be guessed at. For thousands of years the human race ate its food raw, and then between the discovery of how to make fire and the appearance of the Neanderthals, man began to cook his food. So at some point, while using fire for warmth or to ward off wild animals, a discovery was made. Did the spark from a fire catch light and burn down the lair of some wild pigs? Did man smell the roasting fat and try out the first pork scratchings? Or did a grazing mammoth fall into a fire pit, the smell of its cooked flesh wafting on the wind in an appetizing new aroma?

However it happened, man's use of fire to cook was revolutionary. It wasn't just the new flavor that it introduced to food, but the inedible then became edible. Items that could only be eaten when cooked—wheat, barley, rice, potatoes—were then worth cultivating. As man consumed more nutrients, his health must have benefited too. Furthermore, his use of fire for cooking is one of the decisive factors that separates him from other animals. When man cooks, he becomes fully human. Animals may store food—dogs bury bones, racoons douse their food in water—but only humans cook it.

Having learned to roast food, man then got all sophisticated and started boiling it. So where roasting—or burning—food distinguished us from animals, boiling was proof of civilization. The anthropologist Claude Lévi-Strauss muses on this point. In his essay "The Culinary Triangle," he thrashes out his theory on cooked food. "The roasted is on the side of nature, the boiled on the side of culture," he writes. This is literally true because boiling requires the use of a receptacle, a cultural object: "Boiling requires a mediation (by water) of the relation between food and fire which is absent in roasting."

Thus, as we became cultured so roasting was seen as primitive and basic, while boiling was regarded as sophisticated and classy. Until more recently, that is, as we became increasingly sophisticated and decided that roasting was in fact rather more upwardly mobile. After all, the urbane gentleman doesn't take pride in his ability to do a nice "Sunday boil."

But he probably wouldn't roast a goat either. Back in 30 BC, however, Publius Vergilius Maro—Virgil, to his friends—was more than happy to, and his reference to goat, spit-roast on hazel wood, comes in his epic work *The Georgics*. The Roman poet's most famous work after *The Aeneid,* this chiefly detailed methods of running a farm—instruction manuals for those entering the agricultural sector making for perkier reading when in verse. In it he writes of raising crops and planting trees, of keeping livestock and horses and beekeeping.

His reference to roasting goat comes after a section on pruning trees and then a note celebrating vineyards, whose vines teem with "mellowing fruit." With his mention of Bacchus, the goat roasting feels like a celebration of successful farming. The ensuing lines instruct on how to look after the soil with a few notes on hoeing.

As Virgil gracefully instructs one on correct farming practice, so he whets our appetites for a good roast, the flavors of which echo down the centuries as resonant as his poetry. He was writing at a time when Epicurean philosophy was popular, advocating an existence spent enjoying the good things in life. Food and friendship should transcend concerns about self. And how right he was.

7

Another sauce for fowl

AUTHOR: Marcus Gavius Apicius
FROM: *De re coquinaria (Of Culinary Matters)*

Pepper, lovage, parsley, dry mint, fennel, blossoms moistened with wine; add roasted nuts from Pontus or almonds, a little honey, wine, vinegar, and broth to taste. Put oil in a pot, and heat and stir the sauce, adding green celery seed, cat mint; carve the fowl and cover with the sauce.

His predecessor Archestratus (see p. 19) may have had a downer on sauce. Poncey and overelaborate, it engulfed good and simple ingredients. But Apicius was having none of it. He lived during the good times of ancient Rome, long before even the seeds of decline were sown.

If anyone ever asks you, "At which point did Rome reach its zenith and what precisely symbolized that moment?," remember the answer has nothing to do with beating back barbarians at the furthest reaches of the empire or with the building of public latrines. Rome was at its peak when its sauces were at their best, when they were plenty and at their richest. And we can pinpoint when this happened because Marcus Gavius Apicius wrote it all down. He lived between 80 BC and AD 40—during the reigns of both Augustus and Tiberius—and his cookbook is still in print, although unless you speak fluent Latin, I suggest you find an English translation. It's called *De re coquinaria*—"Of Culinary Matters"—and is a bumper read of some 500 recipes. And did I mention sauce? Well, 400 of those recipes are instructions for making a sauce.

Sauce was the trademark of the ancient Roman chef and if Apicius was not the best of them, then he is at least an astonishingly impeccable example. Some scholars argue that Apicius could have been one of several people, or a collection of recipes by several individuals garnered under the name of Apicius, but the good money is on him being the aforementioned M. G. Apicius. He was a chef, a collator of recipes and he endowed a school of cookery. If he were alive today he'd probably be running some Italian equivalent of Ballymaloe (the Irish cookery school near Cork).

He lived and breathed his craft. He inspired those he met with his culinary ideals and he was an exhausting mentor to anyone who could withstand his rigorous teaching methods. He was an obsessive: exacting, precise, detailed and, naturally, opinionated. He also had the good fortune to be well born and wealthy. When we talk about good food during the period of ancient Rome, this was not a democratic idea. Most people would have lived very, very simple lives, with few possessions. The prospect of a decent meal, let alone decadent feasting, was denied to many. For the vast majority meals were a frugal affair at best; the richness of Apicius's recipes therefore reflects only the dining habits of the elite. Of which he was a fully paid-up member.

Apicius had a vast fortune and he spent it on food. His kitchens would have been kitted out with all the latest mod cons. His cooking utensils were far more precious than ours as they would have been handmade, beautiful—works of art, even. By contrast, his apparatus for cooking food would have been basic (pots and a spit for roasting) and he seemed to make a virtue of his lack of chiller cabinets. At least that's the only reason I can think for his creation of a recipe "for birds of all kinds that have a goatish smell."

What he lacked in white goods, however, he made up for in kitchen staff. While good ingredients would have been hard to come by—this was a time when agriculture was haphazard, transportation limited and storage basic—once they were assembled there were plenty of people on hand to prepare and cook them. Perhaps this is one of the great differences between our age and his. Today ingredients are relatively cheap: we have access, within minutes, to ingredients from every corner of the earth. But while food is cheap, labor isn't. Apicius didn't just have cheap staff, he had free staff. What is unimaginable now was normal then—for the very rich, that is.

So we can picture Apicius beavering away with his dozens of kitchen underlings, chopping and prepping from dawn to dusk. Those lucky enough to work in his kitchen would have been dazzled by his ingredients. His larder would have been hung with hare, pork, lamb and endless fowl—from crane and duck to doves and peacocks, ostriches and flamingos. He cooked with truffles, all kinds of mushrooms, sea urchins, mussels, every type of fish. The herbs he used were of such variety that they take the breath away—from lovage and coriander to cumin and fennel seeds. He made wine reductions, pickled offcuts of pork and served up great gravy, and he wrote this all down in his recipes.

Apicius's book is Europe's oldest and ancient Rome's only surviving recipe book. As Joseph Vehling, who translated it into English in 1926, wrote: "The way to a man's heart is through his stomach; so here's hoping that we may find a better way of knowing old Rome and antique private life through the study of this cookery book." Yet it was never plain sailing. Apicius's recipes may paint a picture of luxurious dinners, of exquisite flavors and textures, but he had to deal with a bureaucracy that must have infuriated him.

Marcus Gavius Apicius.

Today, chefs and restaurateurs have to be much more than providers of good food. Aside from creating a restaurant worth eating at, they have to deal with council officials, inspectors and regulators, not to mention listening to the advice of their PRs and tolerating the critics. Apicius had his problems too. History books may carry the legends of Roman decadence but at the time many looked down upon those who enjoyed extravagant lifestyles. Writers such as Pliny and Plutarch disapproved of high living in the form of fine dining, let alone feasting. And they weren't alone—severe laws existed that fixed the amount a household could spend on specific types of food.

Senior politicians and officials felt a need to protect public morals. Not that it stretched to stopping people watching Christians being eaten by lions in the Colosseum. So imperial food inspectors were sent out to perform spot checks on kitchens, not dissimilar to how hygiene officials operate today. Fortunately there was another aspect of life that was rife back then: corruption. So one can imagine Apicius, on being told a posse of ingredient inspectors were on their way, dispatching one of his chefs to entertain the inspectors when they arrived. No doubt the food wardens would have been quickly seduced with promises of some tasty morsels for them to take home, a meal in the kitchen or very likely money, gold even. Because they clearly failed to stop the purchasing of expensive ingredients and the dinners for which they were intended.

Wealthy food-loving Romans thus easily brushed aside the food police and circumvented the law. Which meant they were able to indulge in Apicius's delectable food and, of course, his sauces. And there are sauces to accompany every meat you can think of, from hare and duck to lobster and sardines. But not the oft-mentioned "dormouse"—not so much a mouse as a large rodent that lived in trees (not unlike a squirrel). Apicius stuffed it with pork, nuts and herbs and then roasted or boiled it, but he can't have been that keen on it as he doesn't do a sauce to match. This aberration aside, there are so many sauces it's almost a frenzy. When he can't think what to call it, he just says, "Here's another one"—as you can see from the recipe heading this chapter.

His writing style is chatty when there's detail, of which there is often little. The language is of a busy, harassed man. He can be obscure and unhelpful, assuming a level of knowledge that would frustrate the novice. These days his publisher would have forced a ghostwriter on him. But instead we get the writings of a man focused on his work—after all he was a cook.

But reading between the lines he was also a humane chef. In those days many felt that the worse an animal suffered the better it tasted. Torturing some poor beast, it was thought, would bring out the flavor of the meat. Yet there are very few examples of this in Apicius's writings. The two exceptions being a starter that calls for a disjointed chicken (this being done before the bird was killed) and a fig-fed pig, in which the poor animal would be starved before being force-fed with dried figs and then given mead to drink. The figs then simply expanded or started to ferment, the liver enlarged and the pig died. (For the modern equivalent—foie gras, or "fat liver"—see p. 130.)

Apicius seemed less enamored of this sort of animal cruelty and keener on promoting the cooking of vegetables. If you're ever stuck for a recipe for cabbage, he's your man. He was also a master of the art of disguising food. This was less for economic and practical reasons—think mock turtle soup in later times—than for show. Although the jury is out as to whether his "anchovy paste without anchovy" might have been devised as an exquisite piece of trickery to fool and delight guests or simply concocted on the day he found he was all out of anchovies. With his extraordinary wealth, it was probably the former.

Apicius was a stickler for perfection, determined that his recipes should enlighten his readers and enhance their lives—although he wasn't big on puddings. Despite the Romans love of confectionery, you won't find any sweet dishes in this book. Perhaps this was one thing he sent out for.

But so great was his love of food that it did him in in the end. As he worked his way through his fortune—purchasing the likes of sea scorpions and Damascus plums or refurbishing his kitchen—his outgoings began to outstrip his income. So much so that when he was down to his last few blocks of gold, his last few million *sestertii,* he came to a grand conclusion. If he could no longer live in the manner to which he had become accustomed, if the quality of food that would pass his lips was anything less than what he aspired to, then it was not a life worth living.

So one day he gathered together his most appreciative friends and prepared one final, perfect banquet. Each dish was more exquisite than the previous one. But to one of his own dishes he added an individual twist. We'll never know if it was his "pumpkin fritters," "lentils and chestnuts" or "suckling pig stuffed two ways." But whatever it was, Apicius had poisoned it and he died.

8

Honeyed cheesecakes

AUTHOR: Athenaeus (quoting *Hebe's Wedding* by Epicharmus)
FROM: *Deipnosophistae (The Learned Banquet)*

Wheaten flour is wetted, and then put into a frying-pan; after that honey is sprinkled over it, and sesame and cheese.

One cannot leave the shores of ancient Greece and Rome—for forays around the wider ancient world—without enjoying the taste of honey and various recipes associated with it, courtesy of the Greek scholar Athenaeus. Born in the Egyptian trading port of Naucratis, he was writing in around AD 200. Some of his publications are lost but we are indebted to him because of his fifteen-volume work entitled the *Deipnosophistae.*

Translatable as "The Learned Banquest" or "Philosophers at Dinner," the work purports to be recorded conversations that take place during an epic banquet between a variety of learned people, some of whom may or may not be fictitious. Now you might quite understandably feel that a collection of dinner party discussions in fifteen volumes sounds like proper torture, but what is discussed is so detailed, so many writers and thinkers are quoted, and such a number of customs and ideas are recorded, that it makes the work hugely important. For we are left with a great array of precise detail about life in ancient Rome—where the work was written—not just in AD 200 but going back in history.

The conversation veers from food to music, dance, women and much more. As would happen naturally, topics go off at extraordinary tangents. Poetry, philosophy, myths and legends are quoted at length by various individuals, and there is one of the longest discussions in history on cheesecake. Of the many cheesecakes discussed—and from absorbing myself in the literature, I can assure you that the ancient Greeks and Romans consumed a large number of them, going by different names and all cooked in different ways—the one attributed to Epicharmus, a dramatist and philosopher from around 500 BC, seems the tastiest. Included at the top of this chapter, the recipe is quite straightforward and it uses honey, which, as you'll see, was pretty much a key ingredient.

Reclining on couches, adorned in flowing togas, the guests ate and chatted away while servants fluttered about bringing food and drink as the conversation ebbed and flowed. It was perhaps during the serving of cheesecakes as a second or final sweet course that the epic cheesecake digression took place. "The cheesecakes of Samos are extraordinarily good," we hear one diner say, while another talks of how he has eaten them "set in a mold and made up of egg, honey and very fine wheatflour."

Mention is made of cheesecakes served at a wedding to the bride and bridegroom, drenched in honey—the cheesecake that is, not the happy couple. Others are mixed with honey, then deep-fried and served with honey. Another, a recipe "by that clever writer on confectionery, Chrysippus," is made by first roasting nuts and the seedhead of a poppy. This is pounded in a mortar and added to fruit juice mixed with boiled honey and some black pepper. Added to a cheesy dough, the soft mass that results is flattened and made into squares, then sprinkled with crushed sesame softened with more boiled honey. No doubt it's then cooked, not that the clever Chrysippus is helpful enough to mention this. Still, it's one of a cast of thousands, virtually all of which include honey.

The ancient Greeks and Romans had a pretty high regard for honey, which because of its preservative and antiseptic qualities they associated with longevity and hence immortality. It was both the food of the gods—ambrosia—and a gift from them. The mythical figure of Aristaeus was an apiculture—beekeeping—expert. The son of Apollo and a nymph, he had nectar and honey dropped on his lips as a baby and thus gained immortality. As he grew up, various nymphs taught him how to cultivate vines and olive trees and to keep bees. He then went about sharing his bee know-how with common mortals.

Early excavations on Crete show bee-related motifs on pottery and jewelry; Hippocrates recommended it to everyone, sick or otherwise; Aristotle made an intense study of bees; and Democritus, who spent a lot of time thinking about atoms, had a favorite recipe for a long and healthy life: "One must nourish the external part of his body with oil and the internal with honey."

Honey was mass-produced by the Greeks and used as a traded commodity. A record of 1300 BC shows 110 pots having the equivalent value of an ass or ox. Above all, it was nutritious and tasted good and, as we now know, it was very popular in cheesecake.

Wade through the dinner party monologues of Athenaeus, perhaps imagining him declaim it as a piece of theater, and you learn a thing or two about other foodie subjects. His dinner party guests appear to abhor drunkenness—even during the penultimate volume, when the party was drawing to a close (it must have been a dry night). "We're not of the class who drink to excess, nor of the numbers of those who are in the habit of being intoxicated by midday," declares one. "Those who drink too much unmixed wine are

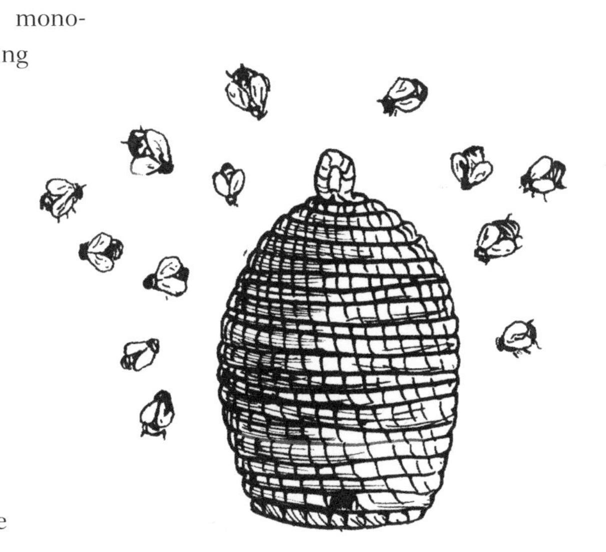

become violent," says another, while a fellow guest opines sagely (quoting Herodotus): "When wine has penetrated down into the body, bad and furious language is apt to rise to the surface."

They recommend songs to calm people at the start of feasts and stop them eating too fast: "Music softens the moroseness of character, for it dissipates sadness and produces affability and a sort of gentlemanlike joy." Not that they were without experience of overdoing it. There is considerable discussion on the subject of hangovers. A comic poet, Clearchus, is quoted as saying: "As we get all the pleasure first... we lose the whole delight in the sharp pain that follows."

But if you want another measure of the spirit of these discussions it comes when referencing one Aristoxenus: "The theatres have become completely barbarised and... music has become entirely ruined and vulgar." No doubt he also felt that young people had no respect.

Still, on food, especially cheesecake, these are precious volumes. And while Athenaeus discourses endlessly on pomegranates, pheasants, suckling pigs and salted crab—to mention just a few of the foodstuffs covered in this work—he's at his best when he waxes lyrical on "tartlets and cheesecakes steeped most thoroughly in the rich honey of the golden bee."

9

Congee

AUTHOR: Linghu Defen, FROM: *The Book of Zhou*

While wearing the mourning of nine months, one might eat vegetables and fruits, and drink water and congee, using no salt or cream.

Of the official twenty-four histories of Imperial China, *The Book of Zhou* stands out—fifty chapters long, some inevitably lost over time—as the one that mentions a dish now enjoyed daily by millions across Asia. As well as recommending it as appropriate to eat during times of mourning, it records how "Emperor Huang Di was the first to cook congee with millet as the ingredient." Today congee is mostly made with rice, but as the emperor showed, where rice wasn't available it might be substituted with another cereal.

The dish has spread to Japan, the Philippines, Thailand, Singapore and South Korea. Each culture has its own way of preparing it, although the basic method is pretty much the same, the rice being cooked in large quantities of water so that it disintegrates in the liquid as it's heated and becomes a sort of thick porridge or soup. It would have been made in this way back in the days of the Tang Dynasty, when *The Book of Zhou* was commissioned by Emperor Taizong to give the official history of the earlier Northern Zhou Dynasty. Although congee was regarded as a little more special in those times—presented as a gift to the emperor's nobles. No doubt given as a measure of respect with no end of bowing, it was then gently brought to the lips with gold-tipped chopsticks made of ivory.

Despite all the ceremony, it was, as now, a plain dish—the humblest gift signifying the greater respect. In fact, served on its own without the addition of other ingredients, it would have been almost tasteless. Think of gruel, stodgy from cooking in the pot overnight and served with little more than a smile. Yet its blandness belies its strength. Congee fortifies the body at the start of the day. It is easily digested, providing instant energy and making it a good dish to wolf down if you're about to be attacked by some aggressive warrior. An expert congee consumer will tell you that by turning a hot bowl of congee in your hands and slurping the cooler parts around the rim, you can get through three bowls in as many minutes. And as it doesn't sit uncomfortably in your stomach, but is absorbed quickly, you won't get a stitch while wielding your sword at your attacker.

Congee is sustaining too, ideal for those who need a quick energy boost after exercise or are recovering from illness. Indeed, its fortifying properties are held in such regard that it is often served at funerals. More than that, it has provided life-saving nutrition in a nation ravaged by famine over the centuries. From 108 BC to 1911, China experienced 1,828 famines—that's almost one a year. The one thing that enabled people to survive, that kept millions of families from starvation, was congee. Congee because of its warming and sustaining qualities and because it is made with rice.

Rice is one of the most important global foods, of which there are some 10,000 varieties. Eight thousand of these are grown for food and they have many advantages over cereal crops such as wheat and barley. Yields are higher and the moisture content is low which means rice can be stored for longer and used during periods of famine. In fact the Tang Dynasty—which lasted from AD 618 to 907—made much of the value of storing rice by building storage depots near their newly built canals so the rice could be transported to areas of greatest need.

Understanding its usefulness, the Tang Dynasty oversaw a period in which the production of rice became a key part of the agricultural industry. Special tools were developed, as were irrigation systems for transferring water to different paddy fields. Rice was just one part of a flourishing empire, the most glistening period in China's history. The economy grew, as did the military. Tax collecting became more efficient as every adult male was given an equal-sized plot of land together with an equal tax bill.

The elite loved their congee and so did everybody else—a poor family might get by on little else, after all. Different types of congee were made at different times of the day. On a cold winter's morning the addition of meat—if you could afford it—warmed the body. At dusk in midsummer as the heat of the day faded, it was made with lotus seeds or hawthorn to cool and refresh. And with the addition of medlar, it would boost the immune systems of the old, feeble and weak.

There is a legend that the recipe for congee was first developed by a fisherman's wife back in the very dim and distant past. According to this story, she took a boiling pot of rice on board her husband's boat to provide them with food at sea. But they were assaulted by pirates and so she hid the hot pot under some blankets. Then, when the pirates had gone, she found that her rice, now cooled, had taken on a fragrant flavor and tenderer texture.

The Yellow Emperor, Huang Di, was the first to cook congee with millet.

Hence most recipes for congee today involve cooking the rice over a very high heat and then resting the pot for half an hour. Often accompanied by small portions of well-seasoned savory dishes, its blandness works well as a foil for stronger flavors and if it wasn't important stuff, there wouldn't be an entire museum dedicated to it in Fanchung County, Anhui Province. I feel a pilgrimage coming on. After all, even Scotland doesn't have a porridge museum.

10

Dried fish

AUTHOR: Unknown, FROM: *The Saga of Grettir the Strong*

He [Atli] went to Snaefellsnes to get dried fish. He drove several horses with him and rode from home to Melar in Hrutafjord to his brother-in-law, Gamli. Then Grim, the son of Thorhall, Gamli's brother, made ready to accompany him along with another man. They rode West by way of Haukadalsskard and the road which leads out to the Ness, where they bought much fish and carried it away-on seven horses; when all was ready they turned homewards.

The Vikings didn't write cookbooks, which rather tallies with their image—too busy dashing off on raids to engage in more cerebral pursuits. While the Roman alphabet had spread across Europe, the Vikings tended to stick to a rather simpler system of lettering called the Futhark, the characters of which are runes. Runes have lots of horizontal, vertical and diagonal lines which made them easier to carve. So when a Viking came to pillage, he might slash and burn your hut and then carve some victorious obscenity on your door. What he wouldn't do was stop to check what local dishes you served for breakfast, before bringing out a pad and making a careful note of it.

In the late 700s, the Vikings outgrew their rocky, somewhat unfertile, land around Scandinavia and became restless. So they set off in their longboats in search of better territory, traveling far and wide in the process, from northern Europe to as far afield as Constantinople in the east and the shores of America in the west. In Britain, they raided the monks on Lindisfarne, off what is now the northeast coast of Northumberland. We know this from an account in the *Anglo-Saxon Chronicle,* which describes how in June 787 "ravages of heathen men miserably destroyed God's church on Lindisfarne with plunder and slaughter."

The Vikings eventually settled in Ireland and Britain, in areas such as Dublin and York. And much evidence remains of their occupation, including their diet. Examination of latrine pits in York—less unpleasant when 2,000 years have passed—shows they consumed a wide variety of foods, including fruit and vegetables (carrots, turnips and cabbage), lamb, pork, gulls' eggs, seafood and fish. They ate plenty of fish, in fact, and were tall as a result. And they had plenty of equipment to cook and eat it with: pots, frying pans and kettles, along with wooden plates and spoons and metal knives.

As Vikings were more talkers than writers, sagas passed down in their oral tradition weren't transcribed until late in the twelfth century. *The Saga of Grettir the Strong* is one such tale. Written in the thirteenth century by an unknown author, it tells the

Landing the herring from Scandinavian waters: a woodcut from Olaus Magnus's Historia de Gentibus Septentrionalibus.

story of a bad-tempered Icelandic Viking called Grettir Ásmundarson. Among the various acts of arson and murder committed by the outlaw we learn how his rival, Atli the Red, travels to somewhere called Snaefellsnes where he buys a large quantity of dried fish. Atli is attacked on his return; most people get attacked at some point in Viking sagas, but that is not the point. Much more relevant are the words "dried" and "fish." Which, written a mere 500 years after the event is, I'm afraid, the closest we'll get to an authentic Viking recipe.

Indeed fish is one of the few foodstuffs mentioned in the sagas, and there is no reference to how it was prepared and eaten. We need to wait until a bit later for this. Olaus Magnus, who wrote about the culture and history of Scandinavia in his 1555 tome *A Description of the Northern Peoples,* gives us an idea of how fish was dried, and it's not unlikely that the method would have survived unchanged from the Viking period:

> When you come in towards the shore [north of an area called Vasterbotten], such an abundance of fish is to be seen as its base on every side that you are dumbfounded at the sight, and your appetite can be wholly satisfied. Some of the fishes of this sort, sprinkled with brine from the sea, are commonly spread out over two or three acres of the flat level ground at the foot of the mountain, to be parched and dried by the wind; some, chiefly, fish of the larger kind, are hoisted on poles or spread out on racks, to be dehydrated by the sun and air. They are all reserved for consumption at home or for the lucrative profit of tradesmen.

The drying fish, as you might imagine, emitted quite a smell. "From the foot then of this crowned mountain there rises such a stench of fish hung up to dry that far out to sea sailors as they approach are aware of it flying out to meet them," Magnus goes on. "As soon as they perceive that smell when struggling beneath the darkness of a storm, they realize it is necessary to preserve themselves and their cargo from impending shipwreck." This use of smelly fish as an alternative to lighthouse illumination did not last the centuries, but the treatment of dried fish, known as *lutefisk,* did. "The dry stockfish [cod] is put in strong lye for two days, then rinsed in fresh water for one day before being boiled," records Magnus. "It is served with salted butter and is highly appreciated, even by kings."

But while food and the act of eating is rarely mentioned in the earlier sagas, much is made of the importance of hospitality. There were no inns, so when a Viking showed up on your doorstep, you fed and watered him, according to the *Hávamál* saga: "Fire is needed/ By him who has come in/ And is benumbed in his knees./ Food and clothes/ Are needed by one/ Who has traveled across the mountain." Although etiquette also demanded—according to a note elsewhere—that guests stay no more than three days. The *Völuspá* saga paints quite a sophisticated picture of entertaining at home. A table set for dinner is described in one instance: "The mother took/ A broidered cloth,/ A white one of flax,/ Covered the table." Clearly the upper echelons of Viking society got out their Sunday best for visitors. And what they ate represents another rare mention of food: "Shining pork/ And roasted birds;/ Wine was in the jug;/ They drank and talked;/ The day passed away."

The sagas don't touch on smoked fish, but this was another method of preserving fish that would have been used at the time. Swedish archaeologists have actually recreated a Viking smokehouse at the open-air Museum of Foteviken. Herring hang on timber beams as smoke slowly wafts over them. But you didn't need a smokehouse to smoke fish. Viking dwellings had an open hearth in the middle of the floor so any meat or fish hung near it would have been smoked naturally.

Over the centuries both dried and smoked fish became entrenched in Scandinavian food culture. Comparisons made between kitchen equipment that was buried with a woman entombed in Oseberg in Norway in AD 834 and the household recommendations of 1585 by the Swedish count Per Brahe for his wife, show how remarkably little had changed—both in the food eaten and how it was prepared—over the course of seven centuries. The Vikings might have bullied their illiterate way around northern Europe, but without them would you be able to seek respite in a plate of smoked herring in an IKEA food court today?

11

Manchet bread

AUTHOR: Unknown, FROM: The Bayeux Tapestry

Here meat is cooked. And here servants serve the food. Here they dined. And here the Bishop blesses the food and wine.

No written recipes for bread survive from the Middle Ages. So one is left clutching, rather desperately, at some thin and disintegrated ancient straws. One such straw is the (rather well-preserved) Bayeux Tapestry, commissioned, most probably, by the Bishop of Bayeux, William the Conqueror's half-brother.

At nearly 70 meters long and created in around 1070, it tells the story of the Norman invasion of England which climaxed with the Battle of Hastings in 1066. William, the Duke of Normandy, invaded the country after Saxon lord Harold took the throne on Edward the Confessor's death. William, meanwhile, reckoned the throne had been promised to him so gathered his army and set sail to lay claim to it.

Detail from the Bayeux Tapestry illustrating William the Conqueror's first meal on landing in England. A man takes freshly baked bread from the oven in preparation for the feast.

His first meal on landing in England is recorded on the embroidered cloth, which is still stored and preserved in the town of Bayeux in Normandy. The Latin captions which accompany the embroidered images state that meat is cooked and that servants bring in food and wine which are then blessed by William before he and his top men get stuck in. The detail of the meal and its preparation isn't conveyed in written form, however, but in the images themselves.

Taking a closer look, you can see how the stewards use shields as table tops in their makeshift field kitchen. There's a portable oven—you can see the flames licking at its base and what might be some steaks cooking on top. And you can also make out some bread, freshly baked, or toasted and clearly too hot to handle. A man uses tongs to take it from the oven, doing this with his right hand and placing it on a tray with his left.

To the left of the oven, soup is being heated in a large cauldron held between two stakes, propped up by a couple of servants. The food then gets passed down the line to William himself, who sits in the middle of the table holding a bowl. A man to his right blows some kind of horn—a little music to help the feast go with a swing—while some small birds, quails possibly, roasted on skewers, are also on their way to the top table.

Wine is served too and that freshly cooked bread. As well as what could be griddle cakes—in the earliest recorded recipe for them, from the fifteenth century, these are flavored with saffron, rolled out thinly and shaped into crescents before being cooked on a hot griddle—there are thicker loaves which could well be manchet bread (leavened loaves made with refined stoneground flour).

Another reason why we are pausing in food history to muse over what type of bread might be recorded in the Bayeux Tapestry is because 1066 was a crucial year in the development of the loaf.

The familiar story of bread goes a bit like this. Man, back in the vague mists of time, discovers that flour and water when mixed makes a dough that once baked makes bread. At some point yeast gets added, possibly naturally or by chance (see p. 14). At some point, too, cereals begin to be cultivated for bread and the resulting grains harvested and ground. The grinding of grain is mechanized around 2,500 years ago when hand-rotating querns appear in Spain. Then the Romans start building mills, driven by wind and water, and by 1086 there are around 6,000 in Britain, as recorded in the *Domesday Book*.

By the seventeenth century, the baking industry is booming but, in London, it suffers a setback when a fire that starts in a bakery in Pudding Lane destroys much of the city and virtually its entire baking industry. The bread story then goes relatively quiet until 1912 when the prototype for a bread-slicing machine is created by an inventor in Iowa, USA (see p. 221). A gap of several decades then ensues before the next big event, in 1961—a moment that makes bread purists shudder—when a production process that both sped up and lowered the cost of the bread-making is developed, known as the Chorleywood Bread Process.

This version of the story, however, misses out a key development, that of the hair sieve. It seems that the device—a sieve with a mesh of woven hair (usually a horse's)—had been around for some time but didn't make its way into general use in England until 1066, after which it is frequently mentioned. Previously and subsequently too, some people sifted, or "bolted," their flour through woolen or linen cloth instead, but it was the hair sieve that, together with the Battle of Hastings, helped bring the country out of the Dark Ages. Just as the seizing of the English throne by William of Normandy marked a significant period in English history, so the proliferation of the hair sieve marked a significant moment in its own way, one that you could call WFL, or White Fluffy Loaf. Hence there is the period BWFL (Before White Fluffy Loaf) and AWFL (After White Fluffy Loaf).

Flour shaken through the sieve, sifting out the bran, could then be used to make what was regarded as a purer, cleaner, lighter—sacramental, even—loaf. Some ascribed to it almost magical properties. The hair sieve was a giant leap forward, both culinarily and socially, for it meant that bread could become a status symbol. In Tudor times the kind of bread you ate reflected your class. The nobility ate white manchets, tradesmen tucked into wheaten cobs and the poor consumed loaves of bran. The Tudor aristocrat could thus impress visitors with his white loaf in much the same way that his social equivalent today might brandish an iPad.

In monasteries the canons (the religious elite) ate white bread, while the lower orders and servants got small brown loaves, for white bread was accorded religious as well as social status. Loaves used in holy communion were stamped with a cross and called "pandemains," from *panis domini* (the sacramental bread or "bread of the Lord"), and even today the bread of the sacrament, or communion wafer, is white.

Although the poor were never meant to get their grubby hands on the stuff, they would have managed to get a taste of it. Perhaps a few hung around the back doors of manor-house kitchens, hoping for scraps. We can imagine a humble peasant grabbing a morsel of white bread and stuffing it into his mouth. Imagine how it would have tasted—the gently risen and baked dough, soft on the tongue, almost melting in the mouth—and how that would have compared to the usual tooth-breaking (if you had any teeth) brown stuff.

But as the elite showed the way, so the rest followed. The making of white loaves in the eleventh century increased steadily and continued progressively over the centuries that followed. Bakeries tended to split into those who provided bread for the poor—brown, coarse, crunchy—and those who baked white loaves—airy, fluffy, melt-in-the-mouth. By the late sixteenth century there were twice the number of white- than brown-bread bakers. And it is from this latter period that one of the first printed recipes for manchet bread dates, published in *The Goode Huswife's Handmaide for the Kitchin* of 1588:

> Take half a bushel of fine flower twise boulted [sifted], and a gallon of faire luke warm water, almost a handful of white salt, and almost a pinte of yest, then temper all these together, without any more liquor, as hard as ye can handle it: then let it lie halfe an hower, then take it up, and make your Manchetts, and let them stande almost an hower in the oven.

The trend continued into the eighteenth century, a writer—one Lewis Magendi—commenting in 1795 that "the flour must be divested of its bran and in a fit state for the most luxurious palate, or it is rejected not only by the affluent but by the extremely indigent."

The white bread supremacy then lasted well into the latter part of the twentieth century. It was perhaps the final push to make it even more mainstream that ended its reputation. While the Chorleywood Bread Process meant you could have a baked and packaged loaf in about three hours, it created a cheap and tasteless commodity. Today white sliced bread is seen as the tip of the iceberg of the worst elements of mass-produced food. To French chef Raymond Blanc it's not even bread, while arch-foodies search out artisan loaves dense with unrefined bran.

The bread served to William of Normandy before he went out in search of Harold's troops and put an arrow in his eye—as depicted in the Bayeux Tapestry—was perhaps the first refined white loaf baked in England. Indeed the Normans found English food plainer and coarser than their own and so they set about improving things. They began to import spices and herbs and introduced new animals for meat—rabbits, for example. And they upped the ante on what they thought was good bread. The Tapestry doesn't show a hair sieve although they must have brought one with them because in the years following 1066, white bread was what a good noble aspired to, right up until the late twentieth century when the posh performed a reverse ferret and sought out brown loaves, the more rustic and potentially teeth-breaking the better.

12

Pasta

AUTHOR: Muhammad al-Idrisi, FROM: *Tabula Rogeriana (The Book of Roger)*

In Sicily there is a town called Trabia, an enchanting place blessed with water year-round and mills. In this town they make a food from flour in the form of strings. Enough is produced to supply, as well as the towns of Calabria, those in Muslim and Christian regions, too.

Had pasta been knocking around much before 1154? Most likely, yes. There is, for example, an Etruscan relief about forty miles north of Rome at Caere. Painted in the fourth century, it shows what looks very much like pasta-making equipment. But 1154 stands out very clearly as the date when pasta got its first decent write-up. The wording is clear-cut, straightforward, honest and there is no reason to doubt its accuracy.

The reference to it comes from a remarkable book written by one Muhammad al-Idrisi, whose full name was Abu Abd Allah Abdullah, Muhammad ibn Muhammad ibn Ash Sharif al-Idrisi. Born in Morocco in 1099, he started to travel the globe at the age of sixteen, visiting Asia Minor, southern France, Spain and north Africa, which must have felt pretty much like the whole world at the time. He was a poet and writer of Arabic prose whose considerable talent came to the attention of royalty, in the shape of King Roger II of Sicily.

King Roger, who had inherited the throne from his father, also Roger—a conquering Norman adventurer—was a Renaissance man before his time who liked the idea of a court of all the talents. He therefore used his reign and position to surround himself with learned individuals—geographers, mathematicians, philosophers, doctors and the like. So when he heard of al-Idrisi, he invited him to join his gang. Under Roger's patronage, al-Idrisi proceeded to map and chart the known world from 1138, working on it for fifteen years. So accurate was the map he made that it was used for the ensuing three centuries.

The map, with its accompanying commentaries, goes by the splendid name of *The Book of Roger*—or *Tabula Rogeriana,* as it's more usually known—and is decently subtitled "Pleasure Excursion of One Eager to Traverse the World's Regions." In matter-of-fact language, al-Idrisi records his knowledge of the land he has both seen and heard about. Some of it sounds mildly derogatory. He describes Britain, for instance, as having "dreary weather." Paris, meanwhile, is a town "of mediocre size surrounded by vineyards and forests on an island in the Seine." But he also makes sensible comments such as "the earth is round as a sphere," not to mention his seminal reference to pasta, which gives rise to plenty of food for thought.

Clearly at the time al-Idrisi was writing, pasta-making was already quite well established. And it was being made in sufficient quantities for export, which suggests it was being stored, but, more importantly, dried. For the key part in the development of pasta is not that the Arabs brought durum wheat to Sicily (around the late seventh century) or that it was later made into strings—not to mention butterflies or little worms—but that it was dried.

That pasta could be dried and stored gives it all the importance of rice as a staple foodstuff (see p. 34). And although there are mentions of what sound like pasta in references to ancient Greece and Arabia, the Italians, quite understandably, claim it as their own.

Anyone wishing to counter their claim should visit the National Pasta Museum in Rome—just opposite the Travi Fountain. It is, the museum states, "the Italian invention that the world envies," adding how its "eleven exhibition halls disclose eight centuries of the history of the first course" (just in case any ignorant foreigner should think it was a main-course dish). Sicily was fortuitous as a starting place for pasta as it was well placed to trade internationally and it had a stunning effect on civilization. As Mary Snodgrass writes in her *Encyclopedia of Kitchen History*:

> Pasta was a momentous addition to world civilization for several reasons. It stored well, thus allowing the warehousing of foodstuffs against famine and fueling monetary speculation during peacetime and war based on predictions of price and demand. More important to the global economy, the formation of hardtack and pasta from durum wheat permitted galley kitchens to feed ships' crews over long ocean journeys of the type that introduced Europe to the Western Hemisphere.

Thus Italy took pasta to its heart. The great Roger II must have eaten it, no doubt to help sustain that vast intellect. "The extent of his learning cannot be described," al-Idrisi said of his patron, while one contemporary historian wrote how "he accomplished more asleep than other sovereigns did awake." *The Book of Roger* was published in 1154 and Roger II died three weeks later. The flag of pasta had been planted on the soil of Sicily—and Italians have been thanking him ever since.

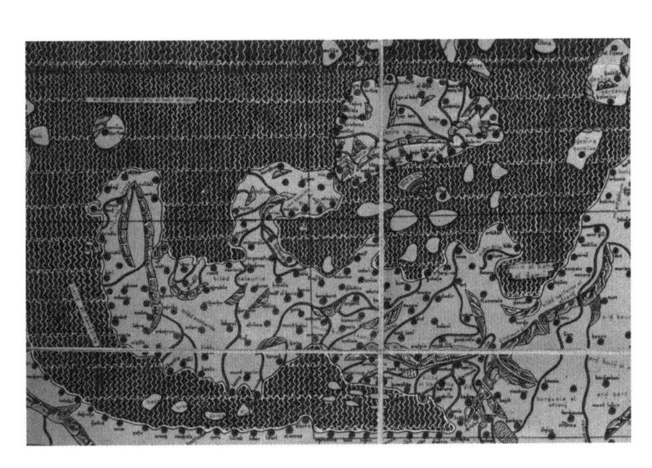

Drawn by al-Idrisi for Roger II of Sicily in 1154–1157 and included in the Tabula Rogeriana, *this map shows Italy, Sicily and the Mediterranean Sea.*

13

Rummaniyya
(Meatballs in pomegranate sauce)

AUTHOR: Unknown

FROM: *Kanz al-fawa'id fi tanwi al-mawa'id (The Treasure of Useful Advice for the Composition of a Varied Table)*

Cut the meat into pieces, put in a pot and cover with water. Bring to a boil while removing the fetid scum. Next add small meatballs the size of a hazelnut. The quantity of broth must be reduced so that when the cooking is done only a residue of light and velvety juice remains. In the meantime, take some sour pomegranate juice, sweeten it with rose water syrup, add some mint and pistachios crushed in the mortar to thicken it, colour it with a little saffron and season with all [the ingredients] of atraf tib [a mixture of spices including black pepper, cloves and ginger]. Sprinkle with rose water and diluted saffron and serve.

Hungry young mouths across thirteenth-century Egypt must have been growing tired of being filled with meatballs. These were pretty much a staple food. So a book circulating in 1250 called *Kanz al-fawa'id fi tanwi al-mawa'id* (or "The Treasure of Useful Advice for the Composition of a Varied Table")—written at the time when the Mamluk warriors, who were descended from slaves, ruled Egypt—must have felt like the first specks of rain after a long, dry desert of a summer.

Its recipes reflect the influences brought about by immigration caused by conflict around the Middle East. New eating habits and dishes came from far and wide, from Greece (turnips, Greek style), for example, Baghdad (a condensed yogurt called *qanbaris*) and the Frankish region of Germany (a salsa for fish). The Crusades in Syria and Palestine, the Mogul invasion of Iraq, not to mention other conflicts, saw armies and their entourages importing and exporting food as they came and went. Returning to Europe, the battle-weary men didn't just bring tales of extraordinary adventures in far-flung places, they had a taste of them in their luggage.

The exotic ingredients they brought back with them, such as rose water and pomegranate, then influenced European cookery for generations to come. Indeed rose water became almost ubiquitous in dishes served at English banquets. Sweet was continually mixed with savory, to the extent that it then took many centuries for sweet dishes to get a final course of their own.

Rummaniyya (which translates as "dish with pomegranate") is a classic example of this: meatballs with the addition of tangy pomegranate juice. The inclusion of exotic ingredients to enliven humdrum foodstuffs would have wowed medieval banqueters back in England at the time *Kanz* was circulating. Other dishes include carrot jam (a sort of a chutney), quince cordial and a recipe for hummus incorporating pickled lemons, cinnamon, ginger, parsley, mint and rue—although as rue is almost toxic, substituting it with rosemary would be a safer bet.

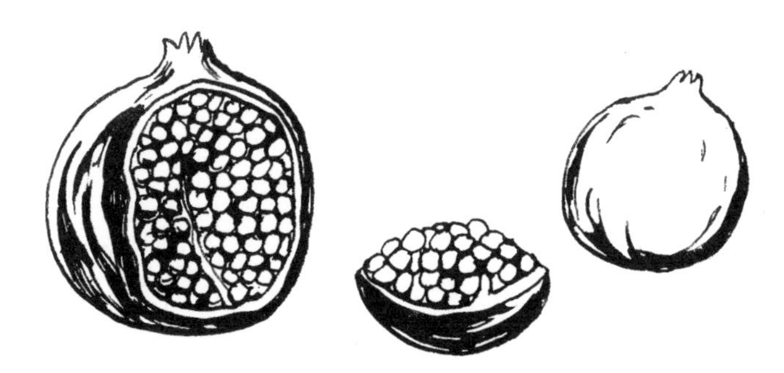

The book also includes plenty of references to the health benefits of particular foods, derived from contemporary or earlier dietetic texts. Cookbooks in Europe followed suit for the next few hundred years, listing recipes because they were thought to be medicinal rather than because they tasted good. Although many of the ingredients they included, pomegranate among them, remain renowned for their health properties to this day.

But this dish would have needed a little care in the preparation as there is a distinct lack of oil and neither is there salt. It might have been medicinal, but it didn't need to taste like medicine. So the trick for the cook would have been to successfully balance the sour and sweet flavors. Which someone must have been doing in Europe as this style of cooking caught on. The likes of lamb stew served with fresh apricots, beef cooked with pistachios, chicken with walnuts or the vegetarian dish of fava beans in a sour sauce with hazelnuts, were seen as rich and exotic and soon mixing sweet and sour became the signature combination of the medieval meal.

14

Pear of pies

AUTHOR: Guillaume Tirel, aka Taillevent
FROM: *Le Viandier (The Food Provider)*

Put upright in paste and fill the hollow with sugar; for three big pears about a quarter of a pound of sugar, well covered and glazed with eggs and saffron then cook them.

As the centuries march by, one needs to rely less on glimpses of cave paintings, random asides in poems, dinner-party recollections or fourteenth-century Swedish surnames to analyze the evolution of cooking. Yet when you do land on a seminal recipe, one that transforms things and pushes you forward to a new enlightened era, it's not all plain sailing.

While Taillevent's recipes are coherent, he makes considerable assumptions about the culinary abilities of his readers as he gives few quantities and no cooking times. But this didn't dent his popularity. Although published in the latter part of the fourteenth century, his *Le Viandier* remained in print—going through fourteen editions—for almost 300 years. The recipe for pear pie that it contains is one of the earliest written recipes for pastry and is extremely sophisticated because not only does the pie hold fruit, it's sweet and you can eat the crust.

But first a word on Taillevent, the pen-name of Frenchman Guillaume Tirel. His story is a classic culinary tale of someone starting at the bottom and rising to the top of the food tree. Many a great chef today started peeling veg and rose to run an empire, but while Taillevent didn't run his own empire, he did cook for a king.

His first job, aged fourteen, was turning the great roasting spit in the kitchen of Jeanne de Bourbon, Queen of France and consort to King Charles V. The work would have been tough beyond belief for anyone, let along a young boy: hours of heaving the heavy metal handle while standing just feet away from a roaring fire. He would have finished the day stinking of smoke and meat fat, but it didn't put him off. Instead, he rose through the ranks, gaining literacy as he went, and as he became more and more skilled, he caught the eye, as well as the taste buds, of the French king.

Charles V, known as Charles the Wise for his sound pragmatism, good governance and learning—one key legacy was the vast library he built—appointed Taillevent as his master cook. This was an important role, especially as the king suffered from gout and had an abscess on his left arm that might have resulted from poisoning. So skilled did Taillevent prove to be as a cook, however, that the king encouraged him to write down a collection of recipes—no doubt both his own and those he had collected from others.

The first known French cookbook, it includes numerous recipes for soups, ragouts, roasts—from piglets to cormorants (you cook them, he says, like heron, which in turn you cook like swan or peacock, which you should prepare like stork—yes, it's one of those books). There are dishes for invalids, fish dishes, sauces, tips and ideas for cooking with wine, as well as a chapter on "desserts and other things," the former including a very tasty milk tart, the latter, hedgehog.

Yet among all these dishes it's the pear tart that stands out because it was so ahead of its time. The earliest example of a recipe for pastry in England didn't emerge until 1545 when *A Proper New Booke on Cokery* came out in London. And even this is more of an aide-mémoire to the cook than a fully fledged recipe book, as it lacks any helpful detail.

No doubt medieval cooks had been preparing pies for some time before Taillevent wrote this recipe, but his was a considerable development. His pear pie has a crust which you eat. Once cooked you cut through it, the pears and their juices oozing out onto the plate. You then mop up the sweet saffron juice with the pastry. But what's so revolutionary about this, you may be wondering. One always eats the pastry from a pie—it's often the best bit. Back in those days, however, this was not the case. Pie crust was not intended to be eaten; it was there to cook the contents in.

And pretty well everything was cooked in this way. As pie historian Jane Clarkson is keen on telling people: "Once upon a time everything baked in an oven that was not bread was pie." Even bread wasn't always baked in an oven (see p. 11), but would have been cooked on a hearthstone or grill, and meat roasted on a spit (see p. 24). An oven, or kiln, was originally just used for firing pottery until it then occurred to someone that maybe the kiln could be used to cook food in. It's a bit like how the Aga was originally just used for drying clothes and for dogs to sleep next to, then someone experimented by putting something in one of the ovens.

As for using the kiln to cook meat, these were days before roasting tins and chicken bricks. Some wrapped their food in leaves, others used a clay pot. Then a bright spark tried wrapping dough around the meat, which not only kept the juices in, but also worked as a container to both transport the meat and preserve it for a short time. It's strange to think that the crust of a pie—the eye-catching casing—was never supposed to be edible. A bit like arriving at a hotel, unpacking and then trying to wear your suitcase—you weren't supposed to do it. But someone did (eat the pie crust, that is, not try on the suitcase) and over time, dough, with the judicious addition of fat, became pastry.

Medieval recipes refer to pastry as a "coffin"—that is, a box—as in the opening lines of this recipe from sixteenth-century Italy: "Make the coffin of a great pie or pastry, in the bottom make a hole as big as your fist..." The title of the recipe, incidentally, is "To Make Pies That the Birds May Be Alive in Them and Fly Out When It is Cut Up."

Taillevent's pear pie doesn't have four-and-twenty, or indeed any, live birds in it—Charles V doesn't sound like the kind of guy who would have appreciated that

Taillevent's Le Viandier *remained in print for nearly 300 years and an engraving of his tomb is depicted in the 1892 edition of the book.*

sort of entertainment. But the ingredients were expensive. Saffron was rare, as was sugar, so this was possibly a dish for a banquet. It might have made a nice pudding after the hedgehog, which, if you're interested, Taillevent chops up finely and mixes with raisins, cheese and herbs and then stuffs into a lamb's stomach and secures with a wooden skewer before cooking. He doesn't say how, of course, but I'd suggest over hot coals.

15

Erbolate

(Baked eggs with herbs)

AUTHOR: Master cook of King Richard II, FROM: *The Forme of Cury*

Take parsel, myntes, sauerey, & sauge, tansey, veruayn, clarry, rewe, ditayn, fenel, southrenwode, hewe hem & grinde hem smale, medle hem up with Ayrenn. do butter in a trape. & do þe fars þerto. & bake it & messe it forth. [Take parsley, mint, savory, sage, tansy, vervain, clary, rue, dittany, fennel, southernwood. Chop them and grind them small. Mix them with eggs. Put butter in a baking dish and put the mixture in it. Bake and serve it in portions.]

Just eleven years after Taillevent published his seminal tome for Charles V of France (see p. 46), English cooks got in on the act. Encouraged by their mentor, Richard II, the master cooks of the royal household brought forth their own volume. No individual takes the glory in this instance; the work is a collaboration of the king's finest culinary artists.

In the form of a vellum scroll, a copy of it lives in the British Library. Its graceful prose, daintily written in soft red ink, details 196 recipes. The recipe for erbolate—in which eggs are combined with an elaborate combination of herbs, from the unusual to the unheard of—encapsulates the spirit of the book, which was written with the approval and encouragement of the court's medical gurus and philosophers. As we saw in Recipe 13 (p. 44), the culinary arts and medicine were inextricably linked at the time. The herbs in this recipe are there primarily for medicinal purposes, reflecting the belief expressed by a contemporary physician, one Dr. Boorde, that "a good cook is half a physician."

Before you leap to the conclusion that this was a book filled with recipes for curry, I should point out the *cury* is in fact the Middle English word for "cookery." And while the book came from chefs of the royal household, their intention was to assist cooks across the land—or at least those of them who could read. This book, the oldest of European instructive cookery manuscripts in existence—and certainly the most famous—was aimed at helping people, as it sets out in the introduction: "commune potages and commune meetis [meats] for howshold as they shold be made craftly and holsomly."

At last here was a cookbook for cooks, not published as some kind of religious tract or philosophical treatise disguised as a collection of dinner-party ramblings (see p. 30). The king believed that the dishes he enjoyed at court should be made available to his people too. But it's not all humble fare. Richard II entertained on a big scale—he would feed thousands at one setting and he didn't just churn out baked eggs with herbs. After the preamble about "common" dishes, the authors then promise "curious potages and meetes and sotiltees for alle maner of States bothe hye and lowe." So you could expect unusually spiced dishes presented in spectacular fashion.

The word *sotiltees* is Middle English for "subtleties." But there was little subtlety in the elaborate sculptures that would be served up at grand feasts. Models of ships, castles and birds—the grander the better; think great big eagles rather than tiny songbirds—made of jelly or sugar would arrive to gasps of approval and applause. Such dishes would often be brought to the table as "warners," notifying guests that dinner was about to be served and giving a clue as to the level of culinary sophistication they should expect. These days chefs present a dainty amuse-bouche or a scented thimble of soup to tantalize the taste buds at the beginning of a meal. When Richard II was entertaining, by contrast, he made his chefs send out edible monuments of the age. Imagine how impressed you'd be if you went round to dine with the king and instead of some delicate titbit the starter that was sent out was a replica of your castle.

Richard II liked his food and had around 300 chefs in his kitchens. He needed a brigade this size, however, judging by the numbers of people he was in the habit of asking over. The provisions are recorded for a feast given by the king and the Duke of Lancaster on 12 September 1387. One hell of a shopping list, it includes: "14 oxen lying in salt... 120 carcas of shepe fresh... 140 pigges... 210 gees... 400 conyngges [large rabbits]... 12 cranes... 11 thousand eggs..." On and on it goes. It must have been one hell of a catering operation too. Today we can't know the meaning of grandiose.

The variety of produce at the disposal of the grand chefs of the time was impressive. Hens, partridge, quail, lark, bittern and woodcock hung in the kitchens alongside a vast array of salted meats and fish. Spices, meanwhile, were locked safely in cupboards. They included ginger, black pepper (prized for its supposed digestive qualities) and exotics such as galangal root. These were brought into the country either by Venetian merchants or by knights returning from the various Crusades (see p. 46).

The kitchens themselves were hothouses. A huge fireplace, capable of holding a whole oxen on a spit, would be at one end, while an open hearth in the middle of the room would have been used as a large grill. Enormous pestles would be pounded in vast mortars by staff whose sole job would be to crush spices, while long tables would be used as chopping blocks and assembly areas. Utensils from the time indicate how hot the fires would have been—they have very long handles. There are deep pans for frying—a lot of food was fried in ale batter. Meat, meanwhile, would be first washed of salt—used to preserve meat in the days before refrigeration—before being boiled to tenderize it and then roasted.

Among the elaborate ways of preparing food in *The Forme of Cury* is a description of how to color slices of lard—each in a slightly different shade—as well as how to dye food dishes in saffron to make them look golden. The cooks were artists, but the king also wanted a decent supper. Which is where the baked eggs come in. While I prefer mine cracked into a ramekin, with some chopped bacon, salt and pepper, the king liked his stuffed with herbs. Perhaps he saw it as a light dinner before bedtime, so the herbs could work their medicinal magic during the night.

From the recipe one can assume the herbs are fresh, taken straight from the garden, and what an herb garden it must have been. Baked and sliced into portions, the resultant dish is more omelette than soufflé. And what might the king have drunk with it? In those days, before glass bottles came on the scene, wine would soon have turned to vinegar, so would have been drunk shortly after fermentation. Instead ale was the drink of the day—consumed by all, as water was still pretty dodgy; not ideal with a light supper of baked eggs. Perhaps the king then called for a spot of jesting to entertain him as he ate, in view of the lack of telly.

Tart de Brymlent [illegible]

Tartes of flessh [illegible]

Tartlet [illegible]

Tart of fysshe [illegible]

Sambocade [illegible]

Erbolat [illegible]

For to make pome dorry [illegible]

The recipe for erbolate is depicted here third from bottom on the scroll of Forme of Cury.

16

Green porray

AUTHOR: Unknown
FROM: *Le Ménagier de Paris (The Householder of Paris)*

Green porray on a fish day. Let it [a cabbage] have the outer leaves removed and be cut up and then washed in cold water without parboiling it and then cooked with verjuice and a little water, and put some salt therein, and let it be served boiling and very thick, not clear; and put at the bottom of the bowl, underneath the porray, salt butter, or fresh if you will, or cheese, or old verjuice.

Sooner or later we have to turn to pottage. Eaten throughout Europe in the Middle Ages, pottage was a dish that united our ancient nations and is so called because it was cooked in a pot. Hence it could be a simple gruel on the one hand, or a rich and elaborate stew. Pottage was eaten by rich and poor alike and there were many kinds, of which one version was porray.

Where most pottage contained some kind of cereal and some onions, porray had greenery—usually cabbage, as in the above recipe. So we're talking soup here: it could be thin and not have very much in it, if you were poor; or it could have meat, breadcrumbs, eggs and more, if you were a noble. These were the days when you could tell the class of man by the type of soup he ate. Meat was enjoyed by the better-off nobles and rarely eaten by peasants, and for very practical reasons. Animals were worth much more alive than they were as food.

Cows, sheep and goats could provide a constant supply of milk, not to mention wool in the case of sheep. Chickens, ducks and geese gave you eggs and they would only be eaten when they finally stopped laying, while oxen would pull your plow. And if you needed blood for cooking or making black pudding, you didn't slaughter your beast, you just made a careful incision on an upper leg and drained some blood.

It's a habit still practiced by the Masai people of Kenya. The idea may make you shudder, as might the method in Colombia of procuring iguana eggs. Hunters will capture a slow-moving, pregnant iguana, slit open her abdomen, gently remove her eggs, rub wood ash into the wound, sew her back up and let her waddle back into the underbrush, dazed and confused, no doubt, but alive. It's a practice that goes back centuries, like pottage cooking. Of which, think of a big pot, boiling away for much of the day, cooking the hell out of any vegetables that at the time people thought were very dangerous to eat if raw. The Romans put barley in it and different pulses; they added leafy vegetables and fish sauce, throwing in cabbage leaves near the end.

Pottage is the ancestor of steamed puddings, a second-cousin of porridge and a precursor to soup. Confusingly, the word *soup* comes from "sop." Sop was the piece of bread that you poured the pottage onto. Bread also served as a poor man's plate, the working man's eating habits still being a few steps away from fine dining. Then, over time, what was the solid part of the mixture became the name for the liquid part. After all, once bowls and plates had been invented, it made more sense to put the bread into the soup rather than the other way round. Next time you have a bowl of soup with croûtons in it, you can bore your friends with this piece of reverse evolutionary epicurean theorizing.

But why, in the history of pottage, stop at 1392? Well, that's because there is an early recipe for porray in a famous French work called *Le Ménagier de Paris*. Published that year, it is by turns creepy, sexist and unusually insightful and valuable.

The author is unknown and we can't be sure whether the narrator is real or fictitious. Although judging by the views and behavior of some men today in Saudi Arabia, he could well have been real. But whatever he was, he was Parisian and elderly. He was a gentleman who had recently procured for himself a young wife—only fifteen years old. And the volume is a manual produced by him for her guidance as she went about her daily life.

Think of it as a sexist bumper version of *Cosmo* magazine. The title translates as "The Householder of Paris" (or *The Goodman of Paris* in a translation from 1928) and it offers a spectrum of lifestyle advice. There are recipes, fashion advice and housekeeping tips, as well as prayers and poems. The advice spans the practical to the spiritual.

Here are some highlights:

> Protect him [your husband] from holes in the roof and smoky fires, and do not quarrel with him, but be sweet, pleasant and peaceful with him.
>
> Make certain that in winter he has a good fire without smoke and let him slumber, warmly wrapped, cosy between your breasts, and in this way bewitch him.
>
> In summer take care that there are no fleas in your bedroom or bed.
>
> As soon as you arrive home ... feed the dogs. Have them put in front of the fire if they are wet or muddy. Let them always be held subject to the whip. If you act this way, they will not pester people at the table or sideboard and they will not get into the beds.

Women, says the author, should also never introduce new fashions, should walk down the street "head upright, eyes downcast." Only the worst wives "go with open eyes, head appallingly lifted like a lion, their hair in disarray spilling from their coifs." And no woman questions her husband's judgment as "it rests on him alone to know all."

And knowing it all he professes to be when it comes to cooking and preparing for meals. The book offers a truly exhaustive list of instructions for every possible culinary episode. There are menus for all kinds of meals—from three- and four-course dinners to intimate his 'n' her suppers, plans for massive weddings and endless miscellaneous pieces of advice. Numbers of staff needed and what they will cost are mentioned, such as the security required for a large banquet, for example: "item: big strong sergeants to guard the door." As if she would forget to hire the bouncers.

The meals themselves are highly elaborate. After the starter for one big dinner of "grapes and peaches in little pies," a course of soups, then endless roast dishes—"five pigs . . . twenty starlings"—there's a jelly course the ingredients for which include "ten young chickens, ten young rabbits, a pig and a crayfish." Doubtless he was trying to emulate Richard II's example (see p. 49) on a more domestic scale.

Then, for one of the quieter moments, there's his recipe for porray. The verjuice he mentions was a popular condiment during the Middle Ages—the acidic juice from unripened grapes or crab apples. It's used as a sharpener for the dish. Perhaps his thick version of pottage was meant as a side dish for some fish—as mentioned in the first part of the recipe. A cabbage broth to go with the fish for which there is a tonne of recipes from eel, to bream, turbot and beyond.

Finally, there is also a brief "recipe": "To write on paper a letter that no one can see until the paper is heated." "Dear XXXX, I'm married to an insane and elderly foodie control freak," his young wife might have wished to write. But one fears little consolation would have been forthcoming.

A cook in the Middle Ages savors the aroma of pottage.

17

Party planning

AUTHOR: Chiquart Amiczo, FROM: *Du Fait de Cuisine*

And in order to do things properly and cleanly, and in order to serve and accomplish it more quickly, there should be provided such a large quantity of vessels of gold, of silver, of pewter, and of wood, that is four thousand or more, that when one has served the first course one should have enough for serving the second and still have some left over, and in the mean time one can wash and clean the vessels used during the said first course.

The history of food sees a lot of talk about feasting. Down through the centuries we come across roll calls of grandiose banqueting, of decadent dinners on an improbable-sounding scale. There are lists of huge numbers of oxen, fowl, poultry and other birds, each more extravagant than the next.

Each master cook seems determined to outshine his rivals — contemporary or historical — in his bid to go down as the most extravagant party giver. Frenchman Chiquart Amiczo is no exception. Here again we have a master cook who worked his way up through the ranks (see p. 46). He did his scullery time. He scrubbed, chopped, served as an apprentice and gradually edged his way up the gastronomic pole. Finally, he came to the notice of the Duke of Savoy who employed his services and then, after many successful years, nudged him into writing a cookbook.

And thus another great tome appears, listing colossal feasts in all their vulgar detail. Except this one was different. Chiquart was a party planner: he doesn't just say "fetch 400 oxen and serve them with a parsley sauce." He tells you how; he is big on logistics. While it's true to say, on the minutiae of recipes, we're not yet into the era of providing cooking times and temperatures, he does actually give quantities — 6 pounds of this herb, 8 pounds of that. Which is a revolution when you consider the vagaries of what went before. He was a more practical recipe writer than his predecessors and had an eye for the bigger picture.

Meanwhile, his boss the Duke of Savoy, also known as Amadeus VIII, was a serial schmoozer. He mixed in the highest social and religious circles and had married the daughter of the Duke of Burgundy, said to be the wealthiest and most powerful man in Europe. It was Chiquart's job to feed Amadeus's friends and contacts and feed them well, which he did. Indeed, so impressed was his employer that (as with previous master cooks across the world) he persuaded him to record his knowledge of cooking, and the planning of it, for posterity.

Chiquart dictated the work and it has lasted in its long, lugubrious, detailed and fabulously un-subbed entirety. There is, for example, a recipe for Parma tarts. It's a big dish. The recipe itself consists of one long paragraph of 1,415 words. One can almost picture Chiquart, the aging, self-glorifying and rather vain chef, reclining on his chaise longue dictating the recipe to a cowering minion. "Again, Parma tarts," he starts with an air of nonchalance, "for the said Parma tarts which are ordered to be made, to give you understanding, take three or four large pigs and, if the feast should be larger than I think, let one take more."

This is a recipe that you should definitely not try at home. The ingredients, in addition to the four large pigs, include 300 pigeons, 200 baby chickens, 100 capons and 600 small birds, although the object of the exercise is actually a very large quantity of small tarts filled with a spicy, herby mixture of the above animals and birds. The presentation of the dish ends with a flourish: "And when one serves it," declares Chiquart, "let on each tart be put a little banner with the arms of each lord who is served these Parma tarts."

Before Chiquart gets stuck into delivering his party-planning advice, he devotes some time to flattering his boss. This must be one of the most oleaginous genuflections in history. He prostrates himself in front of his patron. "To you, the very high, very renowned, and very powerful prince and lord, Monseigneur Ayme, first duke of Savoy, honor and reverence, with the prompt desire to obey your commands, I offer my very humble and devoted respects," he begins, before uttering that he is "no more than the least of your humble subjects." He continues: "I have a low standing and know and have learned too little because through ignorance and negligence I have never sufficiently improved my understanding." This, then, is the introduction to a work that was written onto 236 folio pages, including recipes totaling around 35,000 words—some were, as with his Parma tarts, long, overbearing, unwieldy and rambling.

As humble as he was to his master, he was surely harsh to those who worked for him in order to achieve such spectacular results. And his false modesty cannot disguise his formidable talent for organization. A feast lasting for two days needs four months of planning, he says. Having detailed, at great length, exactly the dishes to be presented for a wedding party, he then considers what might happen if the event has to take place during a religious period—if, for example, there are limitations on what fish, meat or dairy products you can serve. He then goes through the entire menu substituting ingredients with those that would be acceptable. He provides detailed lists of exactly the number of utensils needed for catering a big do; he says how much firewood and charcoal might be needed, and he reminds the reader to make sure there's plenty of money to pay for everything:

> And so that the workers are not idle, and so that they do not lack for anything, there should be delivered funds in great abundance to the said kitchen masters to get salt, pot-vegetables and other necessary things which might be needed, which do not occur to me at present.

Medieval banquets were large and sumptuous affairs, sometimes lasting for a couple of days.

He reminds cooks to invest in enough candles and how to prepare a meal in a kitchen other than your own. He was more than able to plan a Chiquart Amiczo pop-up supper club at the castle of a friend of the duke, for instance. He was mindful too of how visiting nobles brought their own servants. They were not just to be welcomed but afforded every bit of help: "quickly, amply, in great abundance and promptly [supply] everything for which he asks."

As for the crockery and cutlery (part of the instructions that constitute this chapter's "recipe"), 4,000 plates of gold, silver, pewter and wood suggests there was quite a party planned, not to mention a record-breaking amount of washing up. Today's party planners to the rich and famous don't know how lucky they are...

18

Muscules in shelle

(Mussels in white wine sauce)

AUTHOR: Unknown, FROM: *Boke of Kokery*

Take and pike faire musculis, And cast hem in a potte; and caste hem to, myced oynons, And a good quantite of peper and wyne, And a lite vynegre; And assone as thei bigynnet to gape, take hem from þe fire, and serue hit forthe with the same brot in a diss al hote.

The year 1440. Work begins on the Pazzi Chapel in Florence designed by the Italian architect Filippo Brunelleschi. German craftsman Johann Gutenberg of Mainz develops a method of printing using movable metal type. Itzcoatl, Aztec ruler of Tenochtitlan, dies and is succeeded by Montezuma I. In England, Eton College is founded by Henry VI and a Boke of Kokery is published with a recipe for custard.

Actually there are two recipes for custard in this boke, and yes, whoever wrote it—and the author is not known—was into a kind of free-spelling vibe. After all, this was a time when spelling had yet to be standardized and as long as one was consistent—give or take the odd word within an actual document—that was okay. Owning a book was impressive enough, so any strange spelling was small beer.

Most chefs still cooked from memory and that cookery books were so rare indicates that recipes must have been a jealously guarded secret. This particular *Boke of Kokery* includes 182 of them. They're all handwritten of course—the first printed book in English didn't appear until 1473—and the script takes quite a bit of getting used to. When you look at it, the language seems pretty obscure. In addition to the freestyle spelling of otherwise familiar English words, there are colloquial forms of French: the word "let" is used in place of *lait* for "milk," for instance, and "fryit" for *froid,* meaning "cold." But when read out loud, the sentences start to make sense. You can almost hear the strange accent they must have been uttered in. A recipe for green sauce—"sauce verte"—instructs you to take some herbs and "grinde hem smale; And take faire brede, and stepe it in vinegre, and draw it thoug a stregnour." Recite the words in an affected, effete voice and you can almost picture the fellow wafting a handkerchief and demanding that you draw the mixture through a strainer.

a litull in fayre grece. but lete not boyle. then take it oute. and ley on
a faire borde. and kutte it in faire smale peces as thou list And putte
hem ayen into the panne til thei be browne. And then caste Sugur
on hem. and fue hem forth

Pety pernantes

Take fayre floure. Sugur. Saffron. and salt and make paast therof
then make smale coffyns. then cast in eche a coffyn. iij. or iiij rawe
yolkes of eyyes hole. and ij. gobettes. or iij. of Mary couche therin
then take powdre of gyng. Sugur. Reysons of Corans and cast
above. then cover the coffyn with a lyd of the same paste. then
bake hem in a oven. or elles fry hem in fayre grece fressh And
then serve hit forthe.

Aut pety pernantes

Take and make thi coffyns. as hit is aforesaid. then take rawe
yolkes of egges tryede in sugur poudre of Gyngere and reysons
of Corans and mysed mary but not to smalle And caste all
this into a fayre bolle. and medel all togidre and put hit in coffyns
and bake hem. or fry hem as thou diddist be the tother

Custarde

Take vele and smyte hit in litull peces. and wassh it clene. put
hit into a faire potte with faire water and lete hit boyle togidre. then
take percely. Sauge. Ysop. Saverey. wassh hem. hewe hem And cast
hem into flessh whan hit boileth. then take powdre of pep. canel
clowes. Maces. Saffron. salt. and lete hem boyle togidre and a
goode dele of Wyne with all. And whan the flessh is boyled. take
it up fro the broth. And lete the broth kele. whan hit is colde streyne
yolkes and white of eyyes thorgh a streynour. and put hem to the
broth so many that the broth be styff ynowe. And make fair cofyns
and couche iij. or iiij. peces of the flessh in the coffyns then take
Dates. prunes. and kitte hem cast therto powdre of Gyng' and a litull

Cookery books were rare in 1440 as most chefs cooked from memory but the Boke of Kokery contains 182 handwritten recipes, including one for custard.

This doesn't, however, prepare you for the shock of what the author of the book regarded as custard. If you're imagining something thick, warm, yellow and sweet to pour over your apple crumble, think again. Custard in 1440 was a different beast. Far from being a sauce, it was an open pie filled with pieces of meat or fruit. But it was covered with something we might recognize as custard—a sweet and spicy mixture made with egg and milk. As the piece of bread, known as "sop," gave its name to the pottage it went into (see p. 53), so custard gave its name to the sauce that covered it.

One recipe for custard begins: "Take Vele and smyte hit in litull peces, and wass it clene." The rinsed and chopped-up veal is then boiled with herbs, including parsley and sage, and wine is added. The mixture is then left to cool and strained egg whites and yolks are added to thicken the broth. The mixture is then poured into a pastry case (that's right, a coffin—see p. 47) along with chopped dates and prunes and powdered ginger scattered on top.

A recipe for "custard lumbarde" (Lombardy custard), meanwhile, more resembles a fruity custard tart, again baked in a large pie. It's made with cream, egg yolk, herbs and dates. Almond cream and sugar are then poured on top before serving. This type of dish was also known as "crustarde," which, given that it refers to pastry, might suggest where the word "crust" comes from.

If these custard recipes do little for you, then one for another concoction is no less offputting, beginning as it does: "Take some garbage..." This was not an instruction to the servants to put the bins out, however, but a reference to giblets or offal. No doubt the word "garbage" then developed as a response to those who felt these parts of the animal should be discarded.

Critics of the *Boke on Kokery* have said that it works more as a reference book for servants, indicating which ingredients they should have ready for the kitchen and how to chop particular kinds of meat. There is also a section advising kitchen staff on storing food properly, although this is less to do with preserving it and more with putting it somewhere where it wouldn't be stolen. After all, meat, herbs and spices were still the domain of the rich.

But since most servants would not have had the benefit of an education, it seems unlikely that they would have been able to read such instructions. Furthermore, given the luxury that possession of this book would have involved, the tome was probably a cherished volume kept well away from the splashes and mess of a kitchen. But wherever it was stored, and there were no oily stains or flour marks on the copy I saw, what the book does have is an excellent recipe for mussels, hence their being championed here.

What a pleasure it is to see them cooked unadulterated, without lashings of cream, but prepared simply and quickly. Aside from the addition of vinegar and the lack of garlic, you can't go wrong. The author should also be congratulated for the last line of the recipe. After all, how many times have you eaten in a restaurant and felt irritated because you were not given "a diss al hote." Serving hot food on hot dishes is vital and for that reason alone, the *Boke of Kokery* deserves its place in history.

19

Lese fryes
(Cheese tart)

AUTHOR: Unknown, FROM: Harleian Manuscript 4016, British Museum

Take nessh chese, and pare it clene, and grinde hit in a morter small, and drawe yolkes and white of egges thorgh streynour, and cast there-to, and grinde hem togidre; then cast thereto Sugur, butter and salt, and put al togidre in a coffin of faire past, And lete bake ynowe, and serue it forthe.

Don't get too hung up on what might or might not constitute "nessh" cheese—your idea of a nice cheese possibly being rather different to mine. The author of this recipe for a cheese tart is in fact instructing you to use a "mild" cheese. So, if attempting it today, you might try Gouda, for example. And while I'm at it, you'll then need to "pare it clene" (take off any rind or moldy bits), "grinde hem togidre" (whizz the ingredients up in a blender), "then cast . . . al togidre in a coffin of faire past" (pour it into a prebaked pastry case—see p. 47) and bake "ynowe" (enough) or at any rate for 35 minutes in an oven preheated to 200°C (400°F).

Straightforward and delicious, this recipe comes from a fifteenth-century manuscript that rests today in the British Museum. It is one of a number of recipes from manuscripts owned at various points by Elizabeth I and the Earl of Oxford, collected together and published for the first time in 1888 as *Two Fifteenth-Century Cookery-Books*. Although it appears that the editor of the book, one Thomas Austin, did not quite have the stomach for what he was transcribing. "Many of the recipes which are given here would astonish a modern cook," he wrote. "Our forefathers, possibly from having stronger stomachs, fortified by outdoor life, evidently liked their dishes strongly seasoned and piquant."

Austin clearly recoiled from the endless tossing of large quantities of pepper, ginger, cloves, garlic, cinnamon and vinegar into almost everything. Not to mention lashings of wine and ale. "Such ingredients," he wrote, "appear constantly where we should little expect them." Then again he was living in the Victorian age when (see p. 182), the extravagance of flavor was frowned upon.

The cheese tart recipe, however, would have seemed less outrageous and it is one of many that uses milk or a derivative of it. (It is worth noting, however, that nothing is employed more constantly than almond milk—made by steeping ground almonds in hot water then straining—which was used in cooking everything from salmon to pork.)

Milk was a common ingredient for most during the medieval period, with your average peasant keeping a couple of cows on common land. Healthy, flavorsome and versatile, it would have helped to bridge the hunger gap as stores from the previous year's harvest diminished and the first crops of the new year were still to appear. Of course the downside of milk is that it goes off very quickly, particularly in the warmer months. So milk's separation, on heating, into solid curds, which could provide a staple part of a poor man's diet, and whey—a refreshing drink—gave it valuable longevity. The curds themselves could then be turned into a simple cheese by being wrapped in a cloth and then hung up to allow any remaining liquid to drain away.

But by the fifteenth century, cheese-making had become considerably more advanced, right across Europe. While the cheese mentioned in early English manuscripts isn't brand specific, we do know that there was a wide range. English pasture was excellent and the cheeses were delicious and highly varied—there was even one a bit like Parmesan.

This we know because of one man: a cheese-obsessed physician from Italy called Pantaleone da Confienza. Pantaleone traveled around Europe tasting and thinking about cheese and then he wrote a book about it. The reason we know that he took his mission seriously lies in the book's name. He didn't just call it "A Guide to Cheese." *Summa Lacticiniorum* means "Compendium of Milk Products"—not a very sexy title, but it harks back to another *Summa* book, the heavy-weight *Summa Theologica* ("Compendium of Theology") by Thomas Aquinas.

Many people reckon that Aquinas's book is one of the most influential pieces of Western literature, a classic in the history of philosophy. Even during Pantaleone's time it was regarded as the seminal work on the subject. Many just called it *Summa.* But then, 200 years later, came another *Summa,* except this one wasn't about the existence of God, or man's purpose; it was about cheese.

Now I'll leave it to others to discuss which is more important, eternal law or where to find a nice Cheddar, but *Summa Lacticiniorum* was undoubtedly groundbreaking in its own way. Until its publication in 1477 there had been recipe books, a growing number of them—some more useful than others, as we have discovered. Cooking methods were described, ingredients were championed in passing, but no one had ever written a whole book about one single foodstuff.

No one, that is, until Pantaleone traveled across Europe on a serious cheesy mission. As ever, like all the early writers on food, he had a patron. His day job was as a professor of medicine at universities in Turin and Pavia, but he also advised the noble Savoy family on health matters. And the head of the family, the Duke of Savoy of that time, was Ludovico. He loved his cheese and he loved it so much that he suggested his health adviser should write a book about it, the first book in the world dedicated to cheese. (Commissioning employees to pen books on food was in the family, as it happens, because Ludovico's father was Amadeus VIII, who, as we saw on p. 55, had encouraged his chef Chiquart Amiczo to write Europe's first cookbook.)

Ludovico loved cheese almost as much as he loved siring children—he had nineteen of them (by the same wife)—and he dispatched Pantaleone to study the subject at a time when cheese had fallen from favor. The prevailing view during the Renaissance was that it was unhealthy. So perhaps the book was Ludovico's way of arguing for his passion (although sadly the book wasn't published in his lifetime as he died in 1465). He trusted Pantaleone implicitly to do the job and in his favor the latter had a good reputation as a man to be taken seriously on matters of health. Not only was he a professor of medicine, but he had also, while traveling around with his boss in 1464, apparently found a cure for a friend of the King of France, a General Nicolas Tigland, who had been declared incurable by doctors. History does not record what he suffered from, or how Pantaleone cured him, but his reputation soared as a result. Maybe he got him eating cheese.

In the course of his research, Pantaleone visited markets and cheese producers; he questioned those he met about methods of cheese-making, thought long and hard about flavor and texture, and in his book presents a strong case in favor of his subject. The prevailing view may have been that cheese wasn't good for you but, he claimed, he had met "kings, dukes, counts, marquises, barons, soldiers, nobles and merchants" all of whom regularly consumed and loved cheese.

His book begins with a description of the different types of milk used to make cheese, reflecting on the different ages and breeds of animals used—whether cows, goats or sheep—and the variety of places and climates that cheese is made in. He explains the different shapes it comes in, that you can buy cheese with holes, for instance, and that some have crusty edges. And he goes on to detail all the cheeses he has discovered. The list is impressive: there are cheeses from France and Switzerland, there are Flemish cheeses and British varieties—the latter discovered not by crossing the Channel, but in a market in Antwerp. They are, he says, as good as the best to be found in Italy. The German types of cheese he has less time for, however—they are *mediocris saporis* (of unexceptional flavor). Of those he champions in his home country, which include Robiola from Piedmont and a variety from the Aosta Valley, he particularly likes Piacenza Parma, a Parmesan-style cheese.

Panteleone explains how cheese can be good for your health, which type would suit your age, how you should eat it and, interestingly, which cheese you should eat to match your temperament. There is much more going for cheese than just taste, he argues, and it is eminently practical: "Cheese is eaten after lunch, or gluttony, to remove the greasiness which remains in the teeth after chewing meat fat, or to remove any taste in the mouth after other foods." He glories in its qualities as a palate cleanser and bemoans that so many people spurn it. "I grieve at the thought of living in an era when I, a great eater of cheese, should refrain," he writes.

To his great consolation he discovered that cheese-making was flourishing across Europe. Producers were pooling their efforts and creating co-operatives. The product was clearly developing well from its ancient origins.

No one can pinpoint when cheese came into being, although as cheese historian Andrew Dalby says, "It was surely no momentous event." As milk curdles quite quickly if not kept cool, it can't have been long after man (Neolithic, around 7000 BC) started to keep domesticated animals for milk that he discovered cheese.

We can imagine the scene. An Arab nomad jogs through the desert one warm sunny day. Over his shoulder he carries some milk in a container made of animal stomach. Reacting to the rennet in the stomach lining, the milk quickly curdles. Then, when our nomad pauses for a swig, he finds there are white lumps (curds) in the mixture. It might not refresh him, but he likes the taste. Thus cheese is born.

Given that, naturally, milk would be seasonal, cheese becomes the way to store and consume it and its valuable nutrients. Historians describe the discovery of cheese as part of the "secondary products revolution," which marks the time before which animals were just used for their meat, bones and hide.

By the time Pantaleone was writing, cheese-making had become sophisticated, as had its consumption. He champions cheese made in the Aosta Valley as being particularly good when cooked. "It becomes stringy," he says, no doubt having enjoyed a good fondue. In fact cheese-makers from the region still quote his recommendation of their cheese when publicizing it today.

He also discovers cheeses in Piedmont that are ideal for those on a tight budget. These have "a spicy flavor, so much so it is said they are useful to the poor; firstly, because of their hot flavor, they eat very little of it." It's not a very right-on argument but he redeems himself a little as he continues: "Secondly, it is said to be useful to the poor because in the dishes prepared by them, thanks to the sharp taste of the cheeses, there is no need for spices and salt."

Pantaleone was a pioneer of taste. He encouraged a more sophisticated view of food and demonstrated how writing about a specific foodstuff could be used to encapsulate ideas on the economy, well-being and culture. His enthusiasm still encourages one to sniff out a good Brie or cook up some Gouda in a cheesy tart. For my money he's up there with Aquinas.

20

Ravioli for non-Lenten times

AUTHOR: Martino de Rossi

FROM: *Libro de arte coquinaria (Book on the Art of Cooking)*

To make ten servings: take a half libra of aged cheese, and a little fatty cheese and a libra of fatty pork belly or veal teat, and boil until it comes apart easily; then chop well and take some good, well-chopped herbs, and pepper, cloves, and ginger; and it would be even better if you added some ground capon breast; incorporate all these things together.

Then make a thin sheet of pasta and encase the mixture in the pasta, as for other ravioli. These ravioli should not be larger than half a chestnut; cook them in capon broth, or good meat broth that you have made yellow with saffron when it boils. Let the ravioli simmer for the time it takes to say two Lord's Prayers.

For centuries Martino de Rossi played a bit part in culinary history. He was the man who'd got a mention, albeit a very flattering one, in a seminal cookbook published in 1475. Its author was Bartolomeo de Sacchi, a writer and humanist who lived and worked in Rome and went by the name of Platina. His work, *De honesta voluptate et valitudine* ("On Honourable Pleasure and Health"), was credited with dragging cooking from the medieval dark ages to the enlightened Renaissance. With its 250 recipes it was revolutionary in everything from ingredients to techniques. His recipes heralded not just the birth of modern Italian cooking, but the first printed cookbook. It enjoyed wide distribution and was translated into at least four European languages.

As Platina lapped up the praise and adulation, he spares a thought for the man who, he says, inspired his recipe writing. "What a cook, oh immortal gods, you bestowed in my friend Martino of Como," he writes of the man he describes as the "Prince of cooks, from whom I learned all about cooking."

And that's it. We hear no more of Martino, who he was, where he lived, when he lived, who he worked for and whether he himself published any recipes. The man disappears from the culinary radar. That is until 1927 when a studious German-American chef, hotelier and scholar, one Joseph Dommers Vehling, comes across an ancient manuscript owned by an antiquarian bookseller in Italy. The author's name catches his eye and he buys the handwritten manuscript with the title *Libro de arte coquinaria*, or "Book on the Art of Cooking." Having got his hands on it, he begins to translate the Italian text and realizes the discovery he has made. The author, Maestro Martino de Rossi of Como, is the man mentioned in a book he knows well, written, of course, by Platina.

Vehling finally wrote up his findings in October 1932 in the publication *Hotel Bulletin and the Nation's Chefs* and in it he brought to light his most astonishing revelation. Martino didn't just influence Platina's book; all but ten of Platina's 250 recipes were his, word for word. The other ten, incidentally, being those of Apicius (see p. 26). On Vehling's death in 1950, the manuscript was gifted to the Library of Congress in Washington, where it still resides.

Scholars, who had wondered exactly how it was that a man whose main job was writing papal briefs came to know so much about cooking, now had their answer. Was Platina simply the biggest recipe plagiarizer of all time?

Meanwhile, from Martino's own writings we now know a little bit more about the man himself. His recipes show a degree of Spanish influence, he cooked for a time for a family in Milan, and then moved to Rome where his employer was Cardinal Ludovico Trevisan, a powerful and high-ranking Catholic prelate whose name is cited on the book's title page.

But it is the recipes themselves that are revolutionary. Until this point, as we have seen, cookbooks worked more as aides-mémoires for experienced chefs. They listed the ingredients needed for particular dishes and recorded extravagant banquets and feasts. Many were highly illuminating, culturally, but in practical terms at the low end of the helpful scale. Martino's book is different, however. Not only does he give actual quantities, he provides cooking times for the reader.

Take his recipe for game consommé, for example. He mentions "an ounce of salt cured meat, 40 crushed peppercorns . . . three or four garlic cloves, five or six sage leaves torn into three pieces each . . . two sprigs of laurel . . ." And, at last, the bit we've been waiting for since the dawn of time: "let it simmer in the pot for seven hours." When it comes to the minutiae of minutes, he is helpful but is reluctant to throw himself totally into the modern world. His favored method of referring to two minutes, for example, being "the time it takes to say two Lord's Prayers." But given what had gone before, that was pretty useful even so.

Likewise he brings a little color to his description of techniques. In a recipe for a "dainty broth with game," he adds "a generous amount of lard that has been cut up into small pieces like playing dice." Likewise in making pie with deer or roebuck, he instructs you to "first cut the meat into pieces the size of your fist."

Yet his recipes are more than just useful. There are new techniques (he shows how egg can be used to clarify jelly, for instance), his recipes for pastry are all edible, he uses shorter cooking times, promotes the natural taste of food and adds considerable degrees of subtlety to cookery in general. He understands that one drop of olive oil can add flavor, two can ruin the dish. Garlic is "well crushed"; before it was always "roughly" or "finely" chopped. A pedantic detail, perhaps, but one that good cooks will understand. He uses sugar not just to season dishes but to make them properly sweet. He also cooks vegetables al dente. In his recipe for "Roman broccoli" he removes the

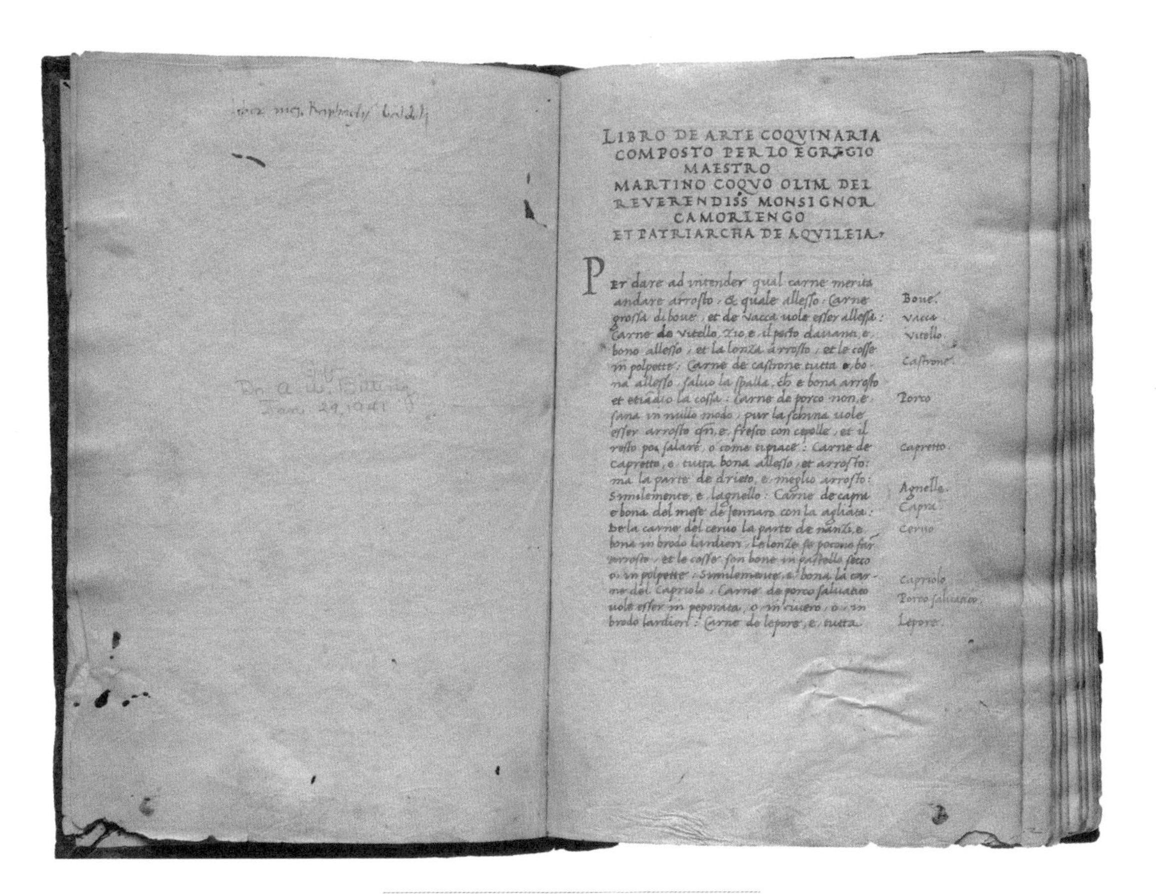
LIBRO DE ARTE COQVINARIA
COMPOSTO PER LO EGREGIO
MAESTRO
MARTINO COQVO OLIM DEL
REVERENDISS MONSIGNOR
CAMORLENGO
ET PATRIARCHA DE AQVILEIA.

Per dare ad intender qual carne merita andare arrosto, & quale allesso: Carne grossa di bove, et de vacca vole esser allessa: Carne de vitello, [illegible] e il petto [illegible], e bono allesso, et la lonza arrosto, et le cosse in polpette: Carne de castrone tutta e bona allesso, salvo la spalla, ch e bona arrosto et etiandio la cossa: Carne de porco non e sana in nullo modo, pur la schina vole esser arrosto [illegible], e fresco con cepolle, et il resto poi salare, o come ti piace: Carne de capretto, e tutta bona allesso, et arrosto: ma la parte de drieto, e meglio arrosto: Simelemente, e lagnello: Carne de capra e bona del mese de Jennaro con la agliata: De la carne del cervo la parte de nanti, e bona in brodo lardieri. Le lonze se porono far arroste, et le cosse son bone in pastello secco o in polpette: Simelemente, e bona la carne del Capriolo: Carne de porco salvatico vole esser in peperata, o in civero, o in brodo lardieri: Carne de lepore, e tutta

Bove. Vacca. Vitello. Castrone. Porco. Capretto. Agnello. Capra. Cervo. Capriolo. Porco salvatico. Lepore.

The first book to mention actual quantities and cooking times in the recipes as well as useful techniques, the Libro de arte coquinaria *was groundbreaking as the first printed cookbook.*

vegetable from the pot when it is "half cooked," at which point he adds a few knobs of chopped lard and finishes it back on the heat, using some of the retained water, for just "a short time."

Gone were the peasant days of boiling veg to the point of mush. It took until my parents' generation in the 1970s to start all that again. In fact he actually introduced vegetables to the nobility that he worked for, demonstrating that although they might be the food of peasants they could very respectfully appear alongside the meat dishes of the rich.

Even so, Martino can't resist a nod to the trickery and extravagance of the grand banquet. There's a recipe for "How to dress a peacock with all its feathers, so that, when cooked, it appears to be alive and spews fire from its beak" (using camphor and cotton wool soaked in alcohol). But his instinct was toward smaller, more convivial dinners, while the fashionable prevailing wind was still for showy feasts. His recipes cater for much smaller numbers. So one could also make the claim that Martino invented the dinner party.

With his recipes for sauces, tortes, fritters, eggs and other dishes he fused traditional ingredients with more modern produce. His cuisine was a fusion of two eras that brought cooking closer to the modern world.

But what of Platina? Should he be cast aside for fraudulence? The answer is actually no. Because, were it not for him, Martino's ideas might have remained in oblivion. By translating his work into Latin and publishing the first ever printed cookbook, Platina ensured these new ideas rightly reached a wide audience. Platina also added an introduction and a chapter on diet and health. Good food was, he argued, not just about decadence and gluttony. His book would "assist the well-bred man who desires to be healthy and to eat in a decorous way." It was not aimed at one who "searches after luxury and extravagance."

Platina's own life was not without discomfort. One might have thought that writing papal briefs would keep him out of trouble. But Platina was a man with opinions and in 1464 he had a row with Pope Paul II, who slung him into the prison of the vast Castal Sant'Angelo, built originally by Emperor Hadrian as a family mausoleum. "It was probably the worst dungeon you can imagine," says a current Vatican curator. A sixteenth-century inmate, the artist Benvenuto Cellini, went further, recalling how his cell would "swell with water and was full of big spiders and many venomous worms," while his hemp mattress "soaked up water like a sponge."

When Platina was released one might have thought he'd play it safe to avoid more such discomfort. But he got into trouble soon after, this time charged with conspiracy to assassinate the pope. Lack of evidence led to another release and he then tried a better tack, which was to write a flattering *Lives of the Popes.* This did the trick. Not only did he stay out of trouble, but he was ennobled by Pope Sixtus IV with an appointment as prefect of the Vatican Library, an event immortalized in a painting by Melozzo da Forli which can be seen in the Pinacoteca Vaticana museum.

Perhaps it was his time in jail that got Platina thinking about food. Perhaps while he dreamed of the dishes he had enjoyed as a free man and recalled his friendship with Martino, he vowed to commit his passion for food to publishing a book about it. Immediately after his second release, he set about translating Martino's work from Italian to Latin, organizing the recipes into fast-day and feast-day dishes and adding the extra chapters and the Apicius recipes.

The book was a quick success, although Platina was not without his detractors. One contemporary writer, Giovanni Antonio Campano, commented how his "mouth was full of leeks and his breath reeked of onions." At least it shows Platina took his food seriously.

Born into a poor family in 1421 in the humid Padanian plains of Italy, he had worked his way up to the higher echelons of Italian society. Without his work the world could have been bereft of the recipes of Maestro Martino, be it his exquisite veal cutlets which "should not be overcooked" or his macaroni or ravioli dishes. The latter delicious, especially if you're mindful not to cook the pasta any longer than a couple of Our Fathers. Platina might have pinched his food mentor's recipes, but isn't that what every good cook does?

21

For to bake quinces

AUTHOR: Unknown, FROM: *This Boke of Cokery*

To bake quinces take iii or iiii quinces and payre them pyke out their cores and fill them full of good syrup made of clarry or of wast pouders and sugre then lette them in coffins and hyle them and back them and serve them.

Now you might well think that one *Boke of Kokery* (see p. 58) must be much like another *Boke of Cokery*. But there are fundamental differences and not just that a period of sixty years saw the progression of the letter "K" being replaced by a "C." While the former was a handwritten manuscript, *This Boke of Cokery* was printed. In fact, it is the earliest known cookbook printed in English. There could well have been others and that they were lost suggests that not a great deal of value was placed on them at the time. These would have been regarded as fairly insignificant works—mere records of banquets, seasonal eating and recipes. More value would have been placed on the printer Richard Pynson's other books—law statutes and suchlike.

As if conscious of this, the title page of the book is humble and modest. "This is the boke of cokery" it states. A longer introduction follows on the next page. This is rather fuller of itself: "Here begynneth a noble boke of festes ryalle and cokery a boke for a princes household or any other estates and the makynge therof according as ye shall find more playnely with this boke."

I turned the ancient pages of this volume, my hands clad in white gloves, as it rested on a pillow in the chilled map room of the Longleat archives in Wiltshire. The book had resided for a couple of hundred years in the Green Library of the house, one of seven libraries, having come into the family collection by marriage. It had rested on a shelf next to titles like *Don Quixote*, *Wars of England*, *The Arabian Nights* and works by Sir Thomas Moore. Today it is carefully preserved in a secure air-conditioned unit in the house's converted stable blocks.

This is not a book for the kitchen and it never was. The pages are as clean as a bible's. It was written as a record and also as an aide-mémoire for the cook. As ever, there are no cooking times and quantities are scarce—save for the quince recipe given above, which at least tells you how many to use.

The author, most likely a senior cook in the royal household, records some memorable banquets from the past—a feast for "King Harry the fourth," who reigned from 1399 to 1413, and a list of the dishes that were served at the coronation of Henry V in 1413. Guess what: the guests were served pottage (see p. 52), boiled pike, gurnard, trout and so on. After the list of banquets there's a dense, dull, list of seasonal cooking: capon stewed, trout boiled, bream in sauce... ad infinitum. It's with some relief that the author then announces: "Here endeth the calendar of the boke of cokery and here beginneth the making."

And a little light detective work—a reread of the *Boke of Kokery*—suggests that these are not original ideas. Like the worst type of plagiarist, the author lifts a number of recipes and then just rewrites them slightly. His recipe for mussels being almost identical to the one that appears in the 1440 book (see p. 58). Except the new version is not quite as good as the old one and lacks the vital detail of the importance of serving the dish on a warmed plate.

But we can forgive this. This work after all was the first printed English cookbook and—as established in the case of Platina, with his pilfering and passing off as his own the work of Martino de Rossi (see p. 65)—the wider dissemination of good cooking is what helps food and society develop. The techniques are enlightening too, revealing much about people's tastes at the time. Vinegar is tossed onto food as we today would drizzle over olive oil. So either contemporary palates favored tangy flavors, or the vinegar was sweetened. The likelihood is that palates acclimatize to what is available. If olive and butter are scarce but vinegar is not and that's what everyone's tossing on their freshly boiled crab, then that's what you use.

Speaking of crab, there is a recipe "For to dight [prepare] crabe or lobster." The author instructs one to "stop the crabe or lobster at the vent with one of his litel claues and boyle them." Since the *vent* is the Middle English culinary term for a creature's bottom, this is an interesting proposition. Is the suggestion that shoving a crab's little claw up its arse will arrest it for a short time, enabling you to grab it and fling it into a boiling pot? Meanwhile, after cooking the crabs/lobsters in either boiling water or baked in an oven, one should again "serve them with vinegar."

When it comes to fish there is equally little mercy, it seems: "Take your tench and scald hym and splat hym and cast him into the pan." Does that suggest the tench is pan-fried alive (after the scalding and splatting) and with its guts? The recipe adds that the fish should be served with "blanched almonds," which adds a rather more luxurious note.

There are then numerous recipes for roasting every bird imaginable. Partridge, quail, crane, heron, egret and goose are among many. As Dr. Kate Harris, archivist at Longleat, comments: "People at the time had a strange interest in cooking and consuming vast quantities of wild fowl. It makes books like this read more like ornithological texts than recipe books."

In fact not long after the publication of *This Boke of Cokery* the first law to conserve birds was enacted, although it was more to protect birds so they could be served at the table rather than to actually save species. But aside from the lists of birds to be netted by princes and noble folk to sate their appetites, there are some recipes more palatable and practical to our modern tastes. Not to mention less offensive.

The recipe for baked quince with sugar is as sensible and worthy as it is delicious. No species of birds were harmed in its preparation and the quince is a mighty and

Quince with sugar and sweet spiced wine baked in a "coffin" is one of the recipes in This Boke of Cokery.

timeless fruit. The recipe calls for "clarry" (sweet and spiced wine) to be poured over the quinces or some sugar and "wast pouders." These were crushed spices—spicy powder—to add a medieval hue to your baked and sugary fruit.

They are cooked in "coffins"—pastry containers (see p. 47)—in the absence of a good ovenproof pot. If made of sweetened edible pastry, the recipe could make a good quince pie. And since *This Boke of Cokery* is not exactly precise with its instructions, who's to say you can't improvise?

22

Hippocras jelly

AUTHOR: Unknown

FROM: *Register of Evidences and Documents Concerning the Family of Stafford, Barons and Earls of Stafford, and Dukes of Buckingham*

Wine 3 gallons
Cinnamon 8 oz
Ginger 2 oz
Nutmegs and Cloves 1 oz
Sugar 3 lb
Graines [grains of paradise spice] 2 oz

This recipe made hippocras–you just needed to add isinglass, hartshorn, calves' feet or ivory shavings to turn it into jelly!

Our experience of jelly today is pretty limited. We serve it at children's parties—normally set in a big dish, having simply dissolved lab-created fruit-flavored tablets in water to create it. We dish it out at student parties using the above method but adding vodka. We then, as adults, serve the student version again in an attempt to bring back those heady days of youth. However, vodka jelly is actually a historic throwback to rather more glamorous times than your own recollections of attempting to maneuver around drunk people and cheap furniture in whatever tip of a flat you might have been partying in.

The earliest recorded alcoholic jelly was served at a dinner thrown by Henry VIII. Blink while perusing the menu of a get-together at Windsor in May 1520 and you might miss it. There are only two words and they come in a long list of dishes served over two evenings of entertainment at the castle. "An ordinance for the King, the Queen, and the Knights of the Garter at Windsor for Saturday Supper and Sunday Dinner the 28 and 29 days of May," is how the event was advertised.

The two meals each had two courses, not that you should think that that made it a simple occasion. Each course comprised between fourteen and nineteen dishes. They flowed out of the kitchen: soups, fish (including salmon, pike, tench and sturgeon), chickens, quail, rabbits and more—the usual story. But the end of three of the four courses that were served over the two days was marked by the arrival of jelly—described in its ancient form of "leche" or "leach," which is jelly served in a more sophisticated fashion. Leach could come in the form of castle, or an animal. It could be multicolored. Doubtless its arrival merited the odd "ooh," "ahh," a possible whoop and probably some clapping.

There is no early recorded recipe for hippocras jelly, but the one heading this chapter, taken from the pages of a manuscript housed in the British Library, is from the same period and just needs a spot of gelatin to turn it into jelly. There were a variety of sources to choose from. Sometimes it was extracted from the bladder of sturgeon (isinglass), at other times from the antlers of male red deer (hartshorn). Calves' feet were another good source, providing a high level of collagen and, more importantly, a neutral flavor. Raspberry jelly made using a calf's foot might not sound appealing, but actually it's rather more appealing than gelatin, the setting agent for modern jelly.

But it is not so much the jellies served at the end of the courses during that Windsor get-together that merit our attention, as the jelly served as the second plate of the second course during the Sunday dinner—in between "A sotelte" and a "Kind Kid." It was "Jely Ypocrass"—that is, jelly hippocras.

Hippocras is an ancient type of mulled wine, its attribution to the fifth-century Greek physician Hippocrates possibly suggesting the drink's health benefits. Certainly mulled wine brings on feelings of warm well-being, although a hippocras is not necessarily heated. A jellied version would have made a spirited addition to the lavish proceedings. Henry's Knights of the Garter enjoyed his favor for the likes of capturing Boulogne, raiding Calais or because they were the father of his current wife. They needed to make the most of their privileged times at the king's court as life was precarious. One moment you'd be guffawing and wolfing down some boozy jelly, the next you might fall from favor and end up in the Tower or worse. And that's a poor place to be when you've got the Tudor equivalent of a vodka jelly hangover.

23

Turkey tomales

AUTHOR: Bernardino de Sahagún
FROM: *Historia general de las cosas de la Nueva España* *(General History of the Things of New Spain)*

Here are told the foods which the lords ate ... turkey pasty cooked in a pot, or sprinkled with seeds; tamales of meat cooked with maize and yellow chili; roast turkey hen; roast quail ... turkey with a sauce of small chilis, tomatoes and ground squash seeds, turkey with red chilis, turkey with yellow chilis, turkey with green chilis ...

Turkeys arrived on the shores of England in the mid-sixteenth century. They must have startled those who first saw them. With their exotic plumage, their strutting, their ugliness and the strange noises they uttered, they characterized the wonder of what merchants were importing from overseas at the time.

The turkey was so named because that was where people reckoned it came from. Merchants had been trading in what was then called the Levant—the eastern Mediterranean—and when they came across these big edible birds they snapped them up. The birds then spread across Europe and while the English thought they were from Turkey, other nations—the Dutch, Danes, Finns, Germans and French—thought they came from India. And so the French today call the turkey *dinde*—the *coq d'Inde,* or "cock of India." Meanwhile, the Danish word *kalkun* comes from the name of an Indian port on the Malabar coast, Calicut. Turkeys were breeding there but they weren't indigenous, having been brought to Calicut by the Portuguese explorer Vasco da Gama. After sailing round the Cape of Good Hope and traveling up the east coast of Africa, he had crossed to India and landed in Calicut in 1498. On board his ship were turkeys, brought by him from Mexico.

And it was from Mexico that they arrived in Turkey. So really we should call turkeys "mexicos." Except that at the time Mexico was called the New Spain as the conquistadors—led by Hernán Cortés—were conquering and killing their way through the country from 1521. These "new spains" had been domesticated by the Aztecs and they called them *huexolotl,* which evolved into the current Mexican word *guajolote.* But "turkey" is easier to say, so we'll stick to that.

Whatever their name, the Aztecs loved them. Fossils of turkeys have been found in the Mexican highlands that date back 10 million years, and by the early sixteenth century they were an important part of their diet. More than that, they were a key ingredient at festivals and feasts. Their meat was devoured and their feathers used as headdresses and to add color to jewelry.

The most detailed accounts of the Aztecs consuming turkey come from a Spanish Franciscan friar, Bernardino de Sahagún, who was dispatched to the New Spain as a missionary in 1529. Having studied at the convent of Salamanca, he was, aged thirty, considered worthy of evangelizing the natives. Doubtless he showed the right degree of religious zeal that it would take to convert to Catholicism those whom Cortés hadn't killed. His companions reported that he never missed Matins and went into frequent ecstasies—of the religious kind.

It was only a few years since Cortés had defeated the Aztec ruler Montezuma, slaughtered thousands and torn down their altars (but not before joining him for a hot chocolate—see p. 77). But life had settled down to a certain extent and Bernardino was tasked with getting to know the locals. "They chose out ten or twelve of the principal old men, and told me that with those I might communicate and that they would instruct me in any matters I should inquire of," he wrote. "With those appointed principal men I talked many days during two years. On all subjects on which we conferred they gave me pictures."

Bernardino is a little modest about his endeavors. The men must have taken to him and his gentle nature and not just because he learned their language and became a fluent speaker. His work, translatable as a "General History of the Things of New Spain," is one of the great works of anthropology, accompanied by 2,000 detailed drawings produced by the Aztecs themselves.

The vivid picture he painted of the Aztecs ran to twelve books and a total of 2,400 pages detailing their society, economics, rituals and, of course, food. On which subject

Friar Bernardino de Sahagún's General History of the Things in New Spain *in mid-sixteenth century Mexico showcased drawings produced by the Aztecs (who liked eating turkey).*

the Aztecs were quite keen, particularly when it came to eating people. But aside from freshly sacrificed and cooked young man, the Aztecs liked turkey, as did Bernardino. Given that in the early months of his arrival much of the food seemed to consist of "tadpoles, ants with wings, and worms," turkey must have been a welcome relief.

He found it "always tasty, savory, of very pleasing odor" and he noted the various ways his hosts cooked it—the section above from the eighth volume of the *Historia* being the closest we'll get to a contemporary recipe—from boiling to roasting, served with different sauces, colored with green, yellow and red chilies. But he was particularly taken by the turkey-stuffed tomales. These early wraps were made with a corn-based dough, usually stuffed with meat. The wrap—a local leaf—was discarded before eating and its contents sustained the conquistadors, who turned their noses up at the human- or ant-type items the menu otherwise had to offer.

Bernardino noted that one of the first things the Aztec women did as a feast day approached was to prepare the tomales, which they had taken to an art form. Young girls would aspire to twist and plait the dough, imprinting them with designs of seashells and shaping them into butterflies. The skill in their construction belies the Americanized reputation of Mexican food as a sloppy pile of lettuce, rice and beans. To honor the various gods, tomales were made with different fillings, be it beans and chili, shrimps, fish or frogs. But our Spanish friar preferred his with turkey. "Very good-tasting, it leads the meat," he wrote. "It is the master, it is tasty, fat, savory."

As brilliant as Bernardino's work was, however, it never saw the light of day in his lifetime—he stayed in Mexico until he died, aged ninety-one. The closer he worked with the natives, the less he believed in the task of converting them all to Catholicism. So honest was his description of their lives, in fact, that the Spanish authorities thought publication would be dangerous. They feared the Aztecs might return to their heathen ways. Much of the work also made uncomfortable reading on the subject of Cortés's conquest, including many firsthand accounts of the terrible massacres he had perpetrated.

The work was quietly buried and didn't see the light of day until an astonishing 250 years later. It was finally published in its full glory in 1829, by which time turkey had become widespread everywhere. Today it is virtually the national dish of Mexico, the ubiquitous *mole poblano* containing a delicious mix of turkey in chili sauce, flavored with chocolate and thickened with seeds and nuts.

It is not surprising the meat took off in Britain and Europe. The King of Spain ordered that each returning conquistador ship bring back ten turkeys—five male and five female. It soon replaced the stringy peacock or goose of banqueting tables. The English were well used to serving big birds and took to it quickly. Championed by Henry VIII, it regularly graced the tables of English and European royalty by the end of the sixteenth century.

By 1600 it had caught the eye of Shakespeare, who mentions it in *Twelfth Night,* clearly amused by the ridiculously aggressive pose of the bird, its puffed out feathers and strutting gait. "Here's an overweening rogue!" says Sir Toby Belch of the posturing Malvolio, to which Fabian replies: "O, peace! Contemplation makes a rare turkey-cock of him; how he jets under his advanced plumes!'

24

Hot chocolate

AUTHOR: Bernal Díaz del Castillo
FROM: *Historia verdadera de la conquista de la Neva España* (*"The True History of the Conquest of New Spain"*)

As soon as the Great Montezuma had dined, all the men of the Guard had their meal and as many more of the other house servants, and it seems to me that they brought out over a thousand dishes of the food of which I have spoken, and then over two thousand jugs of cacao all frothed up, as they make it in Mexico.

The meeting of conquistador Hernán Cortés and Montezuma II, the last king of the Aztecs, is one of the great encounters in history. Two cultures came face to face; one ancient, one modern, each with its own way of life, religion and values. Each had philosophies, dreams and possessions that the other could never conceive of. Cortés was discovering a new world, planting the flag of Spain and the cross of Christ in towns and villages as he went. Montezuma ruled over a kingdom of glorious riches and chilling rituals. Each possessed items the other would find mesmerizing. Cortés had horses; Montezuma had chocolate.

They came face to face on 8 November 1519. After many, many months of negotiations, standoffs, gift offerings and diplomacy, they met outside what is now Mexico City. They were fearful and respectful of each other. Montezuma, a fit forty-year-old, was full of trepidation. Was this foreigner the spirit of the returning god-like ruler Quetzalcoatl coming to save his nation, or an adventurer come to plunder it? His daily ritual of sacrificing youths — especially fattened for the task, to be killed and then eaten — had failed to provide him with a definitive answer.

Cortés, meanwhile, was meeting a man who could stop his adventure in its tracks — whom he feared because of the large number of troops at his disposal — or allow him to build his Catholic churches, take his gold and precious objects, from stones to foodstuffs, and return home in glory.

"It was indeed wonderful," Bernal Díaz del Castillo, who served as a swordsman under Cortés, wrote of the first encounter in his detailed account of it in 1568. "And now that I am writing about it, it all comes back before my eyes as though it had happened but yesterday." He describes how Cortés met his rival, who was carried along by a cortege of obsequious servants — never looking their master in the eye. His dress was magnificent — even his sandals had soles of gold, the upper parts adorned in precious stones. The ground was swept before him, cloths laid in his path.

There were a few awkward pleasantries and then, the conquistadors having been directed to their lodgings for the night, there was dinner—although they didn't actually dine together. Montezuma preferred not to be seen eating, but after he'd finished he shared his magnificent banquet with his court and Cortés's men.

Castillo records how the royal cooks prepared some 300 plates of food for Montezuma to choose from. He sat on a low stool, with a low table beside him covered with a white tablecloth. Little braziers burned beneath the dishes to keep them warm, and after four beautiful women had brought him a bowl in which to wash his hands, he got stuck in. White tortillas, plaited breads and wafers accompanied a variety of roasted duck, rabbit, turkey, pheasant and much more.

A decorative screen was placed in front of him so he could munch in private and some elders gathered about him to keep him company. He fed them morsels of what he liked while they answered questions he put to them. And during the meal, as the historian recounts, "from time to time they brought him, in cup-shaped vessels of pure gold, a certain drink made from cacao, and the women served this drink to him with great reverence."

Having eaten a morsel of fruit and washed his hands again, there was a little light entertainment. A few ugly hunchbacks danced a jig, a jester told some jokes, then, after a puff on some pipes from which he inhaled "certain herbs they call tobacco," he fell asleep.

It was then time for the others to eat. Imagine it as a grand buffet, except that, as other contemporary accounts recount, among the bowls of roast venison and rabbit, you might see a human arm poking out. It was also a chance for Cortés and his men to try a new exotic drink—in "two thousand jugs" of chocolate, "all frothed up," as Castillo describes in his account (quoted in full at the top of this chapter), even if he doesn't go so far as to provide a detailed recipe. "We stood astonished at the excellent arrangements and the great abundance of provisions," he continues, doubtless reckoning Montezuma's catering must have cost what you might inappropriately call an arm and a leg, as he goes onto surmise: "With his women and female servants and bread makers and cacao makers his expenses must have been very great."

But the hot chocolate (which was not necessarily always hot) was worth it and in the ensuing months Cortés drank plenty of it. In a letter to Charles V of Spain, he championed it as "the divine drink, which builds up resistance and fights fatigue." Not all the Spaniards liked it, however. A Jesuit missionary called José de Acosta remarked how it "disgusts those who are not used to it, for it has a foam on top or a scum-like bubbling." And, he added, people "are addicted to it." Heard that before?

In 1528 Cortés returned to Spain with cacao beans (among other things, it must be said) and, more importantly, details on how to turn them into hot chocolate. But it didn't take off and it wasn't until the reign of Charles V's son Philip II that the drink started being served at court.

Hernán Cortés and Montezuma II, the last king of the Aztecs, meet in 1519 just outside what is now Mexico City.

It's likely that Cortés's recipe was too bitter for European tastes. This frothy cocoa was rather different from the mug of sweet hot chocolate that you might sip before bed these days. It might have been prepared with all sorts of additional ingredients, including wine, chili and aromatic flowers. The drink would have been made from mixing the beans and other items into a paste before adding water and then pouring it from jug to jug to froth it up and give it a head like beer.

As other products such as vanilla were brought back to Spain, they were added to the cocoa powder, along with sugar and then milk—used instead of water—and it became more palatable, delicious even. In fact the Spanish royals thought it so good that they kept their hot chocolate a secret for many years. The beans were in short supply and that they needed crushing into a paste before they could be used was information the royal household kept close to its chest.

Progressively, the European world cottoned onto the luxury of chocolate. It was seen as a divine drink, although not in the literal sense that it had been by the ancient Mayans, who predated the Aztec civilization. Images on ancient vases show that nobles were buried with a cup of hot chocolate; a nice mug of cocoa before they went to sleep for eternity. Similar etchings indicate how the beans were picked, fermented, dried and then roasted before being ground to a paste. The drink was used in rituals, but it was so highly valued that it was even used as a form of currency. There really was a time when money grew on trees. The conquistadors in 1521 came across beans stored as capital; there were even fake beans, which suggested someone was counterfeiting the currency. Such was their high value that they were treated like real coins. One Spaniard from the time reports seeing natives drop a few beans when they were trading: "They got on their hands and knees to pick them up as if an eye had fallen."

The properties of chocolate were thought to be numerous. Bernardino de Sahagún (see p. 74), a missionary who spent most of his life in Mexico in the years after the conquest, said it could treat fevers and indigestion. You could drink it to cool down or warm up; it could settle the stomach, help you sleep or wake up. Depending on its preparation, its versatility knew no bounds.

But as has been the case throughout history, this is a product produced by the poor and consumed by the rich. That Montezuma drank and served it on such a lavish scale demonstrated his conspicuous consumption at a time when it was valued as currency. According to an account by Hernando de Oviedo y Valdéz, one of Cortés's men, you could buy a rabbit for four cacao beans, a prostitute for ten and a slave for a hundred.

When Christopher Columbus discovered Mexico in 1503, he also came across cacao beans, but not knowing what to do with them, he carried on in search of "real" gold. So we have Cortés to thank for bringing to Europe one of the most soothing and delicious drinks.

The Spanish should thus be rightly venerated for the proliferation of hot chocolate. A nineteenth-century food encyclopedia reminded its readers of this and Spain's love of the stuff: "The Spaniards are the greatest consumers of cocoa or chocolate in the world and to them it has become so necessary for the support of health and physique that it is considered an extremely severe punishment indeed to withdraw it, even from criminals." I think I know the feeling.

25

To prepare a thick broth called zabaglione

AUTHOR: Bartolomeo Scappi

FROM: *Opera di Bartolomeo Scappi: Maestro dell'arte del cucinare (The Works of Bartolomeo Scappi: Master of the Art of Cooking)*

Get six uncooked fresh egg yolks without the whites, six ounces of sweet malmsey [fortified sweet wine], three ounces of sugar, a quarter ounce of ground cinnamon and four ounces of pure water; mix everything together. Put it through a sieve or a colander. Cook in a small kettle with boiling water – that is, get a copper cooking basin – containing enough water that the kettle is sitting in three fingers of it; boil the water until the zabaglione thickens like a thick broth. You can put a little fresh butter with that zabaglione and, instead of the malmsey, a trebbiano from Pistoia or else some other sweet wine. If you do not want the preparation so fumy, use less wine and more water. In Milan that preparation is given to pregnant women. Although it can be made with whites and yolks, you have to put it through a strainer because of the eggs' tread [sic]. It is served hot.

When the fourteen-year-old Catherine de Medici married a similar-aged French teenager, one Henri, Duc d'Orléans, in Marseilles at a service conducted by her uncle, Pope Clement VII, what consequences did the French foresee? Possibly not that as a result of this Italian/French union future generations would enjoy an enhanced tradition of gastronomy embodied in the likes of richly sweet and yellow zabaglione. The foodie consequences of Catherine's life and her influence on France for generations to come were overshadowed at the time by rather more dramatic happenings. It wasn't until many years after her death that historians picked through the turmoil in her life to assess her legacy in areas such as pastry and cake baking.

Cruel, frightening and short, Catherine's childhood was not what most of us today would regard as regular. She may have been born into the rich Medici family of Florence—the wealthiest and most powerful of what was once a city-state—but her parents died when she was just months old and she became a political pawn. First passed to a grandmother, then after the latter's death a year later, to an aunt, she lived for a time at the family home, the grand Palazzo Medici in Florence. There she was

Catherine de Medici brought Italian food to France and is widely regarded as the mother of French gastronomy.

thrown into the usual rounds of court dances and banquets until rampaging Spaniards, and Italian attempts to appease them, put the ten-year-old Medici in danger and led to her being exiled.

She was placed in a convent for her safety until the Pope, her uncle, decided to move her to Rome. There, barely into her teens, she was eyed by Italian nobility as suitable marriage fodder. Foreign royalty cast their eyes over her too, with the winning hand played by the French court. Not showing much potential as a beauty, she was paired with the French king's second son. Her uncle structured the deal, helping to seal it by marrying the couple himself.

That Henri was also a teenager offered little comfort. His father insisted on watching the consummation and, whatever psychological effects this would have had on the girl, she didn't manage to conceive for ten years. To compound the misery, her young husband took up with his nanny, Diane de Poitiers, who became his mistress, and in the ensuing years had his 'n' her double "D's" emblazoned on monuments and buildings across the city.

And if Catherine thought marrying the second son might at least ensure a relatively quiet life, any such ideas were quashed when she was thrust into the limelight after her husband's elder brother died aged eighteen. Soon her husband became king, she queen, and while she failed to produce heirs, her husband was siring several illegitimate children, courtesy of his mistress. Catherine didn't find much solace with the public either, who rather sniffed at her background. She may have been born of rich bankers but she was not noble by birth. Her detractors called her the Italian "grocer."

Yet she never complained, and was always courteous and charming. She did finally manage to bear children, ten in fact, of which a few survived and, as was the way in those tumultuous times, three became king. Not able to succeed to the throne as a woman, she remained regent. After her husband's death (he was poked in the eye by a lance during a joust to celebrate the marriage of one of their children), she had his mistress removed from the scene and became the adept, Machiavellian even, power-broker behind the throne. All of which history is important to recount before turning our attention back to zabaglione.

As Catherine's power grew, so did her influence. She inspired fashions—from thinner waists to higher heels—encouraged the arts, invested in books, erected buildings and added to them, introduced new dancing, tailoring and perfumes. She may not have been a beauty herself—"her mouth is too large and her eyes too prominent" said a contemporary—but she gathered together a glamorous entourage. "The court of Catherine de Medici was a veritable paradise and a school for all the chivalry and flower of France," recorded one sixteenth-century historian. "Ladies shone there like stars in the sky on a fine night."

And if one wonders how Catherine coped with the apparent isolation of those early wedded teen years, there is a very clear answer: food. When she came to Paris, she was not alone. She brought cooks, and her cooks brought ingredients and know-how.

At the time of her marriage, on 28 October 1533, gastronomy was reaching a high point in Florence. Knowledge had been accumulating since Apicius was writing recipes back in AD 10 (see p. 26). And now new ingredients were arriving, thanks to the Spanish conquistadors (see p. 77). The court menus from the time show considerable Italian influence too. There is macaroni, along with sweetbreads, truffles, sherbets, even ices (records exist of her bringing a Sicilian to Paris to make granitas for a wedding party). Her cooks brought their techniques with them, so that along with deep-frying we see the introduction of béchamel sauce, crêpes and cooking with a bain-marie. The latter crucial for that zabaglione, the device—a container of hot water in which a smaller container holding the food is inserted—enabling the cook to whisk the mixture while it warms gently without burning.

It was brought to France, some say, by Catherine who knew of it from the medieval Spanish alchemist Maria de Cleofa who wrote on medicine, magic and cookery. Although others claim the device was invented far earlier. Was it, for example, alchemist Miriam the Prophetess (also known as Mary the Jewess), the sister of Moses, who is mentioned in Exodus, who invented it? Or did Apicius (see p. 26) come up with the idea, as he appears to have used one to keep food warm when his boss was vague about what time he should serve dinner.

Whoever originally thought up the bain-marie, the Renaissance chef Bartolomeo Scappi didn't appear to have a name for it, as is evident from his recipe for zabaglione.

It was just this type of recipe, published in Italy—during the years that Catherine was the French Queen Mother—and then translated into other languages, that her chefs would have turned out in her kitchens along with her beloved artichoke. The latter ingredient Scappi turns into soup and makes a nice tart with.

She often overdid it on the artichoke front, in fact, specifically on the day of the wedding of one Marquis de Loménie to Mademoiselle de Martigues in June 1576. The French diarist Pierre de L'Estoile records how "the Queen Mother ate so much she thought she would die, and was very ill with diarrhoea. They said it was from eating too many artichoke bottoms and the combs and kidney of cockerels, of which she was very fond."

A great lover of food in general, Catherine kept her own personal recipes, from fish dishes to soups, while her chefs were keen to demonstrate to the French how herbs and spices could be used to enhance the flavor of meat and not just added to conceal the fact that it had gone off, a practice common since medieval times. Nearly eighty years later, in 1651, La Varenne's definitive cookbook *Le Cuisinier François* (see p. 103) reflects this influence. His spices are flavor-enhancers not foils, his touches are more delicate; he uses a roux as a sauce thickener, for instance, rather than just bread.

Likewise Catherine separated sweet dishes from savory, and arranged courses with that in mind, the medieval way to still have plenty of courses, but the table still with an array of puddings (jellies or blancmanges, for example) alongside the meat (see p. 44). Thus, fully laden with olive oil, beans and good cooks, she was able to remain unfazed by her husband's behavior by getting stuck into the catering arrangements.

Her tastes and cooking did not just bring Italian food to France, but helped transform French cooking into a rich discipline, in which French cuisine actually enhanced the Italian contribution, with certain techniques, almost forgotten in Italy, given a new lease of life in France. In this respect, Catherine de Medici is regarded as the mother of French gastronomy. As the twentieth-century writer Jean Orieux has put it: "It was exactly a Florentine who reformed the antique French cooking of medieval tradition; and was reborn as the modern French cooking."

Meanwhile, Catherine's culinary ideas were disseminated across the country. Her cooks demonstrated professional cookery to the staff of other households. Visitors tasted her dishes at her frequent "magnificences" or feasts and they saw her embroidered tablecloths, her porcelain plates and Venetian glass. They also saw her forks (see p. 99), an implement as yet unknown in France and one that still took some considerable time for the French to get used to. With her bread-making, pastries and cakes, Catherine set a new style that reached its zenith 200 years later during the reign of Louis XIV at Versailles. Outliving most of her children, and navigating her way through plots, assassinations and massacres, she had an instinct for survival that carried her through childhood and beyond and ensured that French gastronomy would be nothing if it weren't for the Italians.

26

Earth apples

(Potatoes fried and simmered with bacon bits)

AUTHOR: Marx Rumpolt, FROM: *Ein new Kochbuch (A New Cookbook)*

Peel and cut them small, simmer them in water and press it well out through a fine cloth; chop them small and fry them in bacon that is cut small; take a little milk there under and let it simmer therewith so it is good and well tasting.

The history of the potato rarely relates the role played by the German archbishop of Mainz, Daniel Brendel von Homburg. In the latter part of the sixteenth century, he was selected for the senior role of elector in the Holy Roman Empire of the German nation. It was a time of religious and political shenanigans (when isn't it?) and he worked hard to keep the peace between the Lutherans (thought by many to be obstinate heretics who followed the strict Protestantism of Martin Luther) and the Catholic princes.

How did he keep the peace? Well, given that he had a seriously good chef in his kitchen, it's likely that he entertained them to dinner. And what kind of dishes did he present? A whole manner of fabulous treats—from roasts, pastries, pies and soups to tortes and salads. There was simple fare—stewed pears and tasty plates of fava beans fried with bacon—but there were exotic dishes too, using ingredients never seen before in Germany or more widely in Europe. In particular there was a dish of "earth apples," what we today call potatoes, but the Germans still call earth apples (*Erdäpfel*), as of course do the French (*pommes de terre*) and other nations.

The cook was one Marx Rumpolt and this and around 2,000 other recipes appear in his 1581 *Ein new Kochbuch,* or "A New Cookbook." Rumpolt produced feasts and banquets for his master as he went about his political and religious business. So prolific was his cooking that he wrote his recipes down, publishing them with the specific aim of helping and encouraging young cooks.

Before landing a job with the Elector of Mainz, Rumpolt had worked for a variety of European nobles, learning the cuisines of different regions. He was proud of his knowledge, making it clear in his introduction that these were his own recipes. He had not purloined them from others cooks as many others had, did and indeed would. His cookbook also includes descriptions of wine-making and 150 woodcut illustrations.

His recipe for a potato dish is historic in being the earliest surviving recipe using potatoes. In addition, it demonstrates a good understanding of how to cook the vegetable: Rumpolt simmers his potatoes, before straining and drying them and then, after cutting them into smaller pieces, fries them with bacon and adds a little milk. However delicious the dish was, though, for the princes and religious types who were lucky enough to eat it, perhaps it was ahead of its time for it took another 150 years for the potato to find favor in Europe, although it had been popular for centuries in North and South America, where it had grown as a wild perennial in the mountains.

It was discovered, as were so many exotic ingredients, by the sixteenth-century conquistadors, its arrival in Europe much mythologized by historians and others. Was it Pedro de León, who came across them in Peru in 1553, or Jiménez de Quesada in Colombia in 1537? Possibly both. The latter apparently came upon a village whose inhabitants had vanished—unsurprisingly given the Spaniards' reputation for slaughtering people. There he found maize, beans and what he described as "truffles." They were a delicacy to the Indians, with good flavor. The Italians called them truffles because they were small, misshapen and knobbly, which sound a bit like the Pink Fir Apple variety of potato.

These *tartuffli*—earth truffles—were then brought back to Europe. Some say they arrived in England in the 1580s with the mathematician Thomas Harriot who had accompanied Sir Walter Raleigh. Raleigh himself is supposed to have planted some in his estate garden at Killulagh in Ireland. Unconvinced by them, he got his gardener to dig them up, whereupon the man discovered large quantities of tubers.

Yet, again, they were slow to take off. The French turned their nose up at them, convinced they were responsible for leprosy. Scottish Protestants disapproved of them strongly because they weren't mentioned in the Bible. Then when cultivation of potatoes eventually did spread, it seemed more for the benefit of cattle than of people, until the authorities discovered they made good food for the poor. In 1663 a member of the Royal Society, a gent from Somerset, was encouraging the growing of potatoes across the country, but the 1719 edition of *The Complete Gardener* still completely ignored them, while a sister publication described the potato as inferior to the radish.

They finally took off in the mid-eighteenth century. Some German districts made their planting compulsory and by the 1750s the English Board of Agriculture declared: "Potatoes and water alone, with common salt, can nourish men completely." The clergy urged their flocks to add potato to their diet and before long they became a mainstay of the entire Western world.

Today, of course, there are hundreds of varieties and countless uses—from alcohol to flour—and the potato now exceeds wheat in volume and scale. Marx Rumpolt's *New Cookbook* was a bestseller in its time, yet his recipe for earth apples was overlooked. How tragic that it took almost 200 years before someone built on his inspiration and cooked them *à la dauphinoise*.

27

Trifle

AUTHOR: Thomas Dawson, FROM: *The Good Huswife's Jewell*

Take a pint of thicke Creame, and season it with Suger and Ginger, and Rosewater, so stirre it as you would then haue it, and make it luke warme in a dish on a Chafingdishe and coales, and after put it into a siluer peece or a bowle, and so serue it to the boorde.

Anyone alighting at this chapter and hoping for a recipe for trifle might feel a little shortchanged because if you follow the above instructions you end up with something more like a fool than a trifle. But Mr. T. Dawson's book is indeed a gem and if he calls it a trifle, that's good enough for me. In fact it wasn't until the mid-eighteenth century that the modern trifle made its appearance. Biscuits wetted in wine, placed at the bottom of a bowl, with custard layered on top and then some whipped syllabub were on the scene by about 1755. At that point, Hannah Glasse gives a recipe that "is fit to go the King's table" in her *Art of Cookery Made Plain and Easy.* Her dish has Naples biscuits (like sponge fingers), ratafias and macaroons, soaked in sack (dry white wine) with custard poured on and topped with syllabub, which sounds fairly close to the modern, booze-soaked biscuits and custard dish, just without the jelly.

But even today the French call the trifle a *crème anglaise,* which sounds rather more like the Thomas Dawson version than the kind you might be given at supper with your aunt. Dawson's dish is a slip of a recipe, a mere trifle indeed, inconsequential perhaps, a matter of little importance, a cheeky little dish. Perhaps it deceives you with its sneaky sweetness. Actually Dawson may have had this very dish in mind when he wrote in his brief introduction that the book includes "most excellend and rare Deuises [dishes] for conceites in Cookery."

Little if anything is known of Dawson himself, so one can only offer conjecture as to who he was. But he was a key culinary figure in the Elizabethan era. His book came out in the latter part of Elizabeth I's reign and shows that the aspiration to good cooking had by then reached well beyond just the houses of the nobility.

The middle classes were growing and they needed help; specifically the women needed assistance. As the book indicates, it was clearly not the man who ran the household. And so he offers the English gentlewoman pages of advice, from everyday recipes to drinks, dishes for the sick and tips on keeping animals. For as well as the tips on food, there are, he writes, "also certain approued points of husbandry, very necessary for all Husbandmen to know." He's talking about animal husbandry here. Dawson must have

THE

good husvvifes

Iewell.

VVherein is to be found most excel-
lend and rare Deuises for conceites in
Cookery, found out by the prac-
tise of Thomas Dawson.

Whereunto is adioyned sundry approued
receits for many soueraine oyles, and
the way to distill many precious
waters, with diuers approued
medicines for many
diseases.

Also certain approued points of husbandry, very necessary for all Husbandmen to know.

Newly set foorth with additions. 1596.

Imprinted at London for *Edward White*,
dwelling at the litle North doore of
Paules at the signe of the Gun.

Frontispiece of The Good Huswife's Jewell *by Thomas Dawson: an Elizabethan household companion for women.*

had hands-on experience: he was clearly an accomplished cook who had also kept, or knew well those who had kept, pigs, hens, oxen and the like.

Many of his recipes, meanwhile, still have a distinctly medieval air to them—rich flavors infused with herbs and sweet spices. He lists ingredients such as aniseed, nutmeg, saffron, ginger, rose water, pomegranates, prunes and sugar. There are countless recipes for boiled meats, from veal to chicken, stewed calves' feet and pottage (see p. 52). But there are more modern twists. A custard recipe, for instance, is not the kind we came across in those early pies (see p. 46), but a sweet and heady mixture of eggs, cream, saffron, cinnamon, ginger and butter. He preserves oranges, cherries and gooseberries, makes quince marmalade and tarts with strawberries in red wine. There is a recipe for black pudding not dissimilar to one you would find today—oatmeal and sheep's blood, and using leeks instead of onions.

He presents a fresh, herby leaf salad with cucumber, chopped-up boiled egg and an oil and vinegar dressing, and includes a delicious recipe for a sweet and luxurious almond milk, which is, he writes, "after the best and newest fashion." There's also a brief and rare acknowledgment of a neighboring cuisine: he suggests how to "make a boyled meat after the French waies."

As in many early recipe books, there are medicinal cures for "the Megrime [migraine]...[and] other diseases in the head" and treatments "for all manner of Sores." Not to mention a few miracle solutions for problems that might beset the man in your life. "To restore speech that is lost suddenly," for example, he suggests you push a strange mixture of unheard-of herbs up the victim's nose. There is also the hint that some Elizabethans were worried about their size and needed some weight-loss advice. The Dawson diet plan is simple: "For to make one slender" all you need do is brew up some fennel tea.

Dawson was also clearly a man with a kind heart, especially when it came to looking after animals. His advice on those who have oxen—his target market would have had a patch of land—is that you should not work them if the weather is too cold or too hot but "use them gently...[and] rubbe or kembe [comb] them at night." After a long day their feet should be checked for thorns and their tails washed in nice clean water. You should ensure that their stables are clean, "that the poultrie and Hogges come not in, for the feathers maye kill the Oxen and the dung of sicke Hogges breedeth the murren." And whatever the murren was, it sounds nasty.

He does, however, offer some rather dangerous medical advice. He suggests that when your oxen are ill, bleeding their foreheads is the "uttermost remedie," but also adds that he got that idea from the French. Similarly he has ideas on what to do should "an oxe pisseth bloud" and that if it's unwell from being bitten by a "venomous dogge" you should "noint the place with oyle of Scorpion."

All in all, it is the ideal household companion for the Elizabethan age, although one might finish reading it still pining for a good trifle. But for that you needed to wait another 200 years.

28

Prince-biskets
(Prince biscuits)

AUTHOR: Sir Hugh Plat, FROM: *Delightes for Ladies*

Take one pound of very fine flower, and one pound of fine sugar, and eight egges, and two spoonfuls of Rose water, and one ounce of Carroway seeds, and beat it all to batter one whole houre: for the more you beat it, the better your bread is; then bake it in coffins, of white plate, being basted with a little butter before you put in your batter, and so keepe it.

Sir Hugh Plat was a virtuoso. He was the epitome of a Renaissance man of Tudor England, with a mind so filled with ideas he must have exhausted any companion. He published books and writings with an energetic fervor that is tiring just to think about.

The son of a prosperous Hertfordshire family—his father was a noted brewer who had accumulated property throughout London—he was educated at Cambridge. On graduating, he settled in Bethnal Green from where he set his mind on publishing his thoughts and ideas. Few subjects escape his attention. He wrote about everything, from garden design, munitions manufacture and agriculture (from soil fertility and corn yields to T-budding fruit trees) to children's education, needlework and brewing.

His 1594 book *The Jewell House of Art and Nature* is a "how to" guide for daily living. In it he explains how to deal with smoky chimneys, prevent drunkenness, steal bees, cheat at cards, check the cycles of the moon by studying a glass of water and "how to tell the number of apples, nuts, etc. as they lie in bulk together."

On the subject of ammunition, he claimed to have invented shrapnel and a method of putting a bomb in an empty boat that explodes on impact with an enemy ship. He issued a pamphlet explaining how loam (from silty soil) makes a clean alternative to coal. He was fed up with coal fires, as he put it, "defacing all of the stately hangings and the rich furniture of the house and all of the costly and gorgeous apparel." He didn't just write about loam, he actually sold the stuff. He also peddled pills which, he claimed, could combat the plague. "They were," wrote a twenty-first-century historian, "entirely useless." Although he was probably no worse than other doctors of his day.

But if one interest superseded all others it was food. His first great passion was for pasta, or macaroni as he called it, and which he spuriously claimed to have invented. (The Italians would have had a thing or two to say about that—see p. 42.) He wrote at considerable length about its merits. "It is durable, for I have kept the same both sweet and sound by the space of three years," he said. It was "exceedingly light," "speedily dressed" and "may be as delicate as you please by the addition of oil, butter and such like."

As with his odorless coal there was a commercial motive in his promoting pasta. He'd managed to get hold of a pasta-making machine, the only one, apparently, in London. And he became vocal on the subject soon after Francis Drake had returned from a voyage to the West Indies, during which his men had suffered from severe hunger.

Pasta, he implored Drake among others, was the answer. It made a nice change from the likes of beef, cheese and salt fish, would store well during any voyage, long or short, and was cheap. His pitch to Drake worked and there are records of the explorer commissioning Plat to make a large quantity of pasta for him for at least one voyage.

Plat may have reckoned he had the gen on pasta but, it seems, he didn't actually know how to cook it. He reckoned you soaked it until "it is sufficiently sodden." Nevertheless, buoyed by his success with pasta, he moved to what he thought might be even more lucrative turf—the sweet tooth of upmarket ladies.

Imported sugar was still quite a luxury, yet there was a growing fashion for using it to both conserve and crystallize fruit and to produce elaborate sugary sculptures for dinner parties. This was still a time when sugar was regarded as good for health, a view that remained pretty much current up until the 1970s, when doctors started linking sugar consumption to heart disease and other ailments.

When you didn't come across sugar at the smarter house parties, you found it at the pharmacy, from the apothecary. Recipes for it were considered medicinal and for hundreds of years doctors recommended it. In 1715, for example, a Dr. Frederick Snare wrote a treatise called *A Vindication of Sugars* in which he responds to another physician's attack on what is clearly a personal obsession. As well as listing its many supposed benefits, he states that he practices what he preaches and adds sugar to wine, uses it as snuff and even as toothpaste. He cites the case of the Duke of Beaufort who, he says, lived to a ripe old age because he consumed a large quantity of sweets every night after dinner for the best part of forty years.

So sugar was the best of all worlds, sweet and delicious and really good for you. And when used to crystallize fruit, it added considerable glitz to the table, especially if oranges were involved. Oranges had become a coveted fruit, rich in both flavor and allegory, and before long the wealthy were impressing their friends with the construction of orangeries. If you hadn't got an orangery, you could at least get an orange and cover it in sticky sugar. Plat promoted the practice in his book *Delightes for Ladies* in which he published hundreds of recipes and some very practical advice.

He lists the kitchen tools you need: a deep bronze pan, a ladle, a brazen slice (like a spatula—to scrape sugar off the sides of the pan), among other things. His advice is detailed, precise and very practical. To melt sugar he suggests a proportion of 3 pounds of sugar to "one pint of clean, running water." It must be melted slowly over hot coals without flames: "Let it seethe mildly until it will stream from the ladle like turpentine, with long stream and not drop."

So passionate is Sir Hugh Plat about his sugary ideas that he prefaces the book with a long poem on the subject. His writing is as fruity as his recipes and reveals that he was no mean poet and had a graceful charm with the written word. "Now my pen and paper are perfumed," he writes. "Of sweets the sweetest I will now command/ To sweetest creatures that the earth doth bear." If the ladies weren't titillated at that, he continues:

The walnut, small nut, and the chestnuts sweet
Whose sugared kernels lose their pleasing taste
Are here from year to year preserved
And made by Art with strongest fruits to last.

He then goes a little over the top and suggests that sugar could actually be the solution to the world's problems, a way to end war and violence:

Impalings now adieu ...
Let piercing bullets turn to sugar balls,
The Spanish fear is hushed and all their rage.

Given his other entrepreneurial activities, one wonders whether he actually believed that a little dose of sugar all round might indeed calm one's enemies. Nevertheless, everyone would have applauded his preserved plums, cherries and gooseberries, not to mention his sculptures of sugary rabbits, pigeons "or any other little birds or beasts."

However, since these sweet treats are a little out of fashion today and his "marchpane" or marzipan recipe may be perfect but not to the modern taste, it is his recipe for biscuits that finally makes it to the fore. His "prince biscuits," which are a little like macaroons but without the almonds, are not just one of the earliest recipes for biscuits but they taste good too.

In addition to his recipes for crystallizing fruit, Plat had a section on beauty. There are solutions for "a face that is red or pimpled," as well as tips on making scented water to sprinkle on your clothes. No doubt Sir Hugh himself was as perfumed and decorative as he reckoned others could be. We can only imagine him, a rakish dandy perhaps, going about London seeking a word here and there with his vast network of contacts from whom he derived inspiration. He knew everyone, from kitchen porters and rat catchers, to the Queen's trumpeters and courtiers. He tapped them for ideas and recipes and, thanks to him, we have a unique record of the tastes and aspirations of Elizabethan men and women.

29

To butter crawfish

AUTHOR: Lady Elinor Fettiplace, FROM: *Elinor Fettiplace's Receipt Book*

Boyl the Crawfish and pick the fish out of the bodys tail and claws then take to an Hundred and two or three spoonfuls of water and as much white wine a Blade of Mace or a little nutmeg a little salt and Lemmon peel let it simmer together then put in the crawfish and shake e'm together and when they are through hot put in half a qr of a pd of Butter keep e'm shaking till the butter be metled then put in a little juice of Lemon: you may if you please boyl the shells in the water you put in.

The year 1604 was a bad one for the plague—not much better than 1603, in fact. The summer was hot and people in the countryside waited and listened with increasing anxiety as news emerged of death stalking towns and cities. The previous year had seen some 30,000 deaths in London alone. Those who could fled from the towns, others shut themselves up in their houses, while many, resigned to their terrible fate, wandered around their rose gardens (well, those who had rose gardens) waiting for the inevitable pox to appear.

Countryside folk relied on help and advice not from doctors but from the local big house. While the nobleman collected his rents and dished out reprimands and justice, the lady of the house was more philanthropic, dishing out advice and remedies for ailments. Whether it was a dog bite, stomach pains or a case of melancholy, she'd probably have a cure of some kind, usually some bitter mixture of distilled herbs and roots.

Ladies had increasing power and influence in the home. They organized the household duties—from laundry to food—and mothered not just the family and servants but whole villages. And those who were well organized wrote down their recipes and remedies. Some even had them copied out by professional scribes. They could then be passed down through the family, from daughter to daughter-in-law down through the years.

When twentieth-century literary editor and writer Hilary Spurling went through the possessions of her husband's late and last great-aunt in her semidetached house in suburban London, she came across such a manuscript. With additions and comments added over the years, the recipes were inscribed in the Italian style of the early seventeenth century. It was signed at the end: "By mee Anthony Bridges." There were 225 pages, the date was 1604 and it was copied by Bridges from writings by Lady Elinor Fettiplace. Recipes, household chores, gardening tips and health cures throughout the season were presented with clarity and precision. There were sophisticated dishes and ideas for the new Elizabethan home as well as recipes from yesteryear.

Lady Fettiplace was the wife of a knighted man whose handsome Tudor house was situated a few miles outside Oxford. They were relatively prosperous—although the property was heavily mortgaged—and well connected. They dined well and from a sophisticated range of dishes; indeed, Elinor's recipe for buttered crayfish is one that Mrs. Beeton uses 300 years later unchanged. Served with a green salad, some crusty bread and a cool glass of white wine, it would make a delicious summer supper for friends in the garden.

And it would have taken your mind off the plague back in 1604. It also shows us how food was finally relinquishing its medieval shackles. Lady Fettiplace's crayfish recipe takes our story of food from the feudal to the modern. As, indeed, does her recipe for buttered spinach. "You must boyl yt well wth as little water as you can for the less water the sweeter yr spinage wilbee when yt is very tender," are her first, precise instructions. She then adds verjuice (the sharp, slightly fermented juice of sour grapes or crab apples), some butter and sugar, and lets it stew for a while before adding two egg yolks and cream. To finish, she beats the mixture and adds a bit more sugar before serving.

Creamy but not too rich, this makes a subtle and tasty side dish. You could have it with the crayfish, for instance. It sits among recipes for puddings and meat that are more modest and practical than those presented in previous recipe collections. Lady Fettiplace's recipes serve six, not 600. Eating in larger houses was moving from the great hall—where everyone would eat at the same time, including the servants—to small private dining rooms.

Most of her recipes are modest and practical, as are the suggestions for doing laundry and relieving pox. She had common sense. She didn't recommend bleeding or vomiting or other nastier recommendations of the time. For smallpox she is the model of calm kindness: "When you know certainlie that it is the pocks, let them drink some safron & milk, & let them keep their chamber for fear of taking cold, let them keep themselves warme, but not too hot, for that will doe them much hurt..."

Likewise she helpfully offers fifty-six ways of dressing wounds, as well as cures for insomnia, fevers, coughs and bad backs. She does occasionally succumb to superstition, however, such as when offering a remedy that harks back to the previous monarch. "A medicine of King Henry VIII for the plague or pestilence" is supposedly preventative. "If this Drink bee taken before the markes appear, it helpeth by the grace of God," she writes in the margin.

But her recipes are where we see the distinction of progress. There are fewer mentions of saffron, almond milk and pottage. Like Catherine de Medici (see p. 84), she separates the sweet from the savory, moving away from the medieval habit of laying everything on the table at once, with sugar and spice, meat and fruit not just on the same table but in the same pot. Gone are those artificial colorings and the flamboyant trickery. Neither does she relay one of those long lists of meat and fowl so beloved of older-style cookbooks.

While there are still those Arab influences of rose water, dried fruit and spices, we see egg used to thicken soup rather than bread or flour. French influences now begin to appear instead, as in the emergence of the meringue. And it is from this very moment that we can trace some of Britain's classic dishes and food combinations: roast beef and Yorkshire pudding, mutton with red currant jelly, turkey with bread sauce infused with cloves.

Her house, Appleton Manor, which can still be seen with its twelfth-century Cotswold masonry and Tudor additions, had an open fire for roasting but there were mod cons too. A dish to collect the juices was used; she liked to add a splash of claret to finish her gravy. She had a metal contraption with coals to heat an open pan on one level and a lidded pan above. Some would even have had a charcoal heater. In her recipes she refers to this as a "chafing dish of coals." It might have been installed in a separate room where you would have found distilling equipment and cupboards for drying and storing food.

She would also have had a bread oven. The kitchen of the early seventeenth century would have looked like a cottage industry. Households were very self-sufficient: they would not just have produced their own sickness remedies but the likes of toothpaste, soap, rat poison and weed killer. And housekeepers would have been highly tuned into the seasons. Lady Fettiplace has tips for sowing herbs and vegetables and was mindful of the vegetables that needed growing and storing for the winter months.

Her store-cupboards needed to be well stocked. In the days when deliveries came on foot or using horsepower, the delivery man needed feeding, as did anyone passing by on business. During feasting periods—the twelve days of Christmas, for example, between 25 December and 6 January—there would be endless meals, held twice a day and for up to fifty people.

During the winter months, lean times for produce, the household stores would be much needed. So out would come the pickled samphire and preserved cucumbers and artichokes, along with dried fruit, cheese and biscuits. As spring arrived and summer approached, the kitchen would benefit from harvests of herbs, flowers, honey and fruit. There was "cow whot"—the cream from the top of the milk from the dairy and nothing would be wasted.

The kitchen staff, meanwhile, would be constantly grinding those herbs with a pestle and mortar. They used feathers to take the scum off simmering syrups and to ice cakes. Hollowed-out and dried fennel stalks made a handy test tube to apply eye drops. Of Lady Fettiplace's more sophisticated and ingenious ideas, a recipe for sugar syrup stands out. You blow powdered sugar through a quill into a cleaned pig's bladder which is suspended above a pot of warm water all day "over a very soft fire."

Spurling points out that this was a method still used in France in the 1950s and spotted by Elizabeth David (see p. 256). *Poularde en vessie* ("chicken in a bladder") is prepared by a Madame Baraterro at the Hôtel du Midi in Lamastre in 1958. David tells Madame Baraterro that such a method would not be possible in England. "What do you mean?" replies the indignant hotelier. "Why can you not get a pig's bladder in England? You have pigs, do you not?"

A drawing of Lady Elinor Fettiplace's house, Appleton Manor, by William Bird.

Lady Fettiplace's kitchen was run with exacting efficiency and that she adds handwritten notes in the margin of her book shows she had hands-on cooking experience and, unlike her social equivalent a few hundred years later, did not run the kitchen with just a regular conference with the cook. No doubt she was as firm with her staff and as clear and succinct in her instructions to them as she is in a recipe for an omelette: "Let yor butter bee scalinge hott in yor pan and powre in yor Batter, as yt doth begin to bake stirr yt wth a knife untill yt will frye wthout stickinge."

Her recipes are, says Hilary Spurling, "simple but subtle, and by no means unsophisticated." She goes on to add: "These recipes, standing in much the same relation to modern cooking as Shakespeare's language to how we speak now, are not only entertaining to read but easy to follow, straightforward to make and, in my experience, nearly always excellent eating." Lady Fettiplace's crayfish, which does indeed taste excellent, makes for a particularly entertaining dish when coupled with a conversation about her unusual connections. Her grandmother was a Whittington, as in the thrice-mayoral Dick, while her niece married one Sir George Horner, whose great-grandfather Sir John was reputedly quite small and went by the name of Jack, and she has a recipe from a Dr. Thomas Muffet, whose daughter Patience had an aversion to spiders.

30

An Englishman discovers the fork

AUTHOR: Thomas Coryat
FROM: *Coryat's Crudities: Hastily Gobled Up in Five Moneths Travells in France, Italy, etc.*

The Italian, and also most strangers that are commorant in Italy, doe alwaies at their meales use a little forke when they cut their meat ... This forme of feeding I understand is generally used in all places of Italy, their forkes being for the most part made of yron or steele, and some of silver, but those are only used by Gentlemen. The reason of this their curiosity is, because the Italian cannot by any means indure to have his dish touched with fingers, seeing all men's fingers are not alike cleane.

It was on 14 May 1608 that Thomas Coryat, the thirty-something, Somerset-born son of a rector, finally tired of life in London. He was an educated man who hung around with fashionable types in the company of Henry, Prince of Wales. But while he considered himself an intellectual, his contemporaries saw him as merely eccentric, and while he regarded London life as frivolous, they viewed him as a country bumpkin. His conversation, peppered with tales from exotic places, was not taken seriously. Indeed he was laughed at. There may have been a world beyond the court, but no one within it showed any interest. Apart from him, that is.

So it was that Coryat, one spring morning, put himself on a boat to France. It was a journey that would take him all around Europe. And it was a journey that he seemed mainly to do on foot. On returning to England, he hung up his battered shoes in the parish church by his home in Odcombe. There they rested for many years, right up to the beginning of the eighteenth century. The shoes weren't the only testament to his travels, however; he also produced detailed writings of his adventures, which he published in 1611 in the splendidly titled *Coryat's Crudities.* His account includes two discoveries, both made in Italy and both to prove of considerable consequence to his fellow countrymen.

The first was made in the town of Cremona in Lombardy, where Coryat witnessed the use of "things that minister shadow unto them for shelter against the scorching heate of the Sunne." Of which, he revealed, "they commonly call in the Italian tongue umbrellaes." He described them as "made of leather something answerable to the forme of a little canopy, & hooped in the inside with divers little wooden hoopes that extend the umbrella in a pretty large compasse." He noticed that they were often used by horsemen and that "they impart so long a shadow unto them, that it keepeth the heate of the sunne from the upper parts of their bodies."

Doubtless when Coryat reported this finding to his chums in the English court, they simply scoffed, muttering words like "preposterous." Whereas of course, everyone who has either lived in or visited England since should be endlessly grateful to him for his discovery, if chiefly as protection against the incessant English rain than the scorching English sun.

His second great find came after a rather false start in Turin. "I am sorry I can speak so little of so flourishing and beautiful a city," he writes, this being due to the fact that he was taken ill "by drinking the sweete wines of Piedmont...so that I had but a small desire to walke abroad in the streets." He then offers a piece of advice that his fellow countrymen have been ignoring for centuries. "I would advise all English-men that intend to travel to Italy, to mingle their wine with water as soon as they come into the country, for feare of ensuing consequences."

Recovered from his hangover, Coryat mentions his discovery: "I observed a custome in all those Italian Cities and Townes through which I passed, that is not used in any other country that I saw in my travels, neither do I thinke that any other nation of Christendome doth use it, but only Italy." And he goes onto describe his extraordinary encounter with the fork, as detailed above, adding that those who use their fingers instead of this implement "will give occasion of offence unto the company, as having transgressed the laws of good manners, in so much that for his error he shall be at the least brow-beaten, not reprehended in words."

So impressed was Coryat, in fact, that he took a fork with him on the rest of his travels, around Germany and then back with him to England. His friends, he reports, laughed at his new quirky habit. He was given the nickname "furcifer," which means "pitchfork." To the English forks were over-refined and that the Italians used them was just another example of their being, as another contemporary put it, "effeminate sodomites."

Coryat may have been pioneering in bringing the fork to the attention of a few educated English, but he wasn't the first person to refer to it in print. Its first formal mention came almost a century earlier, in 1526. For that was when the Italian writer and editor Eustachio Celebrino published his *Opera nuova che insegna apparecchiare una mensa,* or "New Work on How to Prepare a Table for a Feast." In his detailed description of how the table should be set, he refers to a piece of bread, a cracker and some cake, with the plate flanked by a knife and a fork.

He calls it a *pirone* and indicates that every smart table setting should have one. Celebrino was after all a helpful soul and he published several manuals of daily living. He'd be a generalist feature writer if he were around today for his range of subjects is diverse, from recipes for good living to cures for syphilis — the latter based on his own experience, which may be too much information here. He also published a book of *Secrets for Ladies who Desire to Make Yourselves Beautiful,* as well as one on how to avoid the plague.

Celebrino published his books in Venice, at the time Europe's center of publishing, having apparently tried his hand at everything from business to the arts. He frequented the courts of Renaissance Europe but also gambling dens and brothels, and legal troubles saw him fleeing the authorities and changing his name before arriving in Venice.

Yet however dodgy his past, he knew how to use a fork. His early mention of its use at formal dinners shows how well-to-do Italians of the time were starting to regard table manners as a sign of culture. The fork was then illustrated for the first time in a major piece of art—Jacopo Bassano's *Last Supper,* unveiled in 1542. While the eye is diverted by the rippling muscles and vigorous poses of those seated around Christ, Peter, the gray-bearded disciple to his right, can clearly be seen gripping a two-pronged fork in one hand.

But still it failed to catch on. Perhaps it was because, as U.S. food historian Clifford A. Wright has argued, "The fork has no practical purpose outside of etiquette; the fingers, knife and spoon are adequate. The fork was invented because of a new consciousness of good taste among a class of people who were urban dwellers, the original meaning of bourgeois."

Indeed, as you can see from an early set of cutlery at the Victoria and Albert Museum, owning your own knife and fork was for a long time a sign of elegance and wealth. It's an ornate French-made set of knife, fork and skewer complete with a leather carrying case from the sixteenth century. Getting them out when you visited friends was bound to impress. Forks from this period are rare but there are many knives. In fact the number that still exist in good order suggests that even they were rarely used and that fingers were the preferred implement.

There are earlier references to forks—much earlier. While large ones were used to lift sacrifices in the temples of ancient Egypt, there is evidence that Middle Eastern courts had some small, two-pronged ones in the seventh century. A record also exists of the utensil being used by a Byzantine princess of the eleventh century who hailed from Greece and was married to a Venetian doge. She was spotted wielding a fork and harshly censured by the Venetian clergy—it was an affront to God's intention to use the fingers. One who observed her fork-habit thought it diabolical. "Such was the luxury of her habits, she deigned not to touch her food with her fingers," wrote a church leader, "but command[ed] her eunuchs cut it up into small pieces, which she would impale on a certain gold instrument with two prongs and thus carry to her mouth."

The fork then seems to disappear for a few hundred years before Celebrino mentions it. Although it takes some time to get going again. Catherine de Medici (see p. 81), who married Henri II of France in 1533, had several dozen in her wedding dowry, made by a famous Italian silversmith, but still they didn't catch on. The French thought them dangerous and the German priest and theologian Martin Luther feared they threatened him for his Protestant inclinations: "God preserve me from forks," he once said.

So Coryat's fellow Englishmen continued to use their fingers to tear apart meat and shove it into their mouths. Indeed, it took another 100 years for the fork to become widely used at every level of society. And this in spite of Charles I of England declaring in 1633: "It is decent to use a fork."

Discoursing on forks seems to have appealed chiefly to the more oddball writers in history. Among the numerous writings of Sir George Sitwell, early twentieth-century eccentric and father of poet Edith Sitwell (oh, and my great-grandfather)—the titles of which included *The Origins of Part-singing, Decorative Motifs Employed in the Leaden Jewellery of the Middle Ages* and *The Introduction of the Peacock into Western Gardens*—is *The History of the Fork.* Sadly, however, no copy of Sir George's seminal work appears to have survived. Indeed, some say that it was concocted by his son Osbert, who virtually made a career out of lampooning his father. Which is perhaps understandable, for when Sir George wasn't writing about forks and other things, he was working on such useful inventions as a revolver for killing wasps.

Coryat and Sitwell were both mocked for their interest in the fork, and eccentric they may both have been, but they at least recognized the value and social importance of this now indispensable utensil.

31

Spargus with white sauce

AUTHOR: François Pierre, Sieur de la Varenne, FROM: *Le Cuisinier François*

As they come from the garden, scrape them and cut them equally; seeth them with water and salt. Take them out, as little sod as you can, it is the better, and set them draining. Then make a sauce with fresh butter, the yolk of an egg, salt, nutmeg, a small drop of vinegar; and when all is well stirred together, and the sauce allayed, serve your spargus.

Spargus with white sauce may not sound revolutionary, ground-breaking or historic. But it was. Look a little closer at the recipe and it's clear that France, in the mid-seventeenth century, had not seen anything like it.

A more modern translation would be asparagus with hollandaise. Take a look at the text and you can see the stunning modernity. As any good gardener or cook will attest, the best asparagus spears are those cut from the soil just as the water is set to boil in the pan. This cook's instruction "as they come from the garden" is a clear endorsement of this. Likewise you don't want to overcook your precious spears, or as he instructs: "Take them out, as little sod as you can, it is the better." And then he goes and makes his hollandaise sauce. Albeit with not quite the precise instructions the domestic cook would like, but then that wasn't his audience.

François Pierre, who went by the nickname of La Varenne, was writing for his professional colleagues. But that he wrote a book at all was revolutionary. No one in France had produced a cookbook since the 1379 manuscript of Taillevent's *Le Viandier* (see p. 46), which was still being printed and reprinted. This, despite printing being increasingly commonplace in Europe. There were presses throughout France but they churned out treatises on every subject except food.

Taillevent's book was the sacred text; it was immortal. This was the seminal work on the subject, so to print others, presumably, was thought to be unnecessary, impertinent even. Perhaps, also, to publish a recipe meant to give away culinary secrets. The world of food was a closed shop, confined to the houses of the great and the good. Recipes were passed on as gift, from mentor to apprentice. Any vacancies were filled from within. If you weren't part of the kitchen hierarchy within a household, you didn't have a chance.

Entertaining was also a form of one-upmanship, a chance to express one's wealth. So you wouldn't want your rivals to get hold of your kitchen secrets. This was also, it seems, a peculiarly French trait. Cookbooks were, after all, being published in England,

Germany and Italy. In Italy the subject of food was discussed with great seriousness. Wealthy families, in the race for opulence—from building to dining—were happy to display their magnificence and elegant good taste and were not averse to having recipes from their glittering dinners and banquets written down.

The French, meanwhile, did not regard even the subject of food as a worthy topic of conversation. Indeed, a Frenchman at the time recalled, almost with disgust, a discussion with an Italian who wouldn't stop talking about food, and in the most serious terms. His conversation "swelled out with rich and magnificent words, the very same we make use of in discussing the government of an empire," he reported.

But this was all about to change. La Varenne had worked his way up through the ranks, like so many before and after. He was very much embedded in that closed cheffy shop. He had started as a boy, scrubbing pots, replenishing coal and turning the spit. But he had risen higher than most for someone of his humble status, attaining the position of kitchen steward in the house of the Marquis d'Uxelles. His master was a wealthy aristocrat, a general, close to the king and, in an era when royalty was attempting to curb the power of the nobles, preeminent.

That he rose to a position normally occupied by someone of gentry status shows how trusted and impressive a man he must have been. La Varenne's position of kitchen steward meant he was responsible for everything in the kitchen, from supplies and accounts to quality control and menus. He would have reported to the maître d'hôtel, who ran the household, and he liaised with the butler and wine steward. It was a setup not dissimilar to the great restaurants of a much later age.

The French at the time were keen to emulate the opulence of the Italians in everything, from housebuilding and furniture to tapestries, dress and dining, so the man in charge of the food carried considerable clout. As ever, displays of wealth were very effective when relayed via the table. Since the innovations introduced into French cuisine by Catherine de Medici (see p. 81), it had come on considerably, but no one had yet published anything.

La Varenne found a publisher in one Pierre David, who may have been a little reluctant to take on the task. He writes an introduction that is almost apologetic in tone. But he recommends it as a useful alternative to books that suggested health cures. If people ate well in the first place, he argues, they wouldn't then need medicines or, as he puts it, "bothersome cures." He then lays out his aims for the book, its purpose being "to provide help and service to anyone who may need it." He recognizes that there were cooks out there who might need help but were too proud to ask: "Some of them think they demean themselves by getting advice in a matter that they ought perhaps to be knowledgeable." His work would "deliver them from their embarrassment." He then ends his introduction by saying that he hopes his book will be "as pleasurable as it is useful." La Varenne's postulating that cooking could be a pleasure, that reading a cookbook a leisurely pursuit, is the first step toward a time when people took their cookbooks to bed as they might the latest bestseller.

But not quite yet. *Le Cuisinier François* recorded the advances that had been made since Catherine de Medici. He writes of omelettes, delicate sauces; he makes a roux to thicken sauces rather than just throwing in breadcrumbs, creates caramel, serves pumpkin pie and makes *beignets* (early doughnuts). He also shows how the French had not just absorbed Italian cooking techniques but built on them considerably. Food had become more sensual and less mysterious. Terence Scully, the Ontario professor who published a modern translation of the book, describes how La Varenne inspired a culinary awakening in France. It was, he says, "a vigorous efflorescence of creativity unlike any that has been seen anywhere before, or, even, since."

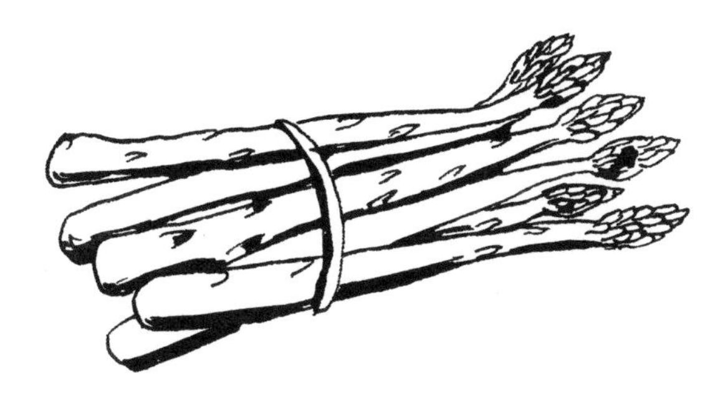

La Varenne was also using more sophisticated equipment. In his kitchen he had a *potager,* which is not as humble and ancient as its name suggests. It was effectively a brick hob. On the top, at waist height, were three of four small openings through which the heat of the fire below would be conducted. Pots could be lifted up, the fire built up or damped down. It gave the cook more control than ever and allowed for more delicate and complex cooking processes.

Such was the success of La Varenne's work that any caution the publisher may have had about publishing it quickly dissipated. Other books followed, from cooks also within aristocratic employ, each claiming his credentials to be superior to those of his predecessor. If La Varenne had broken a taboo, he now opened the floodgates of food publishing in France. Books on tarts and pastries, preserves and confectionery followed. He did have one detractor, however. Written by someone going by the initials "L.S.R." and published in 1674, *L'Art de bien traiter* offered no royal links but claimed to be a "new" book for "everyone." La Varenne's recipes were *"degôutant,"* according to this single dissenter, and gastronomically out of favor. But there seemed little support for this lone voice even if, by the end of the century, cookbooks were being published for more modest pockets and with more readable texts.

La Varenne had started an important trend, however. He respected the ingredient, feeling that it didn't need to be tampered with unnecessarily. His hollandaise sauce adds to the flavor of the asparagus rather than swamping it. While his interest lay more in fine dining than food for the masses, he spawned a populist movement and gave a dramatic rebirth to Gallic cooking. And France has never looked back.

32

A good supper dish
(Mutton baked in breadcrumbs)

AUTHOR: Hannah Woolley, FROM: *The Cook's Guide*

Take a leg of mutton and cut it into thin pieces as long as you can and three or four fingers broad; then take parsley, onions, Penny-royal and Time and chop them fine with mutton suet, season with wine, pepper, cloves, mace and salt, so lay it upon the slices on Mutton and roul them up and fasten everyone with a scure, then roul them in the yolks of eggs and grated bread to roast or bake them in a platter with butter. Thus you may do veal; but then put in some currants. These do well baked in a pye or stewed with wine and butter.

By the mid-seventeenth century, England was seeing a proliferation of cookbooks. As the population steadily grew, so prosperity increased, trade and commerce flourished and more ingredients found their way onto the nation's tables. Meat consumption rose although the bottom 20 percent of the country still subsisted on pottage (see p. 52), to which they added meat if they ever got hold of it, and a diet of bread, cheese and onions. Potatoes (see p. 85) were yet to take off.

As the "withdrawing" rooms in the houses of the upper echelons of English society were filled with Turkish carpets and cushions of Italian velvet, so the kitchens saw the likes of hops from the Netherlands, cherries from France and currants from Greece. While in many households recipes were recorded and passed down by the lady of the house, such as Elinor Fettiplace (see p. 95), cookbooks were becoming increasingly prevalent, all written and published by men. All, that is, except for the lone voice of Hannah Woolley. In 1661 she published her first work, *The Ladies Directory.* It was a bold move and while men like Robert May, whose *The Accomplisht Cook* (see p. 112) won him a healthy advance from his publisher, Hannah Woolley had to fund the venture herself.

Her audacity made her the first woman author of a published cookbook. The venture was a success and three years later she published her second book, *The Cook's Guide,* from which the above recipe comes.

Born in 1623, she learned to cook at the side of her mother and sisters before going into service and working in Essex, aged seventeen, for a noblewoman called Lady Maynard. In her boss she found a kind and sympathetic employer. She nurtured

Hannah's talents and encouraged her to develop her cooking by lending her recipe books and suggesting she buy more interesting ingredients from the market.

Hannah then married a local schoolmaster and may or may not have continued to work for Lady Maynard. But she remained close to the household and in particular Lady Maynard's daughter, Anne Wroth (to whom she dedicates her second book), and her own daughter Mary. After seven years of marriage and with four sons and two daughters, they moved to Hackney to run a small boarding school. This consumed Hannah's time until her husband died suddenly in 1661. With her accumulated knowledge of cooking in a nobleman's house, for her husband and family and no doubt having played a part in the school's catering, she felt she had a thing or two she could impart to a wider audience.

The titles of her various books—*The Ladies Directory, The Cook's Guide* and *The Queen-like Closet*—showed that she had a canny commercial mind. Surely all the best ladies would aspire to have a closet like a queen, while calling her second book a "guide" would have made it seem rather more down-to-earth and accessible, not to mention less patronizing, than the very male titles she was competing with.

There was Gervase Markham's *Country Contentments,* for example, which saw reprints throughout the seventeenth century. A two-part volume, the first concentrates on the men of the house and their spare time, or, as he puts it, how a man "ought to recreate himself after...the heavy toil of more unpleasant (though more profitable) studies." The main ways of spending this spare time seem to be riding, hunting, stalking and keeping kennels, for which Markham provides advice, with the occasional specific tip on, for example, the way to ride a horse if you come across a prince.

He then tackles the housewife. After all, a man's work is "for the most part abroad or removed from the house in the field or yard." As the "mother and mistress of the family [with] most general employments within the house," he suggests how she should behave, dress and even think and talk. She must "suppress contrary thoughts," "shun all violence of rage," avoid fashion and "the gloss of light colors"; she must be patient, witty and not "bitter or talkative." She should also buy local produce, avoid foreign rubbish and focus on keeping her family healthy.

And to help her with these endeavors he has a vast list of remedies for the body, including dealing with "the frenzie." For this you should squirt beetroot juice up the "frenzied" nose and offer the patient ale. Apparently it will "bring him down to a very temperate mildness." There are also cures for "lethargy," "snake bites," "drunkenness" (for which he doesn't suggest the avoidance of alcohol), "stinking breath," "a pimpled fancy face" and how to treat those who can't help "pissing in bed." And yes, there are dozens of recipes too, from salads and pancakes to bread and the boiling and roasting of meat.

This grandstanding tome and others, such as Robert May's *The Accomplisht Cook,* must have meant that Hannah's book came as a welcome relief. While historians believe it was mainly the clergy and gentlemen who read books such as May and Markham's—doubtless striding into the kitchens and dictating their newfound dishes to some unfortunate underling—Hannah's works were directed at the people who actually looked after the house and did the cooking.

Hannah Woolley, author of The Cook's Guide.

Of course while illiteracy was still prevalent among even the wealthier classes, she targeted her books at those who were educated enough to read—literate cooks, upwardly mobile women who wanted to better themselves and improve the efficiency of their households. In addition, she brought character to her writing and understood that you needed to engage your audience rather than just preach to it. Many of her recipes are pared-down versions of fancier dishes. She showed how using just a few more challenging ingredients—anchovies, capers, wine—could enable more modest households to have a taste of glamour enjoyed by the more well-to-do.

She doesn't talk down to her readers: in presenting dishes "I have done . . . in great houses" she adds that "any person who is ingenius, may leave out some, and put in others at pleasure." Thus her readers could choose, for example, from a menu that included spatchcocked eels, fried oysters, buttered shrimps or lobster. This must have been refreshing, if not revolutionary, for her readers who had only ever been dictated to by their pompous culinary masters. What's more, *The Cook's Guide* is a tiny little book, measuring no more than 3 by 5 inches. With this secretive tome, kept in an apron pocket, literate servants really could better themselves.

The book was a follow-up to the earlier *The Ladies Directory,* which focused more on household chores, pressing and scenting linen and gloves, and so on. "All you that have made trial of my first," she suggests, "will I hope be encouraged to the 'cookery' also." Her genuinely humble tone, so different from the obsequious genuflecting of master cooks to their mentors of the past, struck a chord with her readers. She encouraged feedback too. "Ladies," she writes at the end, "I hope you will say I am better than my word. I pray practice them carefully and then censure or esteem."

Her recipes went down well too: the "good supper dish" of this chapter, for which you could use breast of lamb instead of mutton, is smothered in breadcrumbs glistening gold after baking in the oven. While other recipes, presented in no apparent order, include delicious puddings such as lemon cream, lemon syllabub, pancakes and how to make puff pastry.

Her books ran to several editions before she suffered the compliment of serious plagiarism. At least two unauthorized works—one published in 1673 and another in 1685—stole unscrupulously from her earlier work without even a nod of credit to her. It was just the start of such theft. While Hannah put her head above the food-publishing parapet, male writers would swipe her female crown from her for many ensuing years, passing off her and other women's recipes as their own. It would be some time before women food writers were liberated from the shackles of the chauvinistic publishing industry and could reach a wider public.

33

Peas soope

AUTHOR: Lady Anne Blencowe
FROM: *The Receipt Book of Lady Anne Blencowe*

Take about two Quarts of peas and boil them down till they are thick; then put to them a leeke and a little slice of bacon and a little bunch of sweet herbs and let them boyl till they are broke. Then work them with ye back of a ladle thro a corse hair sieve; then take about three pints of your peas and mix with about three quarts of very strong broth and work them very well together. Then set them over a stove and let them boyl very easily. Then as for your herbs, take out the quantity of a gallon of soope; take large handful of spinage and one third of sorrel and one cabbage, Lettice and a little chervil and cresses and a head or two of siliry and indive and ye hear of savoy and a little mint, but mince your mint very small if it be green, but if it be dry, then drie it before ye fire to powder and sift it through a sieve, and mince ye herbs with one leeke very small and put them into a brass dish or saspan with half a pound of butter and let ym stove until they begin to be tender. Then put to them a quart of good gravy or strong broth, but gravy is best, and when ye have mix't it well then putt into ye pott to ye peas and a litle beaten cloves and mace. So let it stove about half an hour, then have a French roll, either dry'd in an oven or toasted by ye fire, in think slices and then season ye soope to your palate and so serve it up. If you please, you may put forced meat balls into it or any other things as pallates and sweetbreads or combs.

When Pierre Koffman put trotters on the menu of London's La Tante Claire in the 1970s, he showed how a staple of the poor could become a noble dish. He won three Michelin stars and his trotters were a deciding factor. There is a certain novelty about dressing up and dining in a smart restaurant and being served food formerly eaten by those in rags. Of course, to succeed, the food in question needs a few magical twists to help it on its way. Koffman's conceit was to laboriously bone the trotters before stuffing them with sweetbreads and scented morel mushrooms.

It's the sort of trick those in his profession have been attempting to master for years; indeed, chefs have been pimping peasant dishes for centuries. An early mention of this occurs in 1669 and is recorded by the diarist Samuel Pepys.

The Royal Navy administrator and Member of Parliament who kept a diary during the turbulent years of the 1660s—when there was, of course, fire, plague and the restoration of the monarchy—loved his food. He frequently refers to what he eats and includes the occasional note on its preparation. And there was this moment on 12 April 1669: "... so walked to White Hall, and, by and by to my wife at Unthanke's, and with her was Jane, and so to the Cocke, where they, and I, and Sheres, and Tom dined, my wife having a great desire to eat of their soup made of pease, and dined very well."

Was this, then, the signature dish of the Cocke Inn? You can imagine his wife Elizabeth's recommendation to friends: "You must go to the Cocke—their pea soup is fantastic." That's right, pea soup. A dish that sustained the poor for centuries, that has featured in the diets of millions across the world, from Canada to the United States, Germany, the Netherlands and England.

We know that the pea soup they served at the Cocke was poshed up because Pepys mentions pea pottage in his diary and he is less enamored of it. On 1 February 1660 he recalls a simple dinner: "In the morning went to my office where afterwards the old man brought me my letters from the carrier. At noon I went home and dined with my wife on pease porridge and nothing else." He sounds vaguely disgruntled about this meal. No doubt he felt that he was a little better than the sort who habitually dined on such a dish.

While his background was humble—his father was a tailor, his mother the sister of a Whitechapel butcher—he was now a successful professional. A man of his standing deserved better than pea pottage. Using peas as a base, it would have had whatever was available added to it, from other seasonal vegetables to meat. But meat was in Pepys's time still the preserve of the wealthier. It was expensive and, as he notes, "hundreds of thousands of families scarcely knew the taste of it... the majority of the nation lived almost entirely on rye, barley and oats."

While I would travel a long way to avoid pea soup, if it is the kind that more resembles mushy peas with its dull, cloudy flavor, the type Pepys liked was probably made with dried peas. It could more resemble the split pea variety, which, coming closer to dahl, is something I would also clamor for.

So what did the pea soup so favored by Pepys's wife taste like? A contemporary recipe for it comes from a Northamptonshire squire's wife, Lady Anne Blencowe, who includes it in her manuscript of "receipts." Very like the one kept by Lady Elinor Fettiplace (see p. 95), it was among other similar books kept over the centuries in the library of my family home, Weston Hall. These scrapbooks filled with pages of spidery, neat writing include a number of loose leaves with other recipes and jottings.

A printed copy of Lady Blencowe's manuscript was published in the 1920s and a further book edited by a descendant of hers came out in 2004. Her recipe for pea soup is the longest in the book and, with the addition of a number of fresh ingredients from the garden (celery, endive, lettuce, chervil, mint and so on), it is quite elaborate. Most of Lady Blencowe's recipes are for entertaining, so this would have been a dinner-party dish. Her husband was a judge and local Member of Parliament and evidently quite prosperous. When his daughter Susanna lost her husband to illness when quite young, he felt sorry for her and her two young children so he bought her a house as a gift on Valentine's Day in 1714. That house is Weston Hall, a property that passed through the female line of the family until my great-grandfather acquired it from an aunt and gave it to my grandfather Sacheverell Sitwell as a present on his marriage to the Canadian beauty Georgia Doble. It was Georgia who showed the original manuscript to her friend George Saintsbury who had it copied and printed in 1925.

The book gives us a good insight into the culinary world of the 1660s. We learn, for instance, that marigold is added when making cheese, to color it, as indeed many cheeses were colored until relatively recently (perhaps Red Leicester is a rare exception today). Lady Blencowe credits the recipes she includes to a variety of people. There is "To do green oranges Lady Stapleton's Way," for example, and "To roast fowl Sir Thomas Perkingses' way." (The latter, incidentally, is stuffed with oysters and onions before being roasted on a spit.) She also includes a recipe "To make Bisketts, Mrs. B's way." Whoever "Mrs. B" was, her recipe is virtually identical to that of Sir Hugh Plat's (see p. 91) for "prince-biskets" back in 1602.

Some recipes would appeal to the modern palate. There is a delicious recipe for Spanish custard, for instance, using ground almonds, orange flower water, eggs, caster sugar, cream and sherry. Other dishes belong more firmly in the past: a "little pye for Entermess" is a spectacular interlude for a banquet, being a chicken in a pie with stuffed larks. There is also an alarming recipe for crayfish which includes the instruction to "bruise" their legs in a mortar while still alive.

In addition to the recipes there are the inevitable "Physical Receipts," including solutions for giddiness, swollen legs, madness even and several cures for indigestion, suggesting it was a common complaint of the time. A remedy for the "bite of a mad dog" sees the patient being drained of 10 ounces of blood, given a mixture of unheard-of dried herbs to be drunk with warm milk before a terrifying program of cold dips in a river or spring every morning for a month.

She also suggests whitening teeth with burned date stones, "to strengthen ye eyes" by chewing on aniseed and having someone blow on your eyes, and "to whiten cloth" by using sheep's dung and then dunking the cloth in a stagnant pond.

However alarming her medical ideas were, she must have fed and looked after her husband well as he lived to the ripe old age of eighty-four. It must have been all that pea soup. As it had saved peasants from starving, so it sustained Sir John Blencowe into old age and delighted the taste buds of Samuel and Elizabeth Pepys. The dish defied the class barrier and became a feature of most cookbooks of the era.

Portrait of Samuel Pepys (1633–1703).

34

Roast fillet of beef

AUTHOR: Robert May, FROM: *The Accomplisht Cook*

Take a fillet which is the tenderest part of the beef, and lieth in the inner part of the surloyn, cut it as big as you can, broach it on a broach not too big, and be careful not to broach it through the best of the meat, roast it leisurely, & baste it with sweet butter, set a dish to save the gravy while it roasts, then prepare sauce for it of good store of parsley, with a few sweet herbs chopp'd smal, the yolks of three or four eggs, sometimes gross pepper minced amongst them with the peel of an orange, and a little onion; boil these together, and put in a little butter, vinegar, gravy, a spoonful of strong broth, and put it to the beef.

OTHERWAYS
Sprinkle it with rose-vinegar, claret-wine, elder-vinegar, beaten cloves, nutmeg, pepper, cinamon, ginger, coriander-feed, fennil-seed, and salt; beat these things fine, and season the fillet with it then roast it, and baste it with butter, save the gravy, and blow off the fat, serve it with juyce of orange or lemon, and a little elder-vinegar.

OR THUS
Powder it one night, then stuff it with parsley, tyme, sweet marjoram, beets, spinage, and winter-savory, all picked and minced small, with the yolks of hard eggs mixt amongst some pepper, stuff it and roast it, save the gravy and stew it with the herbs, gravy, as also a little onion, claret wine, and the juyce of an orange or two; serve it hot on this sauce, with flices of orange on it, lemons, or barberries.

While Hannah Woolley (see p. 106) was gently encouraging the ladies of England to cook better food with her humble prose and sweet tone of reassurance, Robert May had a rather different approach. At the age of seventy-two, this professional cook, who had spent his life serving up dishes for the aristocracy, decided that the world needed him to unleash his knowledge upon them. People required nothing less; it was his duty. "God and my conscience would not permit me to bury those experiences with my silver hair in the grave," he wrote. And so he set about writing a densely packed volume of work that covered every type of recipe he could conceive of.

You're after a recipe for an omelette? He has twenty-one of them. Want some tips on carving? Be careful what you ask for. Robert May doesn't dish out bland generalizations. You "Break that deer, leach that brawn, rear that goose, lift that swan, sauce that capon, spoil that hen, frust that chicken, unbrace that mallard, unlace that coney, dismember that hern [sic], display that crane, disfigure that peacock, unjoynt that bittern, lay that pheasant, wing that partridge, wing that quail, mince that plover, thigh that pidgeon, border that pasty, thigh that woodcock..." You get the picture. But if you're looking for a definitive recipe for, say, roast fillet of beef, one that is unashamedly English, traditional and just right for the restoration of the monarchy, then you can rely on him.

When May took the decision to unburden his knowledge on the public, he was aware that culinary arts were still revered, surrounded as they were in a haze of mystery. His book might attract criticism in the same way La Varenne feared with his mighty French tome in 1651 (see p. 103). They "will curse me for revealing the secrets of this art," he states in his introduction. But he is keen nonetheless to lift the veil of secrecy, and promises that "the whole art is revealed in a more easie and perfect method that hath been published in any language."

That was quite a promise and it is a promise publishers of recipes have been giving ever since. Today the mantras are "easy" and "perfect." And as Robert May shows us, it's nothing new. In fact there is a strong case that Robert May was actually the first celebrity chef, if only self-appointed.

With every previous book or manuscript published, to gain an idea of the individual who wrote it we have to trawl through contemporary accounts and read between the lines of recipes and other writings. Robert May, by contrast, offers a biography of himself. He explains that he was the son of an accomplished chef and how he was at a young age sent to France to learn about cooking. He then returned to London where he began working for a series of well-connected and wealthy aristocrats. As well as reflecting on his early life and inspirations, he also makes it clear that he is a man of strong opinions. All of which makes him ideal celebrity-chef material.

And what better way to demonstrate his opinions than to lay into the French. Perhaps he is defensive of the fact that he spent five formative years there. He does not want anyone to think that, because he was taught in France and learned the language, his cooking and skill as a cook had anything other to do with the fact that he came from a family of good cooks and he was English.

Don't be taken in by the French, he warns. They are ignorant and "have bewitcht some of the gallants of our nation with epigram dishes... their *Mushroom'd Experiences* for *Sauce* rather than *Diet,* for the generality howsoever called *A-la-mode,* not worthy of being taken notice on."

He is kinder to the Italians and Spanish, meanwhile, and gives a nod to their culinary expertise. And while he acknowledges that his is by no means the first major English cookbook, most of them, he thinks, are pretty useless, their methods are "confusing," their experience of using them "barren." All, that is, except for the work of Hannah Woolley, whom he salutes.

May is also at pains to stress that he wishes to produce recipes that are affordable and ideas for dinners that are a practical help to the host. Although the first section of his book focuses on rather more fantastic creations, such as how to make an edible replica of a ship complete with mini stags made of pastry with claret dripping like blood from wounds, and pies filled with live birds and frogs. The climax comes when "while lifting first the lid off one of the pyes out skip some frogs which make the ladies to skip and shreek." But then May also has some down-to-earth recipes for toast—hot buttered, cinnamon-flavored and French, the latter steeped in wine and served with sugar and orange syrup.

His book was an instant success and went into several editions in the ensuing years. Cooks up and down the country tried his dishes and his various ideas for storing and preserving food. Although the jury is still out on his method "to keep lobsters a year very good." After boiling them you wrap them in a rag soaked in brine and then "bury them in a cellar in some sea sand pretty deep."

By its fifth edition he also had a sponsor who both printed the book and took out an advertisement. Obadiah Blagrave sold water that could, apparently, soothe the eyes as it had done "a learned bishop [who] used it and could read without the use of spectacles at 90 years of age."

Robert May, who trained overseas, was exacting, professional, opinionated and overbearing, and seems to be every inch the modern chef. His fillet, roasted on a complex rotisserie system called a spitjack, with the juices either kept in paper or a tray below, is a tasty dish with the added zesty bite of Seville oranges.

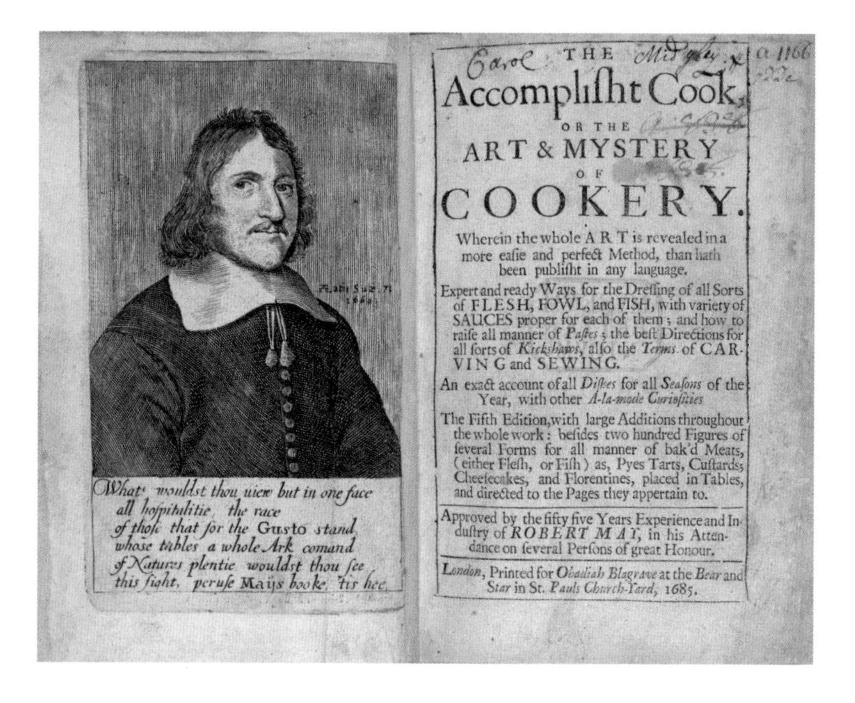

THE
Accompliſht Cook,
OR THE
ART & MYSTERY
OF
COOKERY.

Wherein the whole ART is revealed in a more eaſie and perfect Method, than hath been publiſht in any language.

Expert and ready Ways for the Dreſſing of all Sorts of FLESH, FOWL, and FISH, with variety of SAUCES proper for each of them; and how to raiſe all manner of *Paſtes*; the beſt Directions for all ſorts of *Kickshaws*, alſo the *Terms* of CARVING and SEWING.

An exact account of all *Diſhes* for all *Seaſons* of the Year, with other *A-la-mode Curioſities*

The Fifth Edition, with large Additions throughout the whole work: beſides two hundred Figures of ſeveral Forms for all manner of bak'd Meats, (either Fleſh, or Fiſh) as, Pyes Tarts, Cuſtards; Cheeſecakes, and Florentines, placed in Tables, and directed to the Pages they appertain to.

Approved by the fifty five Years Experience and Induſtry of *ROBERT MAY*, in his Attendance on ſeveral Perſons of great Honour.

London, Printed for *Obadiah Blagrave* at the *Bear* and *Star* in St. *Pauls Church-Yard*, 1685.

Robert May's The Accomplisht Cook *contained every kind of recipe imaginable. It was an instant success and ran into several editions.*

35

Fish experiment XIII

AUTHOR: Denis Papin, FROM: *A New Digester or Engine for Softening Bones*

June 15. I took a Macquerel and put it in a Glass-pot with green gooseberries; I included the Pot in the Engine, and with four ounces and two drams of coals I brought the heat to dry away the drops of water in 10 seconds, and the inward pressure was seven times as strong as the ordinary pressure of the Air. The fire being gone out by little and little, I found that the remaining coals weighed about two drams: the fish was very ready and firm, though the bones were so soft, as not to be felt in eating: the fish, before it was boiled did weigh nine ounces, and after boiling not above seven: so that I had two ounces of good Juyce, which would have been thrown away, if the fish had been boiled after the ordinary way: and moreover the taste was a great deal better, the volatile Salts not having got away, or being dissolved in water: the Gooseberries had a very good taste, and nothing of burning.

Denis Papin was a man bubbling, or rather steaming, with ideas. He had thoughts on all manner of machines, from submarines and air guns to grenade launchers. But his triumph was the invention of the steam digester, what we would call a pressure cooker, although tragically for him the reaction of his fellow members of the Royal Society was less than effusive.

Born and educated in France, he moved to London where he worked alongside the Irish chemist and physicist Robert Boyle. While together they collaborated on a number of projects, including those related to vacuums and steam, and Boyle himself produced his self-named law and wrote a vast array of seminal tracts including his *Occasional Reflections upon Several Subjects,* it was in Papin's spare time that he developed his groundbreaking cooking device.

He built a vessel made of cast iron and with a lid that he could screw tight shut. He then positioned it over burning coals and began his experiments. One can only imagine what the neighbors must have thought. After hours, while Robert Boyle was back home or out with friends discussing and debating resurrection, celestial magnets or describing what happens when you put a snake in a vacuum, his protégé set to work.

Deliveries to his lab included, in addition to the usual potions and powders, haunches of beef, legs of mutton, rabbits and a great deal of veg. Then, as the nights wore on, out from the lab would come smells of food cooking—all unenticing, from the boiled to the burned. The principle of his device was simple: water, heated under increased pressure, has a higher boiling point, enabling food to be cooked more quickly. This would, he felt, make cooking more efficient and hence cheaper as well as tastier.

"Cooking is such an ancient art," he argued, "the use of which is so general and so frequent, and people have been earnest on improving it, that it seems if any could be brought to perfection, this should be it." His contraption could genuinely advance and improve the practice of cooking, he believed. And while he encountered many stumbling blocks along the way, he got there in the end, writing of the "great felicity" of his "discovery... the usefulness thereof may recommend it to posterity."

It wasn't just his experiments that were an uphill battle, he needed money to develop the idea so that improvements could be made to his prototype and it could be marketed for more domestic use. "The hardest cow-beef may be made as tender and savory as young and choice meat," he wrote, arguing about how useful it could be for feeding the poor.

The pressure cooker was invented by Denis Papin (1647–c.1712) but only became popular in the 1970s.

Night after night, month after month, he worked in the laboratory experimenting endlessly with his "engine." He reduced and increased the level of heat from the coals, tinkered with cooking times and with the amount of water added to the vessel. If there was too little, for example, the water dried up in seconds and the meat was burned. He popped in beef, then mutton, then bones and rabbit. He tried old meat, young meat, then pigeons, before moving onto pike, mackerel—as in the "recipe" that heads this chapter—eel, then beans, cherries, gooseberries, plums, quinces, sugar, chocolate even.

And then he tried herbs, from rosemary and cinnamon to aniseed, before seeing what happened to less edible substances—pewter, ivory, horn, tortoiseshell and amber. The answer was, very little: "I will not be tedious in relating particulars of those experiments," he said. "I have found nothing yet that may be brought to use." Nonetheless, he faithfully recorded each experiment in notepads and occasionally got friends round to try the results. He tried them himself too, of course. His experiment with mackerel and gooseberries appears to have been very satisfactory, while his attempt at boiling beef bones to jelly provokes a wry smile from the inventor on sampling the end result: "I may say, I did eat it with sugar and Juyce of Lemmon, I did eat it with as much pleasure, and found it as stomachical as if it had been Gelly of Harts-horn."

His experiments over, he published the results in a book aimed at his esteemed colleagues of the Royal Society. *A New Digester or Engine for Softening Bones* came with deftly drawn and detailed drawings. In the book he focuses on its safe use and enumerates its many possibilities, for "cookery, voyages at sea, confectionery, making of drinks, chemistry and dyeing." Its use for making jelly could vastly improve rations at sea, so there would be no need for the endless salted meat, he notes, which "causeth the scurvy."

Much time is spent dwelling on its costs and the money that could be made from manufacturing the device. He details "the price a good big engine will cost and the profit it will afford." His book was a heartfelt and passionate plea for funding. He needed money to develop a specially constructed furnace that would help his experiments; he was struggling to get the machine to work effectively as he was currently restricted to heating his contraption above coals in a large corner fireplace.

He used every argument he could muster, including the idea that he could brew drinks and make liquor that would "take away the ill quality it hath to generate winds... [and] would not hurt the head either." So here was a device to feed the poor, improve the efficiency and cost of cooking and stop you farting and getting hangovers. Surely providing money for it was a no-brainer?

But even a live demonstration at an event at the Royal Society—at which John Evelyn (diarist and salad expert, see p. 121) pronounced it could "cook mutton to taste like young lamb"—could not muster enough interest. A few years after his initial pitch, he became despondent. "The Digester is a useful invention grounded upon good principles, and confirmed by experience," he wrote with increasing desperation. "Never the less having published this invention five years ago I feel that but very few people have been willing to make use of it."

And his experiments sadly progressed no further. Denis Papin faded into obscurity, ran out of money and lived his last years in poverty, his death going unrecorded. He never patented his design and it was others who copied it, developing it further and becoming rich as a result, as he had foretold that they would.

While the 1970s saw a surge in the popularity of the pressure cooker, the microwave rather eclipsed it. But today the pressure cooker threatens once again to return to favor—its merits as a time- and money-saving device chiming with the mantras of the age. Richard Ehrlich, author of the recently published *80 Recipes for Your Pressure Cooker,* is a big fan, arguing that food prepared in one doesn't all have to taste the same and it won't blow up and scorch you. Perhaps it's time to resurrect the often-maligned pressure cooker and recall a forgotten genius of food history.

36

Tomato sauce in the Spanish style

AUTHOR: Antonio Latini
FROM: *Lo scalco alla moderna (The Modern Steward)*

Take a half-dozen mature tomatoes, then place on the fire to roast, and when they are roasted, peel them carefully and chop them very finely with a knife, and onions chopped very finely to taste, chilli also very finely chopped and a small quantity of (wild) thyme. Mix everything together and dress it with a little salt, oil and vinegar, which will make a very tasty sauce for boiled meat or other things.

The world was pretty slow to pick up on the tomato. While, for example, Catherine de Medici (see p. 81) brought Italian ingredients and techniques to Paris in the 1530s, she didn't bring tomatoes. So we have to imagine the early developments of French gastronomy without this defining ingredient. That means no tomatoes in Provençal food and none in Italian cooking until the middle of the seventeenth century.

While the Spanish did come across them during their conquest of South America (see p. 77), they thought little of it. The Aztecs had cultivated tomatoes—no doubt they ate them—but that didn't convince the Spaniards. After all, the Aztecs also ate people, so it's understandable that the Spaniards may have been circumspect about some of the other things they put in their mouths.

Nevertheless somehow the tomato left the shores of South America and journeyed to Europe, doubtless with cargoes of all the other ingredients plundered, from chocolate to chili, and with it came the word "tomato," based on a misnomer in fact. The word *tomatl* means "plump fruit" in Aztec, while tomatoes are actually called *xitomatl*. But whatever they should have been called, they failed to catch on. An Italian herbalist, Pietro Andrea Matthioli, talked in 1544 of seeing "golden apples." He wrote how, green at first, they turned a "golden color" when ripe and classified them as part of the family of the mandrake, which has in its species nightshade, some of which are toxic, deadly indeed. So given that they were yellow, related to plants that would poison you and had those strange spiky-shaped leaves at the top, it's perhaps understandable that people were suspicious of them.

While Matthioli appears to have been describing yellow tomatoes, ten years later the Swiss naturalist Konrad Gessner painted a watercolor of a red variety and gave

Tomatoes made their appearance in Antonio Latini's book The Modern Steward, *where they were an ingredient in a Spanish-influenced sauce and also added to meat dishes.*

them the Latin name of *Poma amoris*—"love apple." He felt they had an aphrodisiac quality and the Italians obviously liked that idea although they stuck with the name provided by Matthioli—*pomodoro* or "apple of gold," as they still call the tomato today. Whereas the English, Greeks, Danes, French and Spanish—most of Europe in fact—stick with the Aztec-derived word instead.

Coming across them in the 1590s, the English herbalist John Gerard wrote that they were "of ranke and stinking savour." He thought they were poisonous, while the apothecary to King James I, John Parkinson, mentioned that they were grown by British gardeners only for curiosity. But he did mention that they were eaten by people in hot countries, to "coole and quench the heate and thirst of the hot stomaches."

So at some point in the late sixteenth century a few brave souls in Spain or Italy evidently took a bite and maybe tried cooking them. They had certainly entered Italian kitchens by the mid-seventeenth century because Bartolomé Murillo depicts one in his 1646 painting *The Angels' Kitchen.* Here a Franciscan friar is shown in ecstatic prayer while angels lay out plates for dinner and two chubby little cherubs sit on the floor picking through a basket of fruit. On the floor next to them are two aubergines, a pumpkin and a big fat juicy tomato. It looks like the more recently U.S. cultivated type, the beefsteak. Quite what the angels had in mind for it, we don't know and it wasn't until 1692 that, finally, the first known recipes for tomatoes appear.

Antonio Latini was in turn a waiter, cook, a maître d' and a household steward. By the time he published the first volume of his book *Lo scalco alla moderna,* in 1692, he was quite a grand character. He certainly looks it: the portrait of him in his book shows him looking proud, aristocratic even, with a huge curly-haired wig. As the title of his tome boldly suggests, he was the "Modern Steward" and one with considerable clout no doubt.

Not unlike his English contemporaries, Gervase Markham and Robert May (see pp. 107 and 112), his book—with its subtitle "The Art of Good Banqueting"—records the feasts that he was responsible for; he had worked for a cardinal in Rome and then as chef to the Spanish viceroy in Naples. As well as the grander menus, his book details methods of preserving, carving and the kitchen tools needed.

His recipe for tomato sauce was perhaps influenced by his Spanish employer and the dish appears to be intended as an accompaniment for other dishes. But he doesn't put it on pasta. He doesn't use it as a base for pizza either—we have to wait a little longer for that. However, he does add it to meat. In "Another dish, tomato stew," pigeon, veal breast and stuffed chicken are cooked in stock with herbs and spices. Roasted tomatoes are then added to the meat with the note to take "care not to overcook them because they don't take too long."

It was another 100 years before tomatoes saw regular use in the kitchens of Paris and while the *Encyclopaedia Britannica* of 1797 records them as being in "daily British use" many remained suspicious of them. As late as 1831, the British horticulturalist Henry Phillips dismissed the tomato plant as having "a rank smell." Yet the Americans were using it to make ketchup, at which point the wheels of the tomato wagon start turning. Now—be they round, ribbed, big or small, red or yellow—it's hard to conceive of a kitchen without them.

37

Salad dressing

AUTHOR: John Evelyn, ADAPTED FROM: *Acetaria: A Discourse of Saletts*

Let your herby ingredients be exquisitely culled and cleansed of all worm-eaten, slimy, spotted or in any way vitiated leaves. After washing (with spring water) let them remain a while in a colander, to drain the superfluous moisture. And lastly swing them all together gently in a clean, coarse napkin. Use a good knife to cut herbs, one that is (according to the super-curious) silver not steel.

The oil should be very clean, not too rich, or too yellow – a pallid olive green and smooth, light and pleasant upon the tongue (made from Lucca olives if possible). If you have an aversion to oil, substitute butter instead, although it is so exceedingly clogging to the stomach. Use Vinegar, preferably infused with flowers such as nasturtion. Salt must be the best – clean, bright and dry and use a dash of sugar or some honey. Use mustard, preferably from Tewkesbury and made with Yorkshire seeds. Pepper should not be dust but coarsely ground. Also boil until moderately hard egg yolks.

Mingle and mash the egg with the oil, vinegar, salt, pepper and mustard.

Serve the salad in a porcelain dish (not too deep or too shallow according to the quantity of salad ingredients) and with a fork and a spoon stir it until all the furniture be equally moistened.

John Evelyn's unedited recipe for salad dressing runs to 1,400 words. But then you might expect that from a discourse on salads written by a founding member of the Royal Society. He treated such things seriously.

A renowned diarist and scholar, he decided that salads and herbs needed a book of their own, and so while plenty of cooks and chefs had used salads and had mentioned them in recipes, he paused to give them proper thought. (The title of his book, *Acetaria,* means "salad" in Latin.) He pondered on the health benefits of salad leaves and edible herbs, identifying those with medicinal compounds. He also categorized seventy-three separate herbs for use in salad and advised on which were best for cooking and which for flavoring. Evelyn drew a serious nutritional line in the sand: leafy greens were good for your health and if you wanted them to taste their best, make a nice dressing to pour over them.

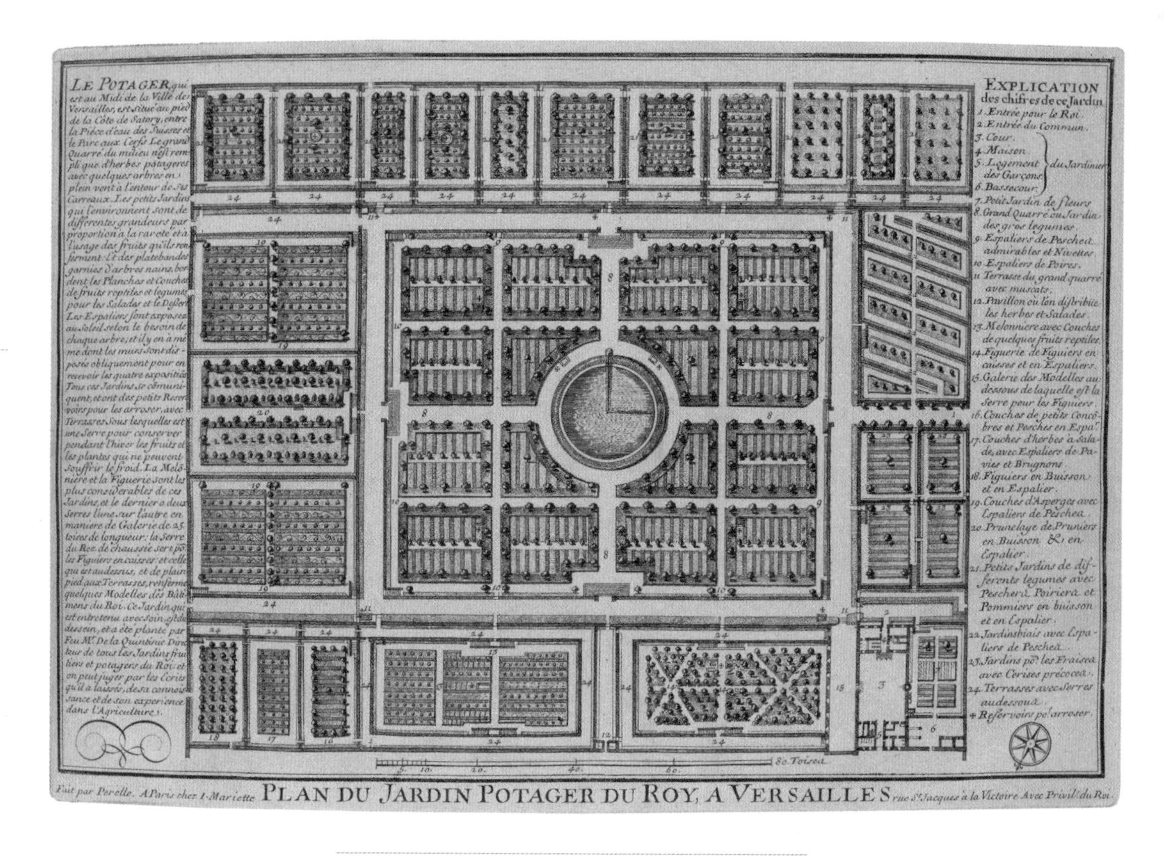

A seventeenth-century plan of the king's kitchen garden, by the Perelle family. It was made up of walled gardens and orchards, producing fruit and vegetables for the court.

This, the first of its kind, was not his only work. He impressed those who knew him with his breadth of learning, but back in his early twenties, when he decided he wanted to be an academic, England was a dangerous place to live in. He feared the consequences of the English Civil War. He was a Royalist and while his family preferred to turn its mind to gunpowder, the manufacture of which had made it a fortune, he was more inclined to ponder on lettuce.

A country at war with itself was not conducive to such thoughts. So in the early 1640s, as Roundheads took on Cavaliers, he was worried. It was, he wrote, "a conjunction of the greatest and most prodigious hazards that ever the youth of England saw." Consequently he left the country to travel round the more peaceful regions of Italy and France before stopping in Paris. There he fell in with the exiled Royalist community and met and married the daughter of an English resident, Sir Richard Browne.

He used the time to study intensely, returning to England in 1652 when life had calmed down a little. Cromwell had by then installed himself as Lord Protector, so he kept his head down living at his wife's family home, Sayes Court, in Deptford. There, as well as building a library, he designed a garden which brought together in physical form his ideas and interests. "The air and genius of gardens operate upon human spirits toward virtue and sanctity," he wrote. His work on the garden, now in the London borough of Lewisham, became hugely respected and influential in its time.

On Charles II's restoration, Evelyn finally raised his head above the public parapet and became involved in public affairs. Although having waited so patiently for the return of the monarchy, he was disappointed by what he saw. The Restoration court was, he said, filled with "fruitless, vicious and empty conversations." It more suited his fellow diarist Samuel Pepys (see p. 109), whom he knew and frequently corresponded with.

So as the royal court didn't offer the kind of serious discourse he craved, he set about writing learned and opinionated treatises. He attacked those who were ripping out forests to build glass factories and iron furnaces and successfully encouraged landowners to plant more trees. Likewise he censured London officials for allowing chimneys to pollute the air and urged them to plant trees to purify the atmosphere. He worried about people's carbon footprint centuries before the term was actually coined.

He advocated a meat-free diet and was an ardent, and possibly the first, high-profile, vegetarian (see p. 177). An appreciation of salad leaves neatly fitted his green philosophy. They were good for the environment and good for the body. Yet he understood that people might think him strange for talking about salad leaves in the same way you might discuss affairs of state. "Some will wonder what my meaning is to usher in a trifle with such magnificence," he wrote, "and end up at last in a fine receipt for the dressing of a salad with a handful of pot herbs."

But he wasn't, he argued, the first to think so seriously about such a subject. Across the ages, dictators, emperors and statesmen thought like him. "After they had performed the noblest exploits for the public, they sometimes changed their sceptres for a spade, and their purple for the gardener's apron," he commented.

And so he produced the world's first A–Z of salad ingredients. He mentions cucumber that can "sharpen the appetite and cool the liver" and watermelons, "brought from abroad," are likewise "exceedingly cooling." There's garlic preferred by "the more Southern people, familiarly eaten with almost everything" but which is a "charm against all infection." Leeks are consumed by "the Welsh, who eat them much," while melon, "which requires sugar to commend it, wants of perfection." There's parsley, "very diuretic, yet nourishing" and he gives some tips on cooking asparagus (more precise but not dissimilar to those from La Varenne in 1651—see p. 103): "They should be speedily boiled, as not to lose the verdure and tenderness which is done by letting the water boil before you out them in."

John Evelyn was a writer and thinker whose thoughts would not go amiss in the modern world. He even had a good idea for how to prepare the then quite rare potato (see p. 85). The type he mentioned must have gone to seed as he talks of "small green fruit the size of a cherry." He suggests you use the root, "roasted under the embers, or otherwise, opened with a knife, the pulp is buttered in the skin of which it will take up a good quantity—season with salt and pepper... the skin has a pleasant crispness." Baked potato with lashings of butter... John Evelyn really was ahead of his time.

38

Ice cream

AUTHOR: Mary Eales, FROM: *Mrs Mary Eales's Receipts*

Take Tin Ice-Pots, fill them with any Sort of Cream you like, either plain or sweeten'd, or Fruit in it; shut your Pots very close; to six Pots you must allow eighteen or twenty Pound of Ice, breaking the Ice very small; there will be some great Pieces, which lay at the Bottom and Top: You must have a Pail, and lay some Straw at the Bottom; then lay in your Ice, and put in amongst it a Pound of Bay-Salt; set in your Pots of Cream, and lay Ice and Salt between every Pot, that they may not touch; but the Ice must lie round them on every Side; lay a good deal of Ice on the Top, cover the Pail with Straw, set it in a Cellar where no Sun or Light comes, it will be froze in four Hours, but it may stand longer; than take it out just as you use it; hold it in your Hand and it will slip out. When you wou'd freeze any Sort of Fruit, either Cherries, Rasberries, Currants, or Strawberries, fill your Tin-Pots with the Fruit, but as hollow as you can; put to them Lemmonade, made with Spring-Water and Lemmon-Juice sweeten'd; put enough in the Pots to make the Fruit hang together, and put them in Ice as you do Cream.

Pinning down the first recipe for ice cream is, frankly, not easy. Experts will happily line up the usual suspects of early guzzlers of iced desserts. For example, there's the Japanese prince who, during the reign of Emperor Nintoku in the fourth century, comes upon an ice pit as he rides through the countryside. "What is this thing before me?" demands the prince of his men. They summon a local who kneels down, genuflects and begs the prince forgive his humble ways. "Why, your most noble and eminent highness, it be an ice pit. Under the thatched roof here lies a bed of straw made of dried reed-grass, what we happen to put ice on," he says, in fear for his life for being so bold as to know something that the prince does not. "And so," continues the disgusting and dirty ice-pit-owning peasant, "come summer, what with the ice having been kept frozen on account of the well-insulated straw and thatch, we use it to cool sake or make ice cream. So, your most high emperor-type-level highness, what will it be? Pistachio or raspberry ripple?" The prince, understandably, has the peasant stripped, whipped and flayed alive for his outrageous temerity.

And what of Alexander the Great tempting in the ladies with his offers of ice, flavored with honey and nectar? Or Nero sending slaves up into the mountains to fetch snow so it could be savored with fruits and their juices? "Watching Christians being thrown to the lions is more fun with a slush puppy," he once remarked.

The veracity of early ice-related yarns (with each retelling) is questionable, of course. More credible are the many references to Catherine de Medici (see p. 81) having enjoyed ice cream. Even the name of her personal ice-cream maker is touted, supposedly a chef named Ruggeri.

The architect and stage designer Bernardo Buontalenti is mentioned as a celebrated director of banquets and feasts of the mid-sixteenth century. A party planner par excellence, he could be relied on by the flash and superrich to produce an extravaganza of fireworks and ice sculptures. He may also have created delightful frozen desserts for the occasion, using zabaglione and fruit. Without question in those days it would have been mightily impressive, midsummer, to be served icy puddings to refresh the palate.

Certainly it seems that Buontalenti, with his architect's hat on, was responsible for constructing ice-houses, although it's hard to know whether they were used for anything other than preserving ice. Indeed ice-houses do stretch back far in time. Athenaeus, in his achingly long, cheesecake-obsessed *Deipnosophistae* (see p. 30), recalls that "in the island of Cimolas underground refrigerators are constructed in summer where the people store jars full of warm water and draw them out again cold as snow."

But it was in the sixteenth century that Italian scientists discovered how the addition of potassium nitrate (saltpeter) to a bucket of snow could be used to freeze a container of water immersed in it. The results of such experiments were published by Giambattista della Porta in his *Natural Magick* of 1558. This magnificent book of alchemy—with its instructions for turning lead into tin, hatching eggs without hens, preserving garden peas and getting better figs from your fig tree (you mix red chalk, oil and human dung and cover the roots with it)—includes his recipe for a wine slush puppy.

He describes how "Wine may freeze in glasses." As wine was the key ingredient at a feast, what could be better than wine "cold as ice [to] be drunk, especially in summer." He adds wine and a dash of water to a glass, then puts it in a mound of snow that has been mixed with saltpeter. The liquid in the glass then freezes. He has this piece of advice for those unaccustomed to frozen drinks: "You cannot drink it but by sucking and drawing in of your breath." It was quite a novelty. It must have caught on because Antonio Latini (see p. 118) in 1692 has a recipe for "20 goblets of lemon sorbet."

But all this is a little off the point because it's all very well serving iced wine and frozen puddings but it's not exactly ice cream. Surely the history of ice cream needs to start at the moment when a decent recipe churns an eggy custard into an ice-crystal-free delight that melts easily and gently on the tongue?

Such a result can be gained from Mrs. Eales's recipe in 1718, although she does make some assumptions on the part of the cook. Her instruction to "Take Tin Ice-Pots, fill them with any Sort of Cream you like, either plain or sweeten'd," assumes that you already know how to make your ice-cream base.

But we can deduce that she herself knew what she was doing and she certainly knew how to use salt in the process. Mary Eales was a pro; she was Queen Anne's confectioner and her little book of recipes contains a whole host of sweet delights, including "chocolate cream." For this she melts a quarter pound of chocolate in a quarter of a pint of water, adds a pint of cream and two well-beaten eggs. She mixes it well before cooling it and then just before serving urges you to "mill it up again, that it may go up with a froth."

Although a previous recipe for ice cream appears in the household manuscript of Lady Anne Fanshawe in the 1660s, she makes no mention of salt, so the trophy for the first ice-cream recipe must go to Mary Eales. And as she also has that delicious recipe for chocolate mousse, her place in food history is assured.

39

Puff past
(*Puff pastry*)

AUTHOR: Edward Kidder, FROM: *The Receipts of Pastry and Cookery*

Lay down a pd of flower & break into it 2 ounces of butter & 2 eggs yn make it into past wth cold water yn work ye other part of ye pound of butter to ye stiffness of yor past yn roul out yor past into a square piece stick it all over wth bits of butter flower it & roul it up like a collar double it up at both ends that they meet in ye midle roul it out again as aforesaid till all ye pd of butter is in.

In the early years of the eighteenth century—when the royal family looked to the House of Hanover to continue its succession, the growth of printing saw the publication of daily newspapers and of books of every kind, coffeehouses spread across London, the rich decked out their houses in luxury and commissioned Lancelot "Capability" Brown to design their gardens (while the poor continued to live in squalor)—a pastry maker called Edward Kidder opened a shop in Queen Street, in London's Cheapside.

As was the new style, he fashioned a shop window in which he placed his fresh pastries and pies. These were filled with the likes of lamb, venison and chicken. There was every kind of pie imaginable, from decorative pasties and sweet tartlets to deep-filled pies with thick golden crusts.

Household servants and cooks bought their pies from Mr. Kidder. A bachelor could keep his, as had long been the habit, on the sideboard in case anyone popped by and needed feeding. Others could be used for entertaining, while some could be taken on longer journeys to sustain travelers between coaching inns.

Mr. Kidder's pies were exceedingly good, and so was his pastry. So much so that having been asked on several occasions to explain, demonstrate even, his pie-making skills he decided to hold regular classes. His students were well-to-do ladies and regularly, throughout the week, he taught them the art of pie-making. He showed them how to make them with hare, chicken, goat, pigeon, swan, turkey, artichokes and much more. He had recipes for fish pie as well as mince pies and a number of sweet-flavored ones too. He then moved onto teach a much wider variety of recipes, from simple roasts and soups, to fricassées and delicious puddings, as well as giving instruction on how to preserve vegetables and meat and make jelly.

Business boomed and he opened a second shop in Holborn and divided his time between the two. History doesn't relate whether he had assistants but it does record that Edward Kidder "teacheth at his School On Mondays, Tuesdays, and Wednesdays, in the Afternoon, in St. Martin's Le Grand And on Thursdays, Fridays, and Saturdays, in the Afternoon, at his School next to Furnival's Inn in Holborn." But that was not all. Not everyone wished to traipse down to his shop. The smarter type of lady preferred to remain at home and have private lessons and so Mr. Kidder advertised that "Ladies may be taught at their own houses."

There are no earlier records of cookery schools in England, so his may well have been the first. Cooking know-how was otherwise passed from cook mentor to protégé, from housekeeper to kitchen maid and from mother to daughter. Like Mr. Kidder, those who taught cookery would have probably recorded their recipes for posterity, as did a lady of the late seventeenth century. A book survives from 1678 called *Rare and Excellent Receipts, Experience'd and Taught by Mrs. Mary Tillinghast,* to which had been added: "And now printed for the use of her scholars only." But how and where she taught is not known. Edward Kidder's teaching venue is known, by contrast, as he makes very clear at the front of the book he published in 1739.

He left the idea of doing a book very late: he was seventy-three by then, although he was still teaching. At first glance, the text of the book looks like manuscript, in a flowing, stylish and elaborate hand. But on closer inspection the words turn out to be printed, from an inscribed copper plate.

Perhaps copies of the book were meant as both instruction and as a souvenir of the lessons. And as his lessons were mentioned at the front, he might also have intended the book to be a marketing ploy, encouraging anyone who was lent the book to enroll for lessons. Those lessons, at 2 guineas a time, were not cheap but they were certainly popular. According to a report in the *Lady* newspaper, albeit many years later in 1851, "he is said to have taught nearly 6,000 ladies in the art of making pastry."

He called himself a "pastry master" and it was clearly the fashion of the time to learn how to make pastry—hence the inclusion here of his recipe for puff pastry. In fact, while he was obviously a fine teacher, his recipes do not seem particularly modern for the age. He was clearly a traditionalist. His book, which he describes as intended "for the use of his scholars," contains all the usual regulars you might expect from the previous 150 years—all those boiled and roasted meats, cakes and soups. But despite the absence of more avant-garde ingredients—potatoes and tomatoes were still to catch on (see pp. 85 and 118)—it didn't stop him being popular.

He was quite wealthy, if his will is anything to go by. He left a gold watch, a diamond ring, sumptuous bedroom furnishings and other trinkets to his wife and two daughters. And the portrait of him printed at the front of his book shows a man in full mid-seventeenth-century wig and costume. He stares out with an exacting expression, the forefinger of his right hand poised as if instructing one to "Shred ye yolks of 20 hard eggs wth ye same weight of marrow & beef suet seasonit wth sweet spice wth citron & lemon piele fill & close ye pyes," as he does for egg pies.

Sadly, the publication of his book brought his career to a close. No sooner had it been published, in all its near-seventy-recipe glory, than he died. The pages serving to record for posterity his pioneering cookery school.

40

Little foie gras pastries with truffles

AUTHOR: Louis-Auguste de Bourbon, Prince de Dombes
FROM: *Le Cuisinier Gascon (The Gascon Chef)*

You have the foie gras which you stick with truffles; you specially make a forcemeat of foie gras; you have small pastries prepared; you line the bottoms with the forcemeat, place a piece of the foie gras on top and a truffle on each side, cover them with the forcemeat, finish them and brown them on top, and put them in the oven. When they are cooked, you open them up and pour a little essence inside and serve.

Using food as currency in business transactions is rarely seen as acceptable. It might happen in the playground—a chewy sweet for a cactus or a football sticker, for example—but beyond childhood it doesn't have much credibility. When it is attempted, the deal never seems totally satisfactory. After Esau sold his birthright to his brother Jacob for some red lentil stew (it must have been good), he came to regret bitterly his side of the bargain.

My great-grandfather, Sir George Sitwell, offered to pay his sons' Eton school fees by sending down a trainload of potatoes, but the school refused. There was, however, a mutually satisfactory deal achieved in 1788 when the Governor of Alsace, Maréchal de Contades, exchanged some pâté de foie gras with the then King of France, Louis XVI, for a piece of land in Picardy in northern France.

No doubt the king had quite enough land, but not enough good pâté. Both partners in the deal were more than happy and word of the transaction spread. Sure the land was good—history does not record the acreage, but much of it was fertile and contained wheat fields and vineyards, even if it's not known why Contades wanted a patch of land that wasn't in his province—but the pâté was sensational.

It was prepared by Contades's pastry chef, Jean-Joseph Clause. Contades was, apparently, tiring of the local Alsatian cuisine—he felt there were only so many dumplings he could eat and rabbit with noodles loses its charm when it becomes an everyday dish. So he challenged Clause to serve up some good and—more crucially—original French food.

It was during a sleepless night that the chef hit on the idea of baking a whole foie gras in a pastry casing stuffed with a veal and lard forcemeat. Contades loved it as did the king who, on tasting it, pronounced it edible gold. In fact he liked it so much that, the property deal aside, he rewarded Clause with the gift of 20 pistoles (inedible gold coins). Clause then used the money to buy a trunk, packed up his belongings and moved to Strasbourg where he opened a shop and spent the next forty years happily selling pâté de foie gras.

By the time his shop was up and running, Clause's pâté contained the added ingredient of truffles. Some records suggest that the original reason the king had loved the pâté was that it already had truffles in it. But the evidence is hazy on this.

Clause called this dish *pâté de foie gras de Strasbourg*. He claims the foie gras moment in food history because he packaged and sold it on a scale that made the product famous. But if Clause ever wrote his recipe down there is no record of it for none survives. And so the prize for the first published recipe for pâté de foie gras—with truffles in it—goes to another cook, who brought out a recipe book some forty years previously.

Le Cuisinier Gascon hit the shelves in 1740. The author was anonymous but it is reckoned that the man to whom the book was dedicated—one Prince de Dombes—actually wrote it. Perhaps it wasn't the done thing—indeed some might think it still isn't—for a noble to be a chef, so he used the cloak of anonymity.

His full name was Louis-Auguste de Bourbon, Prince de Dombes, the second son of the Duc du Maine, and he clearly was a man of taste as the publisher of a 1970 edition of his tome—a neat pocket book of 217 recipes—has described it as "an essential witness of the refinement of life in France in the 18th century." Along with this chapter's foie gras pastries are "eggs in orange blossom water," "chicken à la Caracatacat" and "little pastries of green oysters."

The practice of force-feeding ducks and geese to fatten them up first began back in ancient Egyptian times.

And while the Prince de Dombes was the first to publish a recipe for foie gras pâté with truffles, La Varenne (see p. 103) recorded half a dozen recipes for cooking foie gras—including one in which he dusts it in flour and salt before grilling it and serving it with a squeeze of lemon juice and another in which he adds truffles—though he does not use it to make pâté. An even earlier recipe appears in Marx Rumpolt's huge *Ein new Kochbuch* (see p. 85), where he suggests wrapping the foie gras in calf's caul (the filmy membrane that covers a newborn's head and face—yummy), roasting it and serving it in a brown broth.

Yet it is of course a controversial ingredient. Indeed it has so riled modern-day campaigners for animal welfare that they have succeeded in having it banned in some restaurants, entire supermarket chains and even whole cities. But any cruelty involved in its production is not a modern phenomenon. Anyone wishing to take up their protest with the wise guy who thought up the idea of force-feeding a duck or goose by shoving grain through a tube down its throat will find themselves looking at the ancient Egyptians. They were well into the practice by the third century BC and the evidence can be seen today in the Louvre in Paris.

There, in a series of paintings on stone ornaments taken from a tomb near Cairo, is the clear depiction of men force-feeding domestic ducks and geese. You can even see a man holding a cylindrical tube, apparently for the purpose. The tomb belonged to a man called Ti. A good name because his title, as recorded in Maguelonne Toussaint-Samat's *A History of Food,* is the rather longer "The-Pharoah's-One-Friend-Chief-of-his-Master's-Secrets-in-All-his-Dwellings-Chief-of-the-Royal-Works-Steward-of-the-Pyramids-of-Neferikare-and-Neontsere." He loved long titles almost as much as he loved goose and duck liver, so it was the depiction of "gavage," the force-feeding of them, that he wished to have for his journey into eternity.

But no one taught the Egyptians to force-feed the birds; they do it themselves, come migration time. Before they fly off to different climes, ducks and geese prepare for the ensuing long period without sustenance by cramming themselves with food and thus giving themselves reserves of energy by way of extra fat in the liver. Presumably someone once slaughtered a pre-migratory bird, nicely fattened up for the journey, and found that the liver had taken on a golden, rich and fatty hue. They only then needed to work out that if you force-fed them out of season, you could have foie gras all year round.

The Egyptians loved it, as did the Romans and the Greeks, with Archestratus (see p. 19) describing goose liver as "magnificent." The decadent Emperor Heliogabalus—who reigned briefly from 218 BC before having his, and his mother's, head chopped off—fed it to his dogs. One assumes his servants gave them a good long walk afterwards.

Chefs and foodies can't resist it and the effect of eating it for them eclipses the issue of cruelty. As the American chef Dan Barber has remarked: "There's not a food today that's more maligned... if you're a chef and you put it on your menu you risk being attacked. The problem for us chefs is that it's so freaking delicious." Its rich and fatty unctuousness has made it irresistible to both cooks and diners. As Ben Schott says in his *Food and Drink Miscellany,* foie gras has "killed more gourmands than the plague."

The act of force-feeding a goose or duck so that its liver expands up to eight times its natural size horrifies many, but not those who do the work. The French who traditionally rear ducks and geese for foie gras are in denial at any cruelty. In Richard Olney's *Simple French Food* (1974), he meets a Frenchwoman in Perigord who speaks in loving and almost mystical terms of her métier (and some readers may wish to look away now). She talks of

> the tenderness and gentleness with which the birds are treated and, with mounting enthusiasm and in the most extraordinarily sensuous language, the suspense and the excitement experienced as the moment arrives to delicately slit the abdomen, to lovingly – ever so gently – pry it open, exposing finally the huge, glorious, and tender blond treasure, fragile object of so many months of solicitous care and of present adoration.

Reflecting on the conversation, Olney continues: "One sensed vividly the goose's plenary participation, actively sharing in the orgasmic beauty of the sublime moment for which her life had been lived."

Once Clause incorporated truffles into his pâté de foie gras—one luxury added to another to create something even more sublime—its main ingredient soared in popularity. Enlarging the livers of poultry became a vital cottage industry—particularly in southwest France. Clause's foie gras pâté represented how a shift in food culture took place toward the end of the eighteenth century. Here was a dish that was both a national representation of cuisine and one that was fiercely regional. As the years passed, its producers fought and won protection for their product and its consumption became politicized.

Now with legislation dictating appellations and minimum percentages of foie gras in pâté, it is synonymous with the finest gastronomy not just of France but other cuisines. And with producers now offering "faux" gras, in which birds fatten themselves up thinking they are about to migrate, some chefs hope their menus can be drawn to include fattened goose or duck liver without the threat of protest. But if I were such a protester, I think I'd still be fighting on the side of the goose, liver nicely stuffed, bags all packed and hoping for a pleasant migratory vacation rather than a one-way trip to the farmer's chopping block.

41

Capon de galera

(Fisherman's chicken)

AUTHOR: Juan de la Mata, FROM: *Arte de reposteria (The Art of Pastry)*

The most common gazpacho is called Capon de Galera, and this is how it is made. Take slices of bread (without crust or crumbs), toast them and then dip them in water. Add to a sauce made of anchovies, a couple of cloves of garlic, well crushed together, vinegar, sugar, salt and oil all mixed well together. Leave the bread to soften. Serve on a plate – and add all or some of the ingredients and vegetables of the Royal Salad. An easy way to make the garlic sauce is with a little chopped lemon, rind and sugar, serving the gazpacho as before.

For centuries, the bulk of the world's population has been sustained by soup. Soup in its many guises: it could be gruel, it could be stew, it might be pottage or even porray (see p. 52). Whoever you were and whatever your station in life, from toothless serf to bejeweled nobleman, you ate soup. Soup filled you up; when eaten with bread it could feel like a meal in itself. But whether it was a rich, deep, meaty affair, or just scrapings of a days'-old bubbling cauldron, it was warm. Thick or thin, stodgy or runny, it nourished body and soul, signaling to the heart that this warm blanket of a dish should be loved.

Then man went and did something odd, something that seemed to defy logic. He took this dish of soup, this body-warming, life-giving creation, and reckoned that it could be improved a tad if it was served cold. And then he went a step further and added not a fresh loaf, but bread that was stale—hardened and dried out, preferably about a week old.

Such a step in our culinary history might seem perverse on the face of it, but such a soup did of course come about, and it came to be thought of as not just a dish that could sustain, but one that was both delicious and desirable.

Gazpacho today conjures up an image of nutritious refreshment. So many smart restaurants around the world serve a version of it as a palate-cleansing amuse-bouche. And how delicious it is when consumed in Spain. Especially when the yin of good intentions that gazpacho signals, competes with the yang of a crisp, cold glass of Fino sherry.

The word "gazpacho" seems to have Arab origins, possibly derived from the Mozarab (the language spoken by Muslims who dominated the southern Spanish Iberian peninsula from the fifth to the eighth century AD) word *caspa,* meaning "residue" or "fragments." Which is exactly what soup consisted of in ancient times, except this type was served cold. Or the term might come from the Hebrew word *gazaz,* which means "to break into pieces," referring to the method employed in the recipe of tearing up stale bread.

At its most basic, gazpacho would be made with just bread, water and olive oil. A simple, clean use of easily available ingredients, if one lived in the Mediterranean. So the Moors might have brought the dish to Spain when the country was part of the Muslim world during the Middle Ages, or an earlier version of it might have arrived with the Romans. As vinegar is usually a key ingredient, the trail could indeed lead to Rome. Apicius, after all (see p. 26), often sloshed it into soup and his book *De re coquinaria* features a recipe for barley broth that swims in vinegar.

But however cold soup got to Spain, the Spanish championed it. And just as Jean-Joseph Clause later packaged and sold foie gras (see p. 131) and James Keiller potted marmalade (see p. 138), even though neither invented the foodstuff in question, so the Spanish take the foodie crown for gazpacho as they took this dish to heart, honed it and made it their own.

As ingredients such as tomatoes became more widely available (see p. 118), they were added to it, along with peppers and other vegetables and the more fundamental ingredients of garlic (its bite providing a substitute for the heat of a conventional soup) and onions. It then appears to have traveled abroad out of Spain, to be further disseminated in the nineteenth century, thanks to the Spanish wife of the French emperor Napoleon III, Eugénie de Montijo, although that may not be the reason she had an asteroid named after her.

But when it comes to pinpointing the first ever published recipe for gazpacho, fruitless conjecture can end. For in 1747 in the pages of a book called *Arte de reposteria* ("The Art of Pastry") Madrid-based chef Juan de la Mata presents a variety of gazpacho that he calls *capon de galera* (or "fisherman's chicken"). Quite why it is called "capon" ("chicken"), however, is unclear because it contains no chicken. Perhaps the anchovies provide the answer. Were these salty little fishes thought of as the fisherman's alternative to chicken? Perhaps there was another mid-eighteenth-century dish called "Farmer's anchovy" in which the fish was substituted for chicken.

Juan de la Mata refers to this dish as "the most common gazpacho." Unfortunately, he doesn't also offer up what might have been less common types of gazpacho, in which possibly the bread would not have been toasted, a sauce of anchovies would not have been added and there might have been some tomatoes instead of the "Royal Salad" of unspecified fruit and vegetables. Modern Spaniards might, and indeed do, shudder at this particular recipe, but most nations are ashamed of some aspects of their culinary history.

The author of *Arte de reposteria* does in fact apologize for his recipes in the introduction, his *prologo.* His book was intended, he says, as "a first draft . . . and I'm asking you to excuse my mistakes." After all, his main skill was as a pastry chef and the book's emphasis is on puddings, custards, cakes and cold drinks. His mantra was "to make easy that which is difficult," which seems remarkably twenty-first century of him.

With his recipes for confectionery, sweet things and sauces, Juan de la Mata was following in an already rich tradition of Spanish cookery writing. Many documents survive from the period of Arab rule—particularly in the thirteenth and fourteenth centuries—with the supposed culinary landmark being made in 1599 when a work called *Libra del arte de cocina* ("Book on the Art of Cooking") was published. The author was Diego Granado Maldonado and his reputation survived intact all the way up until the 1980s, when a beady-eyed scholar noticed that Maldonado had actually copied most of his recipes from one Bartolomeo de Sacchi. Bartolomeo's byline was Platina (see p. 65) and his *De honesta voluptate et valitudine* ("On Honourable Pleasure and Health") came out in Italy in 1475. But as we now know, Platina actually stole most of the recipes in his book from Martino de Rossi, who had written them all up some ten years previously.

So Maldonado is actually guilty of handling stolen goods, although he may not have actually realized he was what one might term a recipe fence.

According to Francisco Martínez Montiño, head cook of Philip III of Spain at the turn of the seventeenth century, Maldonado's worst sin was not plagiarism (a crime that went undetected in those days), but that a book which proclaimed to represent Spanish culinary art was in fact mostly filled with Italian cooking. Which does indeed sound like treason.

Montiño attempted to redress the balance in his *Arte de cocina* of 1611 with Spanish pies, pastries, stuffed vegetables and meatballs. And he was followed by a Franciscan monk, a champion of ordinary food whose *Nuevo arte de cocina* ("New Art of Cooking"), published in 1745 under the pen name of Juan Altamira, is bursting with hearty stews and bean dishes.

As for our own Juan de la Mata, as well as his gazpacho dish he has a tasty recipe for drinking chocolate in which cinnamon, orange water and vanilla are added to equal quantities of sugar and cocoa powder. Could this be the recipe for chocolate the Spanish royals had tried to keep secret for so long (see p. 79)? Had Juan let the culinary cat out of the bag? Surely a man responsible for so unremarkable a gazpacho would not have been so underhand as to betray such a confidence?

It appears that Juan de la Mata was not actually such an honest Joe (or José, even) after all.

The recipe that immediately follows *capon de galera* is entitled *Salsa de tomates a la española.* Sound familiar? It's a translation, word for word, of Antonio Latini's "tomato sauce in the Spanish style" (see p. 118) from 1692.

A refreshing slurp of gazpacho might be just the thing to get you over the shock of such news…

Assorted dessert pastries on table next to gazpacho shooters.

42

To make chip marmalade

AUTHOR: Susanna MacIver, FROM: *Cookery and Pastry*

Weigh the oranges, and take equal weight of sugar; clean and grate the oranges; cut them cross, and squeeze them through a searce [sieve]; boil the skins tender, so that the head of a pin will pierce them: when you take them off the fire, squeeze the water out of them, and scrape all the strings from them; cut them into thin chips, and let them boil until they are transparent. As soon as the oranges are grated, pour some boiling water on them, and cover them until you are ready to use them: when the chips are quite transparent, put in the juice, and strain the water through a searce, from the gratings in amongst the marmalade, and let all boil together until the juice jellies, which you will know by letting a little of it cool in a saucer.

The white ceramic pots of James Keiller & Son Dundee Marmalade fetch up all over the world. A fragment was found in the back garden of a house in Nova Scotia, Canada; one was discovered in an abandoned mining settlement in Hawaii. Others have been spotted by snorkelers at the bottom of Lake Placid in Upstate New York, while there are hundreds on eBay.

By the mid-nineteenth century, business was booming and the factory in Dundee, which employed 300 staff, was churning out around 2 million jars of marmalade a year. There were so many of these pots, used to store everything in from pencils to wooden spoons, that it's not surprising they still turn up in the strangest places. People liked the marmalade and Dundee was made famous because of it. It wasn't, however, invented there. As Jean-Joseph Clause had packaged and sold his foie gras (see p. 130) as a tasty pâté in the 1790s, so Janet Keiller did with marmalade at around the same time.

It happened, apparently, by chance. With a storm brewing off the east coast of Scotland, a ship from Europe was forced to take shelter in the port of Dundee. As the bad weather lasted for several days, the men came ashore and word spread of the cargo of fruit and vegetables on board. The ears of grocer John Keiller pricked up at this and he sent his wife, Janet, down to the port to buy some produce for his shop. She returned with a large quantity of Seville oranges.

"We can't sell them, they taste too bitter," he may have remarked crossly, having discovered the large amount she had bought. "Ah," she may have replied, "but there's a recipe for marmalade in Susanna MacIver's *Cookery and Pastry.* And very nice it is too, by all accounts."

At which point, this imagined scenario takes a few steps closer to reality because Janet Keiller makes a great deal of marmalade and it sells like hot cakes or (in view of the weather that precipitated all this) goes down a storm. (One spurious yarn has Janet telling a boy to go back to the ship to buy further oranges: "Mair, ma lad," she cries...) In due course, she finds a regular supplier of the oranges as she churns the stuff out from their shop on Castle Street.

Soon the limited space of her kitchen can't cope and her son James sets up a new business, "James Keiller," in 1797. In 1804 the venture is re-registered, this time as "James Keiller & Son." Which suggests marmalade manufacture was growing, as was his family—who either worked for him or were destined to do so. Here was a product, originally produced at home along with a host of other preserves and confections, that through luck and commercial nous the Keiller family managed to produce on a much larger scale. It was an early example of a brand and one made in a food factory, which would have been rare at that time.

But as historian C. Anne Wilson states firmly in *The Book of Marmalade:* "Janet Keiller did not invent marmalade." Neither was she the first to sell it, but she was different in that she used "chips." Rather than beat the rind smooth using a pestle and mortar, she chopped it. It was less laborious, but just as tasty. Thicker cut and darker, her marmalade contrasted with the usual finer variety.

She didn't need to invent a recipe as there would have been plenty to choose from in contemporary family recipe books. One such volume was by Edinburgh-based cookery schoolteacher Susanna MacIver whose book has two recipes, one for smooth and one for chip marmalade. There were, as she wrote, "not many ways of making it; and I have tried, and found by experience, that these two receipts are the best."

Janet Keiller called her version Dundee Marmalade and it sold so well that it became a byword for Scotland, a key part of the Scottish breakfast, a symbol of excellence, a matter of national pride. Indeed, it is mentioned in accounts of the time. Walter Scott, the Scottish novelist and poet who died in 1832, reminisced about the breakfasts he had with a friend who lived by the banks of the Clyde. "Such breakfasts we used to have at Kilmardinnie," he wrote. "Fresh trout, game pies, cold venison, a baron of beef on the sideboard, home-made scones, potato scones, white puddings, and scotch baps, to say nothing of Dundee marmalade and Scotch bannocks."

The Keillers, as their business grew over the subsequent hundred years and more, were exporting a little bit of Scotland with each jar they sold. And it spread all over the world, its export enabling ex-pats and others, from Australia to South Africa and India to China, to enjoy on their breakfast toast a little taste of Scotland.

Except marmalade isn't remotely Scottish of course. The word itself comes from the Portuguese *marmelo,* which means "quince," and the early incarnation of marmalade was as a quince preserve. While marmalade for the English today refers to an orange preserve, in Greek *marmelada* just means "jam," likewise *marmellata* in Italian. This sweet and solid quince jelly was given as a gift in the fifteenth century and, eaten as a rare treat at the end of a meal, was thought to be medicinal as well. Henry VIII is recorded as having received a pot as a present from "Hull of Exeter" who, in 1524, gave the king "one box."

Recipes for it appear in various sixteenth-century cookbooks before cooks start to apply the quince recipe to other fruit. John Partridge in his 1584 *Treasurie of Commodius Conceites and Hidden Secrets* tells how "To make marmalade of damsons and prunes," for instance. Then, as oranges and lemons begin to arrive in Britain—originally brought to southern Europe by the Arabs—they are used as well. By 1602, Sir Hugh Plat in his *Delightes for Ladies* (see p. 93) is explaining how "To preserve oranges after the Portugall fashion." It then took around another two hundred years for someone to think of making and selling it on an industrial scale.

James Keiller invented a machine that could effectively chop large quantities of peel and by the 1860s the device had been honed by his descendants. Blades on a rotating spindle revolved and chopped the rind into chips. The factory by then was staffed mainly by young women, who fed peel into the machines and stirred row upon row of boiling copper pans. The operation impressed David Bremner, who wrote warmly about his trip to the Keiller factory in his book *The Industries of Scotland* in 1869. "About the whole establishment there is an air of cleanliness and order which the visitor cannot but be gratified to witness," he said. "While the appearance of the workpeople is a sufficient proof that their occupation is by no means unhealthy."

Today the portrait of a benign James Keiller hangs in the McManus gallery in Dundee. He died in 1839 safe in the knowledge that his first factory-produced marmalade was enhancing breakfasts around the world. And all thanks to the ingenuity of Janet Keiller for whom there is today a plaque on the wall of the building on Castle Street where it all started.

43

Sandwiches

AUTHOR: Charlotte Mason
FROM: *The Ladies' Assistant for Regulating and Supplying the Table*

Put some very thin slices of beef between thin slices of bread and butter; cut the ends off neatly, lay them in a dish. Veal and ham cut thin may be served in the same manner.

When Charlotte Mason added a note on how to make a sandwich, it was almost casual, a throwaway line, coming second to last in a section of miscellaneous recipes in her book *The Ladies' Assistant for Regulating and Supplying the Table.* Little did she know that her dissemination of this short recipe was a key part in the genesis of a food monolith, a technique of delivering food to the mouth that today sustains billions in everyday life.

Without doubt it is named after John Montague, Fourth Earl of Sandwich. Exactly how he introduced the sandwich to polite society is an often-told legend. A rake and a gambler, in the best eighteenth-century tradition, he engaged in a gaming session at some point during the year of 1762 which was to last some twenty-four hours. Hence he was disinclined to leave the table for anything save a pee-break or to stretch his slick and slender breeches and stocking-covered legs.

At one point, however, he felt like a snack. But he needed something to sustain him that would not require him to move to the dining room. It was vital that what he ate would enable him to hold his cards and stay in the game but not look inelegant. So he called his man over and asked him to prepare two sides of bread, buttered, and to place in between them a thin slice of meat. As the dish was brought to him, his fellow gamblers murmured words of approval and asked for the same thing, so the fashion to have "the same as Sandwich" was born.

Whatever the date of this seminal food event was (and if he really did call for this "Sandwich" while he was gambling or simply as he sat working at his desk), it happened well before November of that year, by which time the idea had spread. The diary of Edward Gibbon, the historian and Member of Parliament, has the following entry for 24 November 1762: "I dined at the Cocoa Tree... That respectable body... affording every evening a sight truly English. Twenty or thirty... of the first men of the kingdom... supping at little tables... upon a bit of cold meat, or a Sandwich."

Yet while the Fourth Earl of Sandwich may have given his name to this ingenious portable snack, he didn't actually invent it. He had probably come across it during his travels to the eastern Mediterranean, where, among the mezes and canapés were delicate bits of food placed between pieces of bread. The Greeks, as ever, had got in there first and had probably been doing it for ages. But it took an Englishman, and a well-traveled one—he was a politician and a First Lord of the Admiralty, among other things—to lend it a name and make it respectable.

The sandwich itself might have been reputable, but its early incarnation was at events that were less so. It became a popular dish at late-night drinking parties attended by the upper classes, allowing them to sate their hunger as they gossiped and gambled. It spread to balls and grand parties but became more mainstream as, during the nineteenth century, the midday dinner graduated toward the evening. The previous night's roast meals provided cold meat fillings for sandwiches the following day.

As the distance between where people worked and where they lived grew, so the handiness of the sandwich came to the fore. The pasty may have sustained miners working underground—the edible pastry encasing a wholesome meal that could be heated up if necessary—but as men and women traveled in coaches and then trains, they preferred the neater sandwich for their midday snack.

It's surprising, in fact, that it took until the mid-eighteenth century for it to take hold. Bread had been around for a good while, of course, and it had long been used to contain food. Soup or pottage was poured onto large crusts which acted as plates (see p. 53); doubtless other meats were placed on top as well. It would only have taken someone who had to leave the table in a hurry and was still hungry to place another piece of bread on top and thus hold the thing together and make it transportable.

A piece of bread with food on top might be more attractive—it holds no secret of what might be between two slices—but you can eat a sandwich on transport. As H. D. Renner muses forcefully in his 1944 tome *The Origins of Food Habits:* "In the face of these advantages, the physiological and psychological attractions of a single slice with its surface openly displayed could not prevail."

As time went by, the sandwich was eaten at picnics, suppers, for tea, and was served at taverns and other hostelries. When the Temperance Movement gripped

Britain in the nineteenth century—an extreme, though understandable reaction to excessive ale and gin drinking—the owners of taverns offered free sandwiches as a way to entice the drinkers back.

In its infancy, in the era of George III (during which time the king lost the American colonies and went mad), when Charlotte Mason introduced the sandwich to her readers, it was just one of hundreds of dishes she presented. And it was one of many significant advances that she herself heralded. Her book includes a recipe for "a sea dish called chouder," for instance, and a large and inventive section on eggs, among many other gems, from beef olives to "Welch" rabbit and a "floating chocolate island."

Charlotte Mason is an elusive figure; all we know about her is that she was a housekeeper with thirty years' experience and an obsession for suggesting seasonal menus, those "bills of fare" of old. She called it "regulating the table." Page after page is dedicated to her suggestions of what courses can match others. There are no sandwiches of course, which we now know can be a meal in themselves. Her advice, she hoped, would be "of credit to the taste and management of the mistress." If only she'd suggested the lady keep her other half happy with a sandwich, the revolution might have taken off even more quickly.

44

A buttered apple pie

AUTHOR: Amelia Simmons, FROM: *American Cookery*

Pare, quarter and core tart apples, lay in paste, cover with the same; bake half an hour, when drawn, gently raise the top crust, add sugar, butter, cinnamon, mace, wine or rose-water.

It has become an American cultural icon. U.S. soldiers in the Second World War said they were fighting for Mom and it. The sniff of a freshly baked one and the flutter of the Stars and Stripes is enough to bring a tear to the eye of many Americans; stirring enough to get them fired up to happily take on anyone even thinking of disrupting their way of life. But while they don't pretend to have invented it, Americans reckon they perfected it. And so the apple pie's first appearance in America's very first cookbook is pretty goddamn important.

Amelia Simmons has more than one recipe for apple pie, but in her "buttered" version the apples aren't precooked, whereas in another they're stewed and strained before being added to the pie. Baked with cinnamon and mace—the subtle-tasting outer layer of nutmeg—it is not dissimilar to today's all-American version (of which of course there are several), especially if you leave out the rose water or wine and make a nice, sweet and crispy crust.

Americans can be as proud of their apple pie—which is ubiquitous in the States because apple trees were planted by settlers everywhere and the fruit stores well and the pie tends to be eaten at all times of the day—as they can of the author of the first American recipe for it. In writing her book, Amelia Simmons represented the spirit of independence that had long rippled across the country. The British surrender was a distant memory and the Declaration of Independence now twenty years old.

The year her book was published saw the first contested presidential election and the population was beginning to grow rapidly as European immigrants arrived and the USA expanded west. Tennessee became the sixteenth state soon after it came out and, as if to encompass every state, she proudly named it *American Cookery.*

Until that point the only books in circulation in America had been English ones by the likes of Gervase Markham (see p. 107) and Hannah Glasse. There was a book published in America in 1742 by an Eliza Smith called *The Compleat Housewife,* but it was pretty much a rip-off of the other house- and huswife type books that England had seen plenty of over the last 150 years. No recipe book had presented itself as a spirited reflection of this new independent union of states or as one that uniquely grappled with what to do with some of the country's indigenous produce.

Amelia Simmons changed all that—well, some of it at least. She cooked with cornmeal and made a sauce from cranberries to go with turkey (see p. 74). The sauce might have been a descendant of the one made by Tudor cooks from red barbaries to eat with game, but cranberries were indigenous, so Americans have pretty good grounds to claim the sauce as their own. And while a French cookbook included a recipe with cornmeal a few years previously, Amelia Simmons has several and they don't feel very French.

She also makes the first mention of using pearlash—an early baking powder—to leaven dough and smokes bacon over corn cobs. And she renames dishes for the U.S. market, calling oatmeal biscuits "Indian," for instance, and introducing a word that all Americans will be very familiar with—"cookie."

Her greatest triumph was to marry Native American products with English culinary tradition and make it feel like these were recipes for this new and burgeoning country. And she marketed it as such: her book was "Adapted to this Country and All Grades of Life." She priced it cheaply, at just 2 shillings and twopence—around £1 in today's money—and it was so popular she produced a second edition in the same year. "The call has been so great and the sales so rapid," she said.

So who was she? Of that very little is known and has to be deduced from the recipes she writes and a few clues in her preface. What we do know is that Amelia Simmons was an orphan, because she tells us so on the title page. And she's not just any old orphan but "An American Orphan." In fact you get the idea that she was a bit cross, a little chippy about this even. She speaks with envy of those with normal families. "Those females," she says, "who have parents, or brothers, or riches." Then again, perhaps this is understandable.

She has written the book, she says, for "those females in this country, who by the loss of their parents, or other unfortunate circumstances, are reduced to the necessity of going into families, in the line of domestics." There might have been a war of independence, a declaration of it and national pride, but there was clearly misery too for plenty of people. To survive, orphans needed to have "an opinion and determination of their own," she says. And as she learned the hard way, her book was going to help those who didn't have a guiding hand.

The book was also aimed at the young. "Old people cannot accommodate themselves to the various changes and fashions which daily occur," she says, speaking no doubt from experience—it's likely she worked as a servant girl of some sort, a cooking sort presumably—whereas the young can be influenced. They "bend and conform to the taste of the times, and fancy of the hour."

She may have had wisdom but she was very likely also illiterate. In the second edition of the book, she explodes at discovering that the first edition was not all she thought it was. There were "egregious blunders and inaccuracies... occasioned either by ignorance, or evil intention of the transcriber..." she states.

So presumably, filled with knowledge and desperate to impart it in a book, she persuaded someone to take down her dictation of all the recipes. Which in itself is a pretty impressive feat. Then, unable to read the manuscript, it was not until others read it back to her on publication that she discovered the material that had so riled her.

The British surrendered to General Washington after their defeat at Yorktown, Virginia, October 1781.

To us, actually, it seems innocuous because what chiefly caused her anger was the addition at the front of the book of several pages of advice about selecting produce at the market. It includes useful information about spotting, for example, tired fish. You should look for "fresh gills, full bright eyes." The dodgy stuff could have their gills peppered, their tails wetted for display, their bodies splattered with animal blood, their gills even painted.

But this was exactly the sort of information that so many of those English books provided, and she wanted to be different. So to discover there were seventeen pages of this stuff infuriated her. Her audience knew the difference between good and bad produce, so to publish such guidance was patronizing in her view.

Whether or not she was right or wrong was immaterial. Her book was a part of colonial America establishing its identity and because English books gave helpful guides to shopping at the market, she didn't want to. Neither, presumably, did she want pages of tedious "bills of fare"—those seasonal menus that had been appearing for what felt like centuries—and at least the transcriber didn't add those in.

It seems evident that she never married and we'll never know if she made much money from the book, although it was a great success. Perhaps she was able to leave working for the household who employed her, possibly somewhere along the Hudson river valley in New England, judging by where the various editions of her book were published. Maybe this poor orphan was able, one day, to gain the independence she obviously craved.

Needless to say, others plagiarized the book, the most outrageous being the publication in 1805 of *New American Cookery* by "An American Lady," which copied it word for word, and the 1819 *Domestic Cookery* by Harriet Whiting, which was published in Boston and didn't even include the second-edition corrections. To have stolen and republished under a different name the manuscript that even Amelia Simmons hadn't approved of would have made her turn in her grave. But she is remembered less for her anger and the theft of her work than for the way she embodied the spirit of the new America and, more importantly, for her recipe for apple pie.

45

Soufflé

AUTHOR: Antoine Beauvilliers, FROM: *L'Art du Cuisinier ("The Art of the Cook")*

Put in the size of an egg of good butter, a little nutmeg, and the yolks of four fresh eggs, the white of which must be whipped apart as for biscuit; mix them by little and little into the purée though hot, mix all well, and pour it into a silver dish or paper mould, round or square; put it in the oven; when the soufflé is well risen touch it lightly, if it resist a little it is enough; it must be served immediately, as it is apt to fall.

Beauvilliers was keen on his soufflés, which he liked to flavor with poultry or game. It brought a light touch to the dishes he offered at his restaurant, La Grande Taverne de Londres. Located on Rue de Richelieu, this was the first grand restaurant of Paris, if not the world. He is said to have opened a previous, but much smaller, establishment on the same street, and named it Beauvilliers, but as his customers were all aristocrats, when the French Revolution took them down, he went down too. But he escaped the worse fate of his punters and was soon freed, the authorities reckoning he was more useful as a chef than a prisoner.

So on his release he made plans for his triumphant return. On a visit to London, a few years earlier, he had dined at the London Tavern and met its famous chef, John Farley—chef and recipe thief (see p. 135). Farley's establishment in Bishopsgate was a banqueting hall capable of seating up to 2,500 people. The food was sumptuous, as you might expect from a good feast, but there was no choice. This was how it had been, more or less, for hundreds of years. There was nothing new about eating out, but it tended to be a home-from-home experience. Taverns, inns and other eating houses provided customers with what the cook was cooking and it served to soak up the ale.

This frustrated Beauvilliers. He was a cook, born in 1754 and apprenticed at the Court of Provence. He had a wide and detailed knowledge of food preparation and was keen to offer the people of Paris something more. He had catered to the whims of the nobility in their private homes—where there was always a lavish selection of dishes laid out—so why shouldn't the wider public enjoy some choice? And so he opened his restaurant with the novel idea of presenting customers with a menu of food.

Some historians argue that Beauvilliers was not actually the first restaurateur and that the title should go to a man called Boulanger who opened his self-named establishment in 1765. He called it a "restaurant" in the sense of restorative, as his métier was cooking hot soups and broths. One sign on the door apparently read: "*Bou-*

langer débite des restaurants divins" ("Boulanger provides divine sustenance"). While another stated, in a similar vein: "*Venite ad me omnes qui stomacho laboratis et ego vos restauro*" ("Come to me, those who are famished, and I will give you sustenance").

He was said to tout for business outside wearing eccentric clothing and brandishing a sword. But the contemporary American academic Rebecca Spang argues there is no real evidence for any of this. Like so many anecdotes of this kind, she says, they are simply "legends [which] just get passed on by hearsay and then spiral out of control."

Beauvilliers was no legend, however. His restaurant was pre-eminent in Paris for a good twenty years and spawned countless imitations. And if others still try to steal his pioneering crown, we can rely on Beauvilliers's contemporary, the lawyer, politician and epicure Jean Anthelme Brillat-Savarin (see p. 155)—after whom a soft white cheese was named—to put us straight. In his words, La Grande Taverne de Londres was "the first to combine the four essentials of an elegant room, smart waiters, a choice cellar and superior cooking."

Beauvilliers was the classic patron. He both cooked and worked the room. He remembered his customers' names and tastes; he walked them through the menu, suggesting things they might like. And his pièce de résistance was the large key he kept in his pocket. It opened the door to his wine cellar and he would brandish it after suggesting a fine wine to accompany the chosen dish.

As a restaurateur, he was skilled in such a way that customers felt that what they were paying for were actually generous favors dished out by their host. A case in point being his soufflés. While they were savory varieties they were nevertheless popular. His recipe for them appears in his book *L'Art du Cuisinier* of 1814 (literally "The Art of the Cook" but published in English as *The Art of French Cookery* in 1825), in which he urges the cook to serve them up quickly before they collapse. Clearly they kept collapsing for many years because Marie-Antoine Carême, his celebrity-chef successor (see p. 163), devotes pages to the subject of the soufflé (which translates literally as "puffed up"), and how to cook them so that they don't collapse, in his book *Le Pâtissier Royal Parisien.*

Until Carême seized the baton as the next publishing sensation, *L'Art du Cuisinier,* written by Beauvilliers just three years before his death, became the standard text for French cooking in the ensuing years. "Cooking," he writes in his book, "simple in origin, refined century after century, has become a difficult and complicated art." Over his forty years in the trade, he experimented and innovated and now feels he can safely describe his work as "the best": "Those who best understand the enjoyments of the table, have never ceased to rely on me."

He was a man of principle. Bad servants are the result of bad employers, he says. The best masters "exclude the fashionable vice of cards from their halls, and drunkenness from their stables." He is anti-waste, too. Whether you cooked for the richest or poorest, good kitchen economy is vital. "The claw of the chicken or the bone of a fish is not allowed to be lost," he pronounces. Good ingredients are a luxury and the cook shouldn't forget it. "If the good things of life are lavished on us, we ought to use them without abusing them," is his mantra. Time should not be wasted either. A good cook needs to watch and learn and study recipes so he knows them off by heart: "If a cook has to turn over a receipt book, the labor is immense."

Beauvilliers urges people to bring variety to their meals. While he gives detailed bills of fare, like most of his culinary forebears, they should be used just as inspiration. And meals must vary in size and pace. "Real taste does not indiscriminately present turtle and venison on every occasion," he explains. Guests would be just as happy with the "zest of a fine mango... nice salads... and the charms of well-supported conversation."

He includes a vast array of recipes for readers to choose from in order to replicate the "fine dining" experience for their guests. These include curry and béchamel sauces, veloutés, black pudding and the elaborate "*pieds de cochon aux truffes*" (pig's feet with truffles), as well as ice creams, drinks and preserves. Presentation is important too. Of asparagus spears he says, for instance, "when ready to serve, send them to table with butter sauce in a boat." On cooking pheasant, he notes: "If for an English table send up bread sauce with it."

Beauvilliers was also a considerable wine buff. "When new it ferments upon the stomach and goes to the head; and when too old, it attacks the nerves," he says, adding, "those of Chablis are very agreeable, those of Meursault are better but the Chevalier Morachet surpasses them in general." Of champagne he describes its "chief quality is that of raising the spirit," while his tip for the ladies is that "the wines of Languedoc are all very good and favorites of the fair sex."

Such was his attention to detail as a host, Beauvilliers's establishment was one most of us would have been more than happy to spend a long afternoon in.

46

Spring fruit pudding

AUTHOR: Dr William Kitchiner, FROM: *The Cook's Oracle*

Clean three of four dozen sticks of rhubarb, put into a stewpan, with the peel of a lemon, a bit of cinnamon, two cloves and as much moist sugar as will sweeten it, set it over a fire and reduce it to a marmalade, pass it through a hair sieve, then add the peel of a lemon, and half a nutmeg grated, a quarter pound of good butter, and the yolks of four eggs and one white, mix all well together; line a pye dish (that will just contain it) with good puff paste, put the mixture in and bake half an hour.

Step inside the grand interior of the Acropolis-inspired St. Pancras Church, located on Euston Road in London. As the noise of the pounding traffic outside fades to a deep murmur, walk along past the darkened pews on the right and you'll soon see a plaque dedicated to one Dr. William Kitchiner. According to the inscription this was a man "deeply conversant in medical science... an accomplished musical theorist and composer; an improver of the telescope." All very impressive, but little to hold the attention of someone searching for the memorial to a legendary foodie.

In fact Kitchiner, who lived on nearby Warren Street, was not just deeply involved in medicine or music, let alone telescopes, he also plunged himself passionately into the subject of food. Infused with medical know-how, he read every book he could find that had ever been published about food, then carefully and firmly drew a thick line in the culinary sand.

And his contribution to the evolution of cooking is immense. He attempted to standardize cooking measurements, starting a process that was to last many decades, and spelled out the attitudes and manners that he thought should accompany the preparation and consumption of food. He was also a man whose veins coursed with witty and eccentric blood. His seminal book, in which he recorded his many thoughts and recipes, *The Cook's Oracle,* was not just the funniest cookbook printed to date, it was the first that you could genuinely enjoy in bed.

Born in 1777, the only son of a prosperous coal merchant, Kitchiner was educated at Eton and then studied medicine in Glasgow. Not being qualified to practice in England, and believing he would have to live and work in Scotland, he had the good fortune to be left £70,000 by his father. Moving back to London, now a man of independent means, he set about indulging his passion, to cook, talk, think and write about food.

Buying a property on Warren Street, and now with a wife and son, he set about doing two things, collecting books and bringing together a regular group of illustrious diners. After wading through these culinary tomes in painstaking detail, he would begin cooking dishes and testing them on his companions. He could then quite reasonably publish a cookbook of his own.

But food wasn't his only interest. His cathartic rests from the subject of gastronomy saw him tackling a range of subjects from songs to horses. Of the numerous books he wrote here are some of the titles: *The Economy of the Eyes and Rules for Choosing and Using Spectacles, Opera Glasses and Telescopes, The Pleasures of Making a Will* and *The Sea Songs of Charles Dibdin.* It was at the many dinners he organized that his friends and acquaintances discovered his extraordinary range of knowledge or as one contemporary put it, "the optico-musico-medico-epigastro-superabundance of his prolific talent."

Having finishing his mammoth cookbook studying session, he pronounced himself disappointed. It had been "tedious progress," a "Herculean labour" and one that had exposed the many flaws of countless recipe books published up until then. He was unmoved by the pompous advice on subjects such as the deportment of ladies that seemed to feature quite heavily, and was particularly struck by the prodigious recipe theft of the previous century. "Cutting and pasting," he notes in his introduction to *The Cook's Oracle,* was a more common feature than employing "pen and ink." So many writers had been "idly perpetuating the errors, prejudices, and plagiarisms of their predecessors." He was irritated by the vagaries of instructions, "a bit of this, a handful of that, a pinch of t'other." They were of little use to the cook, especially for one lacking experience in the kitchen. Such recipes were, he says, of no more use "than reading 'Robinson Crusoe' would enable a sailor to steer safely from England to India."

He didn't believe many of his late recipe-writing colleagues ever tested their dishes and he vowed to change all that. He would set a new standard: "this precision has never before been attempted in cookery books," he insisted. He published his own guide of standardized measurements in the book, stating that all the cook needed was "a scale and some apothecary measures." Needless to say, his advice was very complicated and required significant refinement.

While the poor still lived on a diet little better than bread, butter, potatoes and bacon, the middle and upper classes, united by all employing servants, had a constantly increasing range of ingredients available to them, and they liked puddings. The ingredients in Kitchiner's spring fruit pudding weren't particularly exotic but the sweetness of the dish would have appealed to them. The population was growing fast and, at the end of the reign of George III—after sixty years on the throne, the longest-reigning monarch to date—Britain was emerging as a leading power in Europe and social habits and customs were becoming increasingly formalized.

The publication of Kitchiner's volume coincided with this move toward greater formalization, in this case in the realm of the kitchen and dining room. And Kitchiner practiced what he preached. To assess his recipes, he put together a regular dining club of people who could evaluate his work and learn from his strict code of culinary etiquette.

Dr. Kitchiner's dining club was "A Committee of Taste" whose guests consisted of a "thoroughbred of grand gourmets of the first magnitude," he writes in his book; indeed, more than that, they were "the most illustrious gastropholists of this luxurious metropolis." They counted among them the Prince Regent, George IV, who ruled while his father suffered a period of mental illness.

Dr. William Kitchiner, medical practitioner, scientist and inventor, was also the author of The Cook's Oracle.

With Kitchiner's aim to bring dignity, courtesy and respect to dining, the rules were onerous. Invitation to dinners needed, he said, to be sent "in writing ten days before and must be answered within twenty four hours at least." Any refusals must be backed up with a decent excuse: "Nothing can be more disobliging than a refusal which is not grounded on some very strong and unavoidable cause." And God forbid the person who accepts and then tries to wriggle out. "Urgent business, sickness, not even death itself" were good enough excuses.

He was a stickler for punctuality. A letter of invitation to a regular guest, William Brockedon, firmly reminds him that for the subsequent dinner the "Specimens will be placed upon the table at Half past Five o' Clock precisely, when the Business of the Day will immediately commence." And above his chimney piece was a sign that read: "Come at seven, go at eleven."

His desire for promptness was nothing less than to assist the cook whose work was governed by the clock. "What would be agreeable to the stomach and restorative to the system if served at five o'clock, will be uneatable and un-digestible at a quarter past," he writes. Those who are late "paralyze" the entertainment; such a guest was a "blundering, ill-bred booby."

It was better to be a quarter of an hour early than half an hour late, and those who didn't arrive at the appointed hour were simply not admitted. "Wait for no one," he demanded; "as soon as the clock strikes, say Grace and begin the business of the day."

Yet it seems he struggled against the fashions of time. "An invitation to come at five seems to be generally understood to mean six," he complains. Five o'clock, he insists, meant "five precisely . . . five o'clock exactly."

As to the predinner meet and greet, he had more firm advice for the host. Introduce people clearly, "name them individually in an audible voice, and adroitly laying hold of those ties of acquaintanceship or progression which may exist between them." This was vital, he believed, "as indispensable a prelude as an overture is to an opera."

And for where people sat, he recommended place cards. There was a habit in France at the time of which he disapproved, where the ladies at a dinner party sat down first and then called out the names of the men they wanted to sit next to. A little like the choosing of players for an impromptu football game. This, he felt, was not ideal because "it may happen that a bashful beauty dares not name the object of her secret desires." The host, meanwhile, in a big party, should sit in the middle of the table, not at one end, so he or she can divide his or her time more equally between the guests.

Then, before the eating commences, there's the issue of Grace. It can be said or sung. In *The Cook's Oracle* he prints his approved musical score, then notes that whether you say or sing Grace it must done in English—"can any thing be more barbarous than to sing [it] in a Foreign Tongue?"

With everyone seated, Kitchiner unleashed his recipes on his guests. The task of eating all these meals was a tough one. He likened his Committee of Taste to the early nineteenth-century explorers: "those determined spirits who lately in the Polar expedition braved the other extreme of temperature, in spite of whales, bears, icebergs and starvation."

And although his mantra was "never affront the stomach," he did like to experiment with his guests. According to one frequent diner, William Jerden, if you didn't like a particular dish, "you were instantly supplied with zest from a phial . . . if three drops did not cure you, you ought to think of making a will." While other diners did seem to tire of Kitchiner's descriptions of the dishes he served, with one reporting: "A tureen of soup was not liked the better for having its ingredients explained."

Still, most enjoyed the food and the conversation and Jerden recalls Kitchiner as being a good-natured host and a witty conversationalist. One evening, discussing the various methods of transport available at the time, Kitchiner suggested people travel not on horseback but on a cow. "The goer could ride on his journey and live on her milk," he exclaimed.

The food eaten, the fine wine drunk, if the party was to stop at eleven, they would have all left promptly. It was a habit resolutely practiced by Kitchiner himself. That is until a dinner party in 1827. Dining at a Mr. Braham's on Baker Street, he was in high spirits—"in his glory," a friend recalled. He was particularly taken by his host's pet macaw, which sat on Mrs. Braham's shoulder all evening and squawked now and then. He forgot the time and when he got up to leave it was, according to a fellow diner, "two hours or more beyond the magic eleven." At 9 a.m. the next day he was dead, aged just fifty-two.

At his funeral his friends toasted the great gastronome, recalling his belief that "a good dinner is one of the greatest enjoyments of human life."

47

Pheasant Brillat-Savarin

AUTHOR: Jean Anthelme Brillat-Savarin
FROM: *Physiologie du Goût, ou Méditations de Gastronomie Transcendante* (*"The Physiology of Taste, or Meditations on Transcendental Gastronomie"*)

After plucking and drawing:

The bird should then be stuffed, and in the following manner:
Take two snipe and draw them so as to put the birds on one plate, and the livers, etc., on another.

Take the flesh and mingle it with beef, lard and herbes fines, adding also salt and truffles enough to fill the stomach of the pheasant.

Cut a slice of bread larger, considerably, than the pheasant, and cover it with the liver, etc., and a few truffles. An anchovy and a little fresh butter will do no harm.

Put the pheasant on this preparation, and when it is boiled surround it with Florida oranges. Do not be uneasy about your dinner.

Drink burgundy after this dish, for long experience has taught me that it is the proper wine.

If there was a moment when France claimed its superiority in the field of gastronomy—or food alone—then this was it. "Tell me what kind of food you eat and I will tell you what kind of man you are," declared Jean Anthelme Brillat-Savarin.

The moment was the publication on 8 December 1825 of his book *The Physiology of Taste.* While, over in England, Dr. William Kitchiner (see p. 151) might have sold 15,000 copies of his book *The Cook's Oracle,* in which he showered his readers with witty and pithy remarks about food and etiquette—including his aversion to the new fashion for tall candelabra (all very good but what's the point in lighting the ceiling when you need to see the plates?) and more—Brillat-Savarin brought a whole new importance to the subject.

He made food not just a key part of philosophy but he argued, succinctly and compellingly, that food—and good food, great food even—was vital to mankind's existence and his continued presence on earth. If an Englishman had taken the subject as seriously as Brillat-Savarin did some 200 years ago, Britain today might have a more embedded food culture.

But even back in the early nineteenth century, France was ahead of the game in this respect. Even Kitchiner remarked on it. The French had, he said, a better understanding of food and not just because they were "surrounded by a profusion of the most delicious wines." "Our neighbors are so justly famous for their skill in the kitchen," he wrote, agreeing with the adage of "as many Frenchmen as many cooks." "They know how, so easily, to keep life in sufficient repair by good eating," he continued, "that they require little or no screwing up with liquid stimuli."

Brillat-Savarin epitomized this state of affairs. His aphorisms are today still so famous that many have become clichés, yet they speak a defining truth about food. Here are a few of them:

> The universe would be nothing were it not for life and all that lives must be fed.
>
> Animals fill themselves; man eats. The man of mind alone knows how to eat.
>
> The destiny of nations depends on the manner in which they are fed.
>
> The discovery of a new dish confers more happiness on humanity than the discovery of a new star.

It was these thoughts among many others that Brillat-Savarin successfully used to argue for gastronomy's place in the world. It was as important as politics, as history, as crucial as the economy; essential for daily life, for enjoying the pleasure that was necessary to mankind. They were views that he came to after a lifetime of studying medicine and science, subjects to which he applied his acute legal mind. In later years he was a judge, and while he lived and died a bachelor, it was not a life of simply study and fine dining.

Brillat-Savarin was born in 1755 in Belley, a town in the Bresse region, to a family of lawyers; his mother was an accomplished cook. When an aunt died and left him her fortune on the condition that he change his name, he added hers to his before going to Dijon to study law, chemistry and medicine. Called to the bar at Belley, he also dabbled in politics, becoming a deputy in the National Assembly. Appointed a judge in the 1790s to the Court of Cassation—France's supreme court of appeal—as the French Revolution took hold, he was censured as a moderate (despite his vocal support of the death penalty), relieved of his post and then summoned to appear at the Revolutionary Court, accused of federalism.

As his detractors sharpened up their guillotines, he got hold of a passport and fled to Switzerland. He then made his way to Holland before sailing for America and spent the next few years eking out a living as French teacher in New York and playing the violin for a small theater orchestra. Then as the troubles calmed in France, when "times had improved" as he delicately put it, he returned in 1797, resuming his position as a judge and once again working at the Court of Cassation.

Now in his early forties, he spent his spare time entertaining friends at his home in Paris and in writing treatises. The piece of work for which he is chiefly remembered was published just two months before his death and, reflecting the author's extreme modesty, was anonymous. But word soon spread about its authorship and as his twentieth-century biographer Giles MacDonogh has commented: "Parisians were mystified by this extraordinary study and by the puckish wit of the tall, portly judge who had put it together." Part of its success is that it is so readable. As a journalist for the *Washington Post* wrote recently: "Every self-respecting devotee of good food, wine and company should have a copy." And indeed if only for the fact that his recipes—such as this chapter's pheasant dish—come with the novelty, for the time, of specific wine recommendations!

"Gastronomy," states Brillat-Savarin in this seminal work, "rules all life" and you can't ignore or avoid it because it "sustains us, from the cradle to the grave...the tears of the infant cry for the bosom of the nurse; the dying man receives with some degree of pleasure the last cooling drink." Good eating affects everyone, from every class, he argues. While the fates of nations are often decided at grand dinners, so the decisions of the powerful can depend on whether or not they have a full stomach. Likewise, "a man who is badly fed, cannot bear for a long time, the fatigues of prolonged labor."

Humans, he argues, do not have taste merely to indulge a hobby: "It invites us by pleasure to repair the losses which result from the use of life." That ability to taste enables us to choose things to eat which will nourish us. And we humans deserve all this. "Man of all the animals who live on the earth, is beyond doubt, the one who experiences most suffering," he states. After all, man loses his hair, goes to war and is always getting ill. More organs cause man the ordeal of pain than can give him the pleasure derived from taste. So to eat good food was a necessity, not a luxury.

This was a message taken to heart by the increasingly prosperous and well-educated bourgeoisie of Paris. To assist his readers in their quest to rightfully eat well, Brillat-Savarin includes a long list of where his favorite groceries, bread and pastries could be bought. Ingredients from England, Germany, Russia, Africa and America were available in the markets: "the world makes its appearance by way of its products," according to Brillat-Savarin.

And he had sage advice that resonates strongly today on aspects of health. He believed that obesity was the result of excess eating, drinking, lack of exercise and too much sleep. "Obesity," he comments, "destroys beauty by annihilating the harmony of primitive proportions, for all the limbs do not proportionately fatten." Although a little sugar can be a good thing: when "mingled with café au lait, [it produces] a light, pleasant aliment...precisely suited to those who have to go to their offices immediately after breakfast."

Today, not just the French but many around the world who argue that good food should be seen as an integral part of mainstream culture persevere in quoting Brillat-Savarin and the book he published in 1825 has, remarkably, remained in print ever since. As one of the most quotable writers on food of all time, the last lines should be left to him: "The pleasure of the table belongs to all ages, to all conditions, to all countries, and to all areas; it mingles with all other pleasures, and remains at last to

Brillat-Savarin was appointed a judge to the Court of Cassation in the 1790s, just when the French Revolution took hold.

console us for their departure." And there's this: "A dessert without cheese is like a beautiful woman who has lost an eye." His extraordinary thoughts down on paper, he still felt bursting with energy, writing as his very last line: "My work is done, yet I am not a bit out of breath."

48

Cupcake

AUTHOR: Eliza Leslie
FROM: *Seventy-five Receipts for Pastry, Cakes and Sweetmeats*

Five eggs **Two large teacupsfull of molasses** **The same of brown sugar, rolled fine** **The same of fresh butter** **One cup of rich milk** **Five cups of flour, sifted** **Half a cup of powdered allspice and cloves** **Half a cup of ginger**	Cut up the butter in the milk, and warm them slightly. Warm also the molasses, and stir into the milk and butter: then stir in, gradually, the sugar, and set it away to get cool. Beat the eggs very light, and stir into the mixture alternately with the flour. Add the ginger and other spice, and stir the whole very hard. Butter small tins, nearly fill them with the mixture, and bake the cakes in a moderate oven.

When she held court in her sixties in 1850s Philadelphia, Eliza Leslie was forbidding, opinionated, haughty, strait-laced and very correct. Any young girl who was brought to see her and failed to display a perfect sense of decorum, decency and politeness was quickly scolded. Miss Leslie, who never married, had very firm views on how to behave and she didn't keep them to herself. Indeed, so wide ranging and detailed were her knowledge and views on etiquette that in 1834 she published a long and exhaustive book on the subject.

Miss Leslie's Behaviour Book: A Guide and Manual for Ladies covered everything from how to dress, speak, eat, travel and more. It was, she hoped, the tome that history would remember her by. She had tried her hand, quite successfully, at children's fiction but behavior made a nation and her volume on it would surely be her lasting memorial.

But she was wrong. It was actually her cookery books that made her famous and her dryly named *Directions for Cookery, in its Various Branches* of 1837 was a triumph. It proved to be the most popular American cookbook of the nineteenth century, selling over 150,000 copies.

Yet it was not with this book that she made real culinary history. A few years before, in 1828, a Boston publisher had brought out her *Seventy-Five Receipts for Pastry, Cakes and Sweetmeats* and it is there that we find the first-ever printed recipe for a cupcake.

These are the little confections that have seen a resurgence in popularity recently in both the United States and Great Britain. American cities boast bakeries making only cupcakes; around the world there are blogs devoted to the subject; clubs have been formed so friends can bake and share their favorite varieties; *Martha Stewart's Cupcakes* book spent eleven weeks at the top of the *New York Times* bestseller list. For some time "cupcake" has been the fastest-rising recipe item searched on Google.

In Britain cupcake fanatics enroll in special courses and dress to match their concoctions. The cupcake is all the rage. And it's not difficult to understand why. A cupcake is individual, it's all yours, it belongs to no one else. It's a whole cake and it's your cake. Cupcakes look pretty and decorative and they feel extravagant. When a hostess produces a whole tray of cupcakes, it seems more generous that just serving up one cake. They can all be slightly different—different flavors and different toppings. They reflect greater glory on the hostess. But cupcakes also have the advantage of being bigger than fairy cakes, and they are naughtier.

There are records of small cakes going back to the eighteenth century, including queen cakes, for example—traditionally made with currants, lemon zest and almonds. But the cupcake seems to have been a relative of the pound cake, so named because it called for a pound of this and a pound of that ingredient. The word "cupcake" comes from the use of "cups" to measure out its ingredients, but also because it was originally baked in cup-shaped molds or, as Eliza Leslie states in her recipe, "small tins."

It is likely that Eliza got her recipes from a cooking school that she attended. She joined Mrs. Goodfellow's Cookery School in Philadelphia in her late teens with a view to helping her mother, who was then running their home as a boarding house. The family had fallen upon hard times. Her father, a watchmaker who had taken the family to live in England for six years when he was starting an export and import business, had died young and left the family with very little means. So her mother took in guests as a way of supporting her young daughter and two sons.

Having learned a great deal about culinary matters in the ensuing years, Eliza decided to write down her recipes to share with friends, before managing to publish them as a book. And in doing so she didn't just make history for her cupcake recipe. *Seventy-five Receipts for Pastry, Cakes and Sweetmeats,* published when she was forty, was a rare book in that it specialized in just one aspect of cooking—baking. (Although, to be totally honest, she couldn't help but throw in a few favorites at the back in a miscellaneous section that includes "a-la-mode-beef," "chicken salad" and several recipes for oysters, among others.)

Her recipes, she promises, are "drawn up in a style so plain and minute, as to be perfectly intelligible to servants, and persons of the most moderate capacity." Having spent some years in England and having read many imported European recipe books, she was not impressed by what had come before her. "Many of the European receipts are so complicated and laborious, that our female cooks are afraid to undertake the arduous task of making anything from them," she scoffs.

Her recipes, she states, are American "in every sense of the word." She was proud of her nationality and it grated her that the English, for example, still looked down on her fellow countrymen. She reflects on this briefly in her book on etiquette. "They have, at last," she says of the English, "all learned that our language is theirs, and they

The Old Custom House on Lower Chestnut Street in Philadelphia.

no longer compliment newly arrived Americans on speaking English 'quite well.'" How dare they, she thought, because after all, "There is no doubt that by the masses, better English is spoken in America than in England." And so her cakes were better baked too.

She urges her readers to cook her recipes also because they would save money, "one half the cost of the same articles supplied by the confectioner," in fact. In those days, though, baking was still fairly arduous. She mentions that butter should be washed, for instance, reminding us that it was still mostly made at home. (The washing was done to remove the buttermilk and any milk solids still left after the naturally soured cream from the top of the milk had been churned.) Sugar, meanwhile, needed to be "powdered" as it was sold in solid cones. And although her measurements are exact, she is less precise with cooking timings. To provide timings simply wasn't possible, she maintains—after all there was no such thing as an oven of standard temperature—so the "Skill in baking is the result of practice, attention, and experience."

Of course for her, too, as it might be for today's cupcake obsessive, it wasn't just how you baked your cupcake, but how you served it, ate it and what you wore when you did so. And for that, the young American woman of mid-nineteenth-century America would need Miss Leslie's etiquette guide. For within the pages one can, among other things, learn the following:

How to behave if you are asked to visit a friend in the country, notwithstanding her advice that you "Do not *volunteer* a visit to a friend in the country." But once there she explains how to make a bed if your chambermaid can't and what to do if a member of staff should "purloin any article belonging to you." (The answer being nothing, unless it's of great value because of the embarrassment you'll cause.)

Then there's the tricky nature of introducing people to English nobility. "Americans," she says, "are liable to make sad blunders in these things." And what to wear at breakfast: "no flowers or ribbons in the hair."

She also advises young girls not "to play a piano in public unless invited" and not to make remarks in French during dinner. Neither should you peel oranges, crack nuts with your teeth and never "take *two* glasses of champagne. It is more than the head of an *American* female can bear."

All this advice, and much more no doubt, she dished out to her many visitors as she handed out cupcakes. Famous in old age, she mostly received people at home because she became rather large and finally too big to be able to walk comfortably. It must have been all those cakes.

49

Petits soufflés à la rose

AUTHOR: Marie-Antoine Carême
FROM: *L'Art de la Cuisine Française (The Art of French Cookery)*

Put in a small basin eight ounces of finely sifted sugar, which form into a firm paste with a white of an egg; work it for ten minutes, and add a few drops of the essence of roses and rouge to tint it of a bright rose; roll out the paste on the dresser strewed with fine sugar, into bands of the size of a finger, cut them in dice, and roll them in the palm of the hand, wet them slightly as you make them, and put each into a small round paper case, three quarters of an inch wide, and one third of an inch high; press lightly on the surface of each with the finger previously wetted, which gives them a fine glaze in baking, and put them into a slow oven; when they rise half an inch above the cases, and have been fifteen minutes in the oven, and are quite dry at the surface, take them out; if not, leave a few minutes longer, but mind them, or they speedily lose their colour.

Carême fitted, broke, renewed and re-designed the mold of chef. His culinary star shone across Europe. He wasn't the first to seek fame, of course, but he became the most famous. Some see him as the first big-time celebrity chef.

If Brillat-Savarin (see p. 155) laid the foundations for the modern gastronomy, arguing for its proper place in daily and cultural life, Carême built the house by devising the recipes and cooking the food. He attempted to redefine cooking, to create new techniques, new utensils, new styles of serving. While he had a penchant for opulent over-the-top showy feasts—and we'd seen that going on for centuries—he was a key player in shifting many aspects of food culture. He helped, for example, to bring fine dining—haute cuisine—from the private house to the restaurant, with recipes such as this chapter's delicate "*petits soufflés à la rose.*" And he lightened many dishes, introducing subtle infused aromas where there had been heavy spices, the latter a hangover from the influence of the Italian Renaissance chefs that had come to France with Catherine de Medici (see p. 81) in the early sixteenth century.

He invented new tools for the kitchen—saucepans that could pour sugar, new types of molds—and he changed the shape of the chef's hat (okay, not ground-breaking, but he did it anyway). He also made kitchens cleaner places, introducing a system of sanitation. The latter was revolutionary given what a stinking place Paris—like other cities—must have been at the time. He reduced the number of courses at dinner, separated meat and fish dishes and encouraged there to be more space between diners, previously bundled together, cheek by jowl.

Above all, he was a product of the post-revolutionary era of Paris. His timing was fortuitous and impeccable, part of what one historian has called "a cyclone of virtuosity." Musicians and dancers thrived, as did chefs. And Carême's own personal story—no doubt a little mythologized by himself, a voracious self-promoter—fitted the age perfectly.

After the French Revolution, self-made men wished to make their mark. They hadn't had invitations to dine with the now defunct and headless nobility and they wanted a taste of what they'd been missing. The new-moneyed establishment had a voracious appetite for luxury and the means to attain it. Egos needed feeding, ambitions fulfilling; these people were hungry for high fashion, smart buildings and, of course, good food.

Born in 1784, Carême was in his late teens when he came to the fore, bringing with him the credentials to make him the perfect culinary foil for the new bourgeoisie. The tale he himself told of his early life only served to make his presence in one's kitchen and the flavor of his impending sauces all the more delectable.

So many of the greatest chefs have risen from humble beginnings and none more so than Carême. Born in Paris, he was one of twenty-five children. His father was an unskilled laborer, his mother, presumably, just permanently exhausted. Life wasn't helped by the fact that the former was frequently not working but drinking. Yet he had, with hindsight, one saving grace. In a seminal, cruel-to-be-kind, moment, he slung his son out onto the street.

It was an evening that Carême remembered well. He was just ten years old and his father had taken him and his brothers for a walk around the city before stopping for supper at a cheap tavern. Arriving back home, possibly the worse for wear, he took his young son aside. "Go my little one, go now," he said (Carême told the story to his secretary, Frédéric Fayot—possibly more than once, and he surely wasn't the first or last to hear it). "There are good trades in the world; leave us; misery is our lot; this will be an age of many fortunes; all that is required to make one is intelligence, and you have that. Go with what God has given you."

Carême's reply was not: "Yeah right, Dad. It's nine o'clock at night, you're drunk and I'm only ten years old." He actually took his father's advice, for the last time, and left the house. He never saw his parents or his brothers and sisters again—which is surprising given how many there were of them.

Without a clue as to where he should go or what he should do, he decided, wisely, to try his luck at the tavern by the Maine gate where they had all eaten earlier in the evening. He managed to get lodging and food there in return for work, and he stayed there long enough to learn basic cooking skills. Whether he worked elsewhere in the ensuing years is not clear, but at the age of sixteen he landed his big break. One of the city's best-known pastry chefs, Sylvain Bailly, had a shop near the royal palace and Carême found a job there.

His boss was astonished at the energy and natural creative flair of the young boy and encouraged him to develop his skills by spending time at the city's National

Library. Somehow Carême had learned to read and he used his time in the library to develop his other love, architecture and design. For two afternoons a week he studied old cookbooks and architectural drawings and then, bringing his two passions together, started sketching out drawings for lavish confections.

"I succeeded in my plans," he later reflected, "but how many nights I stayed up in order to do so." He completed 200 of what he called his "*pièces montées*." "Each one more original than its predecessor," he said, "while remaining easy to execute in pastry." These elaborate confections, sometimes several feet high, were modeled on pyramids, temples and classical ruins as well as themes from nature, from waterfalls to cliffs.

The recipes he later published were not for the faint-hearted. They included a "Small Chinese Ship," a "Venetian Gondola," a "Gothic Tower," an "Indian Pavilion," a "Lyre decorated with emblems of love" and a wide variety of military helmets. His fountains, be they Grecian or Turkish, had sheets of water made of silver spun sugar. He decorated ancient ruins with moss made with a mixture of almond paste, flour, eggs, sugar, salt and natural dyes.

He executed drawings for chefs to follow and exclaimed in the accompanying text: "How great the effect produced! This series of *pièces montées* is generally facile in execution, because the details are short and easily understood."

Designs for pastry decoration from Le Pâtissier Royal Parisien *by Marie-Antoine Carême, published in 1854.*

He stopped working for Bailly and set up on his own, having already come to the attention of several leading Parisians, including the famously scheming diplomat Charles Maurice de Talleyrand-Périgord, who employed his talents at important banquets. He then forged an independent career working across Europe, for the banker James de Rothschild in Paris as well as the Prince Regent in England.

His work didn't simply involve pastry but the complicated logistics of grand feasts. Not all of which were entirely successful. His spectacular creations for a dinner at the Royal Pavilion in Brighton, for instance, were presented on long tables and guests helped themselves to the dishes they fancied. "It was impossible to sustain a conversation because someone was always interrupting," one guest later wrote, presumably referring to the likes of "Would you mind passing the *poulardes à la Périgueux?* Oh, and that *timbale de macaroni à la Napolitaine* looks nice." "The servants," remarked that same guest, "were always on the move."

But money was flowing and Carême's talents were able to blossom across Europe. He was one of the first chefs to have an independent career—not being tied to the house of a rich or noble family—and in doing so raised considerably the status of his profession. "The fine arts are five in number," he wrote, "painting, sculpture, poetry, music and architecture—whose main branch is pastry."

He published several recipe books, which encouraged many more pastry chefs to go independent. His *L'Art de la Cuisine Française* was particularly influential, codifying French cookery and remaining a central reference point in the country's gastronomy ever since. Believing that if he could build towers of pastry he could design whole cities, he also produced several volumes of architectural works. Possibly weakened by a life spent toiling in the kitchen, Carême didn't see old age, dying at just forty-nine. He once wrote that he doubted "a cook has ever made as many pecuniary sacrifices to further the progress of culinary art."

While his famously huge creations do not tally with the spirit of dining today—and they do seem to be extravagant and wasteful of ingredients—most great chefs still pay homage to the man who was for many the first genius of haute cuisine, and he remains an inspiration for those who dream of rising from humble beginnings to achieve greatness.

50

Brussels sprouts

AUTHOR: Eliza Acton, FROM: *Modern Cookery for Private Families*

Free them from all discoloured leaves, cut the stems even, and wash the sprouts thoroughly. Throw them into a pan of water properly salted, and boil them quickly from eight to ten minutes; drain them well, and serve them upon a rather thick round of toasted bread buttered on both sides. Send good melted butter to table with them. This is the Belgian mode of dressing this excellent vegetable, which is served in France with the sauce poured over it, or it is tossed in a stewpan with a spice of butter and some pepper and salt; a spoonful or two of veal gravy (and sometimes a little lemon-juice) is added when these are perfectly mixed. 9 to 10 minutes.

If cabbage is the devil's vegetable, then the Brussels sprout is Satan's second cousin once removed. How many childhoods were blighted by cabbage and its diminutive relative? Mine certainly, although its now singular annual outing is made more tolerable bunched with lashings of gravy and bread sauce amid the turkey at Christmas lunch.

These mini cabbages existed in the Mediterranean for a few thousand years before being propagated in northern Europe. And firsthand—albeit not conclusive—travel experience in the Med indicates that the region was quite happy for it to move further north if not vacate the area altogether as there is little evidence of sprouts in, for example, Greek, southern French or Sardinian cooking.

The Belgians clearly received the sprout gladly, embracing it as one of their own and naming it after their capital, although exactly when this happened is not clear. The sprout receives sporadic mentions during the seventeenth and eighteenth centuries and had hit British soil by the end of the eighteenth century. It gets a mention in Charles Marshall's *Plain and Easy Introduction to the Knowledge and Practice of Gardening* of 1796, in which he describes sprouts as "winter greens growing much like borrowcale [kale]."

Perhaps it was general antipathy toward cabbage that prevented a recipe for sprouts appearing until the mid-nineteenth century. After all there are about 400 varieties of cabbage, which is surely torture enough. Still it took that otherwise blameless culinary heroine Eliza Acton to write the first published recipe, which is why she is uniquely gifted with two chapters in this book (see also p. 169). Actually, she may have understood its unsavory nature, which is why her recipe includes plenty of butter and pepper, not to mention the addition of lashings of tasty veal gravy.

Her version makes the sprout almost tolerable to the young palate, but sadly generations of cooks seemed to ignore her advice, dishing them up overcooked, soggy and altogether dreadful. If only everyone followed her general advice on cooking vegetables. She issues a stern warning that however tenderly cared for, however delicately harvested, "their excellence will be entirely destroyed if they be badly cooked."

She is a firm believer in the very modern mantra about the speed of the journey of vegetables from field to plate. "Their flavour is never so fine as within a few hours of their being cut and gathered," she says. And on their cooking, except for the likes of dried peas and beans, Jerusalem artichokes and potatoes, the water should be "fast-boiling," ready salted, with any scum skimmed.

Care should then be taken that the vegetables are neither overcooked nor left in the water when ready, as "both their nutritive properties and their flavour will be lost." She also advises against undercooking them—or erring on the al dente side, as more recent trends would have you cook veg. She abhors "the tradition of serving them crisp which means, in reality, half-boiled [which] should be altogether disregarded." Such cooking was apparently the fashion, but health, she argued, was more important than any current trend.

Today's cooks would certainly shun her advice for reviving tired-looking vegetables by tossing a little bicarbonate of soda into the pot to liven up their color. Perhaps she was unaware that to add even half a teaspoonful could destroy all the nutrients in veg—or at least obliterate any vitamin C.

Still, this minor slip-up should not detract from her greatness. Neither really should her mention of the dreaded Brussels sprouts, especially as she makes them almost edible. As a contemporary reviewer declared, she is "the greatest and most judicious collector of culinary phenomena that has yet appeared."

51

Kedgeree or kidgeree, an Indian breakfast dish

AUTHOR: Eliza Acton, FROM: *Modern Cookery for Private Families*

Boil four ounces of rice tender and dry as for currie, and when it is cooled down put it into a saucepan with nearly an equal quantity of cold fish taken clear of skin and bone, and divided into very small flakes or scallops. Cut up an ounce or two of fresh butter and add it, with a full seasoning of cayenne, and as much salt as may be required. Stir the kedgeree constantly over a clear fire until it is very hot; then mingle it quickly with two slightly beaten eggs. Do not let it boil after these are stirred in; but serve the dish when they are just set. A Mauritian chatney may be sent to table with it.

The butter may be omitted, and its place supplied by an additional egg or more.

Cold turbot, brill, salmon, soles, John Dory, and shrimps may all be served in this form.

Eliza Acton, according to Delia Smith (see p. 294), is "the best writer of recipes in the English language." It is the simplicity of her instructions and her good advice that Smith finds so appealing. And this posthumous thumbs-up, coming 150 years after the publication of *Modern Cookery for Private Families,* would have gratified Eliza Acton immensely.

After all, she proclaimed that her recipes could be "perfectly depended upon" and to make things simpler she introduced a novel concept that recipe writers have followed ever since. At the end of many of her recipes she lists the ingredients and the quantities of them you'll need for cooking the dish. Mrs. Beeton (see p. 184) developed the idea, putting the list at the start of the recipe, but it was Ms. Acton who set the ball rolling.

It sounds so obvious today, but until that point in history the cook had to run through the recipe to get an idea of what was needed and even then, as we have seen, not necessarily obtain a real picture of what ingredients were actually required.

Eliza's reason for doing this was not just to make the reading of recipes more straightforward, but an attempt to cut down the waste that came from cooking. She was angry—obsessed even—at what she regarded as "a very serious evil," perpetrated in the main by reckless servants, unsupervised by the housekeeper, who had no idea of the true value of money. (So as ever, the poor servants get it in the neck.) "The daily waste of excellent provisions almost exceeds belief," she wailed. So the clearer her recipe writing, the more efficient the cooking and the less good food wasted.

And these poor servants needed all the help they could get. Most of them learned to cook on the hoof, and Eliza castigated charitable institutions for instructing the poor in everything but cooking. They were taught, she said, "half-knowledge of comparative un-useful matters."

Good domestic cooks in the mid-nineteenth century were a scarce commodity and because they were scarce they were expensive. "A rare treasure of English life," Eliza called them and it annoyed her immensely. Despite the progress being made in society—and this was a time of great upheaval during the Industrial Revolution—the English still seemed unable to take cooking seriously. In spite of its varied and abundant produce England's "cookery has remained far inferior to that of nations much less advanced than our own," she said. And when wealthy and aristocratic families did hire cooks, they were usually foreign.

There was a glimmer of light, though, she felt. Cooking was "no longer sneered at as beneath the attention of the educated and the accomplished." But what was needed was some good teaching, not just more publications. "It is not cookery books that we need half so much as cooks really trained," she declared. Her reasoning being just that which Brillat-Savarin (see p. 155) had been arguing some twenty years before in France, to a more intellectual audience.

"The influence of diet upon health is . . . a subject of far deeper importance than it would usually appear to be considered," she wrote, adding, "'Eat—to live' should be the motto." And her passion for good health through food wasn't just to keep families well and happy. She realized she was living in a time of rapid social and industrial change, and that revolution was being driven by the middle classes to whom her book was aimed. "It is from these classes that men principally emanate," she writes in the preface to her book, with the "indefatigable industry, high intelligence, and active genius" to advance science, art, literature and "general civilisation." So they needed to be nurtured and fed well. As Carême (see p. 163) rode the wave of post-revolutionary France, bringing to the bourgeoisie the finer tastes of gastronomy, so Eliza Acton brought to a willing and growing middle class the means of improving their everyday lives through better food.

Born in Sussex in 1799, the daughter of a brewer, she lived in the era captured by Jane Austen and witnessed the changes taking place as the country progressed to the Victorian era. More commodities could be bought in shops, for instance. By the time her first book was published, a volume of poems in 1826, Bird's Custard Powder had been invented and the English kitchen welcomed in the "closed range" cooker with its metal hot-plate covering a coal-burning fire box with rings on which to place pots and kettles. Some models had ovens on either side of the fire box, but temperature controls were still limited. Cleaner, and with the ability to regulate heat, gas cookers arrived, tentatively, from the 1850s.

English grandee of the East India Company riding in an Indian procession.

As kitchen technology enabled cooks to better control their cooking, so the advent of the railway brought further culinary sophistication by way of improved food distribution and a wider variety of ingredients. And ingredients were traveling considerable distances, bringing to Britain new flavors from her colonies. Eliza Acton's recipe for kedgeree describes itself as "an Indian breakfast dish," reflecting how the cuisine of India was becoming increasingly popular in England.

England received its first tastes of India back in the early 1600s when the East India Company was formed and started to trade. As the centuries passed, English trade turned to war and then rule. And when the government of India was taken over by the British Raj from 1858, so the appetites for Indian food increased back in Britain.

While Hannah Glasse had some recipes for curries and pilaus back in 1747, they also appear in an updated edition of *A New System of Domestic Cookery* by Maria Rundell, originally published in 1806 but edited and enhanced by Emma Roberts in 1840. She includes a new section called "Oriental Cookery," by which she meant food from Asia, Persia, Turkey and Hindustan. There are numerous recipes for curry, from Madras prawn and Malay chicken to others credited to "Lord Clive," "Khali Khan" and "The King of Oude." They all feature different kinds of curry powder, which, in a separate section, she explains how to make.

And they are not as bland as you might think. For one recipe she grinds coriander seed, cayenne pepper and turmeric; another has cumin and lemon pickle. While none of the recipes begin with the grinding of fresh garlic and chili, her Bengal curry powder does at least recommend the zesty addition of fresh lime juice.

Emma Roberts includes a recipe for "khicheree," but it is not as we know it—there are no eggs and no flaked fish. It took Eliza Acton to add these. She suggests it as a breakfast dish at a time when breakfast itself was undergoing a renaissance. Breakfast having consisted for centuries of porridge and cold meats, Acton's kedgeree gave the institution an exotic shot in the arm. Much of the rest of the world started its day with rice (the Chinese were still wolfing down their congee, for instance—see p. 33); the British version made it more palatable with the addition of eggs and fish.

Cereals were yet to hit the table. It would be another few years before the Seventh-day Adventists of America started experimenting with baked, ground cereal dough as part of their vegetarian diet; and it wasn't until 1894 that John Harvey and Will Keith Kellogg invented corn flakes to improve the diet of hospital patients (see also p. 246).

By the time Mrs. Beeton had well and truly arrived on the scene (in 1861—see p. 182), eclipsing all in her wake (and stealing plenty of Eliza Acton's recipes while she was at it), the British breakfast had acquired the two staples it's still known for today. Beeton urged households to "relieve the monotony of breakfast" with its "too frequent appearance of bacon and eggs...the sheet anchor of the English cook," suggesting a heart-attack-inducing range of grilled chops, steaks, cutlets and fried potatoes be brought into the bargain.

I'll stick with Eliza Acton's kedgeree, I think, just adding a poached egg on top and eating any leftovers for supper with a big dollop of mayonnaise.

52

Welsh rarebit

AUTHOR: Charles Elmé Francatelli
FROM: *A Plain Cookery Book for the Working Classes*

First, make a round of hot toast, butter it, and cover it with thin slices of cheese; put it before the fire until the cheese is melted, then season with mustard, pepper, and salt, and eat the rarebit while hot.

The story of food tends to alight more frequently on the tables of the wealthy. After all, it is they who can afford better ingredients, employ seasoned chefs and dazzle their friends with the latest culinary creations (from jellies to monumental pastries), exotic ingredients and new dining concepts. So the poorer classes get less of a look in. After all, there is only so much you can do with cabbage, onions, potatoes and bread.

But in the enlightened period of the Victorians, as politicians enacted laws to ban children (albeit only under the age of nine) from working in textile factories and mines and education became increasingly compulsory, so too did some people turn their attention to improving the diet of the poor. One such character was Charles Elmé Francatelli, an Englishman of Italian extraction, and a cook who learned his trade in Paris under the eye of Marie-Antoine Carême (see p. 163). He then worked for a number of wealthy and aristocratic families in England, before landing the plum role of chief cook and maître d'hôtel to Queen Victoria. So he not only cooked for the queen but was responsible for running a substantial part of her household.

His cooking had strong French influences and his first book, *The Modern Cook,* published in 1846—nine years into the reign of Queen Victoria—was crammed full of rich sauces along with dozens of Gallic-named dishes and sophisticated ornamental puddings and soufflés. He displayed his knowledge of desserts in a book devoted to confectionery of 1862 and a year before that—keen to share his recipes with others who ran households—published a mammoth tome, *The Cook's Guide and Housekeeper's and Butler's Assistant.*

Yet there was, he felt, a gap in the market. No one was helping the working classes to cook. And so, prior to his two more upmarket volumes, he set about compiling a book that would give it to them straight: clear culinary advice, recipes that could be achieved on a budget, dishes that could feed and sate the appetites of a family of laborers and their children.

He gave it a name that left you in no doubt about its aim and contents. He called it *A Plain Cookery Book for the Working Classes.* No need for aspiration, it did exactly what it said on the tin. Or did it? How in tune was Francatelli with the needs, desires and cooking abilities of his new audience? And would the book resonate and stand proud in the home of the working man?

As urbanization grew, the range of food available to the poor actually narrowed. Having lived on bread and cheap veg—the cabbage and onion diet—for centuries in the countryside, but now deprived of a smallholding, those living in cities started eating cheap meat instead.

A very clear and remarkable picture of 1840s poor urban living is painted by the journalist Henry Mayhew who, with his small team, observed, met and interviewed hundreds of working-class men, women and children for his book *London Labour and the London Poor.* It was, he said, a "history of a people from the lips of the people themselves."

He describes vividly the markets, streets, houses and people he meets, transcribing long passages of dialogue, recording habits, accents and slang. He meets market traders and laborers—from costermongers to streetsweepers—and absorbs himself in their world. It must have been quite a sight: this portly, well-dressed and benign journalist with his notebook-wielding assistants, dodging the crowds in the markets, peering up alleyways and venturing into the poorest of homes.

One Saturday evening, after pay time, he walks down New-Cut—a market street in Lambeth—with almost impassable crowds. "Little boys, holding their three or four onions in their hand, creep between the people, wriggling their way through every interstice, and asking for custom in whining tones, as if seeking charity." The noise is immense: "the tumult of a thousand different cries of eager dealers, all shouting at the top of their voices at one and the same time, is bewildering."

There are stalls selling new tin saucepans, rows of old shoes along the pavement, families begging: "the father with his head down as if in shame, and a box of lucifers [matches] held forth in his hand." He passes a butcher's shop with the window "crimson and white with meat piled up... the butcher himself, in his blue coat walks up and down, sharpening his knife on the steel that hangs to his waist."

Then there are stalls selling green and white turnips, yellow onions and purple cabbages. The language of the traders was bewildering to say the least. Mayhew found their conversation "clothed in slang, so as to be unintelligible even to the partially initiated." Yet he spends considerable time, for example, among the costermongers, whose hobbies include gambling, rat killing and dog fighting, who encourage fighting and respect anyone who can "serve out a policeman."

They are unschooled, with only an education in learning how to buy in the cheapest market and sell in the dearest. Watching a group gambling, he hears one young man announce he is "going to get an inside lining," referring to dinner, which comprises soup and mashed potatoes. Others he meets eat bread and butter for dinner, and maybe some fried meat. It's largely an "outdoor diet," he comments; many meals are eaten out of the house. Meat, known as "block ornaments," are the cheapest cuts, small dark pieces on the butcher's counter. You could take it to a "tap-room" at the local bar where they would cook it for you.

Mayhew meets a street sweeper with "the dogged look of a man contented with his ignorance." "I don't know how old I am, [but] I's old enough to have a jolly rough beard," the man says before talking about his eating habits. "I buy ready-cooked meat, often cold boiled beef, and eats it at any tap-room. I have meat every day. Vegetables I don't care about, only ingans [onions] and cabbage, if you can get it smoking hot and plenty of pepper." This man, like most Mayhew meets, is illiterate. Although he does have a friend who reads the paper to him, but not altogether successfully. His friend Bill, he says, "has to spell out the hard words so that one can't tell what the devil he's reading about."

Others Mayhew met talked of eating hot pies—made of fruit or meat—and many also lived on a diet of cheap fish. "A fish diet," he writes, "seems becoming almost as common among the ill-paid classes of London as is a potato among the peasants of Ireland." The costermongers sold low-priced sprats and whiting and having poked his head around the doors of several poor homes he reported, "the rooms of our needy metropolitan population always smells of fish; most frequently of herrings." And it wasn't a pleasant smell. You might have smelled fish in a clean kitchen but it would give you "no adequate notion of this stench."

Then on Sundays, if the going was good, a joint of mutton would be cooked. That is, in the words of one man Mayhew met, if you weren't "cracked up." "Many of them drank hard having no other way of spending their leisure but in drinking and gambling," comments Mayhew. In fact many casual laborers, without a steady income lived lives of what he calls "excess both ways...excess of guzzling when in work, and excess of privation when out of it. Oscillating, as it were, between surfeit and starvation."

So what could the Italian-descended, smartly dressed Francatelli, with his proudly grown sideburns, teach such people?

Firstly he supplies a list of necessary cooking utensils—including an oven, in addition to copper pans, frying pans and a potato steamer—which, food historian Colin Spencer works out, would cost the highest-paid artisan six weeks' work at least. Although understanding that, Francatelli suggests you "strive to lay by a little of

The journalist Henry Mayhew is best known for his groundbreaking and influential survey of London's poor in his book London Labour and the London Poor.

your weekly wages to purchase these things." Then, as a chef to the queen and later chef de cuisine at the Reform Club, he can't help himself present recipes for equally unaffordable chickens (for cocky-leaky soup) as well as suckling pig, and geese.

A. G. Payne, who wrote the preface to the influential nineteenth-century *Cassell's Dictionary of Cookery,* was dismissive of much of his work, remarking how "Francatelli wrote for a small class who lead to a great extent artificial lives." Yet in this book most of the recipes are down to earth. The problem is most of them are pretty uninspiring and inedible and there is barely a word encouraging people to look for vegetables or salads.

There are stewed eels, yeast dumplings, potato puddings. A recipe for pig's feet suggests putting them in salt for three days and then boiling them for three hours.

One for toad-in-the-hole (see also p. 225) recommends buying the cheapest meat, but then cutting off the parts which smell rotten and had flies all over them in the shop; "it would tend to impart a bad taste," Francatelli says helpfully and might "spoil the dish."

A potato pie is simply onions and potatoes boiled, put in a dish, covered with mashed potatoes then baked. Fish soup sees onions boiled for ten minutes before adding whatever cheap fish were in the market with a bit of thyme, pepper and salt and boiling for another fifteen minutes. "You may feel occasionally inclined to indulge in a treat of this kind," he says before giving a recipe for boiled tripe. Then there is "How to make toast water." You toast a piece of bread, put it in a jug, then pour over boiling water, "stand until cool" and "it will then be fit to drink."

Given how rank most of these recipes are—and the Welsh rarebit is unique in being tasty—it was probably a blessing that Francatelli's would-be customers couldn't afford his book and, if they could, wouldn't be able to read it anyway.

53

Cauliflower & cheese

AUTHOR: John Smith, FROM: *The Principles and Practice of Vegetarian Cookery*

Boil a cauliflower till tender, drain the water well from it, and divide it; lay it in a dish and pour a quarter of a pint of good white sauce over it; then grate or slice some cheese over it, and brown it before the fire or with a salamander [iron plate heated and placed over a dish to brown it]. Instead of cheese, a few small mushrooms, or very small onions previously boiled, may be put into a saucepan with the cauliflower and white sauce. Serve with toasted sippets.

It was on a September evening at a hospital in Ramsgate, on the English coast, in 1847 that a group of people met to form the Vegetarian Society. This word "vegetarian" was new and the men, including William Horsell—who ran the hospital (it specialized in water cures)—and Joseph Brotherton, an MP, felt it suitably represented their principles. A hundred and fifty members signed up immediately and at the first annual general meeting, which took place the following year in Manchester, their number totaled 265, with an age range of between fourteen and seventy-six. In the ensuing months and years, meetings were held in cities across Britain. A magazine was founded, the *Vegetarian Messenger,* and in 1860 Yorkshireman John Smith published his book *Principles and Practice of Vegetarian Cookery.* It is heavy on theory and light on recipes, the one on cauliflower and cheese coming right at the end of the book, and being a rarity in that he does a bit more than just boil the vegetable. He also gives the dish a nice added crunch with the "sippets"—small pieces of toast.

Smith, meanwhile, didn't just avoid meat, he had firm views on hot food, which he hated. "All food in a hot state, whether solid or liquid, should be carefully avoided, as it acts injuriously on the teeth, debilitates the stomach, and, through it, every organ and portion of the animal system," he wrote. So once Mrs. Beeton (see p. 182) had boiled the vegetables to death, John Smith then dished them out cold. It was yet another low, savage and early blow to British food culture.

But the march of vegetarianism—be its dishes hot, cold or lukewarm—continued. A smattering of veggie restaurants opened in London and by 1897 there were seven of them. The movement looked set to grow throughout the coming century, but with the onset of the First World War, where mere survival was a more immediate concern (men in the trenches were not afforded the luxury of choosing where they might get their protein from), the pace of vegetarianism slowed.

After moving to England in 1881 to further his education, Mahatma Gandhi became a member of the London Vegetarian Society, where he met like-minded people.

It was not the first time those campaigning for a meat-free diet had to struggle against a prevailing wind. But they would soon dust themselves down and progress the movement. Indeed, Second World War rationing—which meant that for possibly the first time in history the nation, rich or poor, all had to eat the same things—brought new opportunities to broadcast the message.

The battle to convince people to abstain from meat has long been tough and challenging, but those who take up the cause do it knowing that they have at their side the illustrious veggie ghosts of history willing them on. In the words of Nadine Abensur, author of the vegetarian cookbook *The Cranks Bible,* "there has always had to be pioneers, cranks and visionaries and we all know that yesterday's folly is today's norm."

We might not have yet reached her vegetarian paradise, but those apparent "visionaries" have included some pretty distinguished individuals (as well as, er, Hitler). There was Leonardo da Vinci, for example, who when he wasn't inventing armored tanks and helicopters wasn't eating meat. And there was Pythagoras, who lived between 570 and 495 BC. Indeed, was there ever such a luminary vegetarian as he? Most of us recall that he was good at math, but so was he an accomplished player of the lyre, a singer and composer. He could accurately guess the number of fish caught in a net, was never seen either laughing or weeping and history also records that not only could he walk on water, but he could be in two places at one time.

Then there was his compassion for animals. He once stopped a man beating a dog because he said that he recognized in the hound's cries the voice of an old friend. And while there was a bit of a tendency in his day to sacrifice animals to the gods, Pythagoras did make sacrifices but he didn't do it with meat; he used cake. Sacrificing one's cake does show quite strong moral fiber, especially if it's made of chocolate.

Then of course there was Buddha (circa 563–483 BC), who also strongly disapproved of animal sacrifice and condemned meat-eating in the same breath as he did war and aggression. Indeed vegetarian principles, say its proponents, go back to the beginning of time. As the food historian Colin Spencer puts it: "In the beginning paradise is vegetarian." The rot sets in, ironically, when Adam eats that fruit—albeit a forbidden one—and culminates in God, fed up with the meat-eating and savage antics of man, sending a flood to destroy the world so he can make a fresh start.

Although anyone claiming that God himself is a veggie has some explaining to do when Noah finally disembarks from his ark. His first act is to sacrifice a couple of animals and, says the Bible, "the Lord smelled the pleasing aroma." He would hardly have gone all "Ah! Bisto" if he'd disapproved of the idea of killing and cooking animals. Although he did also make the point—in several places in the Old Testament—that while eating meat is okay, man is not to drink the blood of an animal. So vegetarians have struggled to land their blows ever since Noah's famous meat-loving gesture in that new post-flood world.

Killing animals for sacrifice has historically been man's hotline to God, while the cooking of meat has been a ritual to unite friends and families, as well as a sign of wealth and power. As we have seen throughout history, slaughtering large numbers of creatures, beast and fowl, has been the hallmark of grand feasting. No rich noble baked an aubergine or cooked up a nut rissole to impress friends or put the fear of God into his enemies.

Meat-eating was what man did. As Colin Spencer writes: come the Renaissance, "meat-eating had become solidly entrenched in the mores of society." Although ironically, as has earlier been noted (see p. 52) meat-eating was a feature of the rich. The poor could not afford it: oxen were more useful pulling plows, chickens producing eggs; and if animals were sold for slaughter, it was so the seller could buy more flour, salt or vegetables. So throughout history the poor have been involuntary vegetarians. And graduating from poverty, they seek out the badge of meat-eater to demonstrate their move up the social ranks.

Vegetarianism of course has two firm pillars upholding it, in the form of a protest against cruelty to animals and an argument about health. And it was the former that galvanized many early veggie crusaders. There is the brutality inflicted by uncompassionate meat producers and the perceived heartlessness presided over by those who hunt for pleasure.

Erasmus, the fifteenth- and sixteenth-century Dutch scholar and veggie sympathizer, mocked the hunters. "When they, the sportsmen, have run down their victims, what strange pleasure they have in cutting them up," he wrote. It was a pursuit fellow sympathizer Sir Thomas More, statesman and counselor to Henry VIII, called "unworthy...the lowest, the vilest and most abject part of butchery...butchers kill their victims from necessity whereas the hunter seeks nothing but the pleasure of the innocent and woeful animal's slaughter and murder."

Given that More would have spent quite a bit of time at Tudor banquets where the conspicuous consumption of meat was a key feature, he must have become well practiced at biting his lip. Perhaps Henry VIII got wind of his veggie and antihunting views and it was that, rather than More's opposition to the First Succession Act, that led to his execution.

More's Utopia was a vegetarian world and with some foresight he attacked the amount of land needed to graze cattle. But it no more chimed with the times than his unpopular political views. Yet he was not a lone voice. His contemporary, the French essayist Michel de Montaigne, was equally horrified by hunting, writing: "I have never been able to see, without displeasure, an innocent and defenseless animal, from whom we receive no offence or harm, pursued and slaughtered."

Likewise, the word welfare was not exactly front of mind for those who kept and slaughtered animals. In his *Cook's Oracle* of 1817, Dr. William Kitchiner (see p. 151) cites some unfortunate culinary practices of the past. There is a recipe where you take a living pig, make him drink his own marinade of vinegar, rosemary, thyme, sweet basil, bay leaves and sage and then "immediately whip him to death and roast him forthwith." Another suggests the cook takes "a red Cocke that is not too olde and beat him to death."

He quotes a more hideous and shocking recipe from a Mr. Mizald that he spotted in a book published in 1660. "How to roast and eat a goose alive" first calls for a "lively creature." Having plucked her and basted her in lard and butter she is set on the ground next to cups of water infused with honey and others with slices of apple. A circle of fire is then lit around the goose and she darts about being roasted alive and taking desperate sips of water. "When you see her giddy with running, and begin to stumble...she is roasted enough. Take her up, set her before your guests, and she will cry as you cut off any part from her and will be almost eaten up before she be dead; it is mighty pleasant to behold."

One can safely assume that this impractical recipe was rarely, if ever, attempted. Yet its very idea symbolizes the worst excesses of an ever-increasing frenzy of spectacular meat-eating.

The dawn of the nineteenth century saw an increased interest in a vegetarian diet as a response to this. So many rich men of the previous century had been obese and gout-ridden. One well-established doctor was said to weigh 32 stone. The idea that a little more veg might be better for you coincided with better distribution of vegetables and a wider variety becoming available in markets.

The early stages of vegetarianism were also encouraged by the temperance movement. The teetotal Reverend William Cowherd advanced the idea of abstaining from flesh among his congregations in the early 1800s with his view that "if God had meant us to eat meat, then it would have come to us in edible form as is ripened fruit." This doesn't, of course, account for steak tartare, neither that many vegetables and fruits also need cooking before eating. But he was a popular man and one of his followers was Joseph Brotherton, who went on to co-found the Vegetarian Society, but his wife, Martha, was the unnamed author of *Vegetarian Cookery: By a Lady.*

In a long and tedious introduction by one James Simpson (in an 1866 edition of the book, originally published in 1812), who was the first president of the Vegetarian Society, readers are urged to embrace the principles of a non-meat diet. "Man is an intermediate animal," begins one excruciating passage, before continuing: "there is an intermediate character of food which precisely suits the various organs of mastication and assimilation that have been considered the standard of comparison..." and so on. Page after page of such stuff being enough to make most people call for a steak.

Yet the message chimed with the reforming spirit of the Victorian era. Those who disparaged tobacco and alcohol happily added meat to the list. Some of the science might have been a bit ropey; Simpson argued that as the nutrients in meat came from the vegetables the animals ate, it made more sense to cut out the middle man (although he didn't quite put it like that). In an age that was championing moralists, new thinking and visionaries, many happily chewed on those meat-free arguments.

54

Roly-poly jam pudding

AUTHOR: Isabella Beeton, FROM: *Beeton's Book of Household Management*

TIME – 2 HOURS.

AVERAGE COST – 9D.

SUFFICIENT – FOR 5 OR 6 PERSONS.

SEASONABLE – SUITABLE FOR WINTER PUDDINGS, WHEN FRESH FRUIT IS NOT OBTAINABLE.

¾ lb of suet-crust,

¾ lb of any kind of jam.

Make a nice light suet-crust, and roll it out to the thickness of about ½ inch. Spread the jam equally over it, leaving a small margin of paste without any, where the pudding joins. Roll it up, fasten the ends securely, and tie it in a floured cloth; put the pudding into boiling water, and boil for 2 hours. Mincemeat or marmalade may be substituted for the jam, and makes excellent puddings.

The Victorian era is perceived as one of morality, order and discipline. Although a modern commentator, "The Age of Uncertainty" blogger, adds that it was also "the true age of the charlatan, when anyone with a passing interest in phrenology and an impressive beard could make sweeping pronouncements about any subject that took their fancy."

But those who aspired to adhere to the upright—if not firmly vertical—spirit of the age needed advice. And in 1861 the book that should have been called "How to be a Fine Upstanding Victorian" was published. In fact it was called *Beeton's Book of Household Management* (simply "Beeton's" at first—named after Samuel Beeton, the publisher—the "Mrs." being added in later editions). A publishing sensation at the time, its popularity has endured ever since and, amazingly, it is still in print today.

It is the most famous cookery book in the English language, but it endures not just because of the recipes. It is a guide to living, not to mention dying (there's a section on registering a death). So this is no mere recipe tome. Such a vast array of knowledge is arranged across its 2,000 recipes and over 1,000 pages. Within the book you'll learn how to deal with bad dreams, calculate your income tax, take in lodgers, apply a bandage, make a bed, clean an oil painting, give the correct duties to a footman, not to mention how to cook that British classic jam roly-poly.

The tome endures for two main reasons. Firstly, as it was continuously updated for some hundred years, it has been continually useful. Secondly, the original 1861 version paints a clear picture of middle- and upper-class life in the latter part of the nineteenth century. So it acts as both a manual for and a mirror on the Victorian age.

One might have expected such a book to have been the culmination of a lifetime of work by someone who had worked in households, cooked and served in every position before, finally, becoming the respected arbiter of all things domestic. A Victorian version of the American Eliza Leslie (see p. 159), who, in her dotage, received visitors eager for her advice on cupcakes or etiquette.

Yet, as is now widely known, Mrs. Beeton was no plump, aging Victorian lady buckled into a corset. She was not just pretty and slender but a mere twenty-five years old when the book came out. It was a work of four hugely intense years. If Mozart stuns the music world by having produced 600 works before his death at thirty-five, so Isabella Beeton shocks everyone at having produced around 1,000 recipes before dying at just twenty-eight years of age.

Her premature death being just the tip of her iceberg of tragedy. She suffered a string of miscarriages, possibly as a result of her contracting syphilis from her husband during their honeymoon (it's said he had a youthful penchant for prostitutes); one child died aged just three and her own death was the result of a fever contracted during the birth of her second surviving son.

Her tragic end also precipitated the demise of her husband. Broken by her death, Samuel became seriously ill and had to bear severe financial strain before succumbing to tuberculosis and dying in his mid-forties. But at least he shared the boom years

A selection of cold collation dishes (left) from Beeton's Book of Household Management *and a portrait of Isabella Beeton (right).*

with Isabella. She had met him in his burgeoning days as a publisher. His publication, the *Englishwoman's Domestic Magazine,* grew in popularity through the 1850s and, having married, the couple settled in a newly built semidetached house in Pinner where Isabella worked on the recipe content while her husband ran the business from Fleet Street.

Her knowledge and understanding of the running of households came partly from her own family background. She was the firstborn of twenty-one children, by two fathers (the first died after siring four), so she understood the need for an ordered house and practical catering.

The monster that was to become her legendary tome was born out of the cooking section of her husband's magazine. Having asked readers to send in recipes, she was inundated. Every post brought more letters and, day in, day out, she tested them. She then arranged them in good order, taking inspiration from her predecessor Eliza Acton (see p. 169), who listed the ingredients at the end, except that Isabella put them at the start (as recipe writers have done ever since). She also purloined many of Eliza's recipes and many others, although in Isabella's defense she acknowledged that her book was very much a compilation of ideas.

Samuel then began publishing the recipes and other instructions and information as part works. He had no marketing strategy or means of advertising, but word of mouth quickly resulted in women across the country keeping each issue and eagerly awaiting the next. Having witnessed the success of this first venture, he then published the whole thing in one single big volume in 1861. There had never been anything like it before. Indeed, any girl seeking solace and help on the domestic front might well have cried out for such a book. Except the weight of it, and depth of information within its pages, could surely have tipped many such young women over the edge.

Of course there had been plenty of books before that offered advice on every conceivable issue, from medicine, through etiquette and food. But Mrs. Beeton's was different. She made no assumptions about what Victorian women might wish to cook. After all, a large number of the recipes had been sent in by her very readers. The book also came out at a crucial time. Women in the 1850s and 60s lived in an era of transition. Industrialization was transforming everything and cooking was entering a new age. "The world is changing very quickly," wrote A. G. Payne in the Victorian *Cassell's Dictionary of Cookery,* "and probably in no previous part of our history have we as a nation undergone so rapid and complete a change as during the past few years."

The cookbooks of old had implored the cook to not just cook some pork but how, having killed the pig, to singe off the hairs before butchering it. Recipes for preserves helped to deal with the glut of fruit in the garden and prepare for the long winter ahead. Hannah Glasse in 1747 had offered something new: "a branch of cookery which nobody has yet thought worth their while to write upon." She pickled, preserved, made pies and collared beef. Yet this was all now irrelevant to so many people. Middle-class life in the cities (and their number tripled between 1851 and 1871) had no plot for the pig, kitchens were smaller and pantries had turned into cupboards. Not only was there no space for hundreds of jars of preserved plums, you didn't need to do it because you could now, come winter, actually buy the stuff.

The improved manufacture of metal containers for food saw shops selling all types of canned food. There was tinned beef from America and canned salmon from Alaska. Why make your own confectionery when Fry's, Rowntree's and Cadbury's could do it for you? Furthermore, smaller houses also meant fewer servants, so there were fewer hands available for all these peripheral kitchen labors.

Men who didn't live in the cities started to commute and life became more regimented. For the first time the experts actively discouraged the likes of baking and preserving. As the editor of the influential late nineteenth-century *Cassell's Household Guide* comments: "Suppose we insist upon having our bread made at home as well as our cakes, and also that we buy our fruit and vegetables for the purpose of making jam and pickles. Unless this work is performed by members of the household who would otherwise be idle, so far from a saving, there is a loss."

"Time is money" said the guide and it became the new mantra in society, with food manufacturers burgeoning on the back of it. In fact anyone looking for a point in history when Britain lost its food culture can locate it to the very moment Mrs. Beeton's book was published. Convenience products came on the market—from dried packets of soup to margarine, tinned fruits, powdered custard and condensed milk—and as food factories churned out cheap pork pies and collared beef, nobody needed to make these themselves.

Mrs. Beeton herself explains how to make a lemonade powder (with no lemon) to create instant lemonade. In fact while her book is aimed at delivering economy and simplicity to the kitchen, it also spells the death of culinary sophistication. None of her recipes, for example, use wine, herbs or spices. A new obsession with health and well-being saw a mistrust of anything that wasn't well and truly cooked. "Vegetables that are cooked in a raw state are apt to ferment in the stomach," she warned, thus starting a British tradition that lasted well into the 1980s, of boiling vegetables to tasteless extinction.

There was also a haughty authoritarianism to the age and Mrs. Beeton was by no means immune to it. She may have been motivated, as she says, by witnessing the discomfort and suffering "brought about by household mismanagement," but did she have to go on to say that "cold or tepid baths should be employed every morning"?

One of her contemporaries was the appalling Dr. Pye Henry Chavasse who, like the classic stereotype of a Victorian abhorring the very idea of pleasure, attacked puddings. "I consider them as so much slow poison," he wrote in his book on child-rearing. "If a child be never allowed to eat cakes and sweets, he will consider a piece of dry bread a luxury."

Only now are we once again yearning to preserve fruit and pickle vegetables. Many today even dream of keeping a pig, yet where it once was for necessity, now it is for flavor or fun, in sharp contrast to the Victorian age in which presentation was everything and the showy trifle, however tasty, simply vulgar.

Still, although Isabella might have scared some with the size of her tome, she inspired many and not just because of her advice. Her book was the first to use colored illustrations, lifting the spirits as no other cookbook had previously. It also stands as a testament to her remarkable tenacity as a compiler. "If I had known beforehand the labor which this book has entailed," she wrote, "I should never have been courageous enough to commence it." Her husband and the publishers—to whom Samuel disastrously sold the rights—kept her death a secret. The brand of Mrs. Beeton with her mythical and austere Victorian image continued to boost sales, which were already 2 million in 1868, three years after her death.

This weighty volume will surely last another hundred years, if only because it makes a useful step to get to that cheeky and distinctly un-Victorian chocolate pudding recipe book on the top shelf.

55

Eggs à la Benedick

AUTHOR: Charles Ranhofer, FROM: *The Epicurean*

Cut some muffins in halves crosswise, toast them without allowing to brown, then place a round of cooked ham an eighth of an inch thick and of the same diameter as the muffins on each half. Heat in a moderate oven and put a poached egg on each toast. Cover the whole with Hollandaise sauce.

There has been some dispute about the origins of eggs Benedict, that delightfully unctuous, salty and creamy combination of ham, muffin, egg and hollandaise sauce (see p. 190).

One claimant to its invention is Lemuel Benedict, a wealthy socialite and resident of New York. According to his descendants, one morning in 1894 he walked into the Waldorf Astoria, toward the end of breakfast service, with a ferocious hangover. A waiter proffered a menu but the card was dismissed. Benedict knew just what he wanted. He ordered toast and bacon with a poached egg on top and with it he wanted a small pitcher of hollandaise sauce. It was not particularly early—in fact lunchtime was closer than breakfast—so not only did he invent this great dish, he also firmly characterized it, albeit unknowingly, as a brunch item.

But this could all be myth, because there's another version of the story. This one goes that in the same year one Mrs. LeGrand Benedict, a regular of the then famous restaurant Delmonico's, arrived there one day in the fussiest of moods. She perused the menu but nothing took her fancy. This was quite a feat as it was famously very long, running to eleven pages—there were, for example, forty-seven veal dishes alone. Yet she was unsatisfied and asked to speak to the chef. His name was Charles Ranhofer, the most famous—and many say the first—chef of New York City.

It was breakfast and the only thing the lady was sure about was that she wanted eggs. So the chef stroked his long, fat mustache before assuring Mrs. LeGrand Benedict that he had just the thing. A few minutes later a dish arrived that triumphed. It brought together Ranhofer's meticulous understanding of French cuisine: a sauce that was creamy—but light enough for a lady—likewise an egg, simply poached (no lashings of fried butter), with the Continental addition of ham (gently browned), and served on an Americanized toasted muffin.

It also looked pretty and, pleased with his invention and having satisfied a customer, he put it on the menu and published a recipe for it in his comically enormous book *The Epicurean*. As Ranhofer actually printed a recipe, the trophy is his, although a slight question mark remains as he spells the dish "Benedick." But then he was French, although, judging by his book, he was also very literate—the dish was, perhaps, much ado about nothing—not to mention exacting.

Ranhofer was head chef of Delmonico's, an establishment that lasted until Prohibition put paid to its wine list, wine-based dishes and sauces in the 1920s and saw it close (there is now a restaurant with the same name at the same location, however). It also functioned at a time of great social hardship in New York. The poor were very poor. Most lived in tenement buildings and slums were beginning to be cleared. *King's Handbook of New York City* of 1892 records that if they did eat out it was at cheap restaurants, which were "feeding places of the vilest kind." Staple items were hash or beans with bread and butter, served with tea or coffee and priced at 10 cents. "A tour [of the city]," wrote the editor, "will reveal much gastronomic atrocity."

Meanwhile, the upper echelons of American society did not share the guilt of their English cousins back in Victorian Britain, busy eschewing puddings and embracing Mrs. Beeton's dishes (see p. 182), with their leftovers and cold meat. A report in 1891 showed how one percent of the population possessed more than the other 99 percent. And the flamboyant rich liked to show off their wealth at the city's top restaurants, the best of which was Delmonico's.

It had been founded in 1827 by two brothers whose nephew Lorenzo had hired Charles Ranhofer in 1862. Having trained in Parisian restaurants since the age of twelve, the son of a restaurateur and the grandson of a distinguished chef, with French gastronomy in his veins, Ranhofer went off to seek his fortune in New York. Lorenzo poached him from the rival Maison Dorée, later recalling his first meeting with this formidable individual: "He was perfect in dress and manner and his attitude was such as to make me feel that he was doing me a great favor by coming into my employment." "You are the proprietor," Ranhofer told his new boss. "Furnish the room and the provision, tell me the number of guests and what they want, and I will do the rest."

The rest included dishes that he had presented at grand banquets in France for Napoleon III. His menus were showy and extravagant, with many dishes referencing their provenance. There was "Rump of beef à la Chatellier," "Macaroni à la Brignoli" and "Halibut with fine herbs à la Reynal," for instance, along with "Columbines of fat liver," "Fine Champagne sherbet," "Parfait of coffee ice cream" and "Chocolate soufflé." These and thousands of other dishes he served and then recorded in *The Epicurean,* along with his stern advice.

It was said by a contemporary that "he brooked no interference... never was there a more unbending autocrat in his own domain." Staff in his kitchen, and he had a brigade of forty-five, were warned never to disregard one word of his or the slightest motion of his hand. "I am responsible and things must be as I direct," he once said.

To the New York dining scene he introduced white tablecloths and printed menus, as well as other dishes he invented, such as "Baked Alaska" to celebrate America's recent acquisition of Alaska from Russia. He insisted on particular dishes being served with particular wines, most of which were French and stored in his enormous cellar. Bordeaux must be served at "between 52 and 60 degrees Fahrenheit depending

One claimant to the invention of the dish Eggs Benedict goes to Lemuel Benedict, who ordered it at the Waldorf Astoria Hotel in New York while suffering from a hangover.

on the vintage" and likewise burgundy at between 42 and 45 degrees. Dessert wines must be served cool and he insisted that fish be accompanied by wines from the Rhine and Moselle.

He was particular, too, about when certain dishes should be served—"suppress oysters in every month not containing the letter R"—and had advice for how to cater for every type of diner: "Should the menu be intended for a dinner including ladies, it must be composed of light, fancy dishes with a pretty dessert." As for the men: "If for gentlemen, then it must be shorter and more substantial." At a private dinner when a gentleman had handed over his coat, the waiter must give him "an envelope addressed to himself in which there will be found a card bearing the name of the lady he is to escort to the dining-room."

Ranhofer reigned over the kitchen until his death in 1899 from a kidney ailment. He'd probably turn in his grave to hear that he is remembered not for an extravagant dish for a banquet hosted by royalty but for an item on a café brunch menu.

56

Hollandaise sauce

AUTHOR: Marthe Distel
FROM: *La Cuisinière Cordon Bleu (The Cordon Bleu Cook)*

It's the simplest of sauces. Melt some butter over a very low heat, or even better in a bain marie. Let it rest then beat in some whisked lemon juice and a pinch of salt. Pass through a fine sieve, add salt and serve in a sauce boat.

In 1861, in the London suburb of Pinner, Isabella Beeton (see p. 182) declared that "Men are now so well served out of doors—at clubs, well-ordered taverns, and dining-houses—that, in order to compete with the attractions of these places, a mistress must be thoroughly acquainted with the theory and practice of cooking." She went on to supply those poor mistresses with a heavy tome that would show them how to cook up good nourishing dishes to ensure that their men had a comfortable and well-ordered home to return to.

But in 1895, in Paris, Frenchwoman Marthe Distel went a very big step further. Good home cooking wasn't enough. The French mistress of the house needed to take those pesky restaurants head on. To this end, she set about publishing an instructive magazine called *La Cuisinière Cordon Bleu* in which well-known chefs and culinary experts provided recipes, cooking tips and advice on good entertaining that would serve as a sort of correspondence course for the reader.

The female cook was a *cuisinière.* She could not call herself a chef; that was a title reserved only for men. But she could be a cordon bleu cook, which was an accolade reserved for women. So while a male cook could call himself a chef, he couldn't call himself cordon bleu.

Although, ironically, the word was traditionally associated with men. In 1578 the French king, Henri III, founded an elite faction of men known as *l'ordre des chevaliers du Saint-Espirit* (Order of the Knights of the Holy Spirit). They rode about, musketeer-like, bowing obsequiously to their Bourbon king, graciously kissing the hands of beautiful maidens and, doubtless, whipping the posteriors of subordinates and peasants.

As they traveled, gathered and dined together, they each wore a blue sash, adorned with medals. These *cordons bleus* reflected the men's high status, their steely reputation and finesse. As time went on, the expression "cordon bleu" became associated simply with anyone excelling in a particular field, gradually attaching itself to the arena of food.

But how did it come to attach itself to women specifically? According to one legend, Madame du Barry, mistress to Louis XV, who ruled France for much of the eighteenth century, was once irritated by a remark made by the king. Only men, he said, could make great chefs. She said nothing but bided her time until a few days later, her own cook, her personal *cuisinière,* prepared a dinner for him. The king was very taken with the food, remarking: "Who is the new man cooking for you?"

"It's not a man but a woman," replied Madame du Barry, "and I think you should honor her with nothing less than the cordon bleu." If true, it would explain why the expression then firmly attached itself to female cooks.

And so in the late nineteenth century Marthe Distel decided to use the name as the title for her new magazine, in which upper-class women of France would learn how to compete with the chefs who were detaining their husbands away from home. Subscription to *La Cuisinière Cordon Bleu* grew steadily and a year later, in 1896, she hit on the innovative marketing ploy of offering free cooking demonstrations to those who bought the magazine.

The first class took place on 14 January in the kitchens of the Palais Royal, a fitting location for learning the whys and wherefores of fine dining. Those who attended watched a top Parisian chef—male, of course—demonstrate several dishes along with some stunning technical wizardry; the kitchens were wired for electricity. The courses gained momentum and popularity—the city's best chefs were procured to teach—and soon rather than marketing the magazine, the magazine was used to advertise the courses.

Dressed in their smartest dresses and hats, the daughters of the bourgeoisie would converge on the Palais Royal for their lessons. The school's influence spread and soon people were arriving from all over the world to be taught—there are records of students coming from Japan in 1905—and gradually it was not just the daughters of the bourgeoisie who came to learn, but men and women who wanted to work in the restaurant trade.

The Cordon Bleu school established French cuisine as *the* gastronomic template, codifying haute cuisine as a French art and making Paris an iconic symbol of it. So by the time Audrey Hepburn's character in the film *Sabrina* came to Paris in the 1950s to finish her education and learn how to make an omelette at the famous cookery school, Cordon Bleu represented the highest level of culinary training.

Now firmly established at No. 8, Rue Léon Delhomme, Cordon Bleu has branches across the world and anyone who's spent a year studying for the *Grand Dimplôme* should easily be able to turn out a superior dinner of lobster, truffles and foie gras. A dinner for which any swashbuckling, blue-sash-wearing knight would proudly doff his flowery hat.

La Cuisinière Cordon Bleu, *by Marthe Distel, was an instructive magazine.*

57

Strawberry shortcake

AUTHOR: Fannie Farmer, FROM: *The Boston Cooking-School Cook Book*

- **2 cups flour**
- **4 teaspoons baking powder**
- **½ teaspoon salt**
- **2 teaspoons sugar**
- **¾ cup milk**
- **¼ cup butter**

Mix dry ingredients, sift twice, work in butter with tips of fingers, and add milk gradually. Toss on floured board, divide in two parts. Pat, roll out, and bake twelve minutes in a hot oven in buttered Washington pie or round layer cake tins. Split and spread with butter. Sweeten strawberries to taste, place on back of range until warmed, crush slightly, and put between and on top of Short Cakes; cover top with Cream Sauce [from elsewhere in the original book]. Allow from one to one and one-half boxes berries to each Short Cake.

In the early 1890s a lady called Fannie Farmer came on the scene in America. If she'd said her name was Mrs. Beeton, you might have believed her. A plumpish, nurse-like, kind yet somewhat severe woman, she was responsible for what became one of the most famous recipe books, *The Boston Cooking-School Cook Book.*

Her edited version of the book—a follow-up to an earlier edition that had come out in very small circulation a few years previously—was published, gingerly, by Little, Brown and Company. In fact, so wary were they that Fannie Farmer had to fund the whole project herself. It was a decision the publishers grew to regret, as by the time of her death, in 1915, some 360,000 copies had been printed. By 1936, the figure was 1,736,000, and ten years later 2,531,000. The book is still in print today. Updated versions have continued to be printed until it was judged the book was more useful in its original form—not dissimilar to what happened to Mrs. Beeton's tome.

The best seller would subsequently be reissued as the *Fannie Farmer Cookbook,* which is worth seeking out if only to enjoy the alliteration of "Fannie Farmer's Fudge." The publishers' initial lack of faith in her seems curious today. After all, a mere glance at just the strawberry shortcake recipe could tell you that the book was a trailblazer.

Building on the recipe presentation of Mrs. Beeton, who developed that of Eliza Acton (see p. 169), Fannie Farmer's culinary instructions were clearer still. Not only were ingredients listed, with the method given in lucid clarity, but her measurements were more precise than any published up until then. The idea that "results may vary" was not on her radar. "A cup is a measured level," she declared. Indeed, so precise and exacting was she as a cook that she became known as "the mother of level measurements." While other culinary heroes might hope that posterity records them in more lively terms, she would have been perfectly happy with this.

Fannie Farmer, after all, was an unlikely star. In her teens she suffered from an illness that left her partially paralyzed. It meant she spent the rest of her life with a limp. She never married but having spent her time recuperating by working as a mother's help and assisting her own mother in the boarding house she ran, she saw the light in domesticity. After completing a course at the Boston School of Cookery, she stayed on as assistant director to the boss, Mary J. Lincoln, and then took over as director on the latter's retirement in 1894.

Two years later she published the book and the recipes that made her famous. It wasn't just that the strawberry shortcake appealed because it was failsafe and delicious. There were many other recipes that, like the shortcake, became staples in American households for generations to come. She offered up brownies, chocolate cake, brown-bread ice cream, pork chops with fried apples, corned beef hash, lobster bisque and Virginia waffles, among many others.

Her cooking, which she taught in practical, no-nonsense sessions at the school, chimed with the developments of the times. As in Britain, more and more women were moving to the cities. They hadn't their mothers by their side, nearby or, quite yet,

Miss Farmer with one of her pupils, Martha Hayes Ludden, at the Boston School of Cookery, where her recipes were kitchen-tested.

on the telephone. Hence Fannie's book was just the prop they needed. Equally in need of assistance were the large numbers of immigrants from countries like Germany and Ireland and from eastern and southern Europe.

They too had lost culinary touch with their families and needed help in their new lives. While at the same time there was a revolution in kitchen equipment. Gas stoves made their first appearance—temperature could now be controlled where before the only way to judge heat was checking with your hand. Clocks and timers found their way into kitchens and standardized measuring cups and spoons were brought onto the market. Fannie knew that if her readers acquired such utensils, they wouldn't go wrong with her recipes.

She was more precise than Mrs. Beeton and a world away in her cooking methods from the lies of the French. While cooks in France were still freewheeling, those in America became obsessed with accuracy and careful measurement, and this still holds true to a large extent today.

But a cooking stove—what Fannie calls "a large iron box set on legs"—was by no means yet universal, as reflected in her definition of roasting: "cooking before a clear fire with a reflector to concentrate the heat." Her book, like other contemporary recipe books, still instructed the reader on how to lay and light a fire for cooking. Refrigeration is similarly defined by Fannie as "the cooling accomplished by means of ice." Although there is a glimmer of light on the horizon—she mentions a "machine where compressed gas is cooled then permitted to expand."

She does occasionally wax lyrical—beginning her book with the words "But for life the universe were nothing; and all that has life requires nourishment," for instance—but her driving force was to be useful. For her, food was not an art form but a practical necessity.

There had, in the century that she grew up in, been major developments in science and understanding of the nutritional values of food, and she attempts to convey this in her book, describing the elements that the body is composed of and the nutrients it needs. She also reaches some conclusions of her own. "Women," she writes, "even though they do the same amount of work as man, as a rule require less food." On the subject of tea in particular she has firm views: "[It] is not a substitute for food [but] it is certain that less food is required where more tea is taken, for by its uses there is less wear of the tissues." But God forbid the consumption of too much of this popular beverage: "When taken to excess, it so acts upon the nervous system as to produce sleeplessness or insomnia, and finally make a complete wreck of its victim."

Fannie Farmer believed her teachings constituted a vital pillar for a healthy lifestyle. "I certainly feel that the time is not far distant when a knowledge of the principles of diet will be an essential part of our education," she comments. Unfortunately it was, and is, rather more distant than she might have hoped, with the recipe repertoire of most people still being at least two cups short of a strawberry shortcake.

58

Preparation of peas

AUTHOR: William Loftus, aka Mr Chatchip
FROM: *The Fish Frier and his Trade*

Peas should be put to soak about seven hours before being required for use. To each pound of peas put a teaspoonful of soda, then pour on boiling water, entirely covering them, leaving 4 or 5in of water for the peas wherein too swell. When required for boiling, pour into a colander, then let cold water from the tap run on them for a few minutes. Afterwards place in one of your metal saucepans filled with cold water; put on the fire, and immediately they begin to boil take them off. Leave the lid on the pan for a few minutes, then take the lid off and do not cover them up again; to prevent them lobbing give them an occasional stir.

It's a measure of quite how popular fish and chips had become in Britain at the turn of the twentieth century that there existed not just a journal dedicated to them but a correspondent whose sole job was reporting on the subject. The correspondent's name was William Loftus and his articles appeared in the *Fish Trades Gazette* under the pseudonym of "Mr. Chatchip." Not only had he owned and run his own fish and chip shop, but he had also held the positions of president and general secretary of the Federation of Fish Caterers.

To further cement his position as number one expert in the field, Loftus wrote a book, *The Fish Frier and his Trade,* published in 1902, which told you everything you might wish to know about the subject and, in particular, how to set yourself up in the business. Indeed the book was subtitled "A Complete Compendium to the Arts and Appliances of the Fried Fish Trade, together with much other useful information relating thereto."

Among that "useful information" were instructions for preparing the fish and potatoes, not to mention the indispensable peas—given in this chapter's recipe, the ingredients for which are neither fresh nor frozen but dried—although he didn't suggest mushing them. He offered advice too on which fish to buy and many useful tips, such as which of the latest potato peeling devices you should invest in and the importance of hygiene when serving customers. "Never smoke in the shop," he said. "Even inveterate smokers such as myself object to having tobacco or tobacco dust served up with their foods."

The business was tough work, he said. Rising early to buy the fish, hours spent washing and peeling potatoes and a late finish, supplying fish and chips to people after they had left the pubs. It was not a job for the meek, nor for the naïve. "A very large percentage of those who enter the trade are landed on their backs with a bump which leaves them sore—or sour—or both, for many a long day after they have left the trade," he commented, adding how "Nine out of every ten people who came into the trade got out of it again as quickly as they could." Which was possibly an exaggeration given the extraordinary growth in fish and chip shops between the late 1880s and the onset of the First World War.

By 1913 there were 25,000 outlets in Britain and a quarter of all fish landed in British ports ended up served with chips. The war then created a lull in the business as fishing, transport and the import of oil, among other things, were disrupted. But the trade then grew in earnest throughout the 1920s. By 1933 there were over 35,000 fish friers; 70,000 people worked directly in the business, with 200,000 working indirectly (in transport, docks, fishing and so on), and 50 percent of all fish landed were ending up at the chippie.

While Loftus sheds much light on the business at the time—writing in the *Fish Trades Gazette* that "the frying trade [in Stockton-on-Tees] seems to be an industry in which anybody with £20 to £25 can start a business"—he does not dwell on the origins of this amazing marriage between the fish and the potato.

It seems to have taken off in the 1850s in both the industrialized north of England and parts of London (Charles Dickens makes a reference to a "fried-fish warehouse" in his 1838 novel *Oliver Twist*). The frying of fish may have been introduced by Jewish immigrants (there are claims that London's first fish and chip shop was opened near Bow in 1860 by one Joseph Malin) and it was certainly prevalent when Henry Mayhew published *London Labour and the London Poor* back in the 1840s (see p. 175). He had been repulsed by the smell of fish emanating from tenement blocks. Widows, apparently, could eke out a meager living by frying fish in their front rooms using old lard. The stench was horrendous, as it was in the shops where they fried fish using oil made from cottonseed imported from Egypt.

With the foul odor of the boiling oil inside and rotted fish discarded outside, shops were obliged to open in the dingiest of places. "A gin-drinking neighborhood suits best for people haven't their smell so correct there," remarked one tradesman quoted by Mayhew, while Loftus reported how landlords in the 1870s "were very unwilling to let shops [to]...the frying trade. Most people with any claim whatever to respectability looked upon fried-fish shops and fish-friers as abominations to be shunned, as one would shun a pestilence or a known rogue." "In those days," continued Loftus, "the frier was drawn from the ignorant classes. He made no pretence to cleanliness, nor did he pay any regard whatever to the laws of sanitation even if he knew them, which was very questionable. His appearance in the shop was often revolting, the same old greasy clothes being worn from day to day."

As to the frying of chipped potatoes, this developed earlier in the century, if not before. William Kitchiner (see p. 151) has a recipe in his 1817 book *The Cook's Oracle* in which he slices them a quarter of an inch thick and suggests you "dry them well on clean cloth" before frying them in lard or dripping. The fat, he says, should be "quite clean" and the potatoes kept moving "til they are crisp." Having drained them, you should "send them up with a very little salt sprinkled over them." All of which sounds thoroughly modern.

History credits no single individual with bringing the fish and the chip together, but the concept clearly took hold and triumphed. Although its early incarnation—before filleting the fish prior to frying became common—would have made the experience less pleasurable. As one early twentieth-century frier commented: "Our customers in the old days must have approached their fish and chip supper in the same manner that one would expect a fox terrier to approach a hedgehog."

Yet bones or no bones, after centuries of the poor enduring cabbage, onions and pottage (see p. 52) and, then in the nineteenth century, such delicacies as bread, dripping, jam and tea, a warm supper of fish and chips, wrapped in paper and sprinkled with vinegar, must have seemed like a dream come true. It meant working-class women could, for couple of nights a week at least, not have to cook supper. Fish and chip shops became social hubs. Their rise, writes social historian John Walton, "coincided with the beginnings of the decline of the pub."

But the fish also provided some much-needed protein at a time when public health was at an historic low. Wages were too meager to ensure a decent standard of living for many; a report on Leeds in 1902, for instance, recorded that half the children had rickets and bad teeth and two out of five Britons applying to enlist during the Boer War were rejected as medically unfit. A Committee on Physical Deterioration was set up to look into the problem because it was recognized that hungry children couldn't concentrate in school, while school boards and the Salvation Army started to supply cheap, nutritious food.

At least fish and chips offered some protein, even if it didn't present an opportunity to eat vegetables, although the gradual addition of peas, mushy or otherwise, and then beans, did add a little extra nutrition. However, the poorest families tended to keep the fish for the adults, offering only chips with scraps of batter to the children.

Of course the late Victorians still disapproved: fish and chip suppers saw women shirking their domestic duties. And did they signal another step in the demise of British food culture (precipitated by Mrs. Beeton encouraging everyone to boil vegetables to death—see p. 185)? It was, after all, the beginning of fast food, of removing the need to cook, of distancing oneself from the basic ingredients of cooking. But it wasn't happening in Europe: the poor were poor, but they were still making their own meals rather than tucking into takeaways. This was because Britain's working classes had become increasingly industrialized, leaving their peasant culture behind them.

By 1900 the medieval monotony of pottage had become firmly replaced by the modern repetitiveness of fish and chips. Industry thrived around it, from fishing to transport. Cheap flour and cheap fish could come together. Manufacturers turned out swanky ranges for deep-frying and couples could run the venture as a family business, with the husband frying the food and the wife selling it at the counter.

In the depressed 1930s, fish and chips featured in George Orwell's list (in *The Road to Wigan Pier*) of working-class luxuries, along with cheap cigarettes, women's stockings and the warmth of a cinema. And they remained a key feature of British life as the country progressed from the Victorian age to the modern era of the twentieth century. They remain so to this day. As commentator Albert Halsey has written: "Fish and chips and Sheffield Wednesday and the monarchy are still parts of the social continuity which is Britain."

59

Peach Melba

AUTHOR: Georges Auguste Escoffier
FROM: *Le Guide Culinaire (The Guide to Cooking)*

Poach the skinned peaches in vanilla-flavoured syrup. When very cold arrange them in a timbale on a bed of vanilla ice cream and coat with raspberry purée.

By the end of the nineteenth century, French cuisine had established itself as preeminent. There was no contest in Britain. Anyone who was anyone procured a French chef—if you had an English one, it wasn't something you bragged about. Indeed the prospering middle classes had a tangible disdain for British cooking. So if fish and chips (see p. 195), the Victorian abhorrence of taking pleasure in food and, thanks to Mrs. Beeton (see p. 185), their persistence in overcooking vegetables didn't destroy Britain's culture, the British acquiescence in the increasing supremacy of French cooking certainly did. As food historian Colin Spencer has noted: "That a whole nation could embrace the cooking of a nation that had been historically its fiercest rival and enemy might seem astonishing."

And France wasn't just busy conquering the Brits in the dining room. Their agents of gastronomy were everywhere. Charles Ranhofer had flown the flag in America (see p. 187), for example. There were French chefs in Russia, such as Hippolyte Gouffé, whose brother Alphonse Gouffé was Queen Victoria's pastry chef. Their other brother, Jules Gouffé, spread the word from his position as chef de cuisine of the Paris Jockey Club via his *Livre de Cuisine,* translated into English as *The Royal Cookery Book.* His watchword was "cleanliness," which he thought should be inscribed onto every kitchen door: "A kitchen may be small, badly arranged and lighted; but it should never, on any plea, be dirty."

All these men and many others, with their firm views and, more often than not, big mustaches, championed the cuisine of France. They were employed at the burgeoning number of hotels and restaurants that grew up around Europe as a consequence of the new and growing rail system. Wealthy Europeans traveling around wanted food that was as good as the meals they were served in their private houses, and French chefs were happy to oblige. While their spiritual home, the capital of France, became a place of pilgrimage for the foodie. As the formative guide to cooking, *Larousse Gastronomique,* comments: "Paris became the mecca of gastronomy."

It was into this world that Georges Auguste Escoffier emerged and rose to reign supreme. Indeed, his writings still influence chefs today, in particular his exhaustive

Georges Auguste Escoffier, author of Le Guide Culinaire.

tome *Le Guide Culinaire,* with its 5,000 recipes. So while his work continues to spread the word of French gastronomy, its impact during his lifetime was immense. Many trained under him and he once proudly remarked: "Throughout my entire career I have 'sown' some two thousand cooks all over the world."

Wherever he was commissioned to organize a dinner, he made a point of bringing French ingredients and French staff to deliver and serve the fruits of his French methods. French cooks were superior, Escoffier argued, simply because the ingredients they used were the best. France had the terroir to produce the best vegetables, fruit, poultry, meat, game and, of course, wine. "Thus," he proclaimed, "it is completely natural for the French to become both gourmands and great cooks." France was the chosen land. It was, as journalist Michael Steinberger puts it, "God's pantry."

Yet it was not in God's pantry that Escoffier spent most of his life. This envoy of French food brought his skills to London. He had worked in kitchens since a boy, beginning, aged thirteen, at his uncle's restaurant in Nice before moving about the country until he met the man who was to become his business partner for the rest of his life, César Ritz.

Ritz was an entrepreneur as well as a smooth-talking hotel manager and got the pair of them employed at the newly opened Savoy Hotel in London. It was 1890 and Escoffier, aged forty-four and no spring chicken, hit the big time. He didn't just bring his French cooking methods to London, he brought his organizational skills. He redrew the way professional kitchens functioned, creating brigades that were part of his assembly-line modus operandi.

In the past, each section of the kitchens of grand houses, hotels or restaurants worked independently, creating specific dishes. Escoffier brought the teams together to work on the same dish. So, for example, one would grill the meat while another made the sauce. Each section was headed by a "chef de partie" with the head chef conducting the whole operation.

It is how most kitchens still operate today. It suited the kind of meals most people wanted, still lavish, but shorter. And instead of taking vast plates out to the tables for people to help themselves to, Escoffier sent out plated food, as ordered from his "à la carte" menu.

Escoffier's kitchens were places of order and, apparently, humanity. His own mantra was *"faites simple."* And not only did he want his chefs to embrace simplicity in their cooking, but to treat each other with respect. Yet his idea of simplicity—while shying away from the monumental pastry towers of Carême (see p. 165)—was technically highly skilled, to say the least. And his own humanity didn't stop him from cooking the books when he was at the Savoy.

In spite of the fact that he had put the Savoy on the culinary map and it had become the foodie hangout for fashionable London, he and Ritz were fired in 1897. Even today the culinary world shirks from facing up to what really happened, such is the hallowed status of this chef legend. Larousse still records that he left the Savoy "for personal reasons." In fact he and Ritz were regularly trousering 5 percent of what was spent on kitchen supplies. So when management found out, they turfed the dynamic duo out.

Shrugging it off as a slight inconvenience, the resourceful Ritz quickly found them new turf for their skills. The Carlton Hotel readily employed them both and soon was renamed the Ritz-Carlton. And, having attracted all their old clientele to their new home, Escoffier then worked there for the rest of his life.

In fact, it was there that he had his best years. The stars came to dine at the Ritz-Carlton and he, happily, flattered them in return. Having created a dish a few years previously for the Australian actress Nellie Melba: poached peaches in ice cream on a swan calved of ice (which he had called "peach swan")—he removed the swan and added a sauce of puréed raspberries and called it "peach Melba."

What greater adulation can there be? Who knows if she was quite as excited when he named a new way of making toast after her. Other actresses received similar tokens, his "Rachel mignonettes of quail," for example.

Egged on by César Ritz, Escoffier eagerly and successfully toadied to the rich and powerful. One can only imagine the backslapping and guffawing when Kaiser Wilhelm II entered his kitchen one day to declare: "I am the Emperor of Germany and you are the Emperor of Chefs."

Escoffier was duly honored back in France by being made a *chevalier* of this and an officer of that as the idolization of French chefs soared to new levels. He capitalized on his fame being the first chef to produce pickles and sauces with his name on the jar, all of which was pretty impressive for the son of a blacksmith. It was a profession he had been unable to enter because he was too short. Cooking, he once reflected, was "not the profession I personally would have chosen." But then, having been sent to work for his uncle when still a child, he never had that luxury of choice.

Having championed French food in London and successfully hammered another nail into the coffin of British cuisine, he surely hoped that future generations would follow his example. In many ways they did. British chefs in due course embraced his Gallic methods, if not, universally, his Gallic temperament.

60

Scotch barley broth

AUTHOR: Marian Cuff, FROM: *A Course of Meals Given to Necessitous Children*

1¼ lb beef (without bones);
½ lb carrots;
½ lb turnips;
¾ lb onions;
5 oz barley; celery or celery salt; parsley; pepper and salt;
4 pints water (or bone stock).

Cut up the meat and put it in the pan with the barley and the water, and bring to the boil. Peel and cut up the vegetables in small pieces and add them to the pan. Cook gently until all are tender. Finely chop the parsley and add it with the celery salt and seasoning. Serve with bread.

NOTE 1. – If celery in season wash and cut up some and add with the other vegetables.
NOTE 2. – Mutton can be used instead of beef, but the large proportion of bone and fat make it more expensive.

Fish and chips (see p. 195) might have provided some much-needed protein for the undernourished poor, but entrepreneurial initiatives alone weren't going to solve what in Britain, by the early 1900s, was turning into a serious social problem.

That so many men were being turned down as army recruits for the Boer War was causing the state to prick up its ears. Young men were physically unfit because they were undernourished as children. If this meant you couldn't raise an army, something had to be done. Thus it was the well-meaning, if depressingly named, Royal Commission on Physical Deterioration that led to the Education (Provision of Meals) Act of 1906, an early example of the interventionist British welfare state gearing into action.

With this piece of legislation, the government gave local education authorities the go-ahead to provide free meals for the really needy and cheap ones for those less so. School lunch became the main meal of the day for many children, the downside being that it removed the responsibility for cooking for children from the parents, something that was revealed in shocking clarity at a school in Bradford.

This northern town had long had a problem with starving children. Parents had been known to literally sew them up in flannel in the winter months to protect them from the cold. Children had been seen fainting during morning assembly. Wealthier locals donated funds to help buy food for them, for until the Act of 1906 it was illegal to use public money to feed schoolchildren.

With funds then available, a local doctor, Ralph Crowley, decided it would be a good idea to monitor the physical progress of the poorly nourished as they tucked into a new regime of free or low-cost meals. He selected around a hundred children, who were fed and then weighed regularly between April and July of 1907. And he joined forces with a lady on the Bradford Education Committee who bore the title of Superintendent of Domestic Subjects. This lady, Marian Cuff, produced a pamphlet of suggested recipes entitled *A Course of Meals Given to Necessitous Children.* These menus then formed the core of what the schools in the area provided for the children.

She proposed a list of seventeen meals, with meat on Tuesdays and Thursdays and fish on Fridays. Breakfast included porridge with milk and treacle or bread covered with margarine or dripping, washed down with hot or cold milk. For lunch there was green pea and vegetable soup or cottage pie with peas and gravy. Puddings were suggested as accompaniments. Miss Cuff's pamphlet had recipes for jam roly-poly (see also p. 182), stewed fruit and buttered rice with sugar. There's also her recipe for Scotch barley broth, with which she suggests a pudding of rhubarb tart. There are no salads on the list, however. It's all cabbage, carrots, potatoes, peas and rice, the veg being incorporated into the main dish—be it a pie or soup.

In addition to Marian Cuff's recipes, Dr. Crowley provided instructions on how the food should be served: tables should be arranged with fifty children seated at each one and older girls working as "monitresses" to serve the food. "The hall itself should be scrupulously clean and freshly color-washed," he advised. "Tables should be covered with table cloths and plants or flowers should be provided... Children should come with clean hands and faces."

It was clear that many of the children were filthy, as Dr. Crowley notes how "the table cloths are very dirty at the end of the week chiefly due to the dirty clothing of the

Children queuing for the Salvation Army "Farthing Breakfasts," c.1900.

children." There was nowhere at the school for children to wash themselves, however. The other major issue was that even though the children were hungry, it took them a while to acclimatize to the food. "Those who at first eat very little it may be necessary to give milk," he recommends, adding that "many of the meals suggested are not such as one is accustomed to find in an ordinary cottage home. The fault lies with the upbringing of the children rather than with the recipes."

And so the hungry school kids munched their way through Miss Cuff's menus and each week Dr. Crowley weighed them. Come the middle of May, the children went home for the Whitsuntide holiday. Then after a twelve-day break, they returned to the school and the doctor weighed them again. He made a startling discovery. They had all lost weight. It was clear they were simply not being fed at home. Not even with fish and chips.

61

Onion butter sauce

AUTHOR: Unnamed home economist, FROM: *Oxo promotional material*

SERVE THIS WITH STEAK, LIVER OR BURGERS.

3 oz butter/margarine

3 oz onions, chopped very finely

1 red Oxo cube dissolved in ¼ pint of boiling water

1 tbsp parsley, chopped

1 tsp Worcestershire sauce

Melt the butter, add the onion and brown slowly for about 10 minutes. Add Oxo stock, parsley and Worcestershire sauce and stir well.

The 1908 Olympic Games were scheduled to be hosted in Rome. Athletes from twenty-two countries were signed up to participate and travel to the Italian city, but then nature got in the way. On 4 April 1906, at an altitude of 1,200 meters, a vent opened on Mount Vesuvius and the volcano erupted. In the ensuing hours and days more vents opened, ash plumes soared into the sky, lava spewed out in fountains and poured down the slopes. The area around nearby Naples was devastated and the town of Ottaviano buried—described by a contemporary commentator as "the new Pompeii." So the government decided it needed to spend considerable funds rebuilding the streets and houses that had been ruined.

Since the Olympic Games also need considerable funds (the 2012 London Olympics costing some £20 billion, rather more than a hundred years previously), Italy held its hands up, citing financial problems, and asked another country to step in as host. So the games came to London. The city proved an efficient organizer and in the short time available built a stadium to seat 68,000 people at White City. It was assisted in the venture by one major sponsor, who not only provided funds but catering. The company's name was Oxo, a brand created nine years previously by the Liebig Extract of Meat Company.

Hot beef drinks were handed out to athletes during the games—be they marathon runners or participants in tug-of-war (for some reason later dropped as an Olympic sport)—and recipes such as this chapter's "onion butter sauce" were published in pamphlets and on the backs of Oxo packets. The link with the Olympics meant that Oxo benefited from the exposure, sending out a message to people that their product was nutritious and a symbol of national pride. After all, the entire British team had been roped into endorsing the product. "Oxo has hugely contributed to my success," proclaims one athlete, A. Duncan, on a poster in which they all give their "written testimony to the sustaining value of Oxo." "As a beverage for athletes," says A. Russell rather stiffly, "Oxo excels every time." Presumably this was Arthur Russell, who went on to win the 3,200-meter steeplechase.

Whether or not sportsmen were genuinely grateful for being given a steaming, hot mug of beef soup during the summer days that the games were held on is not recorded, although, apparently, the early stages were marked by bad weather. But Oxo was run by some sharp marketeers. Produced in innovative square cubes, adverts heralded its thrilling benefits. One contemporary poster shows two slightly chubby blond children skipping along holding giant cubes, accompanied by the words: "Health and joy go hand in hand."

That marathon runners at the games were given the drink seemed to confirm another of their slogans: "For stamina drink Oxo." These were the early days of logos, of increasingly sophisticated branding and of the excitement of food technology.

Food harvested from the garden was all well and good but it wasn't half as exciting as a sparkling, modern product harvested from a big new factory. After all, just a few years previously, in 1895, Bird's Custard Powder had been making just that point. A poster showed two chefs in a kitchen both making custard but one using eggs and the other powder from small, dainty boxes. The chef with the eggs looks unhappily at the shell of one he has just cracked. "What, another!" is the caption. "No eggs! No risk!!" was the main message. Why use boring, old and not so dependable nature when the Victorian age was inventing futuristic products for your kitchen?

"Ladies and housekeepers," the poster also announced, "can add to their list of dishes all manner of choice dainties for the dinner and supper table by consulting a valuable little book 'Pastry and Sweets.'" Bird's would send out the book for free and, of course, every recipe it contained used their custard powder.

The makers of Oxo had a similar wheeze. Its beef extract had been produced many years previously by the German chemist Justus von Liebig, and before inventing the Oxo brand he had publicized the product in a book called *The Liebig Company's Practical Cookery Book,* published in 1893.

Its author was the cookery writer Hannah Young. The labor and drudgery of cooking needed to be reduced, she said, and there were new products that could help you in this endeavor. "The Liebig Company's Extract of Meat holds foremost place in the field," she wrote, before presenting hundreds of recipes all of which used the beef extract. Recipe after recipe shared this star ingredient, even those for fish. Then there was the "Liebig sandwich" and "Liebig on toast." Only puddings escaped its use, though one wonders whether Hannah Young might have tried to push her luck by adding a handful of it to an apple crumble or a jam roly-poly.

A lavish illustration in the book shows a jar of Liebig extract sitting proudly among fresh vegetables, game and lobster. The kitchen portrayed is well appointed, the picture itself sitting in a gilt frame. Using a product such as this was key to good, modern, bourgeois living.

Oxo became a British icon by marketing its products through family-orientated adverts as a cheap way to add flavor to family meals.

In its early days it was also a product people could only aspire to. Beef was expensive. Only the wealthy could afford to add its extract to their dishes. Victorian writers even romanticized about it. Heroines lying desperately ill were revived by a restorative cup of beef extract.

Justus von Liebig was a canny advocator of his product. Through his contacts he managed to persuade one Florence Nightingale to endorse it. As he developed more economic ways of making it and beef prices lowered, soon it was a fundamental ingredient in the kitchens of the armed services, not to mention a vital addition to the provisions of explorers at the turn of the century.

So when the name Oxo was born and the product could be mass-produced and bought from grocers across Britain, people clamored for it. "Oxo cubes are the greatest advance in food invention since men began to eat and women learned to cook," went one message.

Of course its real nutritional value was doubtful. It was more of a stimulant and a flavoring agent, a luxury item in the same way as tea, coffee or wine. Cooks looking for economy in the kitchen would do better making stock from their beef bones than buying heavily salted cubes of beef extract produced from cattle as far away as South America (where the company had many of its farms on the banks of the Uruguay river, in fact, near a town called Fray Bentos . . .).

But the strength of the brand and the appetite for new products meant that common sense and old-fashioned food values didn't have a chance in this early battle in a war between consumerism and mother nature that to this day has not abated.

62

Croque monsieur

AUTHOR: Mrs Brian Luck (recipe by E. Defouck)
FROM: *The Belgian Cookbook*

Cut out some rounds of crumb of bread, of equal size, with a tin cutter, or, failing that, with a wine-glass. Butter all the rounds and sprinkle them with grated cheese – for preference with Gruyère. On half the number of rounds place a bit of ham cut to the same size. Put a lump of butter the weight of egg into a pan, and fry with the rounds in it, till they become golden. When they are a nice colour, place one round dressed with cheese on a round dressed with ham, so as to have the golden bread both above and below. Serve them very hot and garnished with dried parsley.

The history of lunch has as many twists, turns and diversions as the history of food itself. Depending on who wants it, where they want it and how they'd prefer it, the institution can be molded to suit. There are long lunches; epic ones, celebratory and decadent. There can be many courses and much wine. But, frankly, the modern world—weekends aside—simply sees lunch as a sustaining moment during working hours. And that remains the best definition as we creep further into the twenty-first century.

It is only the minority who can pause to wine, dine and schmooze their friends and contacts in the middle of the day. The rest simply require something that is quick to make—if they're making it—swift to consume, appetizing and fills a gap until a meal later in the day.

By the early 1900s the British, depending on their profession and class, were consuming sandwiches (see p. 141), pasties or pies at lunchtime. The French, however, were bringing a little more imagination to the affair. As cafés grew in number, a novel item crept onto the menus in cities across France. It was in 1910, in a café on the long and grand Boulevard des Capucines in Paris, that it first appeared. Called a "croque monsieur," it provided the perfect answer to the lunch question. Hot, crunchy, with cheese and ham, it was both inexpensive and tasty—luxurious even.

There is no one culinary genius who can claim credit for its invention, however. One tale has it that a French workman, placing his tin of cheese and ham sandwiches on a radiator, opened them, come lunchtime, to discover that the cheese had melted. But where did the name spring from? The word *croque* translates as "crunch," but what about *monsieur?* The question mark provides the answer. If the customer wanted his cheese sandwich crunchy, then that's what the kitchen could supply. If the chef then

A postcard showing a typical Parisian café on the long, grand Boulevard des Capucines in 1910.

added some creamy white béchamel sauce over the top, so much the more delicious.

In 1915 a recipe for the dish appeared in *The Belgian Cookbook,* edited by a Mrs. Brian Luck. "The recipes in this little book," she noted in the preface, "have been sent in by Belgian refugees from all parts of the United Kingdom, and it is through the kindness of these correspondents that I have been able to compile it. It is thought, also, that British cooking may benefit by the study of Belgian dishes."

And so the bold claim is made that croque monsieur is Belgian. Credit for the recipe goes to E. Defouck, and quite who that individual was remains a mystery. But he or she would have been just one of the quarter of a million Belgian refugees who poured into Britain as the German Army ravaged their homeland. Such were their numbers that the British government arranged for them to be dispersed throughout the country. Many communities responded warmly to the new arrivals and helped to support them through fund raising. Perhaps Mrs. Luck, on finding she had some new Belgian neighbors, responded positively by compiling a book of Belgian recipes, both to celebrate their culinary heritage and to help raise money for them.

The book includes dishes such as *waterzooi*—a Flemish soup incorporating all kinds of fish with their heads and tails floating in the bowl (although Mrs. Luck suggests these should be removed "for English tastes")—and apricot soufflé. The croque monsieur is suggested as an entrée rather than as a lunchtime snack—but maybe that's how they ate it in Belgium.

Marcel Proust makes mention of the dish in his terrifyingly long novel *À la Recherche du Temps Perdu* (*In Search of Lost Time*), the relevant second volume appearing in 1918. The unnamed narrator returns to his hotel from a morning symphony concert on the beach to a lunch of "croque-monsieur and a dish of creamed eggs." Proust was particular in his description of food—be it madeleines or truffled partridge—as he conjured up the era of the belle époque (that period of optimism and innovation that ended when the horrors of the First World War erupted). His mention of a croque monsieur reinforces the idea that this is a dish of gentle sophistication and elegance.

London cafés might have been serving cheese (and any old cheese) on toast—melted under a grill—but the French melted cheese (specifically Gruyère) *in* toast! It tasted better and looked more elegant and over the years has acquired various relations, such as a "croque madame" (with a fried egg on top) and "croque provençal" (with tomatoes).

The English may have been eating cheese on toast for centuries and calling it Welsh rarebit (see p. 173) but it never developed much sophistication and the only variety, in latter years, was whether or not you plonked Worcestershire sauce on top. Today a Paris-style lunch of croque monsieur with French fries, salad and a glass of red wine is a pretty compelling idea, particularly when compared with a hurried sandwich at one's desk.

63

Chocolate cake

AUTHOR: Miss Maria Parloa for Walter Baker & Co., FROM: *Choice Recipes*

½ cup butter
¾ cup sugar
¾ cup milk
½ teaspoon vanilla
3 beaten yolks
3 ounces Walter Baker & Co.'s Premium No. 1 Chocolate
1¾ cups bread flour
3 beaten whites

Cream butter, add gradually sugar, then beaten yolks, milk, vanilla, chocolate melted, flour mixed and sifted, with baking powder, and fold into the beaten whites last. Turn into buttered shallow cake pans and bake in a moderate oven.

The story of Clarence Saunders is an all-American drama, one of Howard Hughes-type proportions. It's a tale of poverty, ambition, success, ruin and further success, culminating in an exhausting finale. Even if Clarence Saunders hadn't left behind a massive legacy, his story would still be told with considerable wonder. Whatever the twists and turns of his life, he let loose upon the world a culture-changing phenomenon—self-service grocery stores. And few people can claim that these don't play even a minimal part in their lives.

Credited with being one of the creators of twentieth-century culture, his gift to the world was Piggly Wiggly, which still survives in the United States, with 600 stores in seventeen states.

Saunders's childhood was fairly grim, however. Brought up in Palmyra, Tennessee, his mother died when he was five and his father seemed to waste what little money they had. The boy had few possessions and one winter not even shoes. But his life changed when, having left school at fourteen, he joined a local grocery store and discovered his métier. A keen worker, he moved up the ranks, becoming a clerk and gradually learning the business of retail.

A sales job in his early twenties at a wholesale firm allowed him to observe his storekeeper clients who, he reckoned, were lazy—some no better than saloon bar owners in manner; they overcharged their customers and gave poor service. A later job saw him selling stock to a grocer with a small chain of similar stores and who, while being hated by his competitors, was popular with customers for offering them lower prices.

But his eureka moment came on a train journey back from Indiana where he had endured a wasted visit to a store that purported to be laid out in an innovative way. On the way back, he stared despondently out of the window of the train, pondering on life and dwelling on the inefficiencies of the grocery business. At one point the train slowed and he passed a large pig farm. There, in a pen, he saw a large number of piglets gathering round the mother sow to feed. It made him think about how in all the stores he knew—where customers were served at a counter—during the busy times there were never enough clerks on hand, while during the quieter hours those same staff had nothing to do. He hit on the name Piggly Wiggly and, within a few months, on 5 September 1916, opened his first store.

A large crowd surged around the store at 79 Jefferson Street in Memphis, having heard a rumor that there'd be a beauty contest for the first ladies who arrived, with cash prizes promised. In fact all the women were handed $5 or $10 by newspaper reporters posing as judges in the beauty contest, until the money ran out. Children were given flowers and balloons and as shoppers entered they were serenaded by a brass band.

Inside, what they saw was completely new and different. There was no counter to queue at and no staff in white coats to take your orders. Instead, after collecting a basket, you perused shelves and looked at the goods, all at arm's reach. The items included many branded ones that were advertised nationally, such as Campbell's soup (see p. 216) and Walter Baker & Co.'s chocolate bars, products which often came with marketing literature such as the recipe that leads this chapter. The ladies experienced a little tingle of joy that they could take each item off the shelf and pop it into their baskets. There was no sales pressure, no one urging you to buy this or that product and, more unusually, there were price tags on everything.

"One day Memphis will be proud of Piggly Wiggly," declared Saunders, sounding like an evangelical preacher. "And it shall be said by all men that the Piggly Wigglies shall multiply and replenish the earth with more and cleaner things to eat." Ever the canny entrepreneur, he designed a one-way aisle system so that the customer had to negotiate her (and however novel the store concept, there weren't yet many "hims" doing the shopping) way through the shop until arriving at the cash register. There a clerk added up what you had bought, you paid and he gave you a receipt to take home and check.

Fewer staff meant savings and Saunders, opening the store during the First World War at a time when food shortages led to higher prices, well knew what it was to be counting your small change. "Piggly Wiggly will be born not with a silver spoon in its mouth but with a work shirt on its back," he declared.

The stores chimed with an era of increasing convenience and accessibility. "It is all so simple and easy and natural that after your first visit to a Piggly Wiggly you wonder why no one ever thought of it before," wrote one contemporary homes magazine. "Then you wonder why anyone ever should think again of another system."

It was an immediate success, as Saunders noted: "100 people can wait on themselves at Piggly Wiggly... Every 48 seconds a customer leaves Piggly Wiggly with her purchase." He opened nine stores in the first year, setting up franchises where the stores had to be precise replicas and those managing them had to buy the requisite equipment and parts—from turnstiles and units to cash registers and signage—from Saunders.

He attempted to patent his self-service system with varying degrees of success and, by 1918, every region in the country had a Piggly Wiggly. By 1923, just seven years after Saunders had opened his first shop, there were 1,268 stores, each bearing the proud logo "All Over the World." Few businessmen had risen to such prominence in such a short space of time.

Saunders enjoyed his success, building a huge house on a vast estate and purchasing planes and cars. "He seemed to be the mythical king from whose hand everything he touched turned to gold," said a friend. And then disaster struck. A tussle with the New York Stock Exchange, in which he bought excessive amounts of stock in his own company in response to traders shorting on Piggly Wiggly shares, saw him banned from trading. In buying up and cornering stock, Saunders had used up all his company's resources and his own, and in February 1924 he went bankrupt. He lost everything, including his house, which he had latterly decked in pig-inspired pink rendering.

Having lost his own business and the famous name under which he traded, he dusted himself down and started again. This time, in a mad and rather bonkers rage against the unscrupulous traders who had brought him down, he started a new chain of self-service groceries. Unable to use the Piggly Wiggly name, he called these "Clarence Saunders Sole Owner of My Name Stores," which gives you an idea of quite how cross he was.

Thousands turned up to the opening and the new shops proved an instant success. The Sole Owner stores had more products. Each store sold fresh meat, had a bakery and a deli. It was truly a supermarket, although that term wasn't used until some ten years later when stores opened in the vast landscapes of California and it was coined to describe shops that were as big as warehouses.

His new chain expanded quickly and by 1928 he was once again able to call himself a millionaire. He bought another, much bigger house, even grander than the "Pink Palace." He installed an indoor swimming pool, a bowling lane and a film room before constructing one of the country's largest golf courses. But two years later and the Great Depression saw him chased by his creditors and, once again, he went bankrupt. He had also by this time sired four children by two wives.

Not to be put down, he had another idea. This time it was "Keedoozle": a new concept, like an arcade game, consisting of a fully automated store where you fed money into a slot and drove a mechanical arm that put merchandise onto a conveyor belt. "In five years there will be a thousand Keedoozles throughout the U.S.," he announced with characteristic self-assurance. But there weren't and the project was doomed. Items were damaged after being dropped by the mechanical arm and business was lost each time the machines broke down, which was often. So although he had opened twelve franchises, he was forced to scrap the idea, his finances once again teetering on the edge.

Piggly Wiggly, created by Clarence Saunders, first opened a store in the United States in 1916 and still survives today, with 600 stores in 17 states.

Yet Saunders had one more idea in him. His "Foodelectric" was a store concept in which customers wrapped and paid for their own goods using automated machines. The idea was a precursor to the self-checkout of so many supermarkets today. "It can handle a $2 million volume with only eight employees," he claimed, as confident as ever. Unfortunately Saunders didn't open a single store. In 1953, exhausted and worn out, he died, aged seventy-two.

Saunders's detractors see his influence on food culture as malign. Critics see him as starting the rot: his convenience items and branded products divorcing people from the source of their food, from seasonality, and thereby precipitating the gradual slide toward an endless uniformity of product.

But people loved his new, clean and sparkling stores, just as they loved the tins of soup and chocolate bars he stocked. The latter were promoted in recipe pamphlets such as the one that this chapter's chocolate cake is taken from. In 1922 Saunders had placed an advertisement in the *Chicago Tribune* extolling the freedom of choice customers could experience in the firm's stores: "Piggly Wiggly fosters the spirit of independence—the Soul of Democratic Institutions, teaching men, women and children to do for themselves." Across the world millions soon joined in that liberation.

64

Spaghetti à la Campbell

AUTHOR: The makers of Campbell's soups, FROM: *Helps for the Hostess*

1 can Campbell's tomato soup

½ pound smallest tube spaghetti

½ pound sliced smoked ham

1 can button mushrooms (or ½ pound fresh)

2 small onions, thickly sliced

3 small peppers, thinly sliced

½ teaspoonsful thyme

Clove of garlic

2 tablespoonsfuls olive oil

Grated cheese (American or Parmesan)

Boil spaghetti in rapidly boiling salted water, with clove of garlic, until tubes are soft and water absorbed. To a heated skillet add oil, onions, pepper and mushrooms, reserving a few whole mushrooms and pepper rings for garnish, and cook slowly until tender. Add to drained spaghetti. Fry slice of ham, cutting into three or four narrow strips when cooked. Pour Campbell's tomato soup into skillet containing ham dripping, add spaghetti, onions, peppers, and thyme. Mix thoroughly, and mound on round chop dish or platter. Lay ham strips crosswise on top, sprinkling with grated cheese. Garnish base with whole mushrooms and pepper rings.

While the British producers of Oxo (p. 205) were handing out recipe books to their customers, all of which used their magic ingredient, so too were the makers of Campbell's soups in the United States. From the early 1900s, and as they grew their soup range, they endeavored to encourage women to see quite how versatile a humble can of soup could be.

"Spaghetti à la Campbell," from *Helps for the Hostess,* their recipe book from 1916, is possibly the least offensive offering. There was "chicken jelly loaf," made with Campbell's consommé, cold chicken, slices of tongue and stuffed olives. "Campbell's aspic" used their canned bouillon. "Vol-au-vent of rice with beef" had a ring of molded rice filled with Campbell's tomato soup mixed with diced beef, mutton or pork. Even more upsetting was the "broiled halibut steak" in which tomato soup is sandwiched between two layers of fish and then poured over the top before being garnished with an olive and a lemon slice.

Their ingenuity knew no bounds. "Many times unattractive 'left-overs' are thrown away when, by using a can of Campbell's soup, they could have been made into an attractive, appetizing dish." And as with the equally inventive Oxo in Britain, Campbell's also had a pair of chubby children championing their brand. But there the similarities end: the American company took advertising to a whole new level of sophisticated, manipulative, guilt-inducing genius.

It took its name from Joseph Campbell, a wholesale agent who, toward the end of the nineteenth century, teamed up with a small-time tinsmith with a modest cannery called Abraham Anderson. Campbell later bought out his partner and on his death in 1900 his most senior man, John Dorrance, took over. He in turn brought in his own son—a chemist called John T. Dorrance—who developed a method of condensing the soup. (The process of canning itself had developed significantly from 1861, when the experiments of Louis Pasteur with microorganisms led to food being heated to a specific temperature before being sealed inside a can.)

Condensing the soup saw huge savings in production costs. Less water was needed, which also meant lower transport costs. The famous red and white stripes, derived from the shirts of players at a football match, created a distinctive design and with pictures of food overlaid—hitherto cans had been free of labels, blankly mysterious and unappealing—they had an exciting product.

The problem was there wasn't much of a market and sales were modest. The company's early poster campaigns urged women to free themselves from soup-making drudgery. But at the turn of the century, American women were happy to make their own soup and, anyway, it wasn't a key part of their diet. The company's challenge was to convince people that they needed to have something they hadn't previously realized they needed. Their first ploy in 1908 was inventing the eye-catching Campbell kids, who tended to dress as adults, crossed social boundaries and, as the campaign developed, engaged in different activities. The boy layered bricks, did some policing or donned a tuxedo, while the girl looked after her dolls or gazed into a mirror.

But while these images appealed to the American housewife, tugging at her heartstrings, the slogans juxtaposed with them played to her insecurities. If a woman felt inadequate or anxious, Campbell's had her firmly in their sights. They wanted America's women to live in fear of social embarrassment. Imagine if your husband turned up at the house one night and you didn't have sufficient provisions to turn out a nice supper. What could be worse? So sensible women stockpiled Campbell's soup for such an eventuality.

With posters on tramcars and, crucially, in magazines like *Ladies' Home Journal*, Campbell's painted a picture of a society where women were engaged in a constant battle to gratify their husband's desires, culinary or otherwise. The man simply came home and sat in judgment. And woe betide if meals didn't include Campbell's soup in some shape or form.

"The way to a man's heart is through his stomach," advised a poster from 1911. "And many a dainty young housewife has discovered that one of the easiest 'short cuts' is Campbell's tomato soup." An advertisement in 1912 shows a man admonishing his wife for spending so much time in the kitchen. "Take advantage of modern ideas," he scolds her. "Don't bother with homemade soups. Use Campbell soup." Meanwhile, another poster declares: "When a man says it's good... it's good."

The company's advertising may have affirmed their role on the domestic front, but their soup also promised to free women from being a slave to both the seasons and their kitchens. Another poster in 1912 shows one housewife say to another: "And only one maid! How do you manage so nicely?" Freed from the burden of making soup (which ironically they weren't now making much of anyway), a woman became independent and could make some welcome redundancies among her household staff.

And while the Campbell kids had America's children urging their moms to bring home a can, the moms themselves were made to feel they had a moral imperative to buy it. "Housewives of America insist on these soups," declared another poster. Soon enough, America's housewives were wondering how on earth they ever got along without them. They welcomed these new branded and shiny products into their homes.

Meanwhile, John T. Dorrance, who became president of the company in 1914, ran the business with a controlling zeal, managing the supply-chain with ruthless efficiency and constantly striving to force down costs. He once sniffed about his soup-making plant being in Camden, New Jersey—a town, he thought, with far too many bars. "I figure that drink weakens men's efficiency 10 percent," he stated. "And we are moving to Campbelltown soon because we want added efficiency." A reminder that while the image of his soups was one of comforting, wholesome, hygienic modernity, the other side to the story was a rather less savory one of cheap, seasonal immigrant labor and workers battling for a decent wage.

Campbell's soup has become an iconic American product throughout the world.

The mass, industrial production of Campbell's soup saw the product spread across the United States with most households having at least one can in their store-cupboards. It was said that the roads to the Campbell soup plant ran red with the juice and pulp of tomatoes as they bounced off the wagons on the way. The success of the advertising was phenomenal long before Andy Warhol painted the cans in the 1960s and fixed Campbell's soup in people's minds as a truly iconic American product.

65

Creamed mushrooms

AUTHOR: Florence Kreisler Greenbaum
FROM: *The International Jewish Cook Book*

First wash them [the mushrooms] thoroughly in cold water, peel them and remove the stems, then cut them in halves or quarters, according to their size.

Melt one tablespoon of butter in a saucepan over the fire then add the mushrooms and let them simmer slowly in the butter for five minutes; season them well with salt and black pepper, freshly ground. After seasoning, add a gill of cream and while it is heating sift one tablespoon of flour in a bowl, add one-half pint of milk. Stir these briskly till flour is all dissolved, then pour it gradually in the saucepan with the mushrooms and cream, stirring the whole constantly to keep it from lumping. Let it just bubble a moment, then add another tablespoon of butter and pour the creamed mushrooms over hot buttered toast on a hot platter and serve.

Cooked like this mushrooms have more nutritive value than beef.

Florence Greenbaum was, according to her publisher, "a household efficiency woman," a title that, one presumes, she was happy with. After all, that's what's written at the front of her book, one with 1,600 characteristically Jewish recipes.

She taught cooking in New York in the decade leading up to 1920 and her various titles included "Lecturer for the Association of Jewish Home Makers." Designed to help the average Jewish housewife, her book has dishes for many different occasions, including Passover and the Sabbath, for example. But she was also quite into toast. She liked chicken livers on toast, creamed cabbage on toast, cinnamon on toast, as well as mushrooms on toast.

Toast may have been nothing particularly new in the early twentieth century, but making it was given new and exciting impetus by an invention reflecting the increasing electrification of people's homes. For it was 1919, the year that Mrs. Greenbaum decided to share her knowledge with America's Jewish housewives, that Minnesota-based mechanic Charles Strite invented the world's first pop-up toaster, which he then patented two years later.

Of course bread had been toasted for some time by that point. Bread had been sliced and held in front of fires or placed on hot stones for as long as you might care to imagine. It was a natural progression in the story of bread, not to mention a sensible way of preserving it.

Indeed the subject of toast presents some fundamental truths about the wonder of cooking itself. Consider the difference between bread, toast and hot-buttered toast. Bread, the result of chemical processes, human graft and heat, represents an almost magical transformation of the base ingredients of flour and water. Toast then moves that product to a new dimension—a totally different creation, merely courtesy of the way it's sliced and then cooked again. Yet toast itself is plain, dry and dull, bleak almost. But add butter and once again the substance takes on a whole new and wonderful character.

While man has been perfecting the art of making bread for about 6,000 years, he's only nailed the toasting of it in the last hundred, and it happened with the arrival of the toaster, more specifically the one that popped the toast up when it was ready. But this was not just the work of one solitary man. The creation of the toaster is one of the most frantic and fiercely fought battles in food history, one that kicked off in America and soon spread across Europe.

It was Albert Marsh who got the ball rolling in 1905 when he was the first to create a wire that could heat up to 310 degrees Fahrenheit—the temperature required to make toast—without the wire melting. He created Nichrome, a mixture of nickel and chrome, and it did just the job. It was then four years before another inventor, Frank Shailor, put the wire into a workable contraption and the first electric toaster went on sale. Shailor may have beaten toaster-maker archrival Lloyd Copeman to this post, but his toaster required vigilance as the toast had to be manually flipped.

This seemed a reasonable state of affairs, but then onto the scene came Mrs. Copeman. She was walking down the street in New York one day with her husband when the site of a Shailor toaster made them stop in front of a shop window. Seeing the appliance may have narked Copeman but his wife nudged him and said, "Lloyd, couldn't you invent a toaster that would automatically turn the toast."

And that's just what he did, proudly eclipsing Shailor as he unveiled his elaborate toasting and turning device in 1914. A patent was issued, acknowledging the debt to his wife, one Hazel B. Copeman. The patent infuriated Copeman's rivals, who then had to make either very significantly different toasters—some using conveyor belts, others with wild, toast-swinging actions—or pay him royalties. But if the toast was not watched, it still burned. And it took Charles Strite to incorporate springs and a timer and make a simpler device with wires cooking both sides of the bread.

The toast-making frenzy spread to Germany and then the rest of Europe. Dozens of designs, from the beautiful—those more resembling carriage clocks than toasters—to the stylish, funky works in silver plate with delicate wooden handles.

Strite's friends had invested in his invention and he first turned out 100 handmade versions for a chain of restaurants called Childs. His creation was called the "Toastmaster." It took until 1926 for it to become more widely available to the public, heralding a modern age of kitchen appliances.

Strite's toaster was further popularized by another life-changing moment. When Otto Frederick Rohwedder invented the bread-slicing machine in the late 1920s, it was the greatest gift to the toaster since (hand-) sliced bread. By 1933 Americans were buying more sliced bread than unsliced. And having toasted it, they happily put whatever they could get their hands on on top of it. As long as it had butter first. Which then led to another big question—one that taxes the minds of secret snackers everywhere as they greedily butter toast before savoring the delectable results. Why, when dropped, does hot-buttered toast always land butter-side down?

The subject is known as "The Cat and the Buttered Toast Theory," which posits that, just as buttered toast lands buttered-side down, so a cat, if dropped, always lands on its feet. So what happens if you tie a slice of buttered toast to the cat's back? When the cat is dropped, will the two opposing forces of butter and feet cause the cat to hover? Can this form the basis of a high-speed monorail? It would admittedly require a lot of cats, toast and butter. One theorist has suggested cutting out the toast altogether and simply buttering the cat. Although I'm not sure Mrs. Florence K. Greenbaum, graduate in food chemistry from the Hunter College of New York City (and very possibly a cat lover), would have approved.

66

Strawberry ice-cream soda

AUTHOR: Alice Bradley
FROM: *Electric Refrigerator Recipes and Menus: Recipes Prepared Especially for the General Electric Refrigerator*

Fill glass one-fourth full of syrup from canned strawberries or raspberries. Add one large spoonful of Vanilla Ice Cream and fill glass with soda water or charged water. Use other fruit syrups in the same way.

It's not impossible to imagine a world without a toaster (see p. 219) or an Oxo cube (see p. 205). But life without a fridge? Would that be feasible? No cool drinks at the height of summer and no ice cubes (at least not without a trip to the icehouse with a pickax). If you want to have the vaguest inkling about how household kitchens survived until the 1930s, try switching off your fridge for a week and see how long it takes before you start having to throw out most things.

The availability of the domestic refrigerator was yet another factor in the increasing loss of culinary skills—of preserving (be it salting, pickling, smoking)—and the increasing distance placed between the consumer and the source of food. Yet this is not something people tend to complain about. The fridge is not usually blamed for the erosion of food culture because it is generally more favorably thought of. It holds its position as one of the great modern contraptions of the twentieth century. While artificially created light let us ignore nature's message that we go to bed, so the fridge enabled us to tear down the barriers of climate and the seasons.

That it took until the early twentieth century was not for lack of trying. The Japanese were building icepits in the fourth century (see p. 124) and the smart set, for hundreds of years, had icehouses. It had long been understood that chilled food lasts longer and so items were put in cellars, under water even, until such time as scientists worked out how to keep a large box chilled without simply having ice in it, or next to it. The refrigerated railway cars of 1860s America did just that, keeping milk and butter chilled by circulating air over ice bunkers at each end of the carriage.

In fact it was Scotsman Dr. William Cullen, some hundred years previously, who first managed to produce artificial ice. While he established the principles and demonstrated how heat could be removed from an area, leaving it cold—the process of refrigeration—it took many more and longer technical leaps before fridges arrived in kitchens.

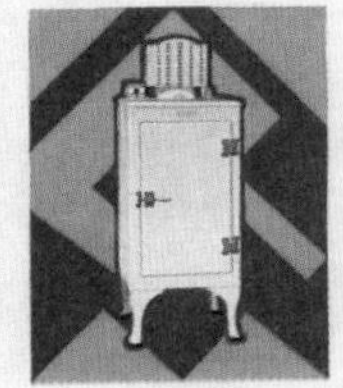

Domestic fridges took over America on a large scale in the 1920s.

In late nineteenth-century America, ammonia was used as part of the process but it took a few explosive and deathly disasters to worry the public. Many were surprised by the fact that an ice-storage plant in Chicago could explode and be engulfed in fire. With so much ice around, you'd be forgiven for thinking a fire was the last thing that would break out. But compressed ammonia is explosive, and equally dangerous was the methyl chloride that leaked in some early domestic refrigerators (also in Chicago), killing a few people in the process.

Soon other chemicals, less toxic, such as sulfur dioxide, were used, before CFCs (chlorofluorocarbons) were found to be decidedly safer, albeit on the domestic front while being lethal for the ozone layer and, ultimately, mankind's very existence.

Britain didn't join the domestic fridge revolution until the 1930s, with many households up until then still receiving milk deliveries twice a day and with meat, fish and green groceries coming daily, or every other day. The country caught the fridge bug from the United States but it was slow to spread. By 1948 still only two percent of the UK population had a refrigerator.

It was in the 1920s that domestic fridges took over America on a big scale. Before then they were the possessions of the rich. Magazine advertisements in 1909, for example, displayed the fridge with grand houses and an Alpine backdrop. It was luxury not necessity. But by 1927 fridges were big business and, as with so many culinary innovations, the makers and marketers set the scene for their product.

If the Oxo cube or the Piggly Wiggly store (see pp. 205 and 212), or indeed so many cookbooks throughout history, were going to set women free, the refrigerator was nothing less than a tool for the "emancipation of womanhood." At least that's what General Electric maintained. The refrigerator "has brought new golden hours of leisure to women" was its claim, and to make sure American women heard the message loud and clear they hired culinary matriarch Alice Bradley to do the talking.

As the principal of Fannie Farmer's Cookery School, founded back in the 1890s (see p. 192), she was something of a culinary authority and what she said about fridges counted. The company persuaded her to put her name to their book of recipes, menus and pro-fridge propaganda.

"According to the United States Department of Agriculture, nature can furnish you with adequate refrigeration only a few days during the year," she declares in the introduction to her book. "The modern American homemaker no longer regards it as a summer luxury." The book then goes on to explain where you should house your fridge ("as near as possible to the place where cooking is done and to the dining room as well"—just in case you thought the damn thing should go in an outhouse) and foretells that "with a General Electric Refrigerator many of your family food problems and your perplexities about entertaining can be solved." Alice Bradley conjures up an extravaganza of fridge-enabled recipes and menus. There are breakfasts of prunes baked with orange juice and cantaloupe melons with crushed ice. Lunches feature frozen pineapple salads and ice-cream pies. There are grapefruit cocktails and stuffed tomatoes in aspic jelly for dinner, not to mention a host of drinks such as this chapter's strawberry ice-cream soda. The faithful disciples of Alice Bradley were surely yearning for a hot meal by the end of it.

With a fridge you can have "week-end guests," "an afternoon of bridge," "after-theater lunches," "children's parties," not to mention dishes "in cases of sickness." The latter having "frapped clam juice" prescribed. In other words, the fridge was a veritable stepping-stone to domestic perfection. Contemporary advertisements see the appliance as being the source of a woman's efficiency, a device to enable her to charm and please her husband. These fridges are bathed in light, children look at them in wonder. They are pictured in houses that have views of verdant landscapes.

One company advertising its "Bandex Model" says that it is "built like a big bay window." To open that fridge is to open a window on the world, a window onto exotic flavor ("Now we can have fresh strawberries all winter!" cry ecstatic children), of foreign, out-of-season foods now at your fingertips. Except it wasn't quite so miraculous as you had probably bought most of the stuff the day before at Piggly Wiggly. As the fridge arrived, so the ice man wasn't required to cometh anymore. New houses were built with spaces for fridges, although it took a good forty years for another object of desire, spawned directly from the refrigerator, to grip the world: the fridge magnet.

67

Toad-in-the-hole

AUTHOR: Unnamed home economist
FROM: *Radiation Cookery Book – For Use with the "New World" Regulo-Controlled Gas Cookers*

¼ lb flour
½ lb sausages
2 eggs
½ pint milk
Salt
2 oz dripping

Make a batter of the flour, eggs, milk, and pinch of salt. Beat thoroughly, and, if possible, allow to stand for 2 hours before using. Make the dripping quite hot in a pie-dish or baking-tin, pour in the batter, drop the sausages in here and there, after removing the skins. Bake for 35 minutes in the oven with 'Regulo' at mark 7.

While the smart cookies in the American refrigerator industry were employing matriarchal figures to spread their message (see p. 222), so too did the UK manufacturers of both gas and electricity. The General Electric Company assembled an Electrical Association of Women led by one Mrs. Ashley, who preached the message that cooking with electricity liberated women from domestic drudgery and was "hygienic, uniform and economical, where cleaning is an easy and pleasant job."

The British Commercial Gas Association, meanwhile, procured the services of the terrifyingly named Maud Adeline Cloudesley Brereton, a Lady Bracknell for the gas world. Through her 1909 book *The Mother's Companion* she had instructed women on keeping budgets and rearing children. Only, she said, by "facing the business side of marriage fairly and squarely, and mastering it, [could there be] any room left for romance."

She lectured across Europe and in America and was the perfect figurehead for the gas industry, which feared competition from its electricity rivals. Under her guidance, the Gas Association erected model homes, hosted cooking contests and held free lectures. She penned articles for the trade and consumer press, successfully preaching the merits of using gas. Certainly in the early year of electric cookers, while the whole business was cleaner, it was also slow. It could take 15–20 minutes to boil two pints of water, for instance. Gas was more powerful and controllable. As food historian Colin Spencer has commented: "the gas oven was an incredible step forward for the cook, because the heat could be controlled from a low simmer to a blazing boil."

These benefits and others were carefully highlighted in a book that came free with every purchase of a "Regulo New World Gas Cooker." Called the *Radiation*

Cookery Book, it featured dozens of recipes, including the one for toad-in-the-hole heading this chapter. The recipes' inspiration seemed to come directly from Mrs. Beeton (see p. 182) as much of the content was down-to-earth fare geared to feeding the working man, from tripe and onions to baked, stuffed heart.

The advantages in technology were so immense, this seems to imply, that the housewife had enough to contend with without actually developing her main cooking skills or trying out more exotic ingredients and ideas. And once again the message of the new technology was that it was an enabler of liberation. The Regulo cooker was the earliest to have thermostat oven control, for instance. It promised "an automated operation; watching, or attention, on the part of the user is unnecessary." The Regulo, said its makers, "is the servant of the housewife enabling her to obtain and reproduce with certainty the cooking conditions she requires."

Clearly the arrival of this cleaner-fueled cooking device must have been greeted with great celebration. No more chopping and hauling in of logs, much less cleaning and a new, previously unheard-of precision in cooking was now achievable. It had been a much more ad hoc business before, as one cook testifies, describing how she attempted to achieve temperature regulation in the pre-gas 1920s:

> Once I had a bed of coals I knew that it took four quarter logs to hot it up enough to bake bread. It only took a crumpled paper and a stick or two to boil the kettle though. If you wanted to cook muffins you stoked up the fire then stuck your hand in and started counting. If you got to eight before it got too hot to stand it, it was right for muffins. Bread was six and pies were ten.

Advertisements in women's magazines at the time focused hard on the Regulo as emancipator. "Marriage won't turn me into a stay at home. I'm a regular 'Regulo' fan!" exclaims one housewife, while another declares: "Cooking won't keep *me* out of the garden. I'm a regular 'Regulo' fan!"

But more compelling was the idea that the Regulo and its newborn technological cousins—the toaster (see p. 219), the electric iron and the water heater, among others—were, as the Gas Association called them, "silent servants." Finally, for the middle classes, technology had replaced servants. In another advert from a contemporary women's magazine a lady acknowledges her lack of domestic staff. She may not have a maid but, she says, "It's the 'Regulo' that does the work. First I set the 'Regulo.' Five! Six! Seven!... or whatever number the Cookery Chart tells me. Then into the oven goes the whole dinner. Not a thing to do once it is in the oven..." Unfortunately the cookery chart she mentions was actually a little vague. Most cooking times were defined as "30–45 minutes," "2–3 hours" or "2 hours or longer," so without doubt these housewives were still dashing in from the garden, opening the oven door and prodding their meat.

Possibly this new technology was more of a boon for those who already engaged in household chores. For many who had previously paid to have the housework done, the replacement of maids and servants for shiny, modern contraptions brought on a new era of lonely domestic drudgery—the one thing the makers of these contraptions claimed they would eradicate.

New technology might have excited the husband, but where was the passion for food? The makers of "Regulo" claimed that cooking should be a "creative activity, not a repetitive, unthoughtful task." The nation's new domestic slaves desperately needed inspiration, a little joy even, in their cooking. And fortunately, it was just around the corner.

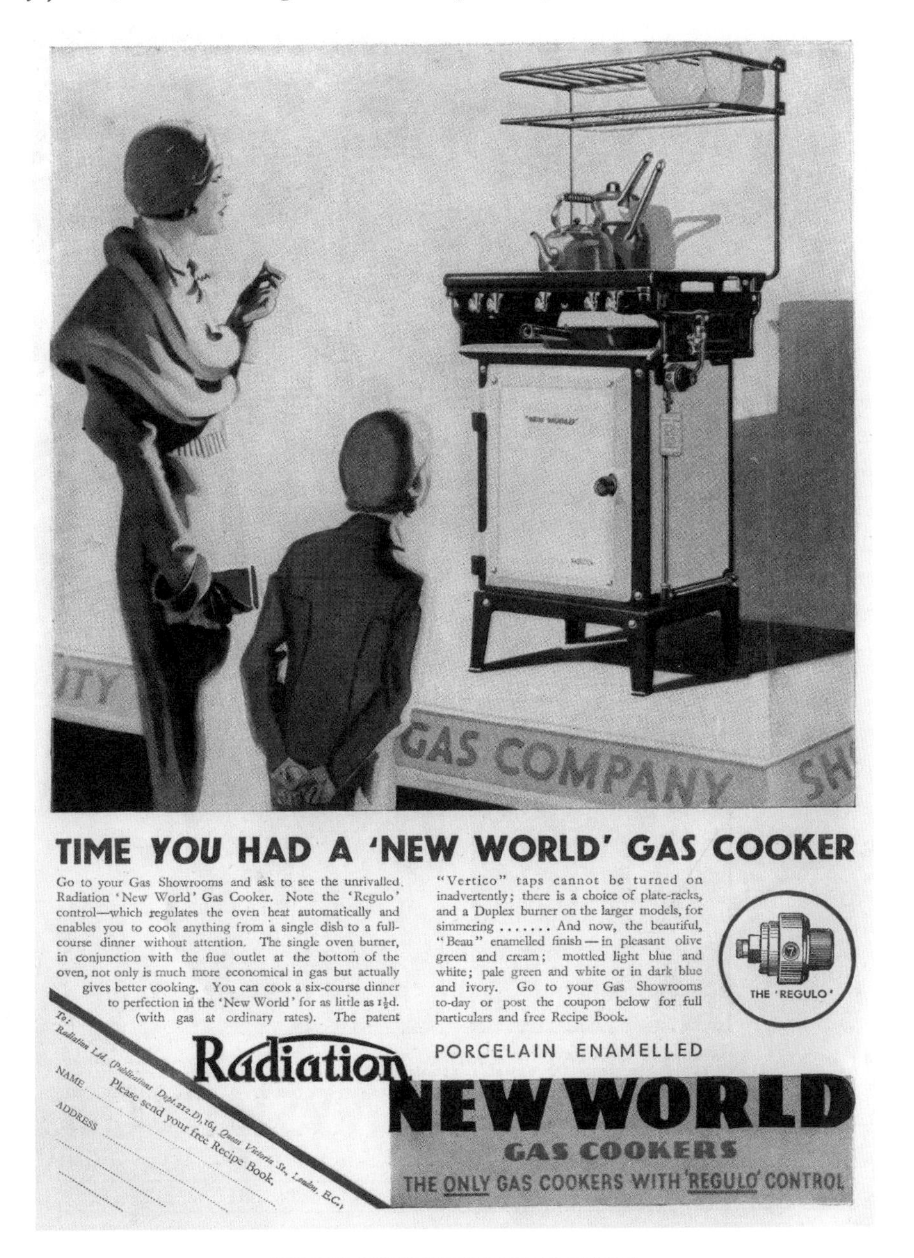

One of the early adverts for the Regulo gas cooker, which was the first cooker to have a thermostat oven control.

68

Quick oatmeal cookies

AUTHOR: Irma Rombauer and Marion Rombauer Becker
FROM: *Joy of Cooking*

ABOUT 3-DOZEN 2-INCH COOKIES

Preheat oven to 350°F.

Measure:
½ cup brown sugar, firmly packed
½ cup granulated sugar

Cream with:
½ cup butter

Combine and beat in until smooth:
1 egg
1 teaspoon vanilla
1 tablespoon milk

Sift together and add to the above ingredients:
1 cup all-purpose flour
½ teaspoon soda
½ teaspoon double-acting baking powder
½ teaspoon salt

When beaten smooth, add:
1 cup uncooked quick rolled oats
(¾ cup chocolate chips)
(1 teaspoon grated orange rind)

Beat the mixture well. Drop cookies 2 inches apart on well-greased cookie sheet and bake until light brown.

Many American women entered the decade of the 1930s with a heavy heart. After the Wall Street Crash of 1929, the Great Depression, which touched most of the world's economies, turned the American dream into a nightmare. America's housewives were at a low ebb. For those who could afford it, the new technology—shiny, gleaming contraptions that stored and cooked and toasted food—sat in the corners of their kitchens with an air of expectation. But now bereft of staff—the price they'd paid for this new equipment (see p. 225)—and with commuter husbands heading home and looking forward to a new array of dazzling dishes courtesy of their culinary investments, many felt even more inadequate.

Besieged by propaganda from the gas and electrics industries, and preached at in haughty tones by the home economists who wrote recipes to match, these ladies needed help. The help they got was unintended. When Irma Rombauer first issued her collection of recipes with the help of her daughter Marion, the circulation was initially small. Published privately at Irma's own expense, *Joy of Cooking* was only ever meant to be the writings of an experienced amateur aimed at helping out inexperienced fellow amateurs or clueless novices. That it went on to become a publishing sensation, with 10 million copies sold in hardback and the same number in paperback by the end of the century, is testimony to the value of the work. Her first print-run of 3,000 successfully sold, by chance, at a bridge game, Irma met the president of the publishers Bobbs-Merrill. A fully fledged proper book was then released in 1936 and it sold, feverishly, from coast to coast.

Each generation needs its culinary prop and when one arrives and speaks in the language of someone who is both mother, best friend, mentor and comforter, it cannot fail to warm the cockles of myriad hearts. Irma Rombauer reached out to thousands of women all desperately wondering how the hell they were going to cater for their husbands, friends and family, and do it in a way that didn't leave them feeling sick with anxiety.

"Will it encourage you to know that I was once as ignorant, helpless and awkward a bride as was ever foisted on an impecunious lawyer?" she asks in the preface to her book. One can see her reader, clutching the book in the corner of the kitchen, a tear trickling from one eye as she thinks, "Yes . . . I think it just might . . ."

"Together," continues Irma, "we placed many a burnt offering upon the altar of matrimony." Her confiding manner and relaxed approach to cooking was infectious, endearing her to thousands of readers. Interestingly, her daughter Marion, who co-produced the book, recalled that her mother "to the end of her life, regarded social intercourse as more important than food."

If those attempting to cope in the kitchen, let alone seeking perfection, could harness some of the joy she heralded, all might not be lost. From the outset, her message is tinged with humor: she gives a witty quote from the British novelist Saki: "The cook was a good cook; and as good cooks go, she went." Follow Irma's book "steadily for a few months [and] you will master the skills the cook walked off with," she continues, before adding these words of encouragement: "What is more, we believe you will go on to unexpected triumphs."

When the makers of a fridge or cooker promised liberation, it rang hollow. When Irma assured you that a better life was possible, you believed her. Study her book and you could "revel in a sense of new-found freedom . . . you will eat at the hour of your choice . . . the food will be cooked and seasoned to your own discriminating taste . . . you will regain the priceless private joy of family living, dining and sharing."

It was the death of her husband, whose family were exiled Hungarians, that spurred her on to distribute her recipes. That and an acute empathy with those who needed culinary help. (Indeed the book is aimed far wider than at just women. Men are acknowledged as having a role in domestic cooking and the book provides recipes for college students (a first) as well as uncertain brides and other innocents.) Finding herself a widow in her mid-forties, she took comfort in work, compiling recipes with her daughter Marion, who would suggest chapter headings and produce charming and simple illustrations to accompany the text.

Irma found it easy to speak to the culinarily dispossessed—and others—because she herself was an outsider. The daughter of German immigrants, the young Irma von Starkloff felt she was not "American." She could offer help without being patronizing and wrote her recipes in such a way that they could be attempted by anyone, however inexperienced.

Her subsequent travels around the world also provided a more varied recipe collection than was currently available. And those travels colored her writing in lyrical tones. She wrote of berries, for instance: "For an attractive way to serve out of doors, make berry cones. We saw them first in the shadows of the rain forest in Puerto Rico, where we were greeted beside a waterfall by children with wild berries in leaf cones held in punctured leaf tops. Glorify your box top with foil."

To write instructional recipes with such anecdotal charm was inspirational. Although many of her recipes also bordered on the eccentric. Her section on game doesn't rest with squirrel, for instance. She has recipes for raccoon, woodchuck and beaver, not to mention opossum: "If possible trap your opossum and feed it on milk and cereal for 10 days before killing." Returning home to see a tethered opossum eating cereal in your back yard is a scenario that might have alarmed even the most open-minded of hungry husbands.

Then there is her recipe for bear. "If marinated at least 24 hours in an oil-based marinade, all bear except black bear is edible," she advises. But once you've caught your bear, don't let it hang around: "Remove all fat from bear meat at once, as it turns rancid very quickly." Not surprisingly these recipes did not make it into later editions. And the book was republished several times throughout the century and into 2006—its most recent incarnation.

Each edition was brought up to date, in time-honored Mrs. Beeton fashion (see p. 182), so that Irma and Marion's cooking could stay relevant for each new generation. And it was a family affair, the 1997 edition, for example, being edited by her grandson Ethan. Tips, from entertaining and place-setting to good health and food safety, being brought up to date according to the times.

Particularly helpful was the 1946 edition with its "emergency chapters" "to meet the difficulties that beset the present-day cook." As well as suggestions for making food stretch, such as adding stale bread to chicken stuffing, Irma addresses her readers with patriotic fervor. America, she says, must defend its "tradition of plenty... with the intelligent use of our mighty weapon, the cooking spoon."

Irma's tome helped to change the perception of cooking from a chore to a joy. It was the only cookbook to make it to the New York Public Library's list of the 150 most influential books of the twenty-first century. So the least one can do is salute the indefatigable spirit of the once-crushed and now, quite possibly, joyful American housewife—and many others across the world—and rustle up her "Quick Oatmeal Cookies." Speedy, delicious and eminently doable, they capture the spirit of the book.

69

Drum roll of colonial fish

AUTHOR: Filippo Tommaso Marinetti
FROM: *La cucina futurista (The Futurist Cookbook)*

Poached mullet marinated for twenty-four hours in a sauce of milk, rosolio liqueur, capers and red pepper. Just before serving the fish, open it and stuff it with date jam interspersed with discs of banana and slices of pineapple. It will then be eaten to a continuous rolling of drums.

Pasta got its first good write-up in 1154 (see p. 42). Abu Abd Allah Abdullah, Muhammad ibn Muhammad ibn Ash Sharif al-Idrisi had spotted it in the form of spaghetti in Sicily, by which time it was no doubt well on its way to becoming what the National Pasta Museum in Rome was to call "the Italian invention that the world envies."

For many centuries it lay at the heart of Italian cuisine: universal, versatile, a delicious emblem of satiety. What Italian would not be proud to acknowledge this central part of his or her cultural DNA?

Well, an Italian called Tommaso Marinetti, for a start. Marinetti was the founder of the Futurist movement whose manifesto was published in 1909. His ideology, with its celebration of youth, industry and violence, was a precursor to fascism and he later became a vociferous supporter of the Italian dictator Benito Mussolini. With a mixture of anarchy and fascism he wanted an end to nineteenth-century romanticism and an embracing of twentieth-century speed and technology.

"We will glorify war—the world's only hygiene," he declared. "We will destroy the museums, the libraries, academies of every kind."

Museums, he said, covered Italy, "like so many graveyards." "We want," he continued, "to free this land from its smelly gangrene of professors, archaeologists and antiquarians."

And how was he going to set about doing that? Well, first of all, by dealing with what his compatriots ate and how they cooked it, for people "think, dream and act according to what they eat and drink." He attacked the "quantity, banality, repetition and expense" of traditional Italian cooking. Futurist cooking, he argued, was "tuned to high speeds like the motor of a hydroplane... its ultimate aim is to create harmony between men's palate and his life today and tomorrow."

And to achieve this harmony one vital thing had to happen. Which is why Tommaso Marinetti called for a ban on pasta. More than that—pasta needed to be abolished. "However agreeable to the palate," he wrote of pasta, "it makes people heavy, brutish, deludes them into thinking it is nutritious, makes them sceptical, slow, pessimistic." Pasta needed to be eliminated because it was "an absurd gastronomic religion. It is completely hostile to the vivacious spirit and passionate, generous, intuitive soul of the Neopolitan."

The Italian people were incredulous at this attack on a food so central to their culture. Huge debates broke out in the newspapers. In cafés, restaurants and in homes across the country, as people tucked into their linguine, tagliatelle and cannelloni, arguments for and against pasta ensued.

How could pasta be so terrible when Italy had thrived on it, had lived on it for so long? It didn't make sense. But the mustachioed Marinetti, who never let a photograph of him be taken without him displaying an air of unremitting arrogance, was having none of it and refused to let up.

Italians may have been heroic fighters, inspired artists and shrewd lawyers but this was, he wrote, "in spite of their voluminous daily intake of pasta."

In the years after he published his manifesto, he collected around him numerous supporters, all eager to stamp out pasta. And meanwhile he worked on a series of recipes and menus that were, for him, as a breath of Futurist air, with no hint of fusilli, penne or conchiglioni.

Finally in 1932 he released what he thought was his finest work. *The Futurist Cookbook* brought together the greatest anti-pasta Italian minds—professors, doctors, lawyers—that Marinetti could muster, together with an extraordinary array of alternative feasts.

The problem with pasta, railed one Professor Signorelli, was that it wasn't chewed properly. It was "swallowed, not masticated," he argued. It was then left to the liver and pancreas to digest the stuff, which led to "an interrupted equilibrium in these organs. From such disturbances derive lassitude, pessimism, nostalgic inactivity and neutralism."

Next up was a "clinician," Professor Nicola Pende, who pronounced that when a man "ingurgitates his biquotidian pyramid of pasta" it left him with a "heavy, bloated stomach [that] does not encourage physical enthusiasm for a woman." Pasta, in short, caused "obesity and exaggerated abdominal volume."

Marinetti presented all these arguments against pasta with tremendous glee, sensing that this "everyday mediocrity" was on the ropes. He savaged "the defenders of pasta," who were, he screamed, "shackled by its ball and chain like convicted lifers" and who carried "its ruins in their stomachs like archaeologists."

He toured the country making speeches in towns and cities where he and his pasta-hating cohorts handed out leaflets and copies of his book. "No more spaghetti for Italians!" went his cry. Then he went one further and called for "no more knives and forks."

And so, wondered those who read his words and listened to his speeches, without pasta and without cutlery—save spoons, which Marinetti had not yet called for a ban on—what and how should one eat?

The answers were in his book. Firstly, people should embrace new technology. The wireless set, gradually arriving in people's homes, was such an enabler and its potential was enormous. Mankind, argued Marinetti, needed to prepare "for the not too distant possibility of broadcasting nourishing waves over the radio." After all, if music on the radio could induce sleep, mightn't broadcasting the sound of dinner being served placate the stomach?

To supplement this idea he called on the state to issue free pills filled with "albumoid compounds, synthetic fats and vitamins." Such food, he maintained, would lower the cost of living and as machines increasingly took over the burden of manual labor, men would be able to spend hours in the "anticipation of perfect meals."

Speaking of which, he then presented a long list of recipes combining food with other sensations, including the one that begins this chapter: poached mullet eaten to the sound of drums.

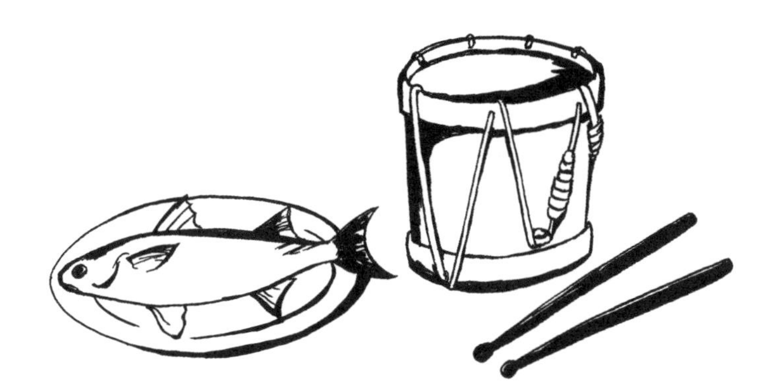

"Aerofood" provides another example of this multi-sensual approach to eating. The dish comprised a slice of fennel, an olive and a kumquat alongside a strip of sandpaper which "need not be eaten." As the diner consumed the fennel, olive and kumquat with his left hand, he would stroke the sandpaper with his right. This would provide "prelabial sensations" which would make the food taste nicer. Meanwhile a waiter would pass by and douse the head of the diner in scent.

In a recipe for "raw meat torn by trumpet blasts" he instructs one to "cut a perfect cube of meat" before passing an electronic current through it and then marinating it for twenty-four hours in rum, cognac and white vermouth. It should then be served "on a bed of red pepper, black pepper and snow." Each mouthful must then be chewed for precisely a minute and in between mouthfuls the diner should make "vehement blasts" on a trumpet.

Perhaps his most triumphant recipe, sandwiched between "surprise bananas" and "Tyrrhenian seaweed foam (with coral garnish)," was "Tactile vegetable garden."

Here the salad is eaten "by burying the face in the plate, without the help of the hands, so as to inspire a true tasting with direct contact between the flavors and the textures of the green leaves on the skin of the cheeks and the lips."

As the eater brings the head up from the plate, a waiter sprays his face with cologne. And then before taking another mouthful, "the guests must let their fingertips feast uninterruptedly on their neighbor's pajamas." Because, of course, they're wearing pajamas.

Having made it through a Futurist dinner, anyone sampling the modern experimental cookery of Heston Blumenthal (see p. 348) or Ferran Adrià (p. 336) would surely consider it child's play.

Seventy-five years later, in 2007, Will Noonan, a professor of the University of Sydney, wrote a lengthy essay considering the arguments and recipes put forward by Marinetti. It was, he declared, "a unique and iconoclastic contribution to the development of Italian cuisine." Marinetti's ideas represented "the movement from a dietary to a sensual and conceptual focus [which] highlights the affinities between Futurist cooking and other forms of artistic praxis."

Was this, he asked, the precursor to Carlo Petrini's Slow Food Movement (see p. 299), or an advance party in molecular gastronomy? The only thing holding Marinetti back, in Noonan's view, appeared to be the unfortunate association with fascism. His "predictions of nourishment by pills and radio waves were never realized" writes Noonan solemnly. Was this because he was "tainted by association with Mussolini's regime"? he asks.

But perhaps Noonan hadn't read the recipes very clearly, let alone attempted to cook them. Perhaps he, like the thousands of Italians who were so riled by Marinetti's writings and speeches, didn't quite spot that *The Futurist Cookbook* was, in the words of Lesley Chamberlain, editor of the 1989 English translation, "one of the best artistic jokes of the century."

A joke even more delicious, perhaps, when savored with "Sicilian headland," a dish that calls for tuna to be chopped with apples, olives and little Japanese nuts. "Spread the resulting paste," implores Marinetti, "on a cold jam omelette."

70

Omelette

AUTHOR: Xavier Marcel Boulestin
FROM: *The Finer Cooking, or Dishes for Parties*

This omelette is quite plain, and the secret of its flavour is just the taste of the eggs and the butter, which must be perfectly fresh: the seasoning is only salt. The eggs are beaten as usual, a good piece of butter is put in the pan, and the moment it has melted the eggs are put in. You stir occasionally with a fork, lifting the coagulating eggs so that the top is allowed to cook.

When the eggs are set the omelette is ready, and served flat, so that it is unlike an ordinary omelette, which is folded, and unlike a Spanish omelette, which is flat but tossed. It is, in fact, as if scrambled eggs had been allowed to set as a whole.

Sitting among the schedules in the *Radio Times Television Supplement* for Thursday 21 January 1937, between "Marks and Mimes" at 9:10 p.m. and the "British News" at 9:40, was a modest notice that read: "9.25: Cook's Night Out." It was ten years since the BBC had become a public corporation and twelve since John Logie Baird had demonstrated the first working television. And here it was, the first food show presented by the first TV chef.

"Marcel Boulestin will demonstrate before the camera the making of the first of five dishes which can be prepared as a separate dish, while the whole together make an excellent five-course dinner," states the rather convoluted caption, adding: "In his first talk M. Boulestin will demonstrate the cooking of an omelette." He had just fifteen minutes and one can only assume it went rather well because M. Boulestin became a regular feature during those early days of the BBC when there was just an hour's telly in the evening, consisting mainly of stuff that had been broadcast for two hours earlier in the day from three o'clock.

These were the first, exciting days of pioneering television. The listings were published as a supplement to the *Radio Times* and Cecil Lewis, cofounder of the BBC, wrote in the same issue of his feverish excitement at what was being embarked upon. "Those who are following its growth are seeing the development of an amazing extension of human powers, the end of which we can hardly foresee," he remarked, with startling prescience. At the time cables were being laid and outside broadcasts were being experimented with. Soon, Lewis continued, "we shall be able to give the viewer a glimpse of the many activities in the life of our capital, visit the theaters, the sports grounds, and the factories around Britain." Then, a microwave transmitter would be able to take viewers "out into the country for fairs and gymkhanas, for open-air plays, river scenes."

His enthusiasm is tangible and as there are no recordings of Boulestin demonstrating his omelette recipe (only in the studio, not a river scene), one can only imagine the curiosity and excitement of those watching in public viewing rooms or at the home of someone lucky enough to own a Marconi TV with its "excellent high-definition [and] flicker-free pictures."

Boulestin was chosen, as the BBC itself said at the time, because, "as well as being a great authority on cookery [he] is a great conversationalist." His TV cookery lessons were, the BBC continued, "greatly helped by the expressiveness of his face and his gestures."

No doubt he was as confident and expansive on camera as he was off. A restaurateur who had run two establishments around Covent Garden, he was a man of many talents, having tried his hand at design, decoration, caricature, music criticism and novel writing. But he shone on the subject of food and, as Elizabeth David (see p. 256) later argued, his work—and that of his contemporary André Simon, a leading wine merchant—"had the most profound influence upon the English attitude to food and wine." It was because they were Frenchmen who wrote, rather than having their work translated into, English. And, as David pointed out, because they came to England speaking little or no English and managed to "assimilate themselves into English life and before long to write and publish books in English" that they became "something of a phenomenon."

Boulestin's graceful prose was often to be seen in *Vogue,* where he had a column, as well as in the several books he wrote, including his autobiography of 1936, *Myself, My Two Countries . . .* , which brings to life his early years in southwest France. Here he writes of his favorite place, the kitchen of an establishment where he once worked. He describes the chicken and partridge that roasted on a spit and whose "subtle perfume filled the kitchen." He remembers crisp salads being prepared and roosters rubbed with garlic. Pork lay salting in cherrywood containers, while the storeroom was overflowing with *confits,* barrels of malting vinegar, honey oozing from combs, grapes and cherries marinating in brandy, along with crates of eggs and sacks of haricot beans and potatoes.

Baskets of fruit included "perfect small melons, late plums, under-ripe medlars, peaches, peas . . . all the fruits of September naturally ripe and sometimes still warm from the sun." It was memories of this profusion that made him loathe the artificially grown and expensively exported produce that was starting to arrive, pre-Second World War, at the smarter restaurants in London.

His food heritage made him a man of firm opinions in the great tradition of celebrity chef, TV or no TV. "Good meals should be the rule, not the exception," he opined and he abhorred the fact that his adopted country was filled with people who disdained the idea of talking about it. A hangover from Victorian times, this peculiarly English belief that talking about food was vulgar, that to enjoy it too much was

Chef Marcel Boulestin cooking for the BBC, November 1938.

immodest and distasteful and that it made for an inferior topic of conversation, irritated him, to put it mildly. "Food which is worth eating is worth discussing," he declared. "The English habit of not talking about food strikes the foreigner, however long he may have stayed in England, as a very queer one."

It was this custom of not according food sufficient merit as a subject that, he felt, held back British food, as it still does in pockets of English society today, preventing it from improving. "If we agree that good food is more important than many so-called 'important things in life,' and surely no one would dismiss lightly an event which occurs at least twice a day, and which is conducive to happiness or bad temper," he wrote in his book *What Shall We Have Today?*, "then we must admit that a cook is an important person in the household, since she dispenses gifts either precious or intolerable."

Boulestin wrote of cookery as an art in the way his foodie forebears had done back in the eighteenth century and early 1800s. Cooks needed to be seen as people with a vocation, as professional artists. "This was," he said, "more than it is now in

England, the attitude taken in other days." The country's acquiescence to the domination of French cooking, coupled with its general lack of interest, had resulted in a world where the quality of food was poor and where women—now bereft of their servants—were expected to cook as well as do everything else: "We take it for granted that the young lady of 1931 [the year the book was published], besides playing a good game of golf, driving her car, dancing gracefully, running a successful shop, is also a capable housekeeper and a happy hostess."

So he offered up hundreds of recipes—all French, of course—as well as practical advice. Don't serve fish in a white sauce if you've just served a creamy soup, for example, and be sure to "arrange your menu in a way that means maximum effect on the dinner table and minimum of working in the kitchen." A mantra which millions would echo today.

He advised women to remember what they served guests the last time, so they wouldn't get the same thing twice, and urged them also to note down which frock they wore to avoid "the quite too awful mistake of appearing in the same creation."

And he urged against an obsession with exactitude. "The dangerous person in the kitchen is the one who goes rigidly by weights, measurements, thermometers and scales... all these scientific instruments are not of much use, the only exception being for making pastries and jams..." Although, as Elizabeth David pointed out, "one has to know roughly what the rules are before one can afford to disregard them."

Boulestin's television career was cut short by the war, during which time TV broadcasts on the BBC were suspended, and he died before the conflict ended, at the age of sixty-five. Yet the Restaurant Boulestin continued on its same Covent Garden site until 1994 when it was sold and became something which would have made the world's first TV chef turn in his grave, a Pizza Hut.

71

Elderberry & apple jam

AUTHOR: Marguerite Patten, FROM: *Feeding the Nation*

COOKING TIME: ABOUT 1 HOUR

QUANTITY: ABOUT 6 LB

3 lb elderberries
3 lb apples
5 lb sugar

Remove berries from stalks and wash. Warm them to draw juice. Simmer for ½ hour to soften skins. Core apples and simmer until quite soft in another pan with very little water, pass through sieve or pulp well with a wooden spoon, add apples to elderberries, reheat and add sugar. Stir until dissolved and boil rapidly until jam sets. Make first test for setting after 10 minutes. Put into hot jars and seal.

The voice of horticulturalist Roy Hay on the Ministry of Information film was emphatic. "Do you like standing in a queue for your vegetables?" he asked rhetorically. "Or do you think it is tiring and a waste of time? Do you ever find your long wait has been useless, that supplies of what you want have run out before your turn comes? It's not your greengrocer's fault, it's up to you." Hay, a gardening author, had been employed by the wartime government to help spread a vital message.

Before the war, Britain had been importing around a third of all the food it consumed. Germany, on the other hand, was rather more self-sufficient, imports supplying just 15 percent of its food. "The health line of the Home Front may become as important as the Maginot Line," nutritionist John Boyd Orr told the government in 1940. As the war progressed, one in four ships bringing in supplies were sunk by the German navy. If Hitler could, he'd sooner starve, rather than bomb, the country to death.

Hay's message was that the men, women and children of Britain should "Dig For Victory." He was joined in the campaign by another familiar gardening figure, C. H. Middleton. Mr. Middleton, as he was known, was recognizable to British audiences through his prewar BBC broadcasts *In Your Garden,* when he appeared in the schedules alongside TV chef Marcel Boulestin (see p. 235). With his gray suit, starched white collar and tie, bowler hat and round glasses, there was even a cartoon character made of him. His animated persona would appear leaning on a garden gate as flowers sprouted, which—grateful for his lessons on good composting—chirped "Thanks, Mr. Middleton!" Using films and eye-catching posters and traveling around the country, Middleton and Hay spread the message that "food is just as important a weapon of war as guns."

English cookery expert Marguerite Patten (left) supervising pianist Geraldine Peppin as she stirs a pan on the BBC TV show Designed for Women, *April 1948.*

Lord Woolton, who had set up the Ministry of Food, wrote of the threat of shortages in his memoirs. "The country never realized how nearly we were brought to disaster," he recalled. "During the course of two hours on Friday afternoon, I received five separate signals from the Admiralty reporting that food ships had been sunk on the Atlantic route. By some extraordinary misfortune, these five ships were largely stocked with bacon." It became Lord Woolton's primary objective not to fail the government's pledge to the public that rations would always be honored. He knew that the country could not fight a war on an empty stomach. There would be public disorder and dire consequences. "It became . . . a constant battle of wits against the enemy, with the harrowing certainty that if we failed people would go hungry," he wrote.

The Ministry of Food became a giant shop that controlled the supply of food, and Lord Woolton and his team hustled for goods to honor rations in every way they could. Each week you were allowed around 4 ounces of bacon or ham, 12 of sugar, 2 of tea, 4 of fat, 2 of margarine or butter and an ounce of cheese. Cereals and canned foods, jam, honey and golden syrup were worth points which you deducted from your monthly allowance. Heavy fines or imprisonment were imposed as punishment upon anyone who breached the rationing restrictions.

Lord Woolton recalled triumphantly how a supply did arrive by ship from America, avoiding the German U-boats, on 31 May 1941. It brought 4 million eggs, 120,000 pounds of cheese and 1,000 tons of flour. "To celebrate I broke my own regulations and handed over for division among the landing staff of 240 a twenty-pound cheese," he wrote. "That there was little or no black market in Britain was a tribute to the British people which I hope historians of this period will proudly record," he later reflected.

But it was Lord Woolton and his team who managed to maintain morale and keep that black market to a minimum. In addition to America, they looked to other, more dodgy, sources for food. They hunted for contacts across the world who could supply the country with everything from flour to sugar. They forged contacts in Singapore for rice, for example. And on the back streets of Egypt, Woolton broke his own rules for using black markets. Except he was careful to keep his own fingers clean, remaining ignorant of exactly how it worked and who was involved. "Just how we got the rice out of Egypt was something into which I never thought it necessary to inquire," he remarked. Indeed, how Lord Woolton and his ministry maintained the ration is one of the great untold stories of World War Two.

Meanwhile, on the home front, women were urged to grow things to eat rather than to look at. "The flower garden will grow beetroot as well as begonias," assured Roy Hay. Wherever there was a patch of ground, it should be dug over and used to plant veg. "Digging can be good fun," Hay insisted. Before long you'd have "peas that will melt in your mouth, carrots that will be a revelation...and cabbages fit for a king." But, he added, for the novice gardener, "for goodness sake, keep your spade clean."

The next challenge for the public was how to cook with their glut of cabbage or meager ration of cheese. So the government called on those same individuals who had been so deft at convincing households to invest in electric or gas cookers (see p. 225). One such person was Marguerite Patten, a home economist who had worked for both the Eastern Electricity Board and Frigidaire. She mixed her cooking skills with a theatrical bent, she recalled, in order to fulfil the "thankless task of persuading people to buy fridges when they all thought a pantry was quite good enough."

In daily radio broadcasts—*The Kitchen Front* aired for five minutes each morning after the eight o'clock news—and through short films, pamphlets and then books, she taught the arts of thrift, making the best of your rations and making it all last. Her passion for economy in leftovers being echoed in two-minute cinema *Food Flashes*. "Don't waste food," they preached. "Food doesn't grow in the shops, you know."

Lord Woolton also became a national figure as he urged people to make the most of what little they had. "Those who have the will to win/ Cook potatoes in their skin/ Knowing that the sight of peelings/ Deeply hurts Lord Woolton's feelings" went one frequently broadcast radio ditty. Woolton was assisted by the more eccentric urgings of French chef Vicomte de Mardit, who wrote a book explaining how one could live entirely on foraging. This included recipes for such delights as grilled squirrel, squirrel tail soup, stewed starlings and sugarless puddings.

Patten, meanwhile, urged women to plan their week's menus in advance and stick to them when they went shopping. It was a mentality that persisted long after the war as British shoppers studiously ignored the idea of being inspired by fresh, seasonal produce, sticking instead to the food they had planned to buy before their trip to the shops. Likewise the government's advice on what people should keep in their store-cupboards—tinned and dried milk, dried eggs, canned vegetables, fruit, meat and fish—also seems to have permeated the larders of the nation well into the 1970s and beyond.

Patten's job was a challenge. While there were extra rations of sugar during the jam-making season, she recalled, "whale meat replaced steak...and even marmalade had to be made with carrots." While children got their vitamins from their ration of concentrated fruit juice, she had to persuade adults to get theirs through the likes of grated raw turnip. But the wartime diet, she once reflected, was "better than I thought it would be... Do you think we could have survived all those years if we were producing inedible food?" Indeed her recipe for elderberry and apple jam that heads this chapter was perfect for those who could simply forage for the ingredients from the garden or in the countryside—except of course the sugar...

By 1945, thanks in part to the "Dig For Victory" campaign, the country had 6 million more acres of land under cultivation and Britain was producing two-thirds of its food. The enforced change to the nation's diet had a tangible effect. Instances of TB lessened, for example, and there was a lower rate of tooth decay. At a time when many of the country's doctors and nurses were overseas supporting the armed forces, the nation actually got healthier. "After two years the public were slimmer and livelier," wrote food historian Colin Spencer. Rations leveled the classes as the rich ate less well than they had and the poor rather better.

Another contemporary cook recruited by Lord Woolton was Irene Veal, who waxed lyrical about the effect the war was having on cooking in her book of wartime recipes. "Never before have the British people been so wisely fed or British women so sensibly interested in cooking," she wrote. "We are acquiring an almost French attitude of mind regarding our food and its careful preparation, and the demand for good and practical recipes is continually increasing."

Her thoughts verge on propaganda. Marguerite Patten did, after all, reflect many years later that "people are inclined to make me say I want to go back to the war years. Well, what a load of nonsense. Who wants to go back to six months without a fresh tomato? Not me."

The end of war did not spell an end to rationing, however. Given that it continued for an astonishing seven more years, it's hardly surprising that habits of frugality, and of making even the stringiest of vegetables last, were perpetuated for decades after it was over. Rationing was not lifted until 1953, by which time those brought up in peacetime on a diet of carrot sandwiches, battered pork rind and spam fritters were certain to revisit those sins on their children, regardless of whether Hitler's bombs were long gone and no matter if there was a fresh melon, or juicy piece of steak on offer at the market.

72

French creamed oysters

AUTHOR: Pearl V. Metzelthin, FROM: *Gourmet* magazine

Put one cup of butter into the top of a lighted chafing dish; add 1 tablespoon English mustard, ¾ teaspoon anchovy paste, salt, pepper, and a dash of cayenne pepper to taste; stir until mixture is thoroughly blended. Add 3 cups finely chopped celery and stir almost constantly until celery is nearly cooked. Pour in 1 quart rich, fresh cream slowly, stirring constantly until mixture comes to a boil. Add 4 dozen oysters, cleaned and free from beard, and cook 2 minutes. Finally, add ¼ cup good sherry wine. Serve on freshly made toast on hot plates, and garnish with quartered lemon and crisp young watercress. Dust each serving with paprika, mixed with a little nutmeg.

It seemed that Marcel Boulestin's (see p. 237) plea that "Food which is worth eating is worth discussing" would fall on deaf ears. How could discussion on aspects of gastronomy possibly be countenanced by a nation at war? As rationing set in and the British government urged people to grow potatoes and eat raw turnips (see p. 241), Europe and the world hunkered down for conflict. Now silenced, as television broadcasts had been suspended, Boulestin left England for his native France. Yet a rejoinder did come, from where it might have been least expected—from across the Atlantic.

In December 1940 a magazine publisher, Earle R. MacAusland, brought out a title called *Gourmet*. It was unlike any magazine published previously and seemed to be strikingly inopportune in its timing. America may have been at the tail end of the Depression, but it was on the eve of war. Yet here was a magazine, written with great passion and beautifully illustrated, whose remit was to celebrate civilized and relaxed dining. Here was an entire magazine—forty-eight pages long and with no advertising at first—that eschewed how food was normally treated in the media. In magazines such as the *Ladies' Home Journal, Good Housekeeping* and *Woman's Home Companion* it was all about practicalities. Families and husbands needed feeding; on a good day cooking might serve to reflect glory on the cook, but otherwise it was no more than a domestic chore.

Gourmet had a philosophy that was entirely different. Here was food as luxury, harking back to great foodies like Archestratus (see p. 19). "*Gourmet* is the synonym for the honest seeker of the *summum bonum* of living," pronounced the letter of welcome in the first issue of the magazine. This was not a language cooks of the day expected to hear when dealing with food. Practitioners in the art of being a gourmet, the editorial went on, "will have the eye of an artist, the imagination of a poet, the rhythm of a musician, and the breadth of a sculptor."

Here at last was a riposte to the stuffy Victorians who refused to lower themselves to discuss anything so vulgar as food. And while the editor was a well-traveled and established female cook and cookery writer, Pearl V. Metzelthin, this was a magazine that could appeal just as much to men as to women.

Although MacAusland loved food, he didn't pretend to be an expert and so built a team that included New York chef Louis P. De Gouy as a consultant as well as commissioning articles by writers with a good knowledge of the subject. The first edition, at the cost of 25 cents and dated January 1941, came out at the start of the previous month and was termed the "holiday issue." It included articles on sourcing and eating great pork, travel through the French wine region of Burgundy, recipes and tips for Christmas and the New Year as well as "Food Questions and Answers."

There was a feature on "Famous Chefs of Today" in which readers were introduced to Georges Gonneau, executive chef of New York City's Hôtel Pierre, "one of the masters of gastronomy" who brought the heritage of French cuisine to the city. His menu of grand-sounding Gallic dishes started with "Le Potage Pierre Le Grand," a gamey mushroom soup of which he remarked cryptically: "winter may let you down, but a hot creamy soup is a stilt without a skid."

A feature on the glories of game had an illustration of a chef and three others worshipping at the feet of a statue of a giant pheasant. De Gouy wrote evocatively of a day's shooting, recalling "the tingling morning, your boots crunching over frosty grass while you slowly follow the vibrant noses of your faithful setters, awaiting the moment when the covey rises and whirls away."

The editor Pearl Metzelthin's recipe for creamed oysters—epitomizing the luxurious leanings of the new magazine—appeared in her section "Spécialités de la Maison," while an article on wine advised what to serve with turkey. "A pretty unattractive meat at the best of times, so often dry and tasteless," opined writer Peter Greig. "Turkey calls aloud for a rich red Burgundy or Rhône wine to instill warmth and flavor into the proceedings." He also urged readers to widen their thinking on wine. Think beyond France, he said, "then the real fun begins, to try to find the wine made in America, or Chile, or Australia..."

The content—confident, helpful, inspiring—could come straight out of a good contemporary food magazine. Yet this was the first ever issue of a new genre of food publishing written on the eve of the Second World War. Earle R. MacAusland and his gang were certainly optimists. "Never has there been a time more fitting for a magazine like *Gourmet* to come into being," continued that letter of welcome.

Within months, America had entered the war and embarked on four years of rationing and food shortages. That a magazine freely admitting that it was devoted to "glorious plenty," "culinary hobbies and amusements," "sensuous enjoyment" and "aesthetic well-being" could be founded in and then survive an era of horror, destruction and austerity is extraordinary.

But perhaps it was its pure devotion to a subject that for a long while people could only dream of that enabled it to thrive. Although it claimed that the ideal of being a gourmet "can be found in a thrifty French housewife with her *pot-au-feu* or in a white-capped chef in a skyscraper hotel," its readers were well traveled and upmarket.

As the culinary historian Anne Mendelson has commented: "Hardship fostered a taste for images of a happier past and perhaps a happier future." At precisely the point when America couldn't enjoy great food, it was able at least to read and engage on the subject. And surely the best food magazines are those you can drool over, their aspirational words and pictures from any corner of the world setting your imagination ablaze with delicious ideas regardless of whether in reality you could actually be either bothered or able to cook them.

73

Rice Krispies Treats

AUTHOR: Mildred Day, FROM: the back of a Rice Krispies packet

¾ cup butter
½ teaspoon vanilla
½ lb Fluffi-i-est Marshmallows
1 package Kellogg's Rice Krispies (5½ oz)

YIELD: 16 X 2¼-INCH SQUARES (10 X 10-INCH PAN).

Melt butter and marshmallows in double boiler. Add vanilla; beat well. Put Rice Krispies in large buttered bowl and pour on marshmallow mixture. Press into shallow buttered pan. Cut into squares.

By the 1940s, cereals were pretty well entrenched in the Western diet. It had been many decades since Dr. John Kellogg, assisted by his industrialist brother Will Keith, had developed ready-cooked breakfast cereals for his patients at a sanatorium in the American city of Battle Creek, Michigan. Back in the 1860s, he had wanted to control the diets of the people he was looking after and he encouraged them to start the day with something that was both vegetarian and nutritious.

In the ensuing years, as production methods were refined and streamlined to roast, puff and shred various flakes of corn, the products successfully infiltrated millions of homes. Families could enjoy speedy and delicious breakfasts that needed no cooking and even less thought. Cereals could happily sit in the store-cupboard, ready to be brought to miraculous life with a simple splash of milk, and in time of war it made the rationed pint of milk for each child that bit more exciting.

More and more brands entered the market and the makers had to think of ingenious ways of convincing people to buy their products. Why, thought some, should cereals be regarded as just breakfast foods? If your children were fussy little eaters, but happily wolfed down a bowl of cereal, why not give it to them at other times of day? "He may indicate he's starved," read a poster ad for Rice Krispies in 1933, "but when nourishing food is placed before him his appetite will suddenly wane." If Kellogg's Rice Krispies are turned down, however, "it's a rare event." After all, they didn't just taste good, they could even speak to you. "As they snap, crackle and pop in milk... they seem to say 'Listen, get hungry.' And it's a joy to see [your children] heed this appeal."

What better joy indeed could there be for tired mothers to discover a dish that needed no cooking and that children would eagerly lap up? It was time, felt

Kellogg's, that their cereals be eaten throughout the day. So they boldly declared in their advertising that while they were good at breakfast they were also "particularly appropriate to serve in the evening." The rationale, while they were at it, being that they're "easy to digest and promote restful sleep." Kellogg's then went one step further and, with the use of their own, staffed-up home economist, Mildred Day, conjured up other reasons to buy Rice Krispies.

One of the early adverts for the popular breakfast cereal.

Mildred, who lived to a ripe old age, dying in Minnesota in 1996, was tasked with developing recipes using their cereals. She, reportedly, confined herself to her Kellogg's kitchen for two whole intense weeks before emerging with her groundbreaking "Rice Krispies Treats." Kellogg's liked them so much that in 1941 they put the recipe on every packet.

Mothers could then turn out a "homemade" dish, albeit made from a processed product. It took them yet another step further away from actual ingredients, and seasonality didn't even enter into the equation. The recipes (published not just on packets of cereal but in promotional pamphlets) were also aimed at the children, as something to keep them occupied. These were sweet and tasty dishes that kids could make, cooking now being seen as a separate activity. How far had the world now traveled to arrive at a place where cooking food was not a necessity, merely something to occupy little hands and minds?

Advertising that targeted children was nothing new of course in 1941. Oxo (see p. 205) and Campbell's soup (see p. 216) had both created well-fed youngsters to promote their products; their chubby features representing good health during times of austerity. But Rice Krispies didn't use the image of kids to attract children; they used chirpy and devious-looking elves. Snap, Crackle and Pop urged you to eat their cereal and not for nutritional reasons but because it could be used to make a naughtily sweet and gooey teatime treat. Today, while the elves are still used on the cereal packets, Kellogg's have cut out the middle man in the Rice Krispies Treats–making procedure and sell them ready-made.

Dr. Kellogg would surely not have approved. Although his honest zeal for health had already been discarded by the early 1900s when Kellogg's told their customers that their Rice Krispies "crackle in cream." Not that the reality of the advertising ever stopped Kellogg's from attempting to make out that it never deviated from Dr. Kellogg's original health mission. In 2009 Kellogg's claimed, in very large writing on their packets of Rice Krispies, that their cereal "Now helps you support your child's immunity." Although after facing a barrage of scornful criticism, they backed down and removed the dubious statement.

Back in 1941, Kellogg's were keen to be seen as a wholesome brand that supported the good health of your family. Their products, they declared, were made "in an immaculate sunlit kitchen," as if people might think they were made in dirty, squalid basements deprived of natural light...

Consumers could also write in for "free literature and advice on child feeding." The only downside being that that free literature mainly consisted of a copy of the *Rice Krispies Treats Cookbook*. But don't, they warned, even think of getting in touch if you want proper advice: "Your own physician should be consulted in the event of sickness—ours is in no sense a medical service." The inventor of Rice Krispies may have been obsessed with his patients getting a rounded and nutritious diet. His commercial descendants had rather less honorable intentions.

74

Cinnamon and nutmeg sponge cake

AUTHOR: Bertha Rosa Limpo
FROM: *O Livro de Pantagruel (The Book of Pantagruel)*

250 g flour
250 g brown sugar
1 egg
2 tablespoons butter
200 ml milk
Cinnamon, nutmeg and lemon zest
2 teaspoons baking powder

Mix softened butter with sugar.

Add the egg (I usually beat eggs in advance).

Add cinnamon, nutmeg and lemon zest.

Mix the milk alternately with flour and the baking powder.

And it is now ready to bake. It is not a very big cake so I usually bake it in a 23 x 13 x 7 cm loaf tin.

It was obvious why Nuno Alves Caetano was so popular, why so many small boys and girls wanted to come back to his house after school, rather than anybody else's. For, almost without fail, lined up on the big kitchen table in his home in 1960s Lisbon would be the fruits of his mother's labors. Each day she would test recipes for the family cookbook. And on the days when puddings and cakes were on the agenda, their home, for Nuno's friends, seemed pretty close to paradise.

"So many times I would come home from school and there would be this amazing and large array of desserts all laid out like a feast," recalled Nuno.

Nuno's grandmother was the celebrated Bertha Rosa Limpo, an opera singer who subsequently became the author of Portugal's greatest cooking manual. And whether you were a daughter or a grandson, it was hard to escape the book.

First published in 1945, it became a culinary monster with each new generation adding to it until today it contains some 5,000 recipes.

Nuno's mother, Maria Manuel Limpo Caetano, had taken over the editorship on her mother's death and one day the baton would pass to Nuno himself.

"I don't know what it must have been like to live in a house where recipes weren't tested every day," he joked. "But it was a normal part of our lives. Sometimes the family seemed to work all day. There were new recipes to be tested and old ones that needed to be perfected."

Bertha was born in Mozambique in 1894. This was colonial Portuguese life, and during Bertha's childhood there was absolutely no need for her to get involved in cooking, the shopping and preparation of food all having been left in the hands of the family's large team of servants.

So when she married and settled into a new life with her husband in Lisbon, she was, she once recalled, "unable to even fry an egg." "I hadn't had time to learn how to cook," she said, "and I was embarrassed to say so."

She was, however, extremely young, only fifteen, and so there was plenty of time to become better acquainted with the culinary arts. Considering the heights she subsequently scaled, she has much in common with another teenage bride who went on to have an extraordinary influence on her nation's cuisine. For back in 1533 Catherine de Medici had married Henri, Duc d'Orléans, at the tender age of fourteen (see p. 81) and in later years, as queen of France, she inspired fashion, the arts and, of course, food, her cooks from Florence bringing with them techniques and ideas from Italy that merged with French gastronomy.

Bertha's first talents, though, were not culinary but operatic. In the 1930s and 40s she became a global star, touring the world as singer. And wherever she sang, she dined. To help keep performance nerves at bay, she decided to take the food she ate seriously and started noting down dishes she enjoyed and then asking the various chefs and cooks who worked in the hotels, restaurants and houses she visited if she could write down their recipes. And, as she later wrote, "captivated by the deference of a lady who spoke to them in their own language and shook their hand like a friend," they readily agreed.

By the eve of the Second World War, Bertha had accumulated a very large number of recipes and her house on Lisbon's Avenida António Serpa had become the venue for the most fashionable parties of the day. Guests, be they artists, writers or politicians, gleefully accepted an invitation to her home, safe in the knowledge that they would not just socialize with the great and the good of Lisbon society, but they would eat extremely well too.

So it was perhaps inevitable that her friends would soon try to persuade her to publish her burgeoning recipe collection, in the tradition of many great culinary legends from the Swedish Cajsa Warg in 1755 to the American Irma Rombauer in 1931 (see p. 228), who also owed it to their friends for talking them into publishing their recipes. It seems that Bertha didn't need much persuasion, however, even if people might at first ask: "Is she a singer or a cook? Does she compose music or stews?" For her nation clearly needed her. As she wrote in the introduction to the first edition of her book, "there is a general ignorance in this country about cooking and frankly this embarrasses me!"

Comprising around 600 recipes, the book also contained instructions on how to use some of the new equipment that was starting to revolutionize kitchens in Europe and America in the mid-twentieth century. Cookers, fridges, mixing machines and toasters were quickly spreading and Bertha thought it sensible to explain how one should use them. This was handy not just in case you had lost the instructions to your

"New World" Regulo-Controlled Gas Cooker (see p. 225), but because such appliances were discussed in nontechnical language that everyone could understand.

A fridge, Bertha said, was "the most valuable jewel one can acquire" and as well as chilling food, it was important, she felt, that you knew exactly how to arrange your vegetables and salads in it. Diagrams aided her explanations on what to put where and

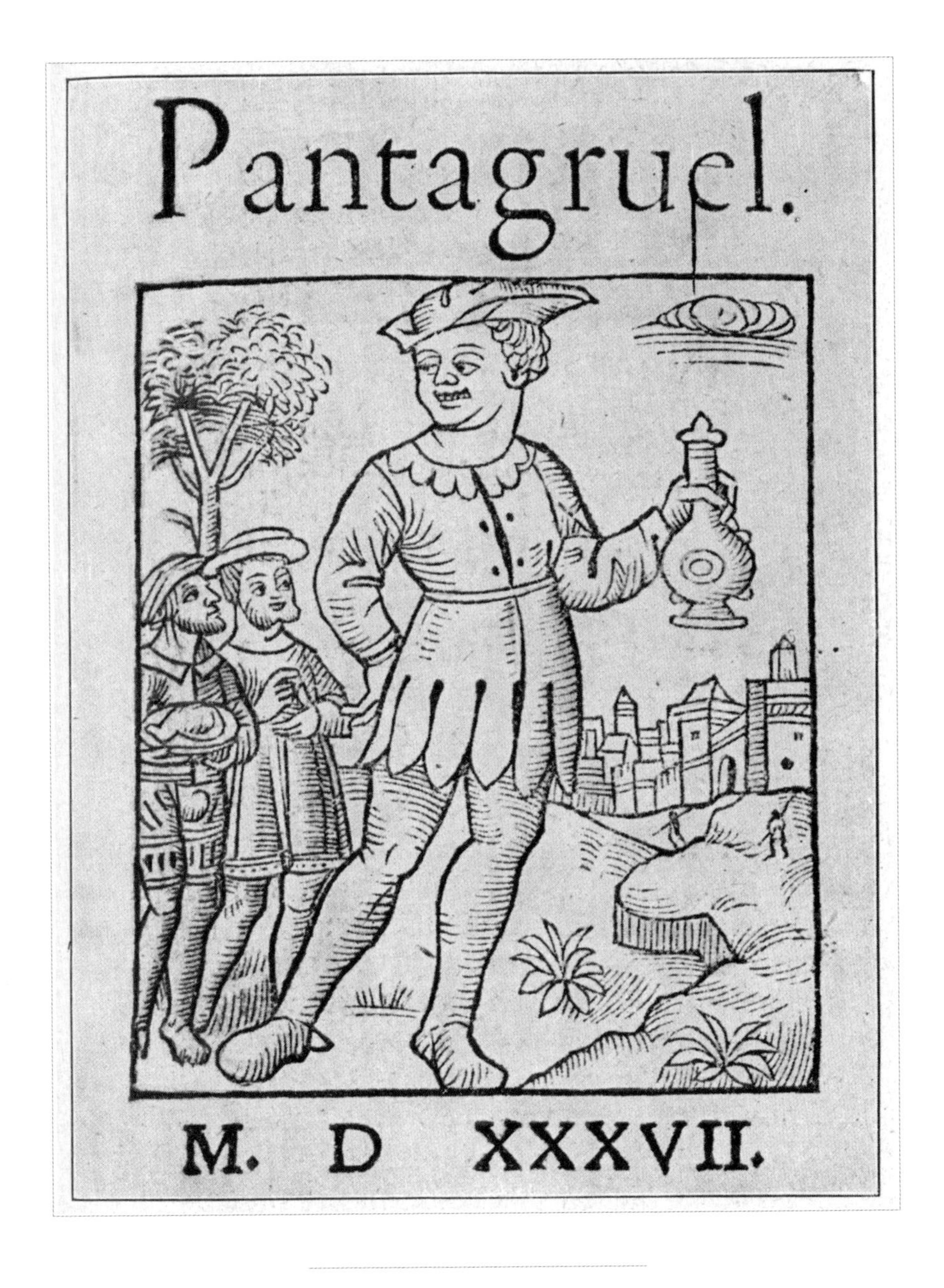

Pantagruel by Francois Rabelais - Engraved frontispiece to the 1537 series. Son of Gargantua. Two giants traveling in a world.

these were all in addition to copious light-hearted illustrations by the Portuguese artist António Serra Alves Mendes—otherwise known as Méco—which portrayed the housewife engaged in various domestic pursuits.

The book was an immediate hit, selling out in the first forty-three days, and a second edition quickly followed.

Bertha's daughter and son were cajoled into working on it, the latter a filmmaker and gourmet who introduced new sections on spices, table decorations and wine. Soon it was on the wedding list of every young bride. Today there is barely a house in Portugal that doesn't have a copy of this now chunky tome. And it's never hard to spot because of its size, with its thousands of recipes from not just Portugal but all over the world. In addition to dishes from Africa and the Middle East, there are mussels from Belgium, for example, snails from France, scones from England and even a recipe for "black velvet" (a mixture of stout and champagne) from Ireland.

Bertha named her work *The Book of Pantagruel* after the greedy fictional giant from the series of novels *The Life of Gargantua and of Pantagruel* written in the sixteenth century by François Rabelais. Pantagruel's main character trait was that he liked to try new things and it was in this spirit of wanting to encourage her fellow Portuguese that she published the book.

Portuguese cuisine had absorbed many influences over the ages, from wheat, olives and garlic brought by the Romans, and Moorish specialities introduced by the Arabs, to spices transported home by explorer Vasco da Gama from India and the Far East.

The melting pot of flavors appealed to Bertha and is represented in her book alongside traditional Portuguese fare, for she felt not enough people knew how to cook national dishes properly, be they fish casseroles or the popular kale, potato and sausage broth known as caldo verde.

She also acknowledges her fellow countrymen's sweet tooth, indulged since sugar cane was planted on the island of Madeira by Portuguese settlers during the fifteenth century.

The recipe she includes for cinnamon and nutmeg sponge cake, presented at the top of this chapter, merges that Portugese love of sweetness with a cinnamon-infused Moorish influence, although it's not known exactly where the dish originally came from.

When Bertha visited a restaurant and asked for the recipe of a dish she liked, no chef could refuse the demands of this culinary queen, even if she would publish it without any reference to the person who actually crafted it.

But she did at least try it out at home first, as she assured readers in her introduction.

"I think the success of the book is principally because all of the 5,000 recipes have been tested by mother, my brother and me," her daughter Maria once said. For which generations of Portuguese continue to be grateful.

75

Victoria sandwich cake

AUTHOR: Unnamed home economist
FROM: *All About Your New Kenwood Chef*

USING K BEATER
6 oz butter
6 oz caster sugar
3 eggs
6 oz self-raising flour

FLAVOUR SUGGESTIONS
VANILLA:
½ tsp vanilla essence

CHOCOLATE:
1 tbsp chocolate powder

COFFEE:
1 tbsp instant coffee powder

ORANGE:
1 tsp grated rind

LEMON:
1 tsp grated rind

First warm the K beater and bowl thoroughly. Place sugar and butter in the bowl and switch to a minimum speed.

When ingredients have combined, increase to speed 2 and beat until light and fluffy, similar in texture to whipped cream. This is very important. The time taken is usually 2–3 minutes but varies according to the temperature of the fat.

Break in the first egg and beat until the mixture returns to a very fluffy texture. Add the second, and the third egg in the same way. A little flour may be added with each egg if desired, but is not necessary, as mixture will not curdle unless eggs are too cold.

Reduce speed to a minimum and tip in all the sifted flour. Switch off immediately the flour is incorporated. This takes only a few seconds. Over beating at this stage will spoil the cake. Using the spatula, turn the mixture into two greased 8" sandwich tins. Bake in a moderately hot oven (375°F) for 25 minutes approximately. When cooled sandwich together with jam or one of the fillings [from the same book]. Dust lightly with icing sugar and decorate as required.

It was while she was working for the Harrods Food Service Bureau in 1947 that Marguerite Patten (see p. 239) was summoned to the electrical department. As she later recalled: “I took a phone call that, although I did not know it at the time, would revolutionize life for the home cook.”

She scampered away from the Food Halls to see the managing director of the store, who introduced her to a man who, she later recalled, “had film star looks.” At his side was an electric mixing device. He walked her through how it worked, showing off its various features with great pride. Her job would be to demonstrate it to the public. Harrods had an exclusive deal to stock the first batch of these machines and the handsome man they did the deal with was one Kenneth Wood.

Patten did some homework and then started her demos. The Kenwood Chef quickly sold out. She gave more demos; she even filled the auditorium at the London Palladium one evening. (There wasn't much on telly in those days.) Soon other stores, such as Selfridges, were stocking the machines. Indeed the craze has barely relented and today, somewhere in the world, someone buys a Kenwood appliance every two seconds.

Its arrival on the scene, however, was particularly timely. Social and technological advances had removed domestic servants from the home, replacing them with fridges and modern cookers (see pp. 222 and 225). But women must have felt a little sore at the deal. They might have had a shiny new friend in the kitchen who made ice and kept food nicely chilled, while gas and electricity entailed less heaving in of coal and wood, but they still had to cook—to chop and stir and mix and strain and beat and whisk. And much of this carried out by those who never even had to do it in the first place.

Help did arrive, however, for the American housewife at least. The firm KitchenAid was the earliest to develop mixers, albeit for factories at first. But models were gradually developed for domestic use and by the 1930s they began to appear in many homes across America. But it took an Englishman to develop the idea in Britain. And while many people will have heard of—and indeed own—a Kenwood, only a few of them may realize that it is named after its inventor Kenneth Wood, who died in 1997, aged eighty-one.

Wood developed his own version in 1947, in a small workshop next door to a fishmonger's in Woking in Surrey. He had just a few hundred pounds in capital and very few backers. Even those who supplied him with parts had little faith in his invention and insisted he pay for what he needed up front. But Wood stuck to his guns, spurred on by what he had seen in food factories, where time-saving, high-tech equipment was being used on an industrial scale. By contrast, as he once commented: "When the whistle went [the workers] went home and in the kitchen stepped back fifty years. I saw that a day would come when women would refuse to go on living in the past. Why should they work in this century and live in the near-Victorian age?"

Although Wood's device looked surprisingly similar to the KitchenAid, it was sturdier. Its bulk and heavy weight were reassuring and early users were mesmerized (as indeed Kenwood virgins still are today) by its "planetary action"—at seeing the beater rotating as it travels around the bowl.

With its bulletproof ruggedness, the Kenwood Chef was the perfect postwar gift in "an era of rationing and kitchen drudgery," as Marguerite Patten has described the 1940s. The machine was a godsend to all those busily baking with their meager rations. It chopped and kneaded and peeled and mixed. Indeed it added a glamorous edge to cooking. For the first time it was possible to whisk up soufflés in seconds, not to mention meringues, mousses and cheesecakes. Cooks no longer needed elbow grease; all that was required was the flick of a switch.

In the subsequent decade, with the help of a new breed of TV chefs—led by the likes of Fanny Craddock who gladly used the latest equipment and reveled in post-rationing freedom—cooking with genuinely time-saving devices made the kitchen an exciting place.

Within just eight years, Wood had 400 employees and a turnover of £1.5 million, and he was soon busy buying up other companies that made household equipment. His firm turned out liquidizers and steam irons, knife-sharpeners and mini rotisseries and by his early forties he was a millionaire. Having successfully traded in Europe and particularly France—where they loved Kenwoods for making mayonnaise—he took his mixer to Canada where U.S. products held sway.

There, he employed door-to-door salesmen who would use the ruse that they were consumer-testing a new brand of powdered milk. While the rehydrated milk chilled in the fridge, the salesman would tentatively ask whether he could display his Kenwood mixer. "We started selling mixers," recalled Wood, "but we also sold a hell of a lot of milk."

He was a man of little formal education, having joined the merchant navy as an apprentice navigator—much to his mother's horror and only two years after his father had died—at the age of fourteen. A born entrepreneur, he bought and sold products from port to port—the likes of leather and tobacco—and traveled abroad for four years. On leaving the navy, he enrolled in night school to study electrical engineering and accountancy before an early career of installing and fixing television sets was cut short by the war.

After the war, he considered going into reconstruction. But he and Roger Laurence, with whom he'd founded a company, Woodlau Industries, didn't have enough funds. "We only had £800," he said, "so we made a toaster instead." Wood and Laurence parted company soon afterwards but it's intriguing to think that, had they continued to work together, couples assembling their wedding list might even now be asking for a Woodlau.

The Kenwood Chef followed the toaster, ushering in a new era of labor-saving devices. It played its part in marital harmony and, rather more importantly, was the ideal machine with which to make that post-war favorite, the Victoria sponge cake.

76

Cassoulet toulousain

AUTHOR: Elizabeth David, FROM: *A Book of Mediterranean Food*

- **2 lb haricot beans (medium-size white beans, not the very small ones which take twice as long to cook),**
- **1 lb pork,**
- **1 lb breast of mutton,**
- **¼ lb rind of ham or bacon,**
- **1 whole garlic sausage,**
- **½ lb preserved goose,**
- **6 oz chopped onion,**
- **3 oz lard or goose fat**

The beans must be soaked overnight, and cooked in an earthenware casserole in the oven with the onion and the bacon rind, and the knuckle of ham, covered with water. They will take from 4 to 5 hours in a slow oven. The pork is roasted separately, and the mutton browned in its own fat. When the beans are nearly done, the meat, the preserved goose, the bacon, and the sausage are cut into convenient pieces and put in alternate layers with the beans. The casserole is then returned to the oven, without the lid, to finish cooking. A crust forms on top of the beans; stir this into the beans, and leave until a second crust has formed; proceed in the same manner, and when the third crust has formed the cassoulet should be ready.

Rationing in Britain still had another three years to run when Elizabeth David published *A Book of Mediterranean Food* and food culture was not exactly at its zenith. David had returned from traveling around the sunny climes of the Mediterranean and the food that greeted her on her return was less than inspiring. "There was flour and water soup seasoned solely with pepper; bread and gristle rissoles; dehydrated onions and carrots; corned beef toad-in-the-hole. I need not go on," she later reflected. To restore her own sanity and bring some of the sunshine that she so craved, into her life at least, she sat down to write her first book.

To those who had a desire for better food, who yearned for a time when the markets would offer a plethora of delicious ingredients rather than not much of what they didn't want, *Mediterranean Food* was a breath of warm, comforting air. David wrote of markets whose stalls were piled high with "pimentos, aubergines, tomatoes, olives, melons, figs and limes." She described the wonders of seeing shiny fish, unfamiliar cheeses and butchers' counters "festooned with every imaginable portion of the inside of every edible animal."

Except that surely this was torture for a country in postwar rationed purdah? Mrs. David might have had the privilege of seeing and tasting "the oil, the saffron, the garlic, the pungent local wines, the aromatic perfume of rosemary, wild tarragon and basil drying in the kitchen..." but what about the poor beleaguered British housewives deprived of such delights?

In fact, they loved the book. Its refreshing tone and evocation of warm and pleasant climates strongly appealed. David wrote about things that might not have been quite within reach and were unfamiliar to many, but it enabled them to dream. As her editor, Jill Norman, once said: "She had a way of capturing the imagination. In the Fifties, there wasn't much else you could do with your rationing—no basil, no tomatoes, no olive oil—except to imagine." That Elizabeth David suggested they think of such things was food for the spirit if not the body. And it also softened them up for when rationing did end and a wider range of ingredients started to return to the shops.

David was quite aware that rationing would not make her book the most immediately useful, but she did also believe that if you looked hard enough ingredients were to be found and that many of her recipes were, in fact, achievable. But then she was also, unabashedly, talking to a well-off middle- and upper-middle-class audience that thought and spoke the way she did. Indeed, she went further in suggesting that people in London might actually find it easier to source Mediterranean ingredients than the inhabitants of Greece, or Italy, might themselves.

Provisions were, she said, "not only easier to come by in London than the materials of plain English cooking but sometimes more plentiful than they are abroad." So she urged people not to be despondent. "Olive oil is good...and plentiful," she wrote, as was cheap wine for cooking. "There is a fishmonger in Brewer Street who sells cuttlefish and octopus...Fresh tarragon can be bought at Harrods...In Selfridges food department there is a display of spices which rivals an Eastern spice market." And there was no excuse not to procure the likes of rosemary or fennel because "everybody knows somebody who grows herbs in their garden."

Whether the postwar privations were being exaggerated, or Elizabeth David lived in an elite foodie fantasy world, is hardly the point, though, because what she said and the way she wrote it had the effect of lifting people out of the culinary dark ages. Her natural and evocative prose style chimed with her contemporaries, speaking to them in a completely new way. She discarded the practicalities of recipe writing, frequently ignoring the convention of listing ingredients before the method.

Her writing alone made the reader salivate. "I hope to give you some idea of the lovely cookery of those regions to people who do not already know them," she wrote, "and to stir the memories of those who have eaten this food on its native shores, and who would like sometimes to bring the flavor of those blessed lands of sun and sea and olive trees into their English kitchens." In the ensuing years, her books—from *French Provincial Cooking* to *An Omelette and a Glass of Wine*—inspired countless cooks to think beyond the shores of Britain and, in particular, bring to their kitchens the spirit of down-to-earth regional French cooking.

Her own inspiration had started when she was sent to Paris on an exchange program. One of four daughters of a Tory MP, she was, as she said herself, "Torn, most willingly, from an English boarding school at the age of sixteen to live with a middle-class family in

Passy." The family, who resided on the Parisian Right Bank, was, she said, "exceptionally greedy and exceptionally well fed." The mother, a rotund woman with a purple face and a shock of white hair, would shop for the family's long-suffering cook in Les Halles, bringing back large bags of food and "looking as if she was about to have a stroke."

The young Elizabeth quickly made friends with her new schoolmates and with a definite naughty streak would hang out after school in restaurants and cafés that were not on her guardian family's list of approved establishments. Released from the dining hall of her English school, it dawned on her how awful food was back home. "Nothing will surely ever taste so hateful as nursery tapioca, or the appalling boiled cod of schooldays," she recalled. Returning home, she realized she had been instilled with a dash of French food culture, her young mind frequently drifting off to dream of the smells, sights and tastes of the markets, cafés and restaurants. It was "unlike anything I had known before."

This teenage taste for France set her pulse racing and, after a brief spell with the Oxford Repertory Company in her early twenties, her naughty side once again came to the fore and she ran off to France with a lover. She spent time in Greece and then in Egypt, where she met and married an Indian army officer, Anthony David. But after the war, having traveled with him to New Delhi, she became ill and returned to Britain alone. Although her husband did return later, their marriage was open, at least from her perspective, and she didn't let it get in the way of other romantic dalliances and, more importantly, her travel. The pair, who never had children, finally divorced in 1960.

Perhaps it was her complicated personal life that made her so private, unwilling to see it unravel by giving interviews. "Elizabeth hated performing and hated public appearances," said Jill Norman. But she didn't shy from expressing her opinions in print, of course, particularly on subjects which caused her irritation. Keen to share her love of French food, it annoyed her to hear of disappointment experienced by the English in France. "Good food is there for those who look for it," she wrote in *French Provincial Cooking* in 1960. "Bad food, too, and rather more than there used to be, but if one gets it, one very often only has oneself to blame." Using a few simple tricks—like not arriving in a town too late and making friends with the patron before ordering—would often prevent culinary horrors from reaching the table, she suggested. It was also necessary to disabuse the French of the disparaging view many of them had of the English. "English people are generally thought only to want beefsteaks or fried eggs and chips," she wrote.

The French had not allowed their food culture to disappear although, like Britain, the country had also suffered from the ravages of two world wars and increases in the cost of living. Yet that and the detrimental effect transportation and preservation had on seasonal food had not affected France as it had the UK. Largely, she argued, because France was still a mainly agricultural society. Good cooks were supported, for example, by good local farmers and butchers.

Yet all was not lost for Britain. "Although there is not such a profusion of raw materials in England," she wrote in *French Country Cooking* in 1951, "we still have much greater gastronomic resources than the national cookery would lead one to believe." She felt that the modern world could actually help rather than hinder good

The front jacket illustration (shown) for the first edition of Elizabeth David's A Book of Mediterranean Food *(1950) is by the artist John Minton and the book was published by John Lehmann Ltd.*

cooking. "Rationing, the disappearance of servants, and the bad and expensive meals in restaurants have led the Englishwoman to take a far greater interest in food than was generally considered polite," she argued.

Her stick-and-carrot approach clearly worked as her audiences warmed to her straight-talking yet elegant prose. "Good food is always a trouble and its preparation should be regarded as a labor of love," she implored, adding that what was needed was "a devoted, a determined, spirit, but not, it is hoped, one of martyrdom."

Thousands have subsequently aspired to that perfect condition where the labor of cooking becomes one of sheer enjoyment. Some achieve it and those who don't are nonetheless quite happy to climb between the sheets with an Elizabeth David perched safely on the bedside table. Indeed, her cassoulet recipe—"of all the great dishes which French regional cookery has produced... perhaps the most typical of true country food," according to David—is as delicious to read as it is to cook.

77

Boeuf bourgignon

(Beef stew in red wine, with bacon, onions and mushrooms)

AUTHORS: Simone Beck, Louisette Bertholle and Julia Child
FROM: *Mastering the Art of French Cooking*

FOR 6 PEOPLE

A 6 oz chunk of streaky bacon
Remove rind, cut bacon into lardons (sticks, ¼ inch thick and 1½ inches long). Simmer rind and bacon for 10 minutes in 2½ pints of water. Drain and dry.

Preheat oven to 450°F, Mark 8.

A 9 to 10 in fireproof casserole 3 in deep
1 tbsp olive oil or cooking oil
Sauté the bacon in the oil over moderate heat for 2 to 3 minutes to brown lightly. Remove to a side dish with slotted spoon. Leave casserole aside. Reheat until fat is almost smoking before you sauté the beef.

3 lb lean stewing steak cut into 2 in cubes (see preceding list of cuts)
Dry the beef; it will not brown if it is damp. Sauté it, a few pieces at a time, in the hot oil and bacon fat until nicely browned on all sides. Add it to the bacon.

1 sliced carrot
1 sliced onion
In the same fat, brown the sliced vegetables. Pour out the sautéing fat.

1 tsp salt
¼ tsp pepper
1 oz flour
Return the beef and bacon to the casserole and toss with the salt and pepper. Then sprinkle on the flour and toss again to coat the beef lightly with the flour. Place casserole uncovered in middle position of preheated oven for 4 minutes. Toss the meat and return to oven for a further 4 minutes more. (This browns the flour and covers the meat with a light crust.) Remove casserole, and turn oven down to 325°F, Mark 2.

1¼ pts of a full-bodied, young red wine such as one of those suggested for serving, or a Chianti
¾ to 1 pt brown beef stock or beef bouillon
1 tbsp tomato paste
2 cloves mashed garlic
½ tsp thyme
A crumbled bay leaf
The blanched bacon rind
Stir in the wine, and enough stock or bouillon so that the meat is barely covered. Add the tomato paste, garlic, herbs, and bacon rind. Bring to simmering point on top of the stove. Then cover the casserole and place in lower part of preheated oven. Regulate heat so that liquid simmers very slowly for 3 to 4 hours. The meat is done when a fork pierces it easily.

18 to 24 small onions, brown-braised in stock
1 lb quartered fresh mushrooms sautéed in butter
While the beef is cooking, prepare the onions and mushrooms. Leave them aside until needed.

When the meat is tender, pour the contents of the casserole into a sieve placed over a saucepan. Wash out the casserole and return the beef and bacon to it. Distribute the cooked onions and mushrooms over the meat.

Skim fat off the sauce. Simmer sauce for a minute or two, skimming off additional fat as it rises. You should have about 1 pint of sauce thick enough to coat a spoon lightly. If too thin, boil it down rapidly. If too thick, mix in a few tablespoons of stock or bouillon. Taste carefully for seasoning. Pour the sauce over the meat and vegetables.

Recipe may be completed in advance to this point.

Parsley sprigs

FOR IMMEDIATE SERVING. Cover the casserole and simmer for 2 to 3 minutes, basting the meat and vegetables with the sauce several times. Serve in its casserole, or arrange the stew on a dish surrounded with potatoes, noodles, or rice, and decorated with parsley.

FOR SERVING LATER. When cold, cover and refrigerate. About 15 to 20 minutes before serving, bring to simmering point, cover, and simmer very slowly for 10 minutes, occasionally basting the meat and vegetables with the sauce.

It may have still been the early days of American television, but it felt a bit bonkers all the same. The show was *I've Been Reading,* normally featuring a studious get-together of talking heads discussing the latest literature. If the program looked different it was because the production team were filming from a chapel as the studio had burned down the previous week. And as the usual tally of serious male authors was not available, the only guest, on this February day in 1962, was a lady. Her name was Julia Child. She didn't own a television, so hadn't seen the show. Nevertheless she decided not just to bring the book she was promoting but, as she said, "to liven things up," a hot plate, a huge copper bowl and a giant whisk.

As the program began, she more or less took over. At six feet and two inches tall, she towered over the presenter, Boston College English professor, Dr. P. Albert Duhamel. She set about madly beating her eggs, speaking loudly in her shrill Bostonian drawl. Backstage the producer, Russell Morash, sat bolt upright: "I thought to myself," he later recalled: "'Who is this mad woman cooking an omelette on a book-reviewing program?'"

The viewers wrote in demanding more: they wanted a cookery show presented by her. They soon got what they asked for and the series *The French Chef,* directed and produced by Russell Morash, was born. Its star was neither French, nor a chef. A studio, built to accommodate her formidable height, was designed like a home kitchen. To the modern viewer it feels like a pastiche. With quirky, quaint *Blackadder*-style music, one half expects this clumsy, blousy housewife to reveal herself as a female impersonator. Was this the real inspiration for Dame Edna Everage?

"How about a dinner in half a minute?" she trills at the start of an early broadcast. "How about a last-minute dinner party? For 300 people? What about an omelette?" As she whisked and stirred, she splattered ingredients onto her shirt, she dropped spatulas into mixing machines, spilt the contents of pans on her hob. Bonkers she may have been but she was the best kind of teacher: real, natural and entertaining. She cooked and talked with charm, her unscripted dialogue naturally engaging. If she tossed a pancake onto her hob, it simply served to demonstrate a vital point about cooking. "If you're going to have a sense of fear or failure," she would say, "you're never going to learn to cook."

She deconstructed and demystified the seemingly difficult art of French cooking for the American public. "A soufflé is only a thick white sauce with a flavoring like cheese or mushroom," she said, "and into that you put stiff beaten egg whites which automatically puff up giving you a soufflé."

Her show became the longest-running program on U.S. television as she turned French cooking into prime-time entertainment, and across America she had legions of devoted fans, all captivated by this tall, exuberant woman in her fifties who would assure them that making lobster bisque was "as easy as toast." "I fell in love with the public and the public fell in love with me," she reflected in old age.

The book that she had been plugging on that first TV show was *Mastering the Art of French Cooking.* It was a thick, chunky tome with long and detailed recipes. Recipes were long, explained Child, when they needed to be. Indeed they were, as

American chef Julia Child taught French cooking to Middle America through her books and on her TV series The French Chef.

this chapter's boeuf bourgignon demonstrates. It's very, very long, but then it's also completely accurate and doesn't leave the novice cook having to read between the lines or clutch for assumed—but not yet attained—knowledge. Cooking was not like free-form jazz and recipes must be followed to the letter.

It was the product of ten long years of work that had begun in France where she had lived with her husband. Until she had arrived in France nothing in her life, as she put it herself, had turned her on. Brought up in Pasadena, California, she was the oldest of three very tall siblings—so tall that her mother once said she had "given birth to 18 feet of children." Her mother never cooked: "she could do Welsh rarebit," Child recalled, but "that was about it." Like most moderately well-off Americans at the time, the family had servants—maids and a cook. "They were cheap and you housed them yourself," she said. "But they all disappeared in the 30s."

The young Child led "a leisurely butterfly life." "In those days women weren't taken seriously," she said. They were "just brood mares." She acted occasionally—"I enjoyed the theater, I'm a natural ham"—although of the kind of roles she played she said, "I was usually something like a fish."

Put into the typing pool—with her fellow Middle American lady fishes—she then found herself, come the Second World War, recruited to the Far East. Filing and typing for the organization that was to become the CIA, she took a longboat to India and ended up in Ceylon, now Sri Lanka, where outside of her filing duties, she found a husband—Paul Cushing Child, a graphic designer making maps and charts for the army—and after the war they returned to the U.S. to marry.

It was when his job took him to France in the early 1950s that her life turned a real corner. Their first meal was in a restaurant near Rouen in northern France. She never forgot that lunch of oysters, pressed duck with a red burgundy sauce and then little French cakes. "I was hooked from then on," she recalled. It was a world away from what she termed "the American food of ladies' magazines"—ready cake mixes and Jell-O-branded no-bake cream pies—of a culture where traditional cooking had surrendered to modern technology.

She fell in love with French food because it was "a real art form, with a history and a background." In Paris she joined Le Cordon Bleu (see p. 190) and then with some new French friends set up a small teaching business for non-French-speaking Americans. Those two friends were Simone Beck and Louisette Bertholle and they had started compiling a book of recipes. "They had a collaborator who I was rather sorry to hear about," she reflected, "and then he died so I took over."

Beck and Bertholle had been given a $75 advance for their book, which Child wrote, as the English speaker. It was a long-term project with no commercial aim. After ten years the work was complete but the publishers were horrified. "Much too long and too complicated" was the response. Yet Child was unapologetic. "There was nobody who had long recipes the way we did," she said. "I insisted things turn out well. [Our] recipes told you exactly how to cook."

Back in America, Child was introduced to another publisher, Alfred A. Knopf, a well-established New York firm, who bought the book. The print-run was small and had it not been for Child's appearance on *I've Been Reading* it might have languished on a few kitchen shelves before fading into obscurity. Instead it became one of the most influential cookbooks in American history, feeding the *Zeitgeist* in the early 1960s, helped along by President Kennedy's wife Jacqueline and her infectious love of all things French.

"This is a book for the servantless cook," the foreword proclaims, the recipes achievable with ingredients bought from supermarkets:

> We have purposefully omitted cobwebbed bottles, the *patron* in his white cap bustling among his sauces, anecdotes about charming little restaurants with gleaming napery, and so forth. Such romantic interludes, so it seems to us, put French cooking into a "never-never" land instead of the Here, which is happily available to everybody.

This seems a deliberate slap in the face of Elizabeth David (see p. 256), who had been wowing British readers with just those interludes. Not that it stopped her from acquiring a copy of the book (the copy that I saw, at the Guildhall Library in the City of London, had her name in the front!).

Julia Child taught French cooking to Middle America with attainable passion. "I find that if people aren't interested in food, I'm not very much interested in them," she once reflected. "They seem to lack something in the way of personality." But not everyone fell for her, hook, line and sinker. However helpful and inspiring she might have been, there was still a growing number of American housewives fed up with the constant burden of culinary expectation.

Their catharsis was to come from American author Peg Bracken, who caused almost as much of a stir with her *I Hate to Cook Cookbook,* written at the same time as Child was putting the finishing touches to her tome. "Some women, it is said, like to cook. This book is not for them," Bracken wrote with refreshing honesty. And then as if she had Julia Child's volume directly in her sights, she continued: "Worst of all, there are the big fat cookbooks that tell you everything about everything. For one thing they contain too many recipes. Just look at all the things you can do with a chop, and aren't going to."

For those unsure of their culinary abilities, Peg Bracken offered some salient advice: "When you hate to cook you should never accept an invitation to dinner," she said. "Sooner or later, unless you have luckily disgraced yourself at their home . . . you will have to return the invitation." Mind you, her recipes could quickly turn you into a social pariah. She suggests, for example, that "a lemon slice isn't the only thing you can float on soup. There's popcorn . . . it looks pretty and is easier than croutons."

Peg Bracken may have finally given voice to the festering burden of homemaker angst but Julia Child would have quickly slapped her down with her big whisk and told her to get a grip.

78

Watercress soup for one

AUTHOR: Jean Nidetch, FROM: *Weight Watchers Cookbook*

Combine in blender and blend until smooth, about 1 minute: ¾ cup water, chicken bouillon cube or envelope of instant chicken broth mix, and ¼ bunch watercress or firmly packed young spinach (remove hard rib). Heat to boiling point and serve immediately or chill.

Perhaps it was only inevitable that humankind, having emerged from the privations of the Second World War and prolonged rationing, gorged itself and then had to go on a diet.

By the 1960s those poor, manipulated housewives must have felt they'd been sold a pup. Fridges instead of servants, that newfangled equipment and glittering processed food all promising to lead them to some domestic nirvana. Then one day, having prepped that special dinner for their expectant husbands, they find they can't fit into that dress he so likes. As the twentieth century progressed, the Pied Piper of domestic bliss played out the sweet tune of dieting. Obesity did not of course premiere in the last century but an obsession with it did, beginning in the 1960s.

There were some notable self-proclaimed experts in much earlier years. Back in 1927, for instance, Dr. Thomas Short, through his treatise *The Causes and Effects of Corpulence,* had advised that the overweight should move to more arid climes as fat people seemed to be more prevalent near swamps. He also argued, citing the usefulness of soap in emulsifying fats, that those who "labor involuntarily under the Incumbrances of Flesh and Blood" should use it both internally and externally. In other words, if you're fat, eat soap as well as washing with it. But he did also offer some rather less eccentric, and more helpful, advice about "keeping the eyes open and the mouth shut."

Further back in time, the Victorian era may have had its fair share of quack doctors but there was common-sense advice from the coffin-maker William Banting. By the 1860s he had eaten so much that he couldn't tie his shoelaces and had to walk down the stairs backwards. He took himself in hand, however, and his *Letter on Corpulence* outlines his diet of lean meat, dry toast, unsweetened fruit and green vegetables, which, he reported, had been "simply miraculous." While he forbade champagne, port or beer, he also offered the following words of wisdom: "I do not recommend every corpulent man to rush headlong into such a change of diet, but to act advisedly and after full consultation with a physician."

Rather less credible was the San Francisco art dealer Horace Fletcher who, in 1903, had advocated his technique of "Fletcherizing," which entailed chewing food thirty-two times—one for each tooth in his head—before spitting it out. The secret being never to swallow anything. "Nature will castigate those who don't masticate," he pronounced. This was little better than the belt-driven fat-massagers that were being developed before the turn of the century, promising, literally, to shake off the excess pounds. Regardless of their value, such devices persisted for many decades.

By the 1950s, diet products were beginning to appear on the shelves of supermarkets. Actresses such as Joan Caulfield were hired to promote the likes of the appetite-suppressant Ayds. You scoffed these before mealtimes—they were available in chocolate, butterscotch, caramel or peanut butter—with Ms. Caulfield proclaiming: "We all agree that Ayds is the most wholesome and natural way to a good figure." What these wholesome and natural sweets actually contained was a chemical called benzocaine, later used to bulk up cocaine. As it is a mild anesthetic, this might explain why cocaine users find that it numbs their gums prior to their high and the discovery of miraculous, hitherto unrevealed insights into the human condition. Come the mid-1980s, however, Ayds suffered an image problem and the product disappeared from the scene when the same-sounding acronym for acquired immune deficiency syndrome was discovered to bring about rather more drastic weight loss.

Alongside appetite suppressants came diet drinks, shakes and other foods. There was Diet Delight, for example, a range of tinned fruit cocktails. "Boy, does that look good," says the man in the early 1960s TV ad as his wife places a bowl of tinned fruit salad in front of him, "but Honey, what'll those calories do to my waistline?" "Relax," she replies. "It's Diet Delight. Has the same flavors as ordinary canned fruit but only half the calories." The man would have found his supper dessert rather less appealing had he known, as studies showed at the end of the decade, that the artificial sweetener, cyclamate, used in the fruit cocktails, gave bladder cancer to laboratory rats.

Mainstream drinks were also latching onto the diet product frenzy. "There's no waistline worry with Coke, you know," a thirsty housewife chirps in another ad as she takes a swig of Coca-Cola. "Actually this individually sized bottle has no more calories than half a grapefruit."

It was in the midst of this cacophony of hype, in 1961, that real New York housewife Jean Nidetch found herself struggling to deal with her 214 pounds of weight. She had tried all the pills, drinks and flesh-wobbling machines. But what she hadn't tried was sharing her problems with like-minded souls in the fashion of Alcoholic Anonymous, which had successfully been helping drunks since 1935.

Nidetch gathered some weight-weary soulmates at her home in Queens and together they battled the bulge. She successfully lost 72 pounds, claiming that much of the credit for her triumph lay in the encouragement she had received at those meetings. Others in the group also lost weight and word spread. Soon there wasn't enough room in her house and before long she and two friends, Al and Felice Lippert, commercialized the concept as Weight Watchers.

They set up their business above a movie theater in Little Neck, New York State, Nidetch intending to promote the diet she had been given by the New York City Department of Health. Expecting fifty to come to their first meeting, they got 400. And in due course members discovered that, like Nidetch, it was the prospect of sharing weight-loss goals with the group, more than the actual diet, that was helping. Those who achieved their ultimate target were then given a maintenance program, to keep any weight gain at bay.

Soon there were three meetings per day, then meeting leaders—who had to lose weight and keep it off to gain the position—were being recruited from all over the city. In just two years Weight Watchers franchises had sprouted across America, spreading to Canada, Puerto Rico, Israel and Great Britain. These days 100 million people attend weekly meetings in thirty countries and the company, having been sold twice, has annual retail sales of over £4 billion.

Joan Caulfield was hired to advertise Ayds, a 1950s diet product.

Nidetch blamed her own weight problems partly on her mother. "I don't really remember, but I'm positive that whenever I cried, my mother gave me something to eat," she once said. Her own recipes, meanwhile, acted as appetite suppressants in their own right. One Weight Watchers cookbook features "Golden Glow Salad," for example, which combines gelatin, bits of grapefruit and orange, lemon juice, sugar substitute, vinegar, salt and cabbage with boiling water. Combined with a steamed chicken dish served on spinach and covered in a fruit sauce, these constitute what the book calls "legal" portions. Still, the watercress soup is not too horrific, as long as there's plenty of cheese and bread to go with it.

While women were being recruited to Weight Watchers, men were offered, in 1964, *The Drinking Man's Diet*. This was the self-help book large-girthed businessmen had been waiting for. There were wine recommendations with each dish and the book promised a diet that would let you have "two martinis before lunch and a thick steak generously spread with Sauce Béarnaise, so that you [can] make your sale in a relaxed atmosphere and go back to the office without worrying about having gained so much as an ounce." Someone could of course have published a book saying that the only way to lose weight was to eat less and exercise more, but it wouldn't go beyond a page and would be commercial suicide.

79

A large cocktail crush for 40

AUTHOR: James Beard, FROM: *James Beard's Menus for Entertaining*

This is one of those parties which starts at about 6 or 7 o'clock and goes on till about 8:30 or 9:00 and provides enough food so that people do not need to go to dinner. I'd set up a full bar and also have some champagne and white wine with cassis. Thus you are apt to satisfy everyone. Coffee is a good idea at about 9 o'clock, with some sweet biscuits, perhaps. Roast Beef with Mustards, raw Vegetables in Ice, Cheese Board, Nuts, Olives.

James Beard had firm views on subjects that graver souls might consider unworthy of their attention. "I really don't like cheese with salad," he once said in an interview with his editor. "Nor do I like cheese with fruit," he added, concluding: "I think people serve salad too much."

But then this man was a food giant (in girth, height and influence) of the 1960s. It was a time for peace not war and if the battleground was the buffet platter, then so be it. Nearly twenty years after the end of war the world felt it deserved a strong vodka martini, and to hell with the consequences. But before they got plastered and swapped keys, the host and hostess needed some reliable advice on throwing a swell cocktail party.

James Beard was the man they—many in America and Britain, that is—turned to, and for several reasons. Not least because he was a man. Women had dominated the scene as dispensers of culinary advice for as long as anyone could remember. Which is perhaps why his book *Cook It Outdoors,* published in 1941, went down so well. As its own dust jacket proclaimed, this was "a man's book written by a man." He had recipes for "man-sized patties" and even his name had a beard in it. That he was also, as an old friend put it, "uncompromisingly, directly, gay" was inconsequential.

He wrote many other books in the years leading up to the mid-1960s, from ones on cooking fish to others that helped one cook on a budget. So when the cocktail-party era got into full swing, Beard was in a good position to offer, and have gratefully received, his expert guidance. "To entertain successfully one must create with the imagination of a playwright, plan with the skill of a director, and perform with the instincts of an actor," he advised in his *Menus for Entertaining,* cleverly flattering his readers with the notion that they could be all three of those people.

He warned against overgenerous and what he called "embarrassing" hospitality. The host should keep things simple and not go to crazy lengths to impress guests.

His idea for "a cocktail party for 30" "embodies my approach to the cocktail hour," he wrote. "Instead of tray after tray of tiny morsels of food, we have a good, hearty offering. Serve the usual variety of drinks, but be sure to include some beer, champagne and chilled dry sherry." The hearty food included steak tartare served in a bowl and surrounded by a selection of breads and crackers, glazed spare ribs, raw peas and raw asparagus tips. He also threw in some roasted peanuts and knockwurst (German sausage) with shallot mustard.

His recipe, meanwhile, for "a small elegant cocktail party for 10" came with considerable flourish. "This is the type of cocktail party you give for a friend who loves the elegant things in life or for a visiting mogul who is tremendously important to you or to the community. In other words, it's a smash!" he exclaimed. He recommended a large silver punch bowl be filled with ice, followed by chilled champagne and vodka. "Bring out small plates, knives and forks and your best linen," he said. And the food, if luxurious, was dead simple: "Caviar, smoked salmon, foie gras."

Author and top chef James Beard creating a Picasso masterpiece in the kitchen in 1972.

He also suggested that martinis be made in advance and then chilled. For those who might grimace at his suggestions for "a large cocktail crush for 40," in particular the idea that raw vegetables in ice could possibly be seen as glamorous, it was of course better than much of the food being served at contemporary cocktail parties. Chicken liver pâté (or canned cheese) was being spread onto crackers and small pieces of toast, and eggs stuffed with mushrooms. And when the mushrooms weren't stuffing something else, they were being stuffed themselves. Likewise cherry tomatoes were stuffed with tuna, if the tuna wasn't stuffing eggs. There were worse sins of course. Just ponder the idea of a gherkin wrapped in salami, itself covered in cream cheese with the whole catastrophe being held together with toothpicks.

As the grown-ups discussed the merits of the Beatles or who might win the next World Cup, children scurried about in between their legs, picking at the exotic tidbits on the side table and wondering at the strange drinks the ladies in polo necks, miniskirts and patterned tights were sipping. Then later they watched curiously as men, sporting crushed-velvet suits and kipper ties and urged on by the giggling ladies, tried to ride their undersized bicycles.

And all the while, much of this was fueled by the influential Beard. That a foundation was set up in his honor after he died is testament to the position he held in America at the time. Julia Child (see p. 260) christened him the "Dean of American Cuisine," while others have credited him with formulating a coherent U.S. gastronomy, pieced together from the different strands of U.S. cooking and its unique ingredients, in what has been called the "American food revolution"—although its definition remains a little foggy.

The only child of a doting mother who instilled in him a love of cooking, Beard's size seems to have prevented him from getting parts in his first love, the theater, and so he started cooking, setting up a cocktail-party catering service called Hors d'Oeuvre. His cooking led to books and an early TV career, although he was uncomfortable with the camera and producers found him too prickly to work with.

His influence on American food came also from the cookery school he founded in New York, about whose guiding principles he was unapologetic. "We have been attacked by one or two people for not being classic," he said. "We're not." But neither was it a money-spinner. So he sought to earn money by lending his celebrity as endorsement to companies such as Green Giant and Planters Peanuts as well as some airlines, which led his detractors to dub him a "gastronomic whore." But he brushed aside such criticism, enveloping himself in his foodie world and, when he wasn't writing or teaching, took time out to eat his way round Europe, one year managing to dine in every Michelin-three-starred restaurant in France.

After his death in 1985, from a heart attack (he was eighty-one), his ashes were scattered over the beach he had so loved as a child growing up in Oregon. The produce of that state had so inspired him; the fruit, fish and nuts he had tasted when young featuring in those buffets he was so keen to roll out in the mid-1960s.

80

Cheese fondue

AUTHOR: Betty Crocker, FROM: *Betty Crocker's Dinner Parties*

1 loaf French bread or 6–8 hard rolls
1 pound Swiss cheese
2 tablespoons flour
1 clove garlic
1 cup dry white wine (Rhine, Riesling, Chablis, Neuchâtel)
2 tablespoons kirsch or sherry
1 teaspoon salt
⅛ teaspoon nutmeg
Dash white pepper

Cut bread into 1-inch cubes. Cut cheese into ¼-inch cubes (about 4 cups). Sprinkle flour over cheese and toss until cheese is coated.

Rub cut clove of garlic on bottom and side of ceramic fondue pot, heavy saucepan or chafing dish. Add wine; heat over medium heat just until bubbles rise to surface (do not allow wine to boil). Gradually stir in the cheese, adding only ½ cup at a time and stirring after each addition until cheese is melted and blended. (Do not allow mixture to become too hot.)

Stir in liqueur and seasonings. If fondue has been prepared on a range, transfer fondue pot to source of heat at table and adjust heat to keep fondue *just* bubbling. Guests spear cubes of bread with long-handled forks and dip into cheese mixture. Stir fondue occasionally. (If fondue becomes too thick, stir in about ½ cup warm white wine.) 4 Servings.

Before the planet needed saving—in response to the likes of Frances Moore Lappé (see p. 276)—there were more pressing issues, such as more dinner parties to throw. Of the ideas being offered up at the start of the 1970s it was those of Betty Crocker that particularly resonated. They oozed with the spirit of hot pants and bell-bottomed trousers. "Today's entertaining," was, she said, "merrier and more relaxed than ever." And the book she brought out on dinner parties was jam-packed with tips on modern dining that reflected "something new on the party circuit," as she put it.

People may have taken a shine to Betty Crocker and her Middle American, reliable, practical and safe persona and portraits of her show a kindly, attractive face, the image of the perfect housewife, but she was of course a work of fiction. A modern-day Mrs. Beeton (see p. 182), perhaps, her name was devised in 1921 by the Washburn Crosby Company of Minneapolis. Her image appeared subsequently throughout the twentieth century, changing from time to time and played by a variety of actresses on television, although one thing that never changed was her combination of red jacket and white blouse.

She was one of the food company's more palatable inventions. After all, these were the people behind Cocoa Pops, Golden Grahams and Count Chocula, the latter being a monster-themed breakfast cereal. Not to mention the strawberry-flavored breakfast offering, Franken Berry. It came with a dye that the human body was unable to break down, the result being that children who ate the stuff produced bright pink turds. Many a parent was alarmed at a symptom that became known as "Frankenberry stool."

When Betty Crocker wasn't putting her name to food products—cake mixes and the like—she turned her fictional self to the dinner party. Her recipes were tested by housewives up and down the country so there would be, she promised, "no snags, slip-ups or semi-successes." This being the start of the 1970s and a new spirit of relaxation, she suggested guests might "sit on plastic cubes, ottomans, footstools or even cushions on the floor." Why not "add to the mood with a roaring fire, or background music from the stereo (keep it turned down low so talk can flow freely)," she continued. James Beard (see p. 269) would surely not have approved.

Dinner itself could be eaten on "trays, TV tables, or whatever surface is solid" while she offered up a "simple memory game" to get the party started. Although "What was the first job you had?" never did seem to really catch on. Still this was the 70s, a time when "some of the best parties end up in the kitchen with everyone singing folk songs while they help with the dishes."

But what of the food itself? This was the era of the "cook-at-the-table dinner." The dinner party had moved out of the dining and into the sitting room, while the cooking equipment had followed it out of the kitchen and settled itself on a low table. Its hero feature was the chafing dish—a metal pan set above a spirit lamp and used for cooking at the table—whose use had ebbed and flowed throughout time. Popular back in ancient Greece, it had disappeared more or less until it became popular once again at the end of the nineteenth century. There was Fannie Farmer's (see p. 192) intriguing book *Chafing Dish Possibilities,* published in 1898, then Frank Schloesser's slightly disturbing-sounding *The Cult of the Chafing Dish* in 1903.

It resurfaced again in the 1970s. Hosts dazzled their guests not just with their sparkling new equipment, but with their flambéing and their crêpes Suzette. Betty Crocker hailed the chafing dish and its trusty sidekick the fondue pot as providing dinners that were "exotic, sophisticated and intimate." And while you could watch your hostess weave her magic over the chafing dish, a fondue pot allowed you to really get stuck in.

"A fondue party can be great fun," said the phantom Betty, but, she warned, "limit the party to five or six." After all, once the fondue's been gobbled, who knows what else could happen? Indeed consider her risqué rules for fondue consumption: "If a man drops his bread in the fondue, he buys a bottle of wine, and if a lady drops hers, she must kiss all the men at the table."

As for her prized menu of which the fondue is the centerpiece, the more sensitive foodie might wish to look away now. It starts with a "Deviled Ham Appetizer Tray." The spreadable ham, which came out of a tin (ironically emblazoned with the image of a little red devil), was mixed with sour cream, horseradish and pepper sauce. It went in a bowl and was surrounded by crackers, celery and apple wedges to dip in.

The next course was the less offensive fondue before a course of "Tossed Greens"—chilled spinach, lettuce, radishes and bottled salad dressing—followed by "Ice Cream Date Pie," a baked mixture of margarine, date bar mix and butter pecan ice cream. At which point, presumably, the orgy was deflecting from any defects in the food.

This seedy, sexy, comic food was inspired by the Alps. A grown-up take on *The Sound of Music,* which was just five years old by 1970. Yet aspects of it live on. The Tiroler Hut restaurant, a tribute to the Austrian mountain cabin, was opened in a basement on London's Westbourne Park Road in 1967 and still thrives. And the fondue never ceases with its threat to make a comeback, almost as insistently as flared trousers, high-waisted palazzo pants and the prawn cocktail.

Fondue parties were all the rage in the 1970s.

81

Mediterranean lemon soup with Middle Eastern tacos

AUTHOR: Frances Moore Lappé, FROM: *Diet for a Small Planet*

YIELD: 6

1½ quarts of vegetable stock (saved from cooking vegetables or beans)

½ cup raw brown rice

Salt, if necessary

¼ tsp summer savory

2 tbsp brewer's yeast

4 eggs, beaten

Juice and grated rind of 1–2 lemons (you can start with lesser amount and add more to taste at the end)

Heat stock to boiling and stir in rice and salt. Cover and simmer about 30 minutes. Mix savory and yeast into eggs. Add lemon juice and rind and mix again. 1 cup of hot stock and slowly add it to the egg mixture. Stir constantly. Remove stock from heat and gradually add egg mixture to it. Serve.

MIDDLE EASTERN TACOS

10 PIECES MIDDLE EASTERN FLAT BREAD OR 10 WHEAT TORTILLAS

YIELD: 10 TACOS

1 cup dry garbanzo beans, cooked

½ cup (heaping) sesame seeds, toasted

2 cloves garlic

2 tablespoons lemon juice

¾ teaspoon coriander, ground

½ teaspoon salt

½ teaspoon cumin, ground

¼–½ teaspoon cayenne

EXTRA GARNISHES

Shredded lettuce

Chopped tomatoes

Chopped cucumber

Chopped onion

1½ cups yogurt (or cheese)

Purée together all ingredients (increase spices to taste). Let stand at least 12 hours at room temperature.

Cut pieces of Middle Eastern flat bread in half and fill "pockets" with bean mixture; or serve on wheat tortillas, fried until soft but not crisp. Add the garnishes and allow everyone at the table to assemble their own "taco."

In 1970 Betty Ballantine, of New York publishers Ballantine Books, traveled to the University of California in Berkeley to see twenty-six-year-old postgraduate Frances Moore Lappé. She wanted to meet the young woman who had authored a seventy-five-page booklet that had found its way to her desk and that argued, with lucid and natural passion, the case for a meatless diet.

The two spent the day together and Lappé cooked her guest a delicious lemon soup with tacos. The originality of her cooking and its fresh and zingy flavors were as delightful and convincing as her arguments, and Lappé gained a commission to write a book that, thirty-eight years later, would be chosen as one of "Seventy-five Books by Women Whose Words Have Changed the World." That book, *Diet for a Small Planet,* is also heralded as a publication that revolutionized the way many Americans eat.

Lappé's thoughts had started as a one-page pamphlet that she handed out to people, and the book's success—3 million copies sold to date—saw her go on to launch research foundations as well as to write a further seventeen books. Its publication in 1971 served as a turning point for how many people viewed food consumption and production. Since the war the growth in world population had led to a frenzy of development in increased food production. Crops were sprayed, hedges ripped out to create larger acreages and ponds were filled in, while factory farming spread, animal rearing became more intensive and highly processed and packaged food increasingly lined the supermarket shelves.

Yet a younger generation refused to sleepwalk into this era of high yield and cheap welfare. When Lappé graduated in 1966 there was a war in Vietnam and the Civil Rights Movement was gaining momentum. The younger, cool set might have been sitting on the floor listening to records hour after hour but they were also swaying to the Beatles and absorbing what they had to say.

All around them they saw forests being cut down and air and water increasingly polluted. Their parents may have liberated the world twenty-odd years previously but the planet's health itself was now deteriorating. Young people weren't looking to government to sort out the problem; the early 70s saw Watergate discredit the upper echelons of politics in the United States, so when the administration said everything was okay, it wasn't an unnatural reaction to disbelieve them.

Sitting in the library at Berkeley, Lappé, having dug deep into exactly why her nation had been at war with Vietnam, moved on to another subject. She was curious as to whether it really was nature's fault that so many people in the world went hungry. How exactly did the global food supply work? The facts she uncovered, she said later, "turned my world upside down."

There had been many passionate advocates of vegetarianism in the past, of course. John Evelyn was putting the case for salad back in 1699 (see p. 121). But the vegetarian cause, given voice by the formation of the Vegetarian Society in England in 1847 (see p. 177), had suffered during the early and middle part of the twentieth century when war had made *that* you ate, rather than what you ate, the priority.

America also reveled in its reputation as a land of plenty, a principle fiercely defended by the likes of cook Irma Rombauer in the 1930s (see p. 228). By the late 1960s, this diet of plenty included a large amount of meat. And the production of this meat, Lappé discovered, was a major reason for why the environment was suffering.

One of the main tenets of her argument was that it took 16 pounds of grain to make a pound of meat and that meat had less than 5 percent of the calories and less than 15 percent of the protein of the grain. Meat production was also depleting natural resources, every pound of meat requiring 2,500 gallons of water, for example, not to mention the damage to topsoil that occurs in the production of corn for livestock feed and the forests ripped out to make way for cattle.

This argument about the large acreage of land needed to farm livestock was not new, though. Plato had raised it his *Republic,* as did writers throughout the seventeenth and eighteenth centuries, including the English poet Percy Bysshe Shelley at the turn of the nineteenth century. "The most fertile districts of the habitable globe are now actively cultivated by men for animals," he wrote, "at a delay and waste of aliment absolutely incapable of calculation."

But Lappé did attempt to do the math. If readers pretended they were in a restaurant eating an eight-ounce steak, she proposed, "the grain used to produce the steak could have filled the empty bowls of 40 people in the room." That cattle were such wasteful converters of grain to meat "confounds all logic," she maintained. So, driven by what she called "simple outrage" she determined to awaken people to the simple fact that "hunger is human made."

Although environmental consciousness was increasing at the time, much of what she said felt almost treasonable. She was calling into question the very heart of the American diet, with its virtual reliance on beef. It amounted to a challenge to the American way of life itself. To question intensive agriculture back then must have looked naïve, but it marked a change in people's thinking. "What was heresy, what was fringe when I wrote *Diet for a Small Planet,*" she later reflected, "is now common knowledge."

So to recruit foot soldiers to her campaign of sticking to a vegetarian diet to ensure there would be enough food for everyone and the planet could remain healthy, she also offered tips and recipes. She urged people to fill their larders with bulgur wheat, nuts, seeds, lentils and sunflower oil and their fridges with tofu, low-fat yogurt and cottage cheese. She suggested shopping at smaller whole-food stores, pointing out how "cooking with grain, legumes, nuts and seeds also means that in one shopping trip you can buy enough for a few months." And her recipes opened people's eyes to food from around the world, from South America to China, the Middle East and India as well as Europe.

In the early 1970s, Greenpeace had 5,000 members. Urged on by the likes of Lappé, they now have 2.3 million in America alone. But as she herself has indicated, as people become more affluent so they increase their consumption of meat. And there are still plenty of people who are quite happy to, temporarily, put off saving the planet for a tender and juicy, medium-rare char-grilled steak.

82

Plum tart

AUTHORS: Alice Waters and Lindsey Shere
FROM: *The menu at Chez Panisse*

8 large plums
1 prebaked 10-inch pâte sucrée tart shell (recipe below)
1 stick unsalted butter
Juice of 1 lemon
2 eggs
¾ cup sugar
1.5 tsp plum brandy, grappa, or kirsch
¼ tsp vanilla extract
⅛ tsp salt
3 Tbsp flour
2 Tbsp heavy cream

Preheat the oven to 370°F.

Cut the plums in half, remove the pits, and slice into ½-inch wedges. Arrange the wedges in concentric circles in the prebaked tart shell. Melt the butter in a small saucepan over low heat. Let it bubble gently and cook until the milk solids turn a toasty light brown. Remove the butter from the heat, add the lemon juice to stop the cooking, and set aside to cool.

Beat the eggs and sugar together with an electric mixer until the mixture is thick and forms a ribbon when dropped from the beaters, about 5 minutes. Add the butter, brandy, vanilla, salt, flour, and cream. Stir just until mixed. Pour the mixture over the plums, filling the tart shell. Bake in the top third of the oven until the top is golden brown, about 35 to 40 minutes. Let cool on a rack for 15 minutes. Serve warm or at room temperature, with lightly whipped cream.

Makes one 10-inch tart; serves 6 to 8.

1 stick unsalted butter, *room temperature*
⅓ cup sugar
¼ tsp salt
¼ tsp vanilla extract
1 egg yolk
1.25 cups unbleached all purpose flour

TO MAKE THE PÂTE SUCRÉE
Beat together the butter and sugar in a medium-size bowl until creamy. Add the salt, vanilla, and egg yolk and mix until completely combined. Add the flour and mix until there are no dry patches. Wrap the ball of dough in plastic wrap and press into a 4-inch disk. Chill several hours or overnight, until firm.

To roll out the dough, first cut two 14-inch pieces of parchment paper. Remove the disk of dough from the refrigerator and unwrap it. Dust one of the pieces of parchment paper with flour, center the disk on it, and dust the top of the dough with flour. Cover with the other piece of parchment and roll out the disk into a 13-inch circle about ⅛ inch thick. If the dough starts to stick to the paper while you are rolling, peel back the paper and dust again with flour, and replace the paper. Then flip the whole package over and repeat on the other side. If there is excess flour on the dough when you are done rolling, peel back the paper and brush it off. Chill the sheet of dough for a few minutes.

To make an 11-inch tart, remove the top sheet of paper and invert the dough into a tart pan. Peel off the remaining paper, press the dough into the corners of the pan, and pinch off any dough overhang. Use the dough scraps to patch up any cracks. Let the tart shell rest on the freezer for 10 minutes before baking.

Just a few streets away from the University of California in Berkeley where Frances Moore Lappé (see p. 276) was recruiting her vegetarian platoon, a right, right again, left, then another right takes you to where an equally tasty food revolution was brewing. That it was happening in the same city would help to make Berkeley a gastronomic center of excellence.

Alice Waters opened her Chez Panisse restaurant, named after a character from a classic French movie of the 1930s, on Shattuck Avenue in 1971. It may have looked like a "run-down hippie crash pad," in the words of Alice's then boyfriend Tom Luddy, but, as ever, appearances can be deceptive for it went on to become one of the most influential restaurants in the United States, revolutionizing the American palate and changing the way people think about food.

The Chez Panisse bug was catching and today Berkeley proudly shimmers in a foodie glow. Tourist websites offer "Culinary Walking Tours" around the "Gourmet Ghetto" so that one can pay homage to this "historical culinary mecca." And you don't just get any old guide to take you round the organic farmers' market, to taste the local cupcakes, slurp the homemade soups, sip fair-trade coffee and eye up the artisanal chocolate. A tour of Shattuck Avenue is led by an "epicurean concierge." And if you hang around long enough, you might get to meet members of the Berkeley Chocolate Club, representatives of the Cheeseboard Collective and other culinary devotees.

Berkeley's current love of food has its origins in the modest aims of Alice Waters, who once said that she opened a restaurant simply because "I was hungry." One of four sisters, Alice was born in 1944 in New Jersey, the family then moving to California as Alice's father climbed the hierarchy of the insurance firm he worked for. She studied at the University of California, at both Santa Barbara and Berkeley, catching in the process an enjoyable whiff of the student protests of the time.

The Vietnam War and the banning of the distribution of political literature on the university campus in 1964 was a gift for students looking for a juicy bit of rebellion.

Some of the protest came in the shape of the Free Speech Movement, whose ideals, according to Alice, "empowered" her. And while friends and fellow sympathizers sat around discussing the pressing issues of the day, she would cook for them. The conversation might have been American but the food was French, inspired by her visit to another revolutionary hotspot—the city of Paris.

Alice's trip to France came as she and a friend signed up to study at the Sorbonne (the University of Paris). And like Julia Child some ten years previously (see p. 264), the moment she got there her taste buds were lit up.

Alice's palate had been deadened by a childhood diet characterized by her mother's insistence on dry, brown so-called "health" breads and oatmeal and vitamin supplements (which she would hold in her mouth and spit out in the bathroom when no one was looking).

But on that first day in Paris, staying in an overpriced hotel recommended by an aunt, the two friends chose the cheapest thing on the menu. It was a simple vegetable soup, recalled Alice, but "so delicious. It felt like I had never eaten before."

This foodie awakening was followed by months of equally good eating, assisted by various boyfriends along the way who showed them around the country and in particular the south of France.

"It was a beautiful moment in time," Alice reminisced. "Food was woven into everybody's everyday life and it wasn't a big deal to eat something that was really tasty."

She saw that best food was produced locally and in season and it was these values that she took back to Berkeley with her, armed with a proselytizing zeal and a copy of Elizabeth David's *French Country Cooking* (see p. 258), picked up from a cookware shop during a visit to London.

Back home she started cooking French-style food, experimenting on family and friends, and it quickly dawned on her that this was something she wanted to do for the rest of her life.

Four years later, on 28 August 1971, she opened Chez Panisse. Aged only twenty-seven, a diminutive figure at just five foot two, Alice wafted through the restaurant wearing a dark lace dress and looking like a "Pre-Raphaelite angel," according to one contemporary.

The menu that first evening was simple and French, using ingredients from local suppliers. And there was no choice: pâté, followed by braised duck in a rich sauce, then plum tart. Alongside her passion for cooking she also displayed a novice's lack of business acumen. There were fifty covers that night and she had fifty-five staff.

Service was a nightmare, even so. There was an hour's delay between the first and the main course but with Alice popping into the restaurant from the kitchen to charm customers, no one seemed to complain. Shouty panic filled the kitchen as the pâté was plated and stock for the duck was reduced and strained, so the plum tart—which heads this chapter—was prepared outside in a shack in the back yard, away from the chaos, by a friend of Alice, Lindsey Shere.

There, wrote Alice Waters's biographer Thomas McNamee, the tart could be put together in relative peace, "protected from the infectious nervous breakdown that had taken hold of Chez Panisse that night."

The pudding that resulted was simple. "Plums," wrote McNamee, "at their peak of ripeness [were] spread across a light custard baked in a buttery crust."

The dish still appears on the menu from time to time some thirty years later.

Back in 1971, the diners gobbled it all up appreciatively, washing it down with local wine from Robert Mondavi's Napa Valley vineyard, and, after coffee, each paying their $3.95 per head.

That first night they served 120 customers and at the end of service there were still people queuing down the street (the upside of having fifty-five members of staff meant that word quickly spread). "I'm sorry we just don't have any more food," Alice told those still waiting. "Come back tomorrow."

Surrounded by culinary buddies, she sat and talked into the early hours of the following morning. "We were so happy. We were so young," she later recalled. "We were in love with what we were doing."

In the days and months, then years, that followed, Alice focused on securing supplies from local producers, encouraging farmers to develop produce for her. She wanted fresh herbs and heirloom vegetables and the dishes she cooked became known as Californian cuisine. A network of organic farms and ranches grew up around the San Francisco Bay Area and the team of people she hired went on to open their own restaurants. The likes of Jeremiah Tower, Paul Bertolli, Lindsey Shere and Mark Miller are now established stars in the American culinary firmament.

Alice Waters did not have a long-term strategy when she started and while her restaurant eventually became a lucrative establishment, it still lost money well into its period of ascendency. She was motivated by food, not finance.

"When we started Chez Panisse I was looking for flavor," she mused many years later. "I didn't have a philosophy about food. I just wanted something that tasted like the food I had eaten in France. Good cooking is about finding the right ingredients and eating the fruits and vegetables exactly in season when they're completely right and have all the flavor."

Gradually she became a standard-bearer for those who preferred her approach, which tallied with the notions of the Slow Food Movement (see p. 299) and challenged the increasingly pervasive influence of the fast-food business.

"When you eat fast food you're not just eating food that is not particularly good for you, you're eating the values of fast, cheap and easy," Alice has said. With her soft mellifluous voice, more reminiscent of someone chanting in church than a chef barking orders in the kitchen, she has argued against the notion that she represents an unrealistic view of food and that she is just the queen bee of snobby, foodie Berkeley. "You either pay up front or you pay up back," is her take on the ills cheap food does, not just to human health, but to animal welfare and the environment as a whole.

Some twenty-five years after Chez Panisse opened, Alice Waters was invited to Britain by French chef Raymond Blanc to attend a conference at his Oxfordshire Le Manoir aux Quat'Saisons. The only female delegate there, she was surrounded by the great and good of the U.S. food scene. "Chefs from the grandest American restaurants arrived laden with produce, imported, canned or frozen," reported an observer at the conference. "Alice just brought a few Californian Meyer lemons and then went out to forage in Raymond's garden."

The resulting meal, according to UK food writer Fiona Beckett, was low-key but "the most memorable... [and] also one of the simplest." Heaped in the middle of the table was a large pile of radishes with their tops still on, along with some sourdough bread and butter to go with it. The main dish consisted of a simple Welsh spring lamb with sweet new potatoes, broad beans and fried herbs. Her lemons she used for a refreshing sherbet. "It was a feast," recalls Beckett, "put together from the best produce available on an early English spring day."

Alice once declared that "your life is changed by the way you eat." Eating food sourced and prepared the Alice Waters way will do that for sure.

83

Lamb korma

AUTHOR: Madhur Jaffrey, FROM: *An Invitation to Indian Cooking*

SERVES 6–8

3 tbsp ground coriander

1 tbsp ground cumin

1 tbsp desiccated unsweetened coconut

4 medium-sized onions, peeled and coarsely chopped

5 cloves garlic, peeled and coarsely chopped

a piece of ginger, about 1½ inches long and 1 inch wide, peeled and coarsely chopped

1 large tomato (tinned or fresh) or 2 small ones, peeled and coarsely chopped

1 tsp ground turmeric

6 tbsp vegetable oil

5 whole cardamom pods

6 whole cloves

7 whole black peppercorns

2 bay leaves

1 cinnamon stick, 2 inches long

2 or more dried hot red peppers (optional)

3 lb boneless meat from lamb shoulder, cut into 1 inch cubes (or from shank, neck, or leg), thoroughly dried

1 tbsp plain yogurt

2 tsp salt

1 tsp *garam masala*

Heat a small heavy frying-pan over medium flame, and dry-roast the coriander, cumin, and coconut, tossing them around with a spoon. Roast for 2–3 minutes until the spices turn a few shades darker, and set aside. Remove frying-pan from heat. Place onions, garlic, and ginger in blender with tomato and turmeric. Blend at high speed for one minute or until you have a smooth paste, and set aside.

In a large, heavy-bottom pot heat 4 tablespoons of the oil over a medium flame. When hot, add the cardamom, cloves, peppercorns, bay leaves, cinnamon, and red peppers. Stir. As soon as the peppercorns begin to expand and the red peppers turn dark, put in a few pieces of meat at a time. Turn the flame higher and brown the meat on all sides. As each batch browns, remove it to a side plate. When all the lamb is browned, cover it and set it aside. Remove the whole spices from the pot with a slotted spoon and keep with lamb.

TO MAKE THE SAUCE:

Keep flame on medium high, and add 2 tablespoons of oil to what is left in the pot. While it is heating, add the paste from the blender; keep face averted. Stir from time to time. As the water evaporates and the paste starts to stick to the bottom, lower heat and stir continuously, for about 5 minutes in all, sprinkling in a little water now and then to prevent scorching. Add the roasted spices and cook for another 5 minutes, then stir in the yogurt, a little at a time to prevent scorching.

GARNISH

Fried onion rings

¼ tsp freshly ground cardamom seeds

Sliced hot green chilies

Chopped fresh coriander

Now put in the meat, the salt, and enough water to barely cover the lamb. Bring to the boil, cover and simmer about 1 hour until done. Lift cover. Sprinkle 1 teaspoon *garam masala,* and cook, stirring for another 5 minutes.

TO SERVE:

Spoon out into serving dish and garnish with one or all of the items suggested. Serve with boiled rice, *pooris* or *chapattis,* and okra or cauliflower or aubergine *bharta.* This dish is also good served with sweet rice, a yogurt dish, and Sweet Tomato Chutney.

The 1960s had seen considerable growth in the number of restaurants in the UK, particularly Italian and Chinese ones. But Indian restaurants had also spread quickly in towns and cities across the country and especially in London. One visitor to the capital in the early 70s was actress and cook Madhur Jaffrey. Indian restaurants, she remembered, "were flourishing in practically every neighborhood." Things were looking up: "I took this efflorescence to signify an increased supply of good quality, authentic regional Indian foods."

By contrast, her first stay in London, in the 1950s—when she had won a scholarship to the Royal Academy of Dramatic Art from a school near her home outside Old Delhi—did not hold happy memories for her. "The city was drab and the food was terrible," she recalled. "There were wonderful fishmongers—one on almost every corner. Everything else was pathetic."

Returning almost twenty years later, she was excited to see scores of restaurants promising to bring her a taste of her homeland. But she was disappointed. "I found most of them to be second-class establishments that had managed to underplay their own regional uniqueness," she later wrote. The cooks, she said, were of poor caliber, "often former seamen or untrained villagers who [had] come to England in the hope of making a living, somehow or other, in alien surroundings." Each one simply copied the menus from other restaurants, the result being food that was "mediocre" and "fake." It also irritated her that the word "curry" was used as a general term for the wonderful variety of food to be found across the country of her birth. It was, she said, "degrading to India's great cuisine."

But the rot had been setting in for the past few hundred years. Indian recipes and ingredients had been reaching Britain as early as the 1600s, at the time of the formation of the East India Company. And the first published recipe for a "curry" appears in Hannah Glasse's recipe book of 1747. By the 1800s the term was ubiquitous when referencing Indian food, or indeed simply oriental (see p. 171). In Emma Roberts's updated edition of *A New System of Domestic Cookery* of 1840, she lumps the food of India, Persia and Turkey under that banner of "oriental" and all the main dishes are curries.

Then there were the recipes made using Madhur Jaffrey's other bugbear: curry powder. While curry is "an oversimplified name for an ancient cuisine," curry powder was not just oversimple, it could actually "destroy the cuisine itself," she declared.

Yet all the Indian restaurants she visited perpetuated this distorted version of Indian cooking, failing to recognize, in her view, that the British had the capacity for a culinary curiosity and adventurous palate. As Jaffrey was not about to open a restaurant of her own, the only way to counteract these crimes against her nation's cuisine was to write a book.

Back in her adopted home of New York, she got a book deal and the result was *An Invitation to Indian Cooking*. "The only way to eat superb Indian food is to learn to cook it yourself," she announces in the introduction, as she set about first to educate the American palate before tackling the British three years later, when the book was published in London.

But that Jaffrey was able to make a career in food writing in the first place was thanks to her friend the filmmaker Ismail Merchant. Merchant had cast her in *Shakespeare Wallah* in 1965 and as part of the publicity drive had suggested the *New York Times* do an article on this Indian actress who cooked. The piece caught the eye of editors who commissioned recipe writing from her, and the career that funded her low-paid acting life began. "It all somehow fell from the sky like rain," she recalled.

Her own cooking was taught via a makeshift correspondence course. Arriving in London in the 1950s and desperate for Indian food, she had appealed to her mother back in India, at whose knee she had not learned cooking. (They were relatively wealthy, living in a home that housed up to thirty members of her extended family. Cooks prepared all the meals and the only thing the young Jaffrey had to do was eat these.) Her mother responded by sending airmail letters filled with recipes which her daughter slowly perfected.

On her thespian forays to London in the 1970s, the BBC had screen-tested her and she landed a major Indian cooking series, largely on the strength of her acting skills. "The first time I had to audition for the BBC they gave me nothing," she remembered. "They said, 'Pretend you're cooking a dish.'" There were no ingredients or pans in front of her, just an empty counter. So she pottered about pretending to rustle up some Indian delicacy and, she said, "they were so impressed, I was hired practically on the spot."

Her ensuing television and writing career has meant that Madhur Jaffrey is today often cited as "the woman who taught the British to cook curry." Which must infuriate her given her views on that word. So it's with that in mind that this chapter treads carefully around this forceful personality, presenting her recipe for lamb korma. This classic Indian dish, while a little time-consuming to make, was written specifically for the American market with the idea that it would demonstrate how delicious, different and inexpensive good Indian cooking could be.

Actress and bestselling author Madhur Jaffrey in 1984.

84

Ginger cake

AUTHOR: Cecilia Norman, FROM: *Microwave Cookery for the Housewife*

½ lb (230 g) flour
1 level tsp bicarbonate of soda
3 oz (90 g) margarine
2 oz (60 g) brown sugar
1½ level tsp ground ginger
1 large egg
5 tbsp milk approx.
2 oz (60 g) crystallized ginger
6 oz (170 g) golden syrup

Place syrup, margarine and sugar in a suitable bowl. *Cook 1½ minutes. Stir well.*

Sieve flour, bicarbonate of soda and ground ginger into a mixing bowl.

Add beaten egg and 2 tbsp milk to syrup mixture.

Combine with flour mixture and beat well.

Add 3 more tbsp milk to make a thick batter consistency.

Chop ginger and mix in.

Pour into lined glass cake dish (9in diameter). *Cook 5½ minutes, turning ¼ turn every 1½ minutes.*

This mixture may be cooked in individual paper cases, each requiring 1 minute. 4 cakes cooked at one time, placed close together on oven base, will take 3½ minutes.

The pushmi-pullyu gazelle–unicorn—or rather donkey–stallion—cross that is British cooking experienced a decisive jolt backwards (or forwards, depending on your view) in the 1970s when the microwave oven became the latest must-have kitchen accessory. While figures such as Madhur Jaffrey (see p. 284) were advocating slow-paced authenticity, UK-based food writers like Cecilia Norman were championing the spirit of "let's just get the food on the table as quickly as possible, for God's sake."

Here, to help you on your way, was a device that could turn out hot food in seconds. Here, following in the tradition of the refrigerator, Regulo oven and Kenwood Chef (see pp. 222, 225 and 253), was another piece of kit for the kitchen that would free the housewife from domestic slavery. Cecilia Norman makes no bones about who her book is aimed at with a title that could have been on the cover of a book published 200 years previously, except that it had the word "microwave" in it.

Technology had initially been used to engage the cook, to encourage those tasked with preparing meals to step bravely into the kitchen. But now, as that process evolved, came a device that ironically managed to eradicate the need to cook. It meant that one could buy an item of processed food from the supermarket, pop it in the fridge to store it until needed and then use another device to heat it, making it ready to eat within seconds. And the stampede to buy that device saw Britain once again lurch away from the prospect of developing a proper food culture.

Norman relished the prospect of a microwave frenzy, as she made clear in the introduction to her book. "During the 1960s the microwave oven quickly proved itself a valuable asset to all types of catering establishments," she wrote, "because of the extreme speed of the facility with which pre-cooked meals can be re-heated ready for serving, and frozen food thawed." It was, she noted, during the Second World War that the heating properties of microwaves were discovered by those involved with radar research. "Now," she gushed, "microwave cookery is proving itself equally valuable in the home, not only for quick re-heating or the thawing of frozen food, but also for basic cooking. The microwave oven will save hours of time in cooking almost any items of food."

She didn't of course say that there were some items that you should decidedly not use the microwave oven to cook them in: steaks, for example, or soufflés, or bread, or any kind of roast. Nor did she mention that if you paused to think about how the microwave actually works, you might consider that you wouldn't in fact wish to cook *any* item of food in it. But the jury is still out on that, although as there still hasn't been enough conclusive research on the subject, that jury has yet to be provided with the full evidence with which to make up its collective mind.

Manufacturers of course insist that microwaves are totally safe. But it is worth reminding oneself how exactly a microwave works. The process is simple. The device emits electromagnetic radiation that, absorbed by the food, sees its molecules rotate millions of times a second, the rapid friction of which creates heat. The heat of those (mainly water) molecules cooks the food. Microwaves work much faster than conventional ovens because the radiation penetrates the food faster than it takes heat to transfer to it from a heating element.

Skeptics don't like microwaves for all sorts of reasons. Some argue that no one quite knows what hap-

Microwaves became the must-have kitchen accessory in the 1970s.

pens to the compounds of food—whether the radiation changes them for the worse. They claim that vitamins are lost in the process, as are other nutrients. And while the good stuff goes, studies have shown that the bad stuff—listeria, for example, in one experiment—stays.

It was indeed, as Norman suggests, during the war that the warming effects of microwaves were discovered. German soldiers, for example, used to huddle around radar stations because they found it warmed them up. A thought which is almost as alarming as the occasion when Percy Spencer, an American engineer, noticed that when fiddling with a radar set one day the chocolate bar in his pocket melted. The point being that as we, like food, are made up of organic matter, if you can cook a piece of meat in a microwave, what's to stop you cooking yourself? Think of that next time you stare through the window at an egg popping. Maybe while you're doing it you can feel the fluid in your eyes nicely warming.

The Russians actually banned microwaves in 1976 as they were so worried about them, but Gorbachev under Perestroika lifted that ban. Today virtually every restaurant, from the humblest to the poshest, has one. And no one is offered the choice of refusing to have their food cooked or warmed up in it.

Making cakes in a microwave, as Norman suggests—and if you don't believe it's possible, try this chapter's recipe for ginger cake and make up your own mind—may be cooking but it's surely not actually baking? However, few minded back in the mid-1970s and she happily churned out books on the device, championing it for cooking fish and vegetables and even for making jams and pickles.

Meanwhile, for those who like to experiment, the following two tricks might appeal. Cook food in a metal dish in a microwave and you can create your own mini thunderstorm. And if you leave a cup of water in the machine and you're lucky enough to get it to superheat—the temperature of the water rising to above boiling point but with no bubbles appearing—when you add a tea bag, the water will instantly boil and the tea bag explode.

Barbara Kafka, self-proclaimed U.S. "microwave gourmet," was once asked whether it was possible to brown meat in the contraption. "You can of course burn food in the microwave," she replied, "which will turn it brown, but not necessarily in the way you want." As to its potential dangers, Cecilia Norman has argued that for some members of the family a microwave is indisputably the best option. "It is safer for the half-asleep husband cooking his own bacon," she writes. He won't burn himself on the fat and then forget to switch off the hob or grill while he looks for a bandage, as the machine has a timer and will automatically switch itself off.

Will microwaves one day be condemned, along with mobiles and transmitter masts? Who knows. But what we do know is that as long as a device makes life easier, most of us are willing to risk frying our brains as well as our, un-browned, steaks.

85

Salmon fish cakes

AUTHOR: Delia Smith, FROM: *Frugal Food*

SERVES 3

A 7½ oz tin salmon

½ lb potatoes, peeled

2 tablespoons chopped parsley

2 gherkins, finely chopped

2 hardboiled eggs, chopped

2 teaspoons lemon juice

1 teaspoon anchovy essence

Flour

Equal parts of oil and butter for frying

Salt and freshly milled pepper

A good pinch of cayenne pepper

I think tinned salmon makes very good fish cakes, as nice as if you'd used fresh.

Begin by boiling the potatoes in salted water, then drain and mash them. Meanwhile drain the liquor from the salmon, discarding any skin or bones, and mash it to a paste with a fork. Then combine the potato with the fish, parsley, gherkins, hardboiled egg, lemon juice and anchovy essence. Mix everything thoroughly, taste and season with salt, freshly milled black pepper and cayenne. Next form the mixture into 6 fish cakes and dust each one with flour (all this can be done in advance). Then fry the fish cakes in the hot fat on both sides until golden. Drain and serve hot, garnished with sprigs of parsley and wedges of lemon.

The storm force that is Delia Smith (over 21 million copies sold to date of some 39 titles) started as a gentle breeze. In the cyclical swing of food publishing, from complex cuisine to simple dishes, she emerged at just the right moment. Robert Carrier might have been televisually exuberant and Elizabeth David (see p. 256) authentically earthy, but Delia just wanted to make things easier.

The book that put her on the map was as cute and cheeky as the pretty girl-next-door that she was. *How to Cheat at Cooking,* which arrived at the start of a British decade of strikes, Ford Cortinas and hot pants, was a paperback that could fit in the back pocket of your flares and cost just 35 pence of the new decimal currency.

"If you're one of those dedicated cooks who's keen on early morning mushroom gathering and wouldn't dream of concocting a salad without using the 'just-picked' variety, then this book is not for you," she declared at the start. Her small tome was nothing less than a manifesto for the time-poor mothers whose husbands were, no doubt, demanding that their wives inject some Robert Carrier–style kerpow into their dinner parties.

The early 70s might have seen an influx of produce from Europe, new cheeses from France, olive oils from Italy, but young women and quite a few young men felt trapped between overweening dinner-party ambition and the realities of what little they had learned, if anything, from their rationing-brainwashed and "make-do-and-mend" mothers.

"You had women's magazines doing six ways with mince and color magazines doing posh stuff and there was nothing in between," is Delia's own retrospective take on it. But there was a middle way, she insisted. Convenience food could be pimped and with some simple sleights of hand you could convince everyone that everything you produced was homemade.

"I was passionately interested in learning to cook," she recalled, but she found contemporary cookbooks—and she had copies of Elizabeth David and Robert Carrier—were frustrating:

> Sometimes I felt there was a lot missing. If you want to drive a car, you have to have driving lessons; you don't just get handed a bunch of car keys and told "here you go, drive," you have to learn. I had struggled myself and I wanted to tell other people how to do it so they wouldn't struggle the way I did. I can remember making marmalade and there was a lemon, but it didn't say the lemon peel, so did you put in the juice? It was just little things like that and I just felt I wanted to reach people with the art of cooking. So the food and the cooking was the star and not me; you know I was just sort of in the background wanting people to understand.

She mocked the pretensions of those who dropped French culinary terms into the conversation (her book, she wrote, was for those who thought "brown rue is a species of butterfly and demiglace a half portion of ice cream") and she disparaged those who professed that there was nothing of greater consequence than gastronomy. "There are more important things in life than cooking," she stated bravely and a nation of flummoxed cooking failures rallied to her cause.

"She was talking to you not as a teacher but as a friend," said her literary agent Deborah Owen, who helped to kick-start her career. Introduced by a photographer with whom Delia had been working as a home economist on shoot for a magazine, Owen asked her, in passing, how she could make the perfect poached egg for her husband. It was the down-to-earth clarity of her response that opened the agent's eyes to the possibilities of this young cook with her pretty looks and sweet smile. "I thought if this woman can do this for my marriage she ought to be able to do it for others as well," she recalled years later, going on to describe Delia's "commonsense mastery of the basics."

Owen helped Delia land a cookery column in the *Daily Mirror*'s new magazine in 1969. In it Delia displayed an innate understanding of what her contemporaries needed. Her little paperback was their shared dirty secret. Keep this book "well hidden," she urged her readers, while you are explaining some tricks to persuade friends that you are indeed a culinary genius.

Delia Smith urged the nation to master the basics of cooking first, from omelettes to treacle sponge.

She suggested hanging dried bunches of herbs around the kitchen, along with a few intriguing jars of spices, before nudging you down to the local supermarket to buy some cheats' essentials. It was important not to run out of "cans of dried milk, Kraft's Parmesan cheese, packets of instant sauce mix, jars of Hellmann's mayonnaise." Not to mention "packets of instant mash potato . . . Batchelor's dehydrated mixed vegetables [and] Marks and Spencer instant chocolate sauce."

Her tips on how to avoid making pastry—aside from buying it ready made or frozen—included a recipe with eight digestive biscuits and 2 ounces of butter. Having melted the butter, stirred in the crumbed biscuits and emptied it into a tin or dish, you should press it down flat "rather like a wall-to-wall carpet."

While her spirit of the 70s meant the inclusion of some convenience foods that would make a true foodie retch, legions of would-be cooks joined her bandwagon. So that by the time she was issuing larger-format cookery books with less reliance on shockers like instant mash, she had a pliant audience.

Likewise her TV shows were intended to be nothing less than accessibly instructional. She didn't flounce around the kitchen reminding the viewer that they were in the presence of genius. In fact she found those early experiences—the first was *Family Fare* and ran for three series with thirty-three editions from 1973—"terrifying." "The program was 24 minutes, 30 seconds," she recalled, "and you had to do it in that time. If you made a mistake in the middle you had to start from the top."

The daughter of an RAF wireless operator, Delia grew up in the London suburb of Bexleyheath. Her mother and grandmother were good home cooks. However, it was perhaps a boyfriend who kept referring to his previous girlfriend's cooking skills that got Delia interested and she started washing up in a small French restaurant, waitressing and then being allowed to help with the cooking. She soon found herself poring over old cookbooks such as those by Eliza Acton (see p. 169) in the British Museum. Armed with such research and her own innate common sense, her emergence onto the British food scene came at a pivotal moment when British home cooks were floundering and needed someone to guide them. With *How to Cheat at Cooking,* Delia won their confidence, sparking a relationship that would grow with each ensuing volume.

Five years on from then, in 1976, Delia published her sixth book, *Frugal Food* (*Recipes from Country Inns and Restaurants* had come out in 1973 and a collection of her *Evening Standard* recipes the following year). But her tone in this new work was much more serious. "I feel our days of unrestricted choice in eating are strictly numbered. There simply is not enough food on this planet to feed all the people who live on it." Eating habits, she felt, had got out of control, and obesity had reached "epidemic proportions." The cheat was out; cheap was in. She attacked so-called labor-saving gadgets, complaining that they "cost a fortune—and then they break down, and when they do you can't get the mending man to come."

Instant food, the cheat's staple, was now shunned as costing "a fortune." Instead economy was paramount—cooking with cider instead of wine, for instance. She was even circumspect about the freezer—"I'm not convinced freezing does always save money"—and condemned bought fish fingers as "outrageously expensive," presenting instead her recipe for salmon fish cakes (the hero of this chapter), along with numerous egg and soup dishes and simple desserts such as caramelized apples.

However, it was two years later, in 1978, that she made what she felt was her "main contribution" to British cuisine when she published *Delia Smith's Cookery Course* to tie in with her BBC series. "At the time I wrote the *Cookery Course,* people who had the money went to Cordon Bleu classes and the people who didn't have the money went to evening classes," she later reflected. "The BBC series and the *Cookery Course* were produced to help teach people to learn to cook in their own homes and not go out on dark evenings to cookery classes."

And she wrote passionately in the book of why she felt the UK had stopped cooking. "When Britain ceased, in the wake of the industrial revolution, to be a predominately rural nation, families lost their links with the country (which is where the roots of good cooking lie)," she argued. Two world wars, with their rationing and shortages, had made things worse. "Till in the end," she continued, "almost a whole generation has missed out on the pleasures of cooking—in many cases where women have to go out to work it has been relegated to the level of a household chore."

Armed with the basic principles outlined in her book, cooking could be, in her words, "enjoyable, fun even." And so she urged that lost generation to get cooking the basics, from omelettes, quiches and fish pies to gravy and every kind of roast, along with sweet dishes from treacle sponge to bread and butter pudding. To counterbalance this, she also gave some firm advice on dieting and slimming: "Unless I'm being entertained, I only allow myself wine at weekends, and again either a pudding or a cake only at weekends."

Whether or not the nation—or indeed the author—really did follow that advice to the letter, what is certain is that Delia Smith herself picked up many stumbling cooks from that generation of the culinarily dispossessed and took them, and then their children, on a cooking journey for the rest of their lives.

86

Sweet & sour pork

AUTHOR: Ken Hom, FROM: *Ken Hom's Chinese Cookery*

SERVES 4

12 oz (350 g) lean pork

1 tablespoon dry sherry or rice wine

1 tablespoon light soy sauce

½ teaspoon salt

2 oz (50 g) green pepper (about ½)

2 oz (50 g) red pepper (about ½)

2 oz (50 g) carrots

2 oz (50 g) spring onions

1 egg, beaten

2 tablespoons cornflour

15 fl oz (400 ml) oil, preferably groundnut

3 oz (75 g) tinned lychees, drained, or fresh orange segments

SAUCE

5 fl oz (150 ml) chicken stock

1 tablespoon light soy sauce

½ teaspoon salt

1½ tablespoons cider vinegar or Chinese white rice vinegar

1 tablespoon sugar

1 tablespoon tomato paste

1 teaspoon cornflour

1 teaspoon water

Cut the pork into 1 inch (2.5 cm) cubes. Put the cubes into a bowl together with the sherry or rice wine, 1 tablespoon of light soy sauce and ½ teaspoon salt, and marinate for 20 minutes. Meanwhile, cut the green and red peppers into 1 inch (2.5 cm) squares. Peel and cut the carrots and spring onions into 1 inch (2.5 cm) cubes. (The uniform size of meat and vegetables adds to the visual appeal of the dish.) Bring a pot of water to the boil and blanch the carrots in it for 4 minutes; drain and set aside.

Mix the egg and cornflour in a bowl until they are well blended into a batter. Lift the pork cubes out of the marinade, put them into the batter and coat each piece well. Heat the oil in a deep-fat fryer or large wok until it is almost smoking. Remove the pork pieces from the batter with a slotted spoon, and deep-fry them. Drain deep-fried pork on kitchen paper.

Combine the chicken stock, soy sauce, salt, vinegar, sugar and tomato paste in a large saucepan. Bring it to the boil. Add all the vegetables, but not the lychees or oranges, and stir well. In a small bowl, blend together the cornflour and the water. Stir this mixture into the sauce and bring it back to the boil. Turn the heat down to a simmer. Add the lychees or oranges and pork cubes. Mix well, and then turn the mixture into a deep platter. Serve at once.

Ken Hom's journey through life has been one that reflects the two extremes of Chinese dietary practice. His childhood in Chicago's Chinatown saw him eating to live; his later—more wealthy—period allowed him to eat for pleasure, and enjoy the wine he so feverishly collected at his home in southwest France. His chance to segue between the necessary (life-sustaining cereals) and the superfluous (meat and vegetables—regarded as of secondary importance) came because the British so took to his BBC series, *Ken Hom's Chinese Cookery,* and subsequent book of the same name, of which he sold 1.2 million copies.

His TV show was in a similar vein to that of Delia Smith or Madhur Jaffrey (see pp. 291 and 284); in fact, as we'll see, the two were responsible for his successful entry into their world.

During his childhood Hom was, at times, almost penniless. He was an only child, the son of a Chinese-American GI who went to China to find a wife. This he did and he brought his bride, happy to escape the perils of the Communist Revolution, back to America. Ken was born in Tucson, Arizona, but his father died when he was barely eight months old. Desperate—her husband had canceled his life insurance cover shortly before he died—and unable to speak English, the young and widowed Mrs. Hom took herself and her baby to where she thought the pair of them might survive: Chinatown in Chicago, where her late husband had some relations.

Ken Hom remained there, ghetto-ized and unable to speak English, until the age of six and was often left alone while his mum (who never learned the new mother tongue) worked long hours at a factory that made tinned Chinese food for the U.S. Army. He recalled one bleak period when his mother, unable to work because of a back injury, eked out their meager provisions of rice with flakes of a single salted fish for two whole months.

Yet she was clearly a good cook and Hom said she always made it fun. His interest was further kindled when, aged eleven, he worked at his uncle's restaurant. He passed all the wages to his mother, keeping only the extra money from bonuses or pay-rises for himself. But it was in his late teens, while studying art at the University of California, that he really got the food bug.

He cooked all the time for himself and for friends and, fortunately, just at the point when he feared a lack of funds might curtail his studies, he was asked to teach Italian cooking to the wife of a wealthy congressman. "I was teaching people to make pasta and they were paying me $300 to do it," he said. "It was like I'd won the lottery." He started giving lessons at his home and then joined the California Culinary Academy as a teacher. A book contract followed and he found himself doing the rounds in New York where, he said, "the chattering classes loved Chinese food."

He was a social creature and it was in 1982 that he met Madhur Jaffrey at a party. Fresh from doing her Indian cooking series in Britain, she

suggested he put himself forward to do the same thing but with Chinese food. Following her advice, he went to London to audition for the role—and sure enough, he got it. It was a straight show, as with Smith and Jaffrey: one presenter in a simple studio carefully walking viewers through the likes of stir-fried beef with orange, and Peking duck.

Smith did Hom the favor of advertising his new series in glowing terms in a newspaper column which, he later said, was "something I'll never forget." But his success was by no means assured. The cleaning lady in the flat he was renting turned her nose up at the Chinese ingredients everywhere. "What's all this Chinese muck doing here?" she ranted. A friend was equally doom-mongering, "Ken," she said, "I think you should prepare yourself—this will never work."

But it did. Hom's series was an instant success. And at a time when ingredients were hard to come by. In the early 1980s the aisles of supermarkets were not filled with soy sauce, rice wine and gingerroot.

Not that Britain was unfamiliar with Chinese food. Immigrants had been arriving in the country since the 1960s, fleeing Maoist China, and by 1970 there were 4,000 Chinese catering businesses, most of which were takeaways. The characteristic flavor combinations, meanwhile, such as sweet and sour sauce, tapped into the British historical subconscious. Medieval cooking, after all, had seen tables groaning with sweet and savory dishes, while many recipes themselves mixed the two (see p. 69). In the words of food historian Colin Spencer, commenting on the success of Chinese food in Britain in the early 80s: "What we were embracing was the return of flavors that once had been part of our own tradition." Although, as Hom states in his introduction to his recipe for sweet and sour pork: "Properly prepared, sweet and sour Chinese dishes are so delicately balanced that one is hard pressed to describe them as either strictly sweet or sour."

Whatever the case, British taste buds had been prepared by Chinese takeaways, enabling Hom to convince many to try the food at home. "I was just in the right place at the right time," he said. "The country was interested, it was hungry. That year I outsold Jeffrey Archer and there was a run on Peking ducks."

Having got Britain hooked on buying woks, Hom went on to bring out a dozen books and several TV series, as well as opening cafés and flogging other Chinese kitchen equipment. But he lamented the fact that he was never able to instill a love of Chinese cuisine that was anything more than skin deep. Thus most of us choose to eat the likes of bastardized dishes such as crispy aromatic duck and fried seaweed, which you'll never find in China. "We [the Chinese] like things that are steamed, soft and chewy," he once bemoaned. "In this country everything people eat is fried. When you try to get them to eat steamed fish they go 'eugh.'" "English people are afraid of food," he continued. "People in the UK don't care where their food comes from. They are poisoning themselves with cheap food."

Ken Hom, in his early TV days, when he appeared on camera with a winning smile and thick black hair was more pragmatic: happy to teach the British what they were happy to learn. "What we [the Chinese] need to learn from the English is the rule of law," he once told an interviewer. "What you need to learn is how to cook a really good stir-fry."

87

Giura
(Slow-braised beef)

AUTHORS: Liliana and Lisetta Burlotto
FROM: The menu at Real Castello di Verduno

INGREDIENTS FOR 4 PERSONS

- **1 kg mature beef (usually neck)**
- **2 large white onions**
- **2 carrots**
- **2 celery sticks**
- **3 garlic cloves**
- **1 sprig of rosemary**
- **1 piece of cinnamon bark**
- **15 black peppercorns**
- **Salt to taste**
- **1 laurel leaf**
- **2 spoonfuls of extra-virgin olive oil**

PREPARATION:
Cut the beef into large chunks, clean and finely slice up the vegetables and mince up the rosemary and cinnamon. Mix together with the remaining ingredients in a preheated oiled large terracotta pot (or thick-based saucepan). Cover with a tight-fitting lid and cook for 2½ hours on a low heat on the hob or in the oven. Serve with slices of partially hollowed thick stale bread, or polenta and boiled vegetables.

It was on 26 July 1986, in Serralunga d'Alba, in the Italian region of Piedmont, that Carlo Petrini was elected president of a gastronomical league. The organization, Arci (Associazione Ricreativa Culturale Italiana), would later merge with other like-minded groups and become known as Slow Food. But whatever words were uttered on that day in late July, and there were more than a few and some of them were quite long, it was the food they ate, its provenance and how it was cooked that spoke volumes.

That evening delegates descended on a restaurant, Real Castello di Verduno, owned by three sisters, Liliana, Lisetta and Gabriella Burlotto. While Gabriella seated Carlo and his fellow guests in the dining room, her two sisters prepared dishes that represented the cornerstones of Slow Food. Each dish was born of the distinct local culture and cooked with care. That the food was also exquisite was equally important. The American chef Alice Waters once called Slow Food a "delicious revolution," which was vital because if it tasted as worthy as it sounded even fewer would pause to consider its merits before walking into a Burger King.

That night they dined first on a peasant broth with chicken livers and herbs. Main course saw the arrival of a meltingly good braised beef stew—a *giura*—with cream of courgettes. Pudding was *bonet,* a Piedmont speciality made with chocolate and amaretti.

The centerpiece of the meal, *giura,* is a humble and economic dish which uses the meat of elderly cows past their milking prime—*vacche stracche.* Sometimes marinated and then gently stewed in the local Barolo wine, it would be put into the oven as the farmers set out to work and relished after a hard day's labor in the fields. Which is how it went down with Petrini and his cronies that night. And each time they subsequently met, single-minded dishes would cut through the cacophony of linguistic exercise. Which is a relief to those who spend time attempting to penetrate the Slow Food manifesto, for those who champion its cause tend to mix philosophy with apocalyptic invective.

The Slow Food purist believes that each bite of a Big Mac brings society closer to extinction. "We are enslaved by speed and have succumbed to the same insidious virus: Fast Life, which disrupts our habits, pervades the privacy of our homes and forces us to eat Fast Food," is a typical utterance. Or as Slow Food supporter Tom Bruce-Gardyne, a journalist and drinks writer, once put it: "Westerners have become a parody of their own self-indulgence. As they waddle into the new century, they have grown fatter, more toothless and more constipated than ever before."

Carlo Petrini himself, as with many of his fellow believers, emerged from the left wing of Italian journalism. While hoping to save the world from degradation, he also aimed to improve the culture of the poorest; it was they, after all, who were so often a part of distinct culinary tradition, be it cooking or cheese-making.

So when they gathered together, the food needed to be as good and authentic as their words. A vital meeting in Paris, for example, where the Slow Food manifesto was drawn up, saw a starter of flan of sturgeon with black cabbage sauce, potatoes and thyme. Then came pasta stuffed with veal and served with white truffles, before a dish of lamb tenderloin with coffee. Pudding was honey jelly with balsamic vinegar and wild strawberries.

If the food served at their meetings was not up to scratch, all hell would break loose. In October 1982, for example, Petrini had led a merry band of Arci followers to Montalcino, in the Tuscan hills, where some fellow lefties were celebrating the Festival of the Thrush. The feast, which heralded the end of the Brunello and Barolo harvest, was an opportunity for the Petrini gang to meet fellow socialists and communists and discuss their anxieties and political strategies. But Petrini left enraged: the quality of the conversation was fine, but the food had been terrible.

Back in his hometown of Bra, Petrini wrote a furious letter on behalf of Arci to those who had organized the festival. "We are writing this letter to discuss the lunch we had at your club," he began. It was "a spread worthy only of an army barrack or a fifties diner." The food, he said, was "hideous" and "unacceptable" for it had included "cold pasta, inedible ribollita, unwashed salad greens, a dessert made inedible because of the crowd pushing everywhere for its turn." If he'd cooked food like that in Bra, he said, he'd "be publicly lynched."

So it was hardly surprising that when McDonalds reared its ugly head in Rome in 1986, Petrini and Co. lost their temper again. Its site was by the ancient and beautiful Piazza di Spagna. "It's as if a bomb has hit the city," cried one architect. The urban planner and critic Bruno Zevi asked: "Will Piazza di Spagna become a garbage dump identifiable by the nauseating smell of fried food?" He talked of the "ruin of Rome." Others saw the arrival of the Big Mac there as nothing less than the insidious "colonization by the United States."

Carlo Petrini gathered his troops and staged a sit-in on the famous Spanish Steps that led from the square to the Trinità dei Monti. Defiantly they ate pasta—apparently in a light tomato sauce with a hint of garlic and chili. Slow Food found its voice that day and decided from then on to use the name in English to garner a wider following and take on the Big Mac in its own language.

The McDonalds was built anyway and was by then one of almost 30,000 outlets that had spread across the world since the first had opened in Des Plaines, Illinois, on 15 April 1955. For Petrini it could not have been further from the philosophy of one of his own mentors, Brillat-Savarin (see p. 155), the Frenchman who had urged others to "eat slowly and savor thoughtfully." Although many of his other utterances are neatly applicable to McDonalds. "Tell me what kind of food you eat and I will tell you what kind of man you are," he once wrote, for instance.

Petrini, meanwhile, deplored the increasing interest in food, feeling it bred ignorance rather than good culture. "We're all full of gastronomy and recipes," he once told a journalist. "Turn on a TV anywhere in the world and you will see an idiot with a spoon. And every newspaper and magazine has recipes and a photo of the dish taken from above like a cadaver. It's a form of onanism and is masturbatory. We must normalize food rather than put it on a pedestal out of reach."

Cooking, he believed, must not be seen as a chore, because it then alienates the cook, who doubtless then seeks refuge at McDonalds. Yet the irony is that Petrini himself, as one of his sidekicks admitted, did not cook regularly. And he risked accusations of elitism as he preached the Slow Food creed: "The cultural goals of the international Slow Movement are to defeat all forms of chauvinism, to re-appropriate diversity, and to indulge in a healthy dose of cultural relativism." You might want to fill yourself up with a nice burger and fries before you attempt to digest that.

88

Tagliatelle of oyster with caviar

AUTHOR: Marco Pierre White, FROM: The menu at Harvey's

SERVES 4

20 fresh oysters (shelled, retaining their juices and the rounded shell)

FOR THE SAUCE BEURRE BLANC:

4 shallots, very finely chopped

75 ml/3 fl oz white wine vinegar

225 g/8 oz unsalted butter, cut into cubes

Salt and freshly ground white pepper

Lemon juice to taste

TO SERVE:

225 g/8 oz cucumber (as dark a green as you can find)

25 g/1 oz butter

225 g/8 oz tagliatelle

Fresh seaweed and/or rock-salt

2 tbsp black caviar

TO MAKE THE SAUCE:

Put the shallots in a pan with the vinegar and bring to the boil. Continue to boil for a minute or two to drive off the acidity and concentrate the flavours. Add a few drops of cold water and bring the mixture back to the boil.

Remove the pan from the heat and gently but quickly whisk in the butter, piece by piece.

Leave the sauce to infuse for 20 minutes. Then season with salt and pepper and a little lemon juice. Pass through a muslin-lined sieve. Taste and adjust seasoning again, if necessary. Warm through just before serving.

TO PREPARE THE TAGLIATELLE AND CUCUMBER GARNISH:

Peel, de-seed the cucumber and cut it into julienne strips, about 4 cm/1½ inches long. Place in a pan with just enough water to cover and half the butter. Bring to just beneath the boil and simmer until the cucumber is just tender. Drain, pat dry and keep warm.

Just before serving, gently warm through the tagliatelle in just enough water to cover, along with the remaining butter and seasoning to taste.

TO COOK THE OYSTERS:

Thoroughly scrub clean the rounded oyster shells. Place them in a small pan, cover with water and bring to the boil. This will both sterilize and warm the shells.

Strain the oyster juices to remove any traces of shell. Place the juices in a small pan and bring to the boil with a little water, if needed, to cover the oysters. Add the oysters and poach them gently over a low heat until they are just firm to the touch – about 1 minute *only!* Drain the oysters, pat dry with a clean cloth and keep warm.

TO SERVE:

Dress each plate with a bed of either seaweed or rock-salt – if you have neither, a little mashed potato under each shell will serve to keep the oysters stable. Place the 5 warmed oyster shells securely on each plate.

Wind the well-drained tagliatelle around a fork to make a nest to settle inside each shell. Place an oyster on top, then cover with a few strips of cucumber.

Spoon the beurre soy sauce gently over the oysters and then place a few grains of caviar on top of each. Garnish the plate with seaweed if you wish.

On a blisteringly cold night in 1987, twenty-four-year-old chef patron Marco White stood with his young female maître d,' a couple of chefs and two waiters by the door of his restaurant. They stared out across Wandsworth Common as a blizzard raged. The restaurant was completely empty. It was a few days after the place had launched and the weather wasn't helping. "We were dead," White later recalled. "Any more nights like that and we were going bust."

But if anything would drive him on, it was the stars he had in his eyes, Michelin ones. And the food that it rewarded was indisputably French. Marco White knew this: he had been trained in the art of classical French cooking, the kind of food that was all the rage in restaurants during the 1970s and early 80s. As the British had acquiesced to the dominance of French cooking at the end of the nineteenth century, so it did in the postwar years of the twentieth.

From the early 1970s the Roux brothers, Michel and Albert, for example, had towered over the London dining scene. Le Gavroche, which opened in 1969, was *the* place for a young chef to get his training. And there were others. Pierre Koffmann (La Tante Claire) and Michel Bourdin (the Connaught) ran London establishments that the fashionable dined out in, and then, in 1984, the self-taught chef Raymond Blanc opened Le Manoir aux Quat'Saisons in Oxfordshire. It was in the kitchens of these Frenchmen that every ambitious chef sought work. And one such budding culinary talent, who ended up working for all of them, was Marco White.

A working-class boy from Leeds, he was in his late teens when he began toiling at the Hotel St. George in Harrogate. It was 1978 and he was cleaning shoes when he wasn't peeling vegetables. It was here that he first came across an Egon Ronay guide. Leafing through the pages, his eyes lit up at the possibilities of such glittering, fine dining. Then he came across a copy of the little red book with its sought-after and very rarely given stars. Those who received such accolades were few and far between and it fired the young White with an extraordinary sense of ambition. "Money was not a concern," he once wrote. "My success would be measured in Michelin stars."

Celebrity chef Marco Pierre White (right) became the first and youngest British chef to have won three Michelin stars by the age of thirty-three.

His dream of Michelin success set him off on a journey that led him to train in the country's best restaurants and then work to get a coveted star for himself. It was a tough road to success that would see his passion for stars eventually turn to loathing for the very institution that handed them out.

The Michelin Red Guide—the one that strikes such terror into the hearts of so many chefs, who work every hour to gain stars and endure sleepless nights in the days leading up to its release in January each year—began in 1900. At a time when cars were rare and good garages rarer, the two brothers, André and Édouard Michelin, who had started the tire company in the 1880s, decided to launch a guidebook that would tell potential customers where they could change their tires and where they might like to stop for a meal on the journey.

Intended initially as a marketing vehicle for the tire company, it quickly gained in popularity as well as influence. In 1926 it started awarding stars to what it regarded as the best establishments. One star denoted "Very good cooking in its category," two, "Excellent cooking, worth a detour" and three, "Exceptional cuisine, worth a special journey." And it was these stars that, by the early 1980s, were obsessing White.

Having worked at the acclaimed Box Tree in West Yorkshire, he traveled to London and knocked on the door of the Le Gavroche HQ in Wandsworth. There he saw Albert Roux himself. "Go back to Leeds," said Roux, evidently impressed. "Get your belongings and then come back down on Monday. Report here on Tuesday." White lived up to his potential. His journey to Michelin success was well and truly under way, stoked by Roux who once told him: "If I don't get three stars, I'll throw myself in the Thames."

So that bleak winter's night in 1987, when the only customers who came in from the cold were a prison officer and his wife, was a mere blip. The restaurant was Harvey's and its forty-four covers were soon filled once the restaurant critics had visited. Fay Maschler wrote of "the volatile but rather beautiful Marco, his intensity can glaze a crème brûlée from ten yards." Then the man who had inspired White's interest in the first place came in himself. Egon Ronay reviewed it and, said White, "bookings never stopped from that day on." Ronay also called him Marco Pierre White, adding his middle name, which appealed to White as a neat refinement and it stuck. Once business improved, White focused on turning out dishes that would impress Michelin. And he did it in a way that transformed the reputations of many chefs in the 1980s and 90s.

But while the restaurant was a place of refined elegance and the dishes small works of art, the kitchen was a different kettle of fish. "In Harvey's I had found my adrenaline heaven, a pain paradise," White recalled. On a table in the center of the kitchen, he worked to bring together the dishes that started as sketches on a piece of paper. With his tousled, curly hair hanging over his face, he counted down the seconds before the component parts of each dish needed to reach him. "We were like wolves," he said, "darting round each of us doing a bit of everything." Any mistakes were rewarded with vicious assaults, mental and physical. Miscreants got thrown in the bin. Complaints that the place was too hot saw him turning off the air-conditioning or slicing holes in his employees' clothing. By contrast, those who prospered under him, such as Gordon Ramsay, were rewarded with huge success.

White didn't contain his rage to the kitchen. Obnoxious diners, those who were late or those who clicked their fingers at waiters, were thrown out. He was behaving more like a rock star than a chef and he loved the press attention it brought him. A journalist in the mid-1980s once asked him: "Someone told me you kicked eight people out of your restaurant in the last two weeks..." "Eight people in two weeks," replied a brooding White, drawing on an ever-present Marlboro. "God, I'm below par."

But nothing would detract him from the goal of achieving stars, which he knew could only be won with a combination of perfection and consistency. His menu featured classic French dishes such as pigeon in pig's bladder, pig's trotter, pottage of shellfish, ravioli of oyster and his own creation tagliatelle of oyster with caviar. Of which he later commented: "[It] succeeds in every way. It's not enough for a dish to have great flavor, it's only when the taste of the dish equals its visual appeal that you know you're onto a success. This is one of the few dishes I know which actually does that. It's very rare."

All the hard work and ingenuity paid off. Within the year he'd won a star. Two years later, he gained a second, while in 1995 he became the first British chef to win three stars and, at thirty-three, the youngest. "To win a star was rare," he later remarked. "To win two stars was rarer. To be told I'd won three stars... it was the end of my race. I had danced to the Michelin drum. I understood the rules and did what was expected of the system."

He held those three stars for five years and then in November 1999 he put a call through to Michelin. "Just to let you know. I stop cooking on December 23," he told the man who dished out the stars, Derek Bulmer. "Please don't include me in your next guide."

Michelin dismissed his antics as a PR stunt. White's view was he didn't want to "live a lie." If he wasn't in the kitchen, he shouldn't get stars. Deftly he cast aside the pressure of star-gazing and then turned his venom on Michelin. "Today they dish out stars like confetti," he said in 2010. Those secretive inspectors had less knowledge and ability than those they judged and, he said, when stars were being given to chefs who spent more time on television than in their kitchens, "you have to question the integrity of the guide." The whole institution, he argued, had become "unhinged."

The acclaimed chef Nico Ladenis once said of White: "Marco has a mad, mad passion in food such as I've never encountered in anyone. It's total madness. But you have to forgive him. He's a near genius." Unreliable and self-centered he might be to some people, but the chef—who quit the kitchen to go fishing—brought a feverish glamour and notoriety to cooking such as had never been seen before. He also learned to cook the finest French food without ever even visiting France. "It was a revolution," he reflected. "The French guys had dominated British kitchens, but I got our British boys going."

89

Chicken & goat's cheese mousse with olives

AUTHOR: Rowley Leigh, FROM: The menu at Kensington Place, London

2 large breasts of chicken
2 egg whites
100 grams goat's cheese
700 ml double cream
Butter for moulds
2 tablespoons black olives
Additional clarified butter for sauce
200 ml red wine
50 ml red wine vinegar
45 grams soft brown caster sugar
50 ml port
1 dessertspoon cracked white pepper

Remove skin and any obvious sinew from the chicken breasts. Cut into small pieces and purée in a food processor. Add the egg whites and continue to blend to a smooth and homogenous mass. Pass this mixture, a little at a time, through a drum sieve. Recuperate all the passed meat and chill in a large steel bowl, covering the meat with film.

Cut the goat's cheese into small pieces and blend this in turn in the (washed) bowl of the food processor. Add 100 ml of the double cream and continue to blend until absolutely smooth. It should not be necessary to sieve this mixture.

Place the bowl with the chicken on to a bed of ice in a larger bowl. Very slowly, add 100 ml of the cream to the chicken mixture, beating it constantly with a wooden spoon as you proceed. Take care to clean the sides of the bowl with a rubber spatula and ensure the mixture is thoroughly blended. Continue to beat in another 100 ml of cream, beating in air as you make the mixture lighter and smoother.

Now incorporate the goat's cheese and cream mixture, beating the two mixtures together. Test the mixture by poaching a teaspoonful of the mixture in a little pot of simmering, salted water. It should still be quite firm when cooked but be smooth and not grainy. Continue now to beat in the remainder of the cream, testing the mixture again to make sure it will still hold when cooked. Once the desired consistency is reached—very light and smooth—season the mixture with salt. Adding the salt will tighten the mixture (it is disastrous to add it too early) and a little more cream can be added to loosen the mixture again. Taste the mixture for seasoning.

Brush six 150 ml moulds with softened butter. Rinse the olives, stone them and then chop them extremely finely with a large knife. Squeeze the olives dry in a piece of kitchen paper and then line the bottom of the moulds with the olives, pushing them down into the butter to make a compact layer. Now pipe in the mousse mixture, tapping the moulds to make sure there are no air pockets and smoothing the tops flat with a palette knife. Place the moulds in a tray of hot water, cover with foil and then bake in a cool oven (120°C) until just set, around 25 minutes.

Boil the wine, vinegar and sugar mixture in a small pan and reduce by two thirds. Add the port, reduce slightly and then add the crushed pepper. Turn the mousses out on to six plates. Pour a tablespoon of clarified butter on to each plate and then dribble half a dessertspoon of the red reduction into the butter. Decorate with two or three plucks of chervil.

While Marco Pierre White (see p. 302) was turning out French food in his uniquely brutal way, there was a very different kind of revolution happening on the other side of London. Rowley Leigh had also trained at Le Gavroche, but his approach to cooking was a world apart and distinctly laid back.

Perhaps he was an unlikely figure to lead the British fight back. He had been slung out of various academic institutions for, in his own words, "appalling behavior" before spending his early twenties playing snooker. Needing money, he got a job turning burgers in Covent Garden and was unexpectedly bitten by the food bug. He toiled his way through some of the city's best restaurants, his work at Le Gavroche catching the eye of Albert Roux who made him head chef at the smart Roux brothers–owned City hangout Le Poulbot.

"By the time I was head chef of Le Poulbot I lived and dreamed cooking," he said. But something on the scene was lacking, he felt. There was either fine dining or cheap and cheerful pubs. In fact Le Poulbot represented both of these. The restaurant had two sections—a posh part upstairs and a brasserie downstairs—but nothing in between. "I wanted to merge the two," he said. "There wasn't anywhere in London with any ambition that wasn't fine dining."

So Leigh got together with Nick Smallwood and Simon Slater, who already ran the successful and upmarket Launceston Place in South Kensington, and created Kensington Place. The idea was for innovative and exciting food but produced at a budget for a bigger market.

The restaurant had one large room, designed by Julian Wickham with floor-to-ceiling windows looking out on the streets of Notting Hill, for which Leigh drew up a menu that many believe made him the architect of contemporary British cooking. You could order a simple omelette (made in the Elizabeth David fashion with finely chopped herbs), there were chips and mash, sausages and then Leigh's own creations such as a whole oozing wedge of griddled foie gras served on a sweet-corn pancake or his exquisitely soft chicken and goat's cheese mousse, offset to perfection by the bitterness of its chopped-olive topping.

"It was a revolution," recalled Cath Gradwell, one of the chefs who worked with Leigh at the time. "And it was brave. No one else could have put chips on the menu and got away with it. If you'd opened a smart restaurant up north and written that kind of menu there would have been a riot. It was definitely the moment when things changed."

Leigh's chicken and goat's cheese mousse was not a dish he'd been particularly serious about. The idea had come from Michel Roux's Waterside Inn where the Frenchman had created a chicken mousse with Roquefort and walnuts. "I just wrote it on the menu and thought it sounded fun. I don't think I'd actually ever made the dish. It was the red finch in the window," Leigh recalled, referring to the marketing trick of enticing people in with a red finch knowing they would only ever buy the white variety.

"I never thought people would actually have it and like it. But it was amazingly popular and I never took it off the menu." So it remained the chief weapon in Leigh's armory until he left the restaurant to start Le Café Anglais in Bayswater some twenty years later.

After passing the blitzed chicken breast through a fine drum sieve and mixing it with the soft goat's cheese, it was put in a mold with chopped olives on the base. So when turned out after cooking in a bain marie, it had a dark topping. Leigh added clarified butter around the dish as well as a port and wine reduction and then three sprigs of chervil as a final touch.

Extraordinarily, he may have cooked it thousands of times but he studiously avoided consuming it. "I never ate it once," he said. "I thought that if I did I might want to improve it. I thought I'd just leave it alone. It's a demanding recipe and had to be perfect. But I took a great deal of pride watching the kids do it along with the omelette."

The restaurant was, as Leigh put it, "rammed within the [first] week." And on Saturday the restaurant critic Jonathan Meades heralded its arrival in *The Times*. "This is the place and about time too," he wrote. "That was real blast off," recalled Leigh. The growth of the London restaurant scene subsequently gathered pace, encouraged by the changing climate in Margaret Thatcher's Britain where eating out was becoming a wider pursuit, a regular part of social interaction rather than simply something the posh and wealthy indulged in.

Leigh was joined in his revolution by other budding British cooks. Simon Hopkinson brought his adept and passionate home-cooking skills as chef and co-owner of Terence Conran's restaurant Bibendum and Notting Hill also saw the opening of Alastair Little's unfussy self-named restaurant. While on the other side of the street from Kensington Place, Sally Clarke opened Clarke's with its fixed menu promoting the joys of the British season. "The whole scene was bursting open," said Leigh. "And Alastair, Simon and myself became absolutely obsessed with food."

Leigh may have been taught by the French and inspired by Quentin Crewe's book on the great chefs of France, but suddenly his Gallic soulmates were left for dust. When the self-taught Frenchman Raymond Blanc arrived, he steered clear of London altogether, opening a brasserie in Oxford instead.

Rowley Leigh at Kensington Place restaurant, London.

Leigh had no intentions of starting a restaurant revolution, however. Like so many other radicals in the food world, he was just doing what came naturally. He didn't want kitchens to be fierce places; indeed his own view on cooking was that it was therapeutic. As engaging and holistic an experience as savoring his iconic chicken and goat's cheese mousse.

90

Quails with couscous

AUTHOR: Joan Bunting, FROM: *MasterChef 1990*

1 tablespoon olive oil or melted butter
Salt
8 oz (225 g) couscous
2–3 tablespoons pine nuts, toasted
2–3 oz (50–75 g) large plump raisins, soaked in Armagnac
4 pairs quails
8 rashers bacon
A little red wine
Pepper
A few sprigs of fresh coriander or parsley, to garnish

Put 10 fl oz (300 ml) water and 1 tablespoon of olive oil or butter in a large saucepan. Add a pinch of salt and bring to the boil. Remove from the heat, add the couscous, stir and leave to swell for 15 minutes. Stir again and add the pine nuts and raisins. Stuff the quails with some of the couscous mixture, and secure with cocktail sticks. Cover each quail with bacon and place in a roasting dish. Pour in a little red wine and season with salt and pepper. Bake for 8–10 minutes at gas mark 7–8, 425–450°F (220–230°C), until very tender. Strain the sauce and serve separately. Pile the reheated remaining couscous in the centre of a suitable dish and surround with the quails. Pour over the sauce and garnish with coriander or parsley.

Joan Bunting had returned to her hometown of Gosforth near Newcastle from a long teaching assignment in the Bahamas when she picked up a copy of the *Radio Times*. Flicking through it she saw an advertisement from the BBC. They were looking for contestants for a new cooking competition. She tore out the page, drew a ring round the ad and picked up the telephone.

Bunting had long been interested in cooking, taking lessons from her mother. In fact she'd learned to do a full Sunday roast by the age of ten. The criteria for this new competition didn't seem too terrifying, although she did wonder what it would actually be like as there weren't any other cooking contests on television at the time.

The first episode broadcast on 2 July 1990. The show pitted her skills against two other amateur cooks and she made it through to the semifinals and then the final—there were nine heats and three semifinals. On 24 September she cooked her way through a menu of mussels with *pistou* (a Provençal mixture of garlic, basil and oil), a Moroccan dish of quails (rather than the traditional pigeon) with couscous, accompanied by spring cabbage with garlic and juniper, before finishing with a pudding of Mediterranean islands. The latter being meringue pieces floating in a sea of custard and decorated with small pieces of fresh fruit.

The cooking and tasting over—there were two judges that night, the chef Anton Edelmann and the art historian Roy Strong—and the show's presenter Loyd Grossman addressed the camera. "We've deliberated, cogitated and digested," he said—echoed, immediately, by millions of viewers at home up and down the country, attempting to imitate his bizarre Bostonian, mid-Atlantic drawl—before announcing that Joan Bunting was the winner.

The end of the series saw the start of a revolution in food television. The show, said Grossman, was "pioneering" and "kick-started the proliferation of food programmes on TV." "I hadn't thought I'd get through to the final," muttered a modest Mrs. Bunting, who went on to write a cookery column for her local Newcastle paper, the *Journal,* for the next thirteen years before retiring to the place that had inspired the cornerstone of her winning menu, Provence.

MasterChef had been devised by the film director Franc Roddam, who had notched up such success with the late-1970s mod-revival cult classic *Quadrophenia.* Roddam selected Grossman to present the show as he was currently a copresenter with David Frost of what Grossman himself has called "one of the most successful television programmes ever," *Through the Keyhole.* As he was also a long-serving restaurant critic for the *Sunday Times* and *Harpers & Queen* magazine, he had, as he put it, "a lot of food credibility."

He also had one of the strangest accents on television, which, when mixed with his catchphrase, made for a moment in each show of strangely enjoyable anticipation. "I knew, because of my experience in light entertainment television, how important a catchphrase was," he recalled. "And I knew that people would start repeating it. It became a viral thing."

Of course it was the subject matter itself that so appealed to the British television-watching public. "I knew from writing about food for ten years and getting out and about around the country that the dam was soon going to burst," said Grossman.

"It had been repressed for so long, for all sorts of social and cultural reasons. And it burst at just the point *MasterChef* was starting. We accelerated the process."

It did that by making the food look slick—on a dark set, moodily lit. It was unlike any other cookery program and the food establishment loved it too. The list of chefs, who appeared with celebrity counterparts ranging from Michael Caine to George Melly, was a roll-call of the great and good from the culinary world. There were the Roux brothers—Albert and Michel—Simon Hopkinson, Alastair Little, Raymond Blanc and Pierre Koffmann, among many others.

While the show was serious about food, it gained an audience much wider than those involved in cooking. But although Grossman and others were confident they would have a hit on their hands, those who ran the schedules were less sure. "We went out at 7 p.m. on a Monday against *Coronation Street,*" recalled Grossman of the first series, "and that was the graveyard slot. But our program was novel. People watched it and then started talking about it."

Grossman believed *MasterChef* was responsible for nothing less than "a huge transformation. It opened up food culture to a mass audience and it has stayed there." Two years after *MasterChef* started broadcasting, Grossman was accosted by a waiter in a London restaurant. He told him that before the show had started he had never heard people talk about food—they would discuss golf or business. But now they talked about what they were eating. "Food had not been regarded as a legitimate subject for conversation," said Grossman. "It was almost rude."

MasterChef went on to become a huge global brand with different formats broadcasting across the world, be it *Celebrity MasterChef Australia* or the German *Deutschlands Meisterkoch.* It had moved well away from the graveyard to prime-time viewing. Loyd Grossman, with a little help from Joan Bunting, showed that good food and the pleasure of it, in Grossman's own words, "was no longer just for the cynical and we were part of that phenomenon."

91

Individual sausage, tomato & artichoke-heart pizzas

AUTHOR: *Gourmet* magazine (where the recipe originally appeared in 1991)
FROM: *epicurious.com*

MAKES 2 SERVINGS

TIME: CAN BE PREPARED IN 45 MINUTES OR LESS

1½ cups unbleached all-purpose flour

1¼ teaspoon (half of a ¼-ounce package) fast-acting yeast

½ cup hot water (130°F)

1 tablespoon olive oil

1 teaspoon sugar

½ teaspoon salt

½ pound hot Italian sausage, casing discarded and the sausage chopped

½ cup finely chopped onion

1 large garlic clove, or to taste, minced

½ teaspoon dried oregano, crumbled

½ teaspoon dried basil, crumbled

Yellow cornmeal for sprinkling on the baking sheet

A 14-ounce can Italian tomatoes, drained, chopped fine, drained again in a colander

A 6-ounce jar marinated artichoke hearts, drained, rinsed, and patted dry

½ cup coarsely grated mozzarella

⅓ cup freshly grated Parmesan

In a food processor combine ½ cup of the flour and the yeast, with the motor running add the water, and turn the motor off. Add the oil, the sugar, the salt, and the remaining 1 cup flour, blend the mixture until it forms a ball, and turn it out onto a lightly floured surface. Knead the dough 8 to 10 times, form it into a ball, and let it rest while making the sausage mixture.

In a small heavy skillet cook the sausage over moderate heat, stirring, until it is cooked through, transfer it with a slotted spoon to a bowl, and discard all but 1 tablespoon of the fat remaining in the skillet. In the fat cook the onion, the garlic, the oregano, the basil, and salt and pepper to taste over moderately low heat, stirring, until the onion is soft and transfer the onion mixture to the bowl.

Halve the dough, form each half into a ball, and stretch each ball into 7-inch round, making the rounds slightly thicker around the edges. Transfer the rounds to a baking sheet (preferably black steel, for a crisper crust), oiled and sprinkled lightly with the cornmeal, top the rounds evenly with the sausage mixture, the tomatoes, the artichoke

hearts, the mozzarella, the Parmesan, and salt and pepper to taste, and bake the pizzas on the bottom rack of a preheated 500°F oven for 10 to 12 minutes, or until the crusts are golden brown.

Fifty-eight years after television first transmitted food programs to British audiences (see p. 235), a new medium sprang to life that would revolutionize cooking all over again.

On a summer's morning in 1995, Rochelle Udell, a high-flyer at New York publishing company Condé Nast, sat on the floor of her handsome Greek Revival home in Westchester County, New York. The light pouring into her sitting room, she sat with magazines and cookbooks strewn all around her. It was the weekend and time out from her day job as Vice President of Creative Marketing and New Media.

The daughter of a baker, she had spent many a happy hour as a child helping her father out at his bakery in Brooklyn. It had instilled in her a love of food and a passion for fine ingredients. But this particular morning she was getting frustrated. "All I wanted was a decent recipe for chicken breast," she said. A good cook, Udell was expected to have a few tricks up her sleeve when she gave a dinner party and she was determined to find something a little different to do with the chicken breasts she had in the fridge.

Recently appointed at Condé Nast to look into ways of taking advantage of the new phenomenon that was the World Wide Web, she was struck by a sudden thought. If only there was a place to go on the Internet where she could find such a recipe. If only such a website existed. But in 1995 it didn't exist. She looked up from the floor and forgot about the chicken breasts. She had had a rather bigger idea.

"It was an epiphany," she recalled years later. And she certainly couldn't remember what it was she did to those chicken breasts to impress her friends that evening. But on Monday morning she went to see Si Newhouse, the big cheese at Condé Nast, about her idea.

"I started lobbying to do a website," she said. "What had occurred to me was that the web could do two important things. It could connect people and it could sort information. Food seemed a safe place to play and a good subject with which to learn the web business." The result was epicurious.com, the first food website on the Internet, launched quietly at the end of the summer and with Udell as the president and founder.

The idea of epicurious was that it would be a brand. A magazine could follow, as might a TV show and food products. But then Rochelle had another, slightly smaller but associated, epiphany just before Thanksgiving that same year.

It was warm in New York that November, where she and her husband and family lived during the week. "I was up early, at around 5:30 a.m.," she recalled. "The forecast was for 21 degrees and I was wondering whether there was a way of cooking the turkey on the grill. So I logged onto aol.com, where I saw a 'turkey talking hotline.' At

6 a.m. I put a question up on the site asking for ideas. Half an hour later I had around 30 answers."

So Udell's next idea was to add a recipe swap dimension to Epicurious, much of whose recipe content came from *Gourmet* magazine, which was also in the Condé Nast stable. The sausage, tomato and artichoke-heart pizzas, originally published in *Gourmet,* was one of the first recipes that went up on the website when it launched, the artichoke hearts lending an element of sophistication to a popular dish. It was just the sort of recipe that got people commenting on, cooking and then reviewing it.

From that moment the site didn't just grow but the idea of food on the Internet blossomed into a frenzy. More than fifteen years later, the site had some 30,000 recipes—all new dishes created bespoke for Epicurious and tested before being published. Ninety-six percent of those recipes were being rated by users, of which there were between 6 and 8 million each month. And the Internet couldn't have been more crowded.

The site's success, meanwhile—aside from advertising revenue—could be measured in the same way that recipe books were measured in their ascendency in the late 1700s and early nineteenth century. Plagiarism became rife. "People steal our recipes. Our content shows up in places we never agreed to," said Tanya Steel, who became editor-in-chief in 2005. "But it's the nature of the beast and we take it as a compliment. We're one of the dinosaurs but with age comes wisdom and we don't worry too much about our imitators."

Sixteen years after she had invented the first food website, Rochelle Udell brushed aside the idea that her own creation could kill off her original passion, cookbooks, which she devotedly read at night in place of novels. "Cookbooks have an

epicurious.com

emotional resonance that you don't get online," she said. "And as cooks and people who love food are passionate tactile people, they'll never give up buying cookbooks and food magazines. The Internet can build someone's interest in food but it also drives people to cookbooks."

Today Epicurious gets its highest volume of traffic just before Thanksgiving, showing that new technology can be a prop to support the oldest traditions.

92

Pecan waffles with pecan & banana syrup

AUTHOR: Emeril Lagasse, FROM: *Emeril's TV Dinners*

MAKES 4 TO 8 SERVINGS

- **¼ pound (1 stick) plus 2 tablespoons unsalted butter, melted**
- **1 cup pecan pieces**
- **2 medium-size ripe bananas, peeled and cut crosswise into ½ inch-thick slices**
- **2 cups pure maple syrup**
- **1 cup ground pecans**
- **1½ cups bleached all-purpose flour**
- **½ cup sugar**
- **1 tablespoon baking powder**
- **¼ teaspoon salt**
- **2 large egg yolks**
- **1 teaspoon pure vanilla extract**
- **1¾ cups milk**
- **2 large egg whites**

Heat 2 tablespoons of the butter in a medium-size sauté pan over medium heat. Add the pecan pieces and cook, stirring, until golden, 2 to 3 minutes. Add the banana slices and syrup and bring to a simmer. Set aside and keep warm.

Combine the flour, ground pecans, sugar, baking powder, and salt in a medium-size mixing bowl. In a large mixing bowl, beat the egg yolks and vanilla together slightly. Beat the milk and the 1 stick of melted butter into the egg mixture. Fold the flour mixture into the egg mixture. Stir until combined yet still slightly lumpy. In a small mixing bowl beat the egg whites until stiff peaks form. Gently fold into the batter, leaving little fluffs.

If using a Belgian waffle iron, pour 1 cup of the batter onto the grids of a pre-heated and little greased waffle iron. (Regular waffle irons will take only about ½ cup.) Close the lid. Do not open during cooking time. For the Belgian waffle iron, cook until golden and crisp, 3 to 4 minutes. Small waffle irons will take 1½ to 2 minutes.

Serve hot with the pecan and banana syrup.

Reese Schonfeld had formed in the world of television. In 1980, with Ted Turner, he had co-founded Cable News Network (CNN). A New York journalist who moved to the business side of his profession, he saw CNN as a newspaper in audio-visual form. There was, he reckoned, plenty of news to keep its presenters and reporters busy over a constant twenty-four-hour cycle, not to mention the viewers watching.

Some ten years later and he thought it was time to do a similar thing with the subject of food. So he conceived the idea of TV Food Network (TVFN). It was simply, he said, "transferring another page of the newspaper to TV." And asked whether he thought there was really enough interest to launch a channel that did nothing but broadcast food content day and night, he replied simply: "Everybody eats."

It was, of course, a little more complicated than that. This was an era, in the U.S., when cable channels were springing up all over the place. There was MTV (Music Television), for example, alongside CNN and Nickelodeon. But to survive, "category" broadcasting, as the cable industry called it, had to deliver an audience to advertisers whose funding Schonfeld needed along with the revenue from subscribers willing to pay for this niche content. So the programs needed to have broad enough appeal.

There were already plenty of daytime food programs on TV, most of them instructional. Schonfeld reckoned that if America was ready for twenty-four-hour food TV, it needed to be entertaining. He had a target market in mind. There were amateur chefs who would probably tune in anyway, but he wanted to attract those eighteen- to thirty-five-year-old women who had to balance their jobs with cooking for husbands and children. And he needed to reach them. So along with partnering a newspaper company, he teamed up with a major TV station and nine other cable companies which gave his new channel access to 7.5 million American homes right from the start.

He then chose a big foodie moment in the U.S. calendar, launching on 23 November—Thanksgiving Day—in 1993. The channel, at the start, broadcast six hours of programs, which were repeated four times a day. This was food as entertainment, as reflected in the programs that were aired. These included an anchored, news-style show, *Food News and Views, Molto Mario* with Mario Batali, *Chillin and Grillin* with Bobby Flay, *How to Feed Your Family on a Hundred Dollars a Week* and *Essence of Emeril.*

Emeril Lagasse was a large, boisterous chef and restaurateur working in New Orleans when a producer approached him about recording a pilot. Lagasse wasn't sure he'd have the time. But he sorted his schedule, the pilot got the thumbs up and his *Essence of Emeril* show debuted at the channel's launch. Recording up to seven shows a day, Lagasse found a way of keeping the crew awake during the long hours of filming in studios in New York. Adding a dash of salt or a sprinkling of sugar to a dish, he would yell "Bam!" at the top of his voice.

It kept the crew awake and became his catchphrase. He also became one of the most familiar faces on U.S. television and later was given his own late-night chat show where he cooked in front of a studio audience and had a band, to boot. His inimitable style is retained in the tie-in book, *Emeril's TV Dinners,* which came out five years later. Introducing his pecan waffles recipe, for instance, he says: "If you're a waffle lover, this is the one for you, babe. The pecan and banana syrup is out-a-sight."

TVFN, which changed its name to Food Network after Schonfeld sold out, gradually picked up audiences. It repeated classics presented by the likes of Julia Child and James Beard (see pp. 260 and 269) and also brought to the U.S. British shows such as *Two Fat Ladies* in 1997 and *The Naked Chef* in 1999. In fact so popular was Jamie Oliver (see p. 341) that Food Network subsidized further episodes to guarantee the show's return.

By 2002 there were 71 million subscribers to Food Network; some ten years later and the figure was closer to 90 million. It launched in Britain in 2009 (where the UK Food channel had been in place since 2001) and in Asia in 2010.

Food Network proved Schonfeld's conviction that food content could be seen as pure entertainment. And other channels then filled their schedules with cooking and eating shows. That in turn drew more viewers to subscribe to Food Network, eager to sate their appetite for the subject. The channel brought a glamour to the

culinary profession and also led to a distinct rise in the number of people enrolling on cooking courses. Except their dreams were not to run restaurants but to be TV chefs. Schonfeld had a huge success on his hands, even if not in quite the way he had perhaps envisaged. Entertaining the Food Network surely was. Millions tuned in, but most with absolutely no intention of cooking anything.

Food became a spectator sport, both in America and across the pond. Surveying the state of British cooking at the time, the journalist Joanna Blythman commented: "In 2002, UK TV screened 4,000 hours of food programmes; 900 food books and 25 million words about food and cookery were published. But we seem to spend more time watching chefs than cooking ourselves." Britain, she said, had become a nation of "food voyeurs." Still, it helped people to order in restaurants and gave them things to talk about. And if you do try to watch telly while you cook, you'll probably end up cutting yourself anyway.

93

Salmon tartare with sweet red onion crème fraîche

AUTHOR: Thomas Keller, FROM: *The French Laundry Cookbook*

CORNETS

¼ cup plus 3 tablespoons all-purpose flour

1 tablespoon plus 1 teaspoon sugar

1 teaspoon kosher salt

8 tablespoons (4 ounces) unsalted butter, softened but still cool to the touch

2 large egg whites, cold

2 tablespoons black sesame seeds

SALMON TARTARE
(makes about ¾ cup)

4 ounces salmon fillet (belly preferred), skin and any pin bones removed and very finely minced

¾ teaspoon extra virgin olive oil

¾ teaspoon lemon oil

1½ teaspoons finely minced chives

1½ teaspoons kosher salt, or to taste

Small pinch of freshly ground pepper, or to taste

SWEET RED ONION CRÈME FRAÎCHE

1 tablespoon finely minced red onions

½ cup crème fraîche

¼ teaspoon kosher salt, or to taste

Freshly ground white pepper to taste

24 chive tips (about 1 inch long)

FOR THE CORNETS:
In a medium bowl, mix together the flour, sugar, and salt. In a separate bowl, whisk the softened butter until it is completely smooth and mayonnaise-like in texture. Using a stiff spatula or spoon, beat the egg whites into the dry ingredients until completely incorporated and smooth. Whisk in the softened butter by thirds, scraping the sides of the bowl as necessary and whisking until the batter is creamy and without any lumps. Transfer the batter to a smaller container, as it will be easier to work with.

Preheat the oven to 400°F.

Make a 4-inch hollow circular stencil [see instructions below]. Place a Silpat on the counter (it's easier to work on the Silpat before it is put on the sheet pan). Place the stencil in one corner of the sheet and, holding the stencil flat against the Silpat, scoop some of the batter onto the back of an offset spatula and spread it in an even layer over the stencil. Then run the spatula over the entire stencil to remove any excess batter. After baking the first batch of cornets, you will be able to judge the correct thickness; you may need a little more or less batter to adjust the thickness of the cornets. There should not be any holes in the batter. Lift the stencil and repeat the process to make as many rounds as you have molds or to fill the Silpat, leaving about 1½ inches between the cornets. Sprinkle each cornet with a pinch of black sesame seeds.

Place the Silpat on a heavy baking sheet and bake for 4 to 6 minutes, or until the batter is set and you see it rippling from the heat. The cornets may have browned in some areas, but they will not be evenly browned at this point.

Open the oven door and place the baking sheet on the door. This will help keep the cornets warm as you roll them and prevent them from becoming too stiff to roll. Flip a cornet over on the sheet pan, sesame seed side down, and place a 4½-inch cornet mold (size '35) at the bottom of the round. If you are right-handed, you will want the pointed end on your left and the open end on your right. The tip of the mold should touch the lower left edge (at about 7 o'clock on a clock face) of the cornet. Fold the bottom of the cornet up and around the mold and carefully roll upward and toward the left to wrap the cornet tightly around the mold: it should remain on the sheet pan as you roll. Leave the corner wrapped around the mold and continue to roll the cornets around molds: as you proceed, arrange the rolled cornets, seam side down, on the sheet pan so they lean against each other, to prevent them from rolling.

When all the corners are rolled, return them to the oven shelf, close the door, and bake for an additional 3 to 4 minutes to set the seams and colour the cornets a golden brown. If the colour is uneven, stand the cornets on end for a minute or so more, until the color is even. Remove the cornets from the oven and allow to cool just slightly, 30 seconds or so.

Gently remove the cornets from the molds and cool for several minutes on paper towels. Remove the Silpat from the baking sheet, wipe the excess butter from it, and allow it to cool down before spreading the next batch. Store the cornets for up to 2 days (for maximum flavour) in an airtight container.

To make the stencil: Cut the rim from the top of a plastic container. Trace two concentric circles on the lid, the inner 4 inches in diameter, the outer about 4½ inches. Sketch a thumb tab that will make it easy to lift the stencil off the silicon-coated Silpat. Trim around the tab and outer circle. Remove the inner circle so that you have a hollow ring. The batter gets spread to the stencil's edges then it's lifted off, leaving perfectly shaped rounds.

For the salmon tartare: With a sharp knife, finely mince the salmon fillet (do not use a food processor, as it would damage the texture of the fish) and place it in a small bowl. Stir in the remaining ingredients and taste for seasoning. Cover the bowl and refrigerate the tartare for at least 30 minutes, or up to 12 hours.

For the sweet red onion crème fraîche: Place the red onions in a small strainer and rinse them under cold water for several seconds. Dry them on paper towels. In a small metal bowl, whisk the crème fraîche for about 30 seconds to 1 minute, or until it holds soft peaks when you lift the whisk. Fold in the chopped onions and season to taste with the salt and white pepper. Transfer the onion cream to a container, cover, and refrigerate until ready to serve, or up to 6 hours.

To complete: Fill just the top ½ inch of each cornet with onion cream, leaving the bottom of the cone empty. (This is easily done using a pastry bag fitted with a ¼ inch plain tip or with the tip of a small knife.) Spoon about 1½ teaspoons of the tartare over the onion cream, and mold it into a dome resembling a scoop of ice cream. Lay a chive tip against one side of the tartare to garnish.

Back in October 2011 American chef Thomas Keller was sitting in an ornate tearoom in London department store Harrods having a rather fractious conversation with a journalist (the author of this book). It was almost twenty years since Keller had first cast his eyes on the French Laundry in California's Napa Valley. The restaurant that he had created there, in a building that during its first ninety-two years of life had served as a saloon bar and a brothel as well as a laundry, was the conduit to making Keller one of the biggest stars of the U.S. culinary scene.

Now he was offering a taste of it to London, bringing some fine-dining flavor to the capital's latest craze for restaurant "pop-ups."

Keller's job that afternoon was to publicize his forthcoming chef residence at Harrods' Georgian Restaurant. He wanted to chat through his menu, but instead he found himself being challenged about his environmental responsibilities. As a high-profile chef, wasn't it his duty to worry about how the world needed to be fed, to preach the importance of sustainability? asked the journalist.

"It's not my job to be a policeman for the environment," Keller retorted, although he admitted that his "biggest fear" was "how we are going to feed everyone in fifty years' time." While this was not a problem that he intended to tackle himself, he conceded that he has had to make adjustments in his own cooking.

"I've decided to serve less people," he said. "You see every day it becomes harder and harder to find great ingredients as produce becomes scarcer and scarcer. So I have restricted the numbers of guests—it's the only way I could improve quality. I am comfortable with being an elitist."

Keller was refusing to use his celebrity (seven coveted stars for his various establishments in the respected U.S. editions of the Michelin guide, plus countless other awards) to campaign on food ethics in the way that cooking colleagues such as Alice

French Laundry chef Thomas Keller preparing salmon.

Waters (see p. 282) had done. He didn't see it as his job. "We live in times that are complicated and harsh," he said to the journalist, "but don't ask me to have an impact on the world."

It was an opinion that he expressed again the following year, in 2012, during an interview for the *New York Times* when he caused consternation by stating about chefs: "Is global food policy our responsibility, or in our control... I don't think so."

Their role rather, as he had explained that day in London, was to "offer an escape from reality. And you can criticize me for that. We all need a recluse somewhere. I just want guests to have the memory of a great experience. On your deathbed, what do you have left? You have your memories."

And lunch or dinner care of Thomas Keller is certainly memorable, although of such complexity that it might need jotting down on a notepad to help proper recall. His tasting menus include such gems as "Sabayon of Pearl Tapioca with Island Creek Oysters and White Sturgeon Caviar, Moulard of Duck Foie Gras, Peanut Génoise, Concord Grape Gelée, Celery Branch and Petite Sirah Reduction," while his sweet, butter-poached Maine lobster comes with "Cauliflower, Royal Blenheim Apricot, Young Coconut, Marcona Almonds, Cilantro and Tahitian Vanilla."

Before you prepared to meet your maker, could you calm your thoughts with memories of his "Caramélia Chocolate Crémeux" made with "Gros Michel Banana, Candied Pine Nuts, Dentelle and Salted Popcorn Ice Cream"?

Given that Keller was planning on reducing the numbers of guests he served, only a lucky few would be able to recall such a dessert before they drew their last breath.

Yet his influence goes far beyond the indulgence of a privileged elite. As he himself has said: "What appears on a menu in a chef's restaurant soon finds its place on a supermarket shelf. Chefs have brought exposure to all sorts of ingredients." And not just ingredients but cooking techniques too. It was Keller who popularized the refined method of cooking known as "sous vide" (literally, "under vacuum"), in which vacuum-packed food is gently heated in a temperature-controlled water bath. Based on the ancient method of cooking using a bain-marie (see p. 83), the process had been developed in France in the 1970s, but many viewed it as unsafe and the equipment was expensive.

Keller was shown the technique by French catering expert Gérard Bertholon in 2000, and he marveled at the level of control this industrial device—a metal box with a plastic lid and a few controls and knobs—could give the cook. The heat was low enough to cook food properly but no more than that, while the plastic bag protected the food from direct contact with the water.

Keller discovered how just one degree centigrade could create a difference in texture and flavor. It was, he later wrote in a book devoted to the subject, Under Pressure: "a step in our culinary evolution to apply heat in the most exacting way... it gives us the extraordinary ability to cook food at the same temperature we want it to reach."

Keller brought the technique to prominence and taught those he was mentoring about it, and today there is barely a fine-dining restaurant kitchen in the world that does not boast sous-vide equipment (as exemplified by the last recipe in this book—see p. 348).

The scientist and author Harold McGee has heralded the technique as "one of the most important culinary inventions of all time [which has] opened up new realms of texture and flavor that weren't discernible before." If heat is the most important element in cooking food, then sous vide, for the first time, enabled it to be heated with absolute precision.

Yet Keller himself has downplayed the effect his championing of sous vide has had: "I don't believe there's anything that's new in cooking. We just manipulate it.

Sous vide is an old method of cooking. We can say that we had an impact or influence but if we think we are doing something new then we have to re-examine who we are."

Such modesty comes from a man who was largely self-taught and whose early experiences of restaurants were during his school holidays in Florida when he washed dishes in a restaurant managed by his mother. He then gradually moved up the ranks, spending time during his twenties in some of the best kitchens of Paris. By the late 1980s he had opened a restaurant in New York but it wasn't until he was forty that he opened the French Laundry.

It was there that he developed his more elaborate menus. And it was there that he began to regularly serve—and continues to serve to this day—the recipe that heads this chapter, salmon tartare with sweet red onion crème fraîche, a dish that set him on the path of extraordinary ingredient combinations, striking presentation and, crucially, incredible flavor. It was the dish that, like so many that followed, pushed the boundaries of what seemed acceptable to put on a plate.

Keller had conceived it one evening in New York after a stressful day planning menus for a forthcoming function for which he was doing the catering. He had dug deep into his repertoire of dishes to find something original but inspiration still deserted him.

After dinner with friends the group popped into an ice-cream shop. Keller made his choice and, he recalled, "This guy put [the ice cream] in a little holder—you take it from the holder—and said, 'Here's your cone.' The moment he said it I thought, there it is! We're going to take our standard tuiles, we're going to make cones with them and we're going to fill them with tartare."

Almost every meal at the French Laundry now starts with this dish. "People always smile when they get it, it makes them happy," he says of the signature salmon served in a cone.

In appearance Thomas Keller is not your archetypal chef. He is not a jolly, rotund man who looks like he enjoys eating what he cooks. To anyone seeing him chatting with the journalist that day in Harrods in 2011 he could have been mistaken for a city gent. Tall, slim, with distinguished flecks of gray in his swept-back hair and sporting a well-cut suit and silk tie, he doesn't look like someone who spends his days in a kitchen.

But then, as he himself has admitted, those who practice the culinary arts have undergone a radical change. "Being a chef today is very different than in the past," he explained during the Harrods interview. "In the past we didn't have to talk to the media and we didn't run businesses. Now we write books and we have to smile for photographers. Paul Bocuse [a famous French chef] once told me that in my father's time chefs ended their careers as drunks. Look how far we have come." He then paused and looked across at the journalist, scribbling in his notebook in between firing off awkward questions, and said finally, "You see how far we have come? Today, for example, I'm sitting here talking to you..."

94

Fairy cakes

AUTHOR: Nigella Lawson, FROM: *How to Be a Domestic Goddess*

MAKES 12

125 g unsalted butter, softened

125 g caster sugar

2 large eggs

125 g self-raising flour

½ teaspoon vanilla extract

2–3 tablespoons milk

500 g packet instant royal icing

12-bun muffin tin lined with 12 muffin papers

Preheat the oven to 200°C/gas mark 6.

It couldn't be simpler to make fairy cakes: just put all the ingredients except for the milk in the processor and then blitz till smooth. Pulse while adding milk down the funnel, to make for a soft, dropping consistency. (If you do want to make by hand, just follow the method for the Victoria sponge [elsewhere in the original book].) I know it looks as if you'll never make this scant mixture fit 12 bun cases, but you will, so just spoon and scrape the stuff in, trying to fill each case equally. Put in the oven and bake for 15–20 minutes or until the fairy cakes are cooked and golden on top. As soon as bearable, take the fairy cakes in their cases out of the tin and let cool on a wire rack. I like my cherry-topped fairies to have a little pointy top, but for all floral and other artistic effects, darling, you need to start with a level base, so once they're cool, cut off any mounded peaks so that you've got a flat surface for icing.

I've specified a whole packet of instant royal icing because the more colours you go in for the more you use, though really 250 g should be enough. I make up a big, uncoloured batch, and then remove a few spoonfuls at a time to a cereal bowl and add, with my probe (a broken thermometer, but a skewer is just as good), small dots of colours from the paste tubs, stirring with a teaspoon and then adding more colouring, very slowly, very cautiously until I've got the colour I want (pastel works best here, whatever your everyday aesthetic). I then get another spoon to spread the icing on each cake (it's important to use a different spoon for icing than for mixing or you'll end up with crumbs in the bowl of icing) and then I leave it a moment to dry only slightly on the surface before sticking on my rose, daisy or whole bouquet of either.

This was the recipe that spawned a million cupcake cafés," Nigella Lawson reflected several years later. She had seen cupcakes in America (see p. 159 for the first printed recipe) and brought her slightly less sweetened version to the British market. It became one of the most popular of all her recipes and had been chosen to adorn the cover of her book, *How to Be a Domestic Goddess*.

The book, ostensibly about baking, had an impact far beyond the realms of cooking, its title and content provoking leader writers in newspapers into mad rages about the role of women in society. Throughout the century there had been a love–hate relationship between women and their stoves. Technology had failed to set them free and now, at the turn of that century, as more and more joined the workforce, Lawson seemed to be urging them back into the kitchen. "[At] times we don't want to feel like a post-feminist, overstretched woman but, rather, a domestic goddess trailing nutmeggy fumes of baking pie in our languorous wake," she wrote in the preface to her book. "Cooking," she continued, "has a way of cutting through things, and to things, which have nothing to do with the kitchen. This is why it matters."

The response from some quarters of the press was vitriolic. "Could it be that the real reason women hate baking is because cake-baking epitomizes us as domestic slaves," screamed writer Nicola Tyrer in the *Daily Mail*. "Most men secretly love the idea of a Stepford wife, programmed to eager servitude, be it sex or baking." It was, said Tyrer, just a "short step from baking to domestic enslavement."

Others joining this bandwagon of fury included journalist Anna Burnside in the *Sunday Herald*. "Now, as if we're not already racked with guilt trying to be everything, along comes TV's newest cookery star, Nigella Lawson, to tell us that we should also be able to bake," she wrote, adding mockingly that the book was "affirming stuff...for women who have given up career jobs to make packed lunches and sew Tweenie costumes."

Burnside—livid anyway that Lawson was, as she put it, "gut-stabbingly beautiful with mascarpone skin and huge expressive eyes"—was irritated at what she saw as a woman preaching to the UK from her own rarefied and well-off, middle-class confines. "The problem," she explained, "is all this is designed for Lawson's version of the way we live now, which is pretty much the way people who write for London newspapers, drive large, sleek cars, employ au pairs and have their own television series live now." And then Suzanne Moore, the left-wing columnist, properly lost her temper in the *Mail on Sunday*, fuming about the "fantasy that Nigella [was] peddling." Her book could take the nation back to the "pre-feminist world of backstreet abortion," she cried.

But Lawson, a journalist, restaurant critic, and food writer for *Vogue*, took the criticism on the chin, understanding how columnists work. She had given up being a columnist herself when she found herself thinking: "I know I've written on this subject before but I can't remember what view I took..." Her book did spring from a genuine premise, however. Reflecting on its genesis over a decade later, she recalls how, during a bread-making class, she was "somewhat radicalized": "I found that mixing and handling the dough was very liberating, to actually feel it in your hands. Also while you can understand how a stew works there is something miraculous about mixing eggs, butter and flour together and getting cake."

This insight, along with the realization that so many women, herself included, just seemed to "work, work, work, get home, crash and then work, work, work," turned into the germ of an idea. "I wrote a piece for *Vogue* on how to feel like a domestic goddess and talked of my new-found love of baking," she recalled. "And I got a very big response including from quarters you would not believe."

At the time, although there were plenty of books on baking they were by no means fashionable, while people who baked, said Lawson, were regarded as "brisk and efficient." She wanted to demythologize the subject. And she knew from the children's parties she threw that the parents always loved the fairy cakes more than the children did.

"I had a fake nostalgia," she said. "It was a nostalgia for the childhood I didn't have. Baking meant I could re-create it for myself and my own children. It creates a safe, cosy and restorative feeling in the kitchen." As for accusations that she was sending women on some kind of culinary penance, she said of baking: "It doesn't shackle women to the kitchen, look how many bring cakes to the office these days. Neither is it just women. I have signed countless books for men over the years and just cross off the 'dess' [on the title page] and add an exclamation mark."

Meanwhile, there were many plaudits for the book. "She is not issuing matronly instructions like Delia [see p. 291], she is merely making sisterly suggestions," opined *The Times.* The cook and writer Tamasin Day-Lewis was equally positive, commenting in the *Daily Telegraph:* "It takes an I-dare-you kind of confidence to write about cakes, fairy cakes and sponges in a post-modern way rather than about Tuscan char-grilled vegetables."

Britain also warmed to the theme, ignoring the journalistic invective, and *How to Be a Domestic Goddess* sold 180,000 copies in the first four months. It followed on the heels of Lawson's first book, the acclaimed 1998 hardback *How to Eat,* in which the author had announced: "I have nothing to declare except my greed." Her writing and TV career blossomed; the audience loved seeing a real woman stuffing her face with her own food, especially one who expressed what she called a "reluctance to worship at the great God of Thin."

Nigella Lawson succeeded in persuading many people that it wasn't quitting, but engaging in, the kitchen that could liberate you. "What I'm doing here," she once said, "is seeking to offer protection from life, solely through the means of potato, butter and cream. There are times when only mashed potato will do." The same, of course, goes for cake.

Nigella Lawson at the launch party for her successful book, How to Be a Domestic Goddess.

95

Bacon, leek & potato gratin

AUTHOR: Jane Baxter, FROM: Riverford Organic Vegetables newsletter

SERVES 6

2 leeks, sliced

1 knob of butter

100 g bacon, cooked and chopped

300 ml double cream

100 ml milk

2 garlic cloves, crushed

800 g potatoes, peeled and cut into 2–3 mm thick slices

1–2 tbsp freshly grated Parmesan

Sea salt and black pepper

Sweat the leeks in butter for 10 mins, then add the bacon and garlic. Add the cream and milk and bring to the boil. Season and mix in the potatoes. Transfer to a gratin dish. Cover with foil and bake at 180°C for about 50 mins, until potatoes are tender. Remove the foil, sprinkle with Parmesan and bake for another 10 mins, until golden brown.

Frances Moore Lappé (see p. 276) may have attempted to galvanize a generation of Americans to care about the planet and eat less meat in the early 1970s, but the march of consumerism was a tide few had the mettle to fight against. As a consequence Britain, like America, saw a feverish growth in supermarkets throughout the 1970s, 80s and 90s, buoyed by financial boom and the cash-rich days of Thatcherism. With the twin temptations of convenience and labor-saving gadgets, all hyped endlessly through television—be it advertising or actual programs—the parlous state of the earth was unlikely to get a look in.

Most British shoppers, by the end of the 1990s, were buying their food from supermarkets that fought to offer more choice and cheaper food. Walking their aisles became an attack on the senses. Vast arrays of produce were shipped from all over the world, each competing for your attention. And such was the glorious triumph of transport and communication that if you wanted strawberries in December then there was bound to be a country somewhere in the world warm enough to grow them.

The horrors of rationing were finally put to bed when Britain entered an era in which the consumer could buy whatever exotic ingredient he or she wanted, at any time of year and at any time of day. By the turn of the twenty-first century, food in Britain was also well and truly a trendy subject. No longer just a permitted topic of conversation at the dinner parties of the chattering classes, it was becoming compulsory. The London restaurant scene had been transformed and young chefs from around the world were flocking to the capital to train in the kitchens of British chefs. Food publishing blossomed, both in books and the birth of new magazines: *Food Illustrated,* launched in 1998, was followed by the likes of *Olive* and *Delicious.*

And as food writing—not to mention being a restaurant critic—became a career many aspired to, so thinking rather more deeply about the subject became popular. Which was rather bad news for the shopper, who was just getting used to negotiating all the aisles and throwing everything into his or her trolley, from Colombian coffee to Mediterranean bluefin tuna. All of a sudden a whole array of new buzzwords started spreading through the food-writing ether. It started simply with terms such as "local" and "seasonal," which most people could sort of get the hang of, before moving on to the likes of "organic," "sustainable," "ethical" and "Fairtrade."

For those who prided themselves on having a conscience, shopping suddenly became a guilt-inducing minefield. Where once you bought coffee simply because you liked coffee, now, before making your purchase, you had to weigh up which of the Fairtrade beans in front of you offered the better school or clinic that would be built with the proceeds of your generosity.

At least you could then sleep well that night—provided you had chosen the decaf variety—except that with this new term "food miles" perhaps you should have shunned the whole coffee idea and just had some hot water and a slice of lemon. Then, hang on, it's winter. Where do those lemons come from?

Vying for market share, the supermarkets soon recognized the growth potential in investing in organic food. But not before one man had come on the scene, and for rather more altruistic reasons.

Guy Watson grew up on a farm in north Devon and in the 1980s joined others of Thatcher's children as a management consultant. He soon realized his heart was not in the New York office he'd found himself in, however, but back where he'd spent his childhood. So, returning home one Christmas, he decided to stay put, opting to lease some land from his father in order to pursue his idea of farming organically. "I had always had my suspicions about the intensive use of chemicals," he said, admitting that it had also "seemed like a bit of an emerging market."

Watson knew that there was a growing interest among consumers in knowing where their food came from and in eating locally and seasonally. "A lot of people do want to do what's right but with so much conflicting information they end up in despair and the default position is then just to be lazy," he commented. So to make it easy for them,

he started the first home-delivery scheme for organic vegetables, dropping off boxes containing a variety of seasonal veg sourced from local organic farmers. His early customers received boxes hand-delivered by Watson in his beaten-up Citroën. This he did in addition to selling fruit and veg to wholesalers and retailers, which constituted the bulk of his business for many years.

Yet organic farming proved much harder than Watson had realized as he battled against weeds, disease and pests. And, like Odysseus tempted by the sweet song of the Sirens to their dangerous isle, he was continually assailed by offers inviting him to use pesticides. "All the while the chemical salesmen were whispering in my ear," he remembered. But he tied himself to his own mast of organic destiny and sailed on.

He steadily grew his business and then in 2001 decided to franchise deliveries to specific areas. At which point the business became transformed. "It was just amazing," he recalled. "It absolutely took off."

"The veg boxes had been ten percent of my business but without any marketing push," he went on. "So it made sense just to concentrate on that." A colleague and his sister also persuaded him to think about his brand. "I didn't know what they were talking about," he said. But he went with their idea and ten years later Riverford Organic Vegetables was seeing annual sales of £34 million, with 47,000 organic veg boxes being delivered each week throughout England and South Wales. The only downside for the customers being the dilemma of having to think of ways to cook all the damn stuff. Watson helped by way of publishing regular newsletters, featuring the likes of bacon, leek and potato gratin devised by chef Jane Baxter—who went on to head up the restaurant he opened on the farm in Devon. He later published cookbooks to further broadcast the organic message.

Meanwhile supermarkets waded into battle, fighting tooth and nail to claim that prized organic torch. "They bullied their conventional suppliers into it," said Watson. "And with the exception of Waitrose were absolutely brutal." But for him, it was about much more than hard-headed commercialism:

> For me organic farming is a philosophy. It's about our relationship with the planet and not trying to dominate everything. The supermarkets may have created a situation where the people who supplied organic food were no longer a bunch of unreliable hippies, but their idea of organic – while it might adhere to the letter of certification – does not compare to my idea of organic. Harvesting food from huge farms, wrapping it in cellophane before sending it half the way round the world, loses some of its spirit...

Watson was an early pioneer of organic farming and offered an alternative and more earthy shopping experience. His vegetable boxes also became hugely fashionable. Meanwhile, lovers of fish, happily taking advice to eat more of it, were about to be shocked into their own guilt trip.

96

Asian salad with ponzu ginger dressing & wasabi peas

AUTHOR: Jennifer Chandler, FROM: *Simply Salads*

MAKES 6 APPETIZERS OR SIDE SALADS

SALAD

1 bag (5 ounces) Spring Mix [includes baby lettuces, such as baby green and red romaine and lolla rossa, baby greens, such as red Swiss chard, frisée and radicchio]

1 cup wasabi peas

PONZU GINGER DRESSING

¼ cup soy sauce

2 tablespoons water

1 tablespoon red wine vinegar

1 tablespoon freshly squeezed lime juice

½ teaspoon grated freshly peeled ginger

1 scallion, thinly sliced

In a small bowl whisk together the soy sauce, water, vinegar, lime juice,
ginger and scallion. Makes about ½ cup.

In a large bowl, toss together the Spring Mix and wasabi peas. Add the dressing to taste and gently toss. Serve immediately.

The bright and breezy Jennifer Chandler, a young American mum, recipe writer and occasional TV chef, may have studied at the Cordon Bleu cookery school (see p. 190) in Paris but the traditional idea of preparing meals from scratch was not her bag. Having run a food shop, Cheffie's Market & More, in Memphis, dedicated to selling prepared foods, she turned her mind to prepackaged salads.

Her book *Simply Salads* was devoted to it, and unashamedly so. The "Spring Mix" salad that starts this chapter effectively combines about eight different types of salad—helpfully introducing people to the range! But nevertheless, with the dressing, it's very tasty and you can use salads straight from your garden to alleviate any prejudices against the concept of bagged salads.

Meanwhile, the book's cover promised "more than 100 delicious creative recipes made from pre-packaged greens..." "Packaged salads," she wrote, "have changed the way I enjoy salads... Whoever decided to make these blends 'ready-to-eat' is a genius in my book." She was long done with cleaning "sand and dust out of fresh spinach" and if she could find her salad spinner at the back of a cupboard, it would definitely have "a layer of dust on it."

Millions of her fellow Americans agreed with her. As they did in Britain. A little tardy to catch up with the habit of bagged salads, the UK saw them introduced into supermarkets in 1992 and within ten years the industry was worth £1.25 billion. That was bigger than sliced bread, a larger chunk of the market than breakfast cereals.

Its nascent years were in 1960s California where lettuce growers packaged shredded leaves. But consumers resisted them and the only market was restaurants whose chefs were happy to forgo a little lettuce chopping.

As lettuce has a habit of decomposing once it is picked, it needed some technological assistance to extend its shelf life. When cut, lettuce—along with its salad and vegetable relations—breathes in oxygen and it gives off carbon dioxide, water and heat. This process sees it wilt, and it was a company called the TransFresh Group who worked out a way of reducing the oxygen and upping the carbon dioxide during packaging to prevent that happening. Their "modified atmosphere packaging" (MAP) gave the salads longer shelf life, which they then extended by adding nitrogen to the bags, which lowered oxygen levels further. McDonald's and Burger King bought the salads in large quantities in the 1980s and then, at the end of the decade, the concept took off in the consumer market.

Bagged salads promised speed and convenience, especially for those time-poor, cash-rich, two-income households. The early 1990s then saw a wider variety of salads introduced, from radicchio to baby arugula. There was more novelty too, with the likes of Caesar salad complete with a dressing kit and Parmesan croûtons. So with the promise of such healthy food at just the tear of a bag away, sales soared. TransFresh, which became Fresh Express, saw its revenues in bagged salads increase nearly six-fold between 1991 and 1994. By the mid-2000s, the number of Americans who ate bagged salads each week reached 20 million.

By 2002, two-thirds of the British public, meanwhile, were buying them regularly. This frenzy for bagged salads tallies with the astonishing decrease in the amount of time we spent cooking in the kitchen during the course of the twentieth century. In the 1930s it was three hours a day, by the 1970s it was one hour and by the turn of the millennium the average figure was just fifteen minutes.

While Jennifer Chandler and countless others were celebrating this wonderful statistic, others were less impressed, however. The British journalist Felicity Lawrence voiced her concern, commenting how "in our wish to remove the labor from feeding ourselves, we have lost the cultural significance of meals." But more than that, it seemed that the simple act of opening a bagged salad opened a Pandora's box of food horrors of the kind that make the followers of the Slow Food Movement (see p. 299) and their ilk froth at the mouth.

There was the chlorine that bagged salads were washed in, for example—not that that worried Chandler, who acknowledged that there was "a big debate about whether

Bagged salads were introduced into supermarkets in 1992 and were a huge success as they promised speed and convenience to time-poor, cash-rich households.

to wash the salad blend or not," before concluding that it "is not necessary." Then again, as we have established, she wasn't sure she could even find her salad spinner.

Lawrence reported in 2004 the findings of one toxicologist, who found that the average Briton has 300–500 chemicals in his body that weren't present fifty years previously. Not that she is suggesting they all come from eating bagged salads, of course. But it's worth noting that between 1992 and 2000, the period, Lawrence pointed out, that saw bagged salads take off, 6 percent of food-poisoning outbreaks were associated with bagged salads, and ready-prepared fruit and veg.

There is the system, too, that produces the salad which causes concern. It depends on "cheap, casual labor," as Lawrence has stated, consisting of an immigrant workforce living in conditions of "appalling squalor." So think Iraqi Kurds, Brazilians, Lithuanians, Russians, Ukrainians; all living crammed into smelly little caravans whose gangmaster bosses are linked to prostitution and drug rings.

And what of the soil in which the salads grow? In southern Spain, where the industry moves after the English salad season ends—and where there are acres of greenhouses—the soil is so depleted by pesticides that they have to ship in new earth.

In Lawrence's seminal book *Not on the Label,* which she published in 2004, she despaired at what the bagged salad represented—its destruction of food culture and eradication of the time spent cooking and eating together. "Ninety-nine pence for a few leaves is a lot of money," she continued. "But 99p for an unlimited supply of servants to wash and pick over it all, hidden not as in the old days below stairs, but in remote caravans or underneath plastic hothouses—that is cheap."

Jennifer Chandler and millions of others, meanwhile, would simply shrug their shoulders and ponder that the salad spinner always was a rotten wedding present anyway.

97

Steamed brioche with rose-scented mozzarella

AUTHOR: Ferran Adrià, FROM: *A Day at elBulli*

Brioche Dough
375 g (3 cups) plain (all-purpose) flour
100 g (⅓ cup) sourdough starter [see note below]
67.5 g (⅓ cup) milk
32.5 g (2¼ tbsp) sugar
6.5 g (¼ oz) fresh pressed yeast
140 g (¾ cup) beaten eggs
115 g (1 x 4 oz stick) softened butter
Salt

Place the flour and sourdough starter in the bowl of the mixer.
Start the mixer at three quarters of the full speed with dough hook attached.
Dissolve the sugar and yeast in the milk and add to the mixer.
Wait for one minute before adding the beaten eggs.
Knead until the dough is smooth.
Add the salt and knead for one more minute.
Add the butter in chunks and knead until the brioche dough comes away from the sides of the mixing bowl and the butter is fully incorporated.
Keep refrigerated in a covered bowl for 12 hours.
Note: A sourdough starter is a mixture of flour and water that is left to ferment and collect natural yeasts. It is used as a rising agent when making sourdough bread.

Fermented Brioches
200 g (⅔ cup) brioche dough, previously prepared

Knead the brioche dough into a long strip.
Cut into 10 x 12 g (½ oz) pieces.
Shape into balls.
Place the 10 brioche balls on parchment paper.
Keep at room temperature for 30 minutes, then ferment at 32°C/90°F for 3 hours.
Cover well to prevent them from drying out and keep at room temperature until needed.

Rose Air Base
500 g (2 cups) milk
4 drops rose essence
2.5 g Lecite [a type of emulsifier]

Mix all 3 ingredients in a 25 cm (10 in) deep container.

Crumbled Mozzarella
2 x 150 g (5 oz) fresh buffalo mozzarella balls

Remove the outer layer of the mozzarella balls (set this aside for another dish).
Break up the creamy interior of the mozzarella by hand.
Refrigerate.

Finishing and Presentation
Work a hand-held blender over the surface of the rose air mixture until it emulsifies and the air foams.
Steam the balls of brioche dough for 16 minutes.
Once the brioches are cooked, cut open the top with scissors and put 7.5g (⅓ oz) crumbled mozzarella into each one.
Heat the mozzarella brioches under the salamander grill (broiler) for 30 seconds. Remove and place a spoon of rose air on top of each brioche.
Serve on a black slate with satin paper.

How to Eat
Hold the brioche by the base and eat it in 2 mouthfuls.

Ever since the dawn of time, man has sought food for survival. In roasting food (see p. 24), he distinguished himself from other animals. In boiling it he became civilized, the cooking pot being a cultural object. Over time he also used food to demonstrate hospitality, to impress people with audacious dishes or simply to show kindness through sharing.

But whether a nobleman is putting the fear of God into his enemy by serving him a cake that is a replica of his castle, or a peasant shares his last crust of bread with a stranger, food has one vital function. It is there to feed and to nourish.

Or at least that was the case until 1984, when a Spanish chef called Ferran Adrià took the helm of elBulli, a former beach bar on the Spanish coast two hours north of Barcelona, and food acquired a new function. "People will come to my restaurant not for nourishment," he said, "but for experience."

While Tommaso Marinetti (see p. 231) had written about avant-garde cuisine and proposed menus in his *Futurist Cookbook* of 1932, he hadn't cooked the dishes. No one actually ate his "Tyrrhenian seaweed foam" or his "immortal trout"—fish wrapped in calf's liver and fried with nuts and oil. It was Adrià who converted culinary whimsy into reality. He didn't just write down recipes such as "monkfish liver fondue with ponzu and white sesame-flavored kumquat" or "charcoal-oil flavored lamb's brains," he also cooked them.

Whereas Marinetti's "aerofood"—a slice of fennel, an olive and a kumquat to be eaten while stroking a piece of sandpaper—was fantasy, Adrià's "orange nitro-sorbet with its balloon," in which the diner was instructed to eat a sorbet while a balloon containing orange-flower essence gradually deflates, was no joke.

Adrià saw himself as an artist who could achieve something that a painter could only dream of. People would eat his "paintings." And eating was a more intense experience than viewing art.

"Painting is for the eyes. Music may be beautiful but it is only for the ear," he declared. "Eating is the most intense experience. There is no other creative moment that uses all the senses."

And to deliver such experiences he didn't just do away with the dessert and cheese trolleys. He discarded the idea of first courses, mains and puddings. He created new types of cutlery—spoons made from paper, for example. His waiters dispensed firm instructions about how to eat dishes (the order in which ingredients should go into the mouth, for example), and he didn't offer guests menus.

In fact he did the opposite; he handed out the menus after dinner. He had total control of the dining room and the whole dining experience. He didn't offer salt or pepper—and certainly not ketchup or mustard—and the diner would eat whatever arrived at the table; up to forty courses on some occasions.

"When you eat, you smell, you listen, you hear, you taste. Eating is so complex," he said. "But because we eat everyday we don't see it as complex."

The restaurant he created had just one sitting per day, for fifty guests. There were about seventy members of staff, including around forty chefs. The place only opened for six months per annum, to give Adrià and his team time to create and plan. And while 8,000 did get to dine there each year, vastly fewer didn't—there were some 2 million reservation requests.

Born in 1962, in a suburb of Barcelona, Adrià was far removed from the world of restaurants as a child. And there would have been little to inspire him culinarily: his father was a plasterer and his mother a terrible cook. His passion in his younger years was football, not cooking, and he played for a local team throughout his teens.

Having enrolled on a business course after leaving school, he dropped out and took a job washing up for a smart restaurant so he could save money for a trip to Ibiza. But the chef of the hotel introduced him to classical cooking—mainly French—and Adrià got hooked. He sought other jobs in good restaurants, ran a kitchen during his stint in national service and finally got an apprenticeship at elBulli, which was still, in the early 1980s, owned by a German homeopathic doctor, Hans Schilling.

Impressing the manager, Juli Soler, he was invited to return the following year as chef de partie, in charge of one particular area of the kitchen. Showing considerable talent, he quickly worked his way up the hierarchy and by 1985 was head chef.

In 1990 Adrià teamed up with Soler, bought the place off Schilling and dispensed with its traditional French menu. "Turbot on a bed of spinach soufflé" would make way for "roses with ham wonton and melon water."

The pair shut the restaurant for an extended period over the winter and Adrià traveled the world for inspiration, finding ingredients along the way. There was dried seaweed from Japan, pickled daisy buds from North America, gelling agents from China. Then, using the best local produce, sourced from as close to elBulli as possible, he gathered his growing army of creative supporters in the workshop near the restaurant and started plotting recipes.

Jotting notes onto endless scraps of paper, he recorded ideas, sketched out how food should be arranged on a plate and conceived of completely new ways of cooking.

Adrià was insistent that every dish had to be completely original. "We look into the past to make sure we don't copy and we analyze ourselves continuously," he said. The Spaniard was determined not to have any association whatsoever with that great culinary tradition of plagiarism.

"When you eat a traditional meal you have references to things you have had before," he explained. "When you have a dish of avant-garde cooking, something new, you have no references. It's like you're on a different planet. It's a new world."

On a trip to America in 2009, he was asked by the TV interviewer Charlie Rose what he called his type of cooking.

"It took us twenty-five years to come up with a name," replied Adrià, having dismissed the notion that he and his team had anything to do with so-called molecular gastronomy. Rose was all ears: would Ferran Adrià finally reveal the term that described his extraordinary contribution to the culinary arts, one that had given him three Michelin stars and the title of best chef in the world working at the world's best restaurant?

"I call it elBulli cooking," said the thick-set Adrià in his fast, gruff and best Spanish (he always refused to answer an interviewer in English, although he appeared more than able to understand the questions).

Whatever one termed it—and he sometimes called it "deconstructivist"—there were many new techniques he discovered. He transformed ingredients using extreme cold, pouring liquid nitrogen, for example, over a Caipirinha cocktail to turn it into a sorbet. He would produce savory dishes frozen; his version of chicken curry included curry ice cream, for instance. And he worked out a way of serving jelly warm (the "Roquefort sorbet with hot apple and lemon jelly" being a case in point). He served up non-pasta ravioli, soups that were sweet, and turned savory dishes more associated with the main course into desserts.

Food was served as a series of acts: the chef, he said, was the "emitter," the waiter the "transmitter," and the guest the "receptor." Whereas conventionally the chef might walk into the dining room to greet guests, at elBulli the guests walked through the kitchen and saw the chef as a matter of course.

Ferran Adrià was fêted across he world. The eminent French Gault Millau guide added to those three Michelin stars with a 19/20 score and, as British food writer Tim Hayward once noted, Adrià had "perhaps unintentionally, become the figurehead of a global rebellion against the culinary hegemony of France."

Yet for all its success elBulli couldn't make money and Adrià became frustrated at how the restaurant was becoming less famous for its food than the near impossibility of getting a reservation.

One way to overcome this, suggested Tim Hayward, was to book a week's holiday in Barcelona and then call each morning to get onto the cancellation list, keeping one's mobile telephone on and hoping for the best. If no table was forthcoming, at least the food from the other "merely brilliant" restaurants in Barcelona could keep you happy.

"My life has become about getting somebody a table," said an exhausted Adrià in 2011. "ElBulli has become almost a monster." Then to his shocked fans he announced he was closing the restaurant. It would re-open in 2014 as a creative center. Meanwhile his other businesses, including a high-end chain, Fast Good, and numerous consultancies would continue.

"We will no longer have to worry about Michelin, or awards or reservations," he declared. And for those who would miss his food there was his massive, heavy tome *A Day at elBulli*, published in 2008 and featuring the recipe for a dish that was a restaurant staple for many years—"steamed brioche with rose-scented mozzarella"—and which heads this chapter. The book also comprises such delights as "Thai nymph"—cucumber with a Thai-style filling—and the inimitable "chocolate air LYO [short for 'lyophilized'—freeze-dried] with crispy raspberry sorbet and eucalyptus water ice."

But those wishing to recreate a dish that Tommaso Marinetti would surely have been proud of, "banana salad with mojito ice and mint jelly," will have to search elsewhere. They could wait until 2014, attempt to enroll on a course at the new elBulli "creativity center" and then ask Ferran Adrià nicely.

98

Steamed salmon with tomato basil couscous

AUTHOR: Jamie Oliver, FROM: *"20 Minute Meals" app*

YOU'LL NEED:

2 x 200 g salmon fillets, preferably higher welfare (pinboned)
100 g ripe cherry tomatoes
150 g couscous
1 small bunch fresh basil
1 medium red onion
1 small bulb fennel
½ tsp fennel seeds
1 medium fresh red chilli
1 fresh bay leaf
1 lemon
2 tbsp natural yoghurt
Olive oil
Sea salt
Black pepper (freshly ground)

EQUIPMENT:

• kettle • chopping knife • chopping board • medium wide saucepan with lid (approx x 25 cm) • wooden spoon • pestle and mortar • mixing bowl • box grater

1. Put your kettle on to boil. Preheat your oven to the lowest setting and place your plates in the oven to warm.

2. Lay your salmon fillets out on a plate, drizzle with olive oil and season lightly with salt and pepper.

3. Pick the basil leaves and put to one side, finely chop the stalks. Place the pan on a medium heat.

4. Peel the onion and trim the fennel, then chop both finely. Halve, deseed and chop the chilli.

5. Add a splash of olive oil to your hot pan with the basil stalks and prepared veg. Cook gently for 5 minutes, stirring now and then, until the vegetables are soft. Meanwhile…

6. Pound the fennel seeds in a pestle and mortar until fine and add to the pan with the bay leaf.

7. Place the couscous in a mixing bowl, and pour over 150 ml of boiling water. Stir with a fork to break up any lumps.

8. Cut the cherry tomatoes in half and add to the pan with the softened vegetables. Season everything with salt and pepper and mix well. Flatten out a little.

9. Tip the couscous over the vegetables and smooth out. Carefully pour over another 150 ml of boiling water, then place the salmon fillets on top of the couscous.

10. Finely grate the zest of a lemon over the salmon then cut the lemon in half and squeeze the juice from one half over the fish.

11. Cover the pan with a lid, and cook on a medium heat for 7 to 10 minutes until the couscous has fluffed up and the salmon is just cooked. Turn the heat off.

12. Make your table look respectable – get the cutlery, salt and pepper and drinks laid out nicely and get your warmed plates out of the oven.

13. Drizzle over some extra virgin olive oil and sprinkle over a pinch of black pepper. Roughly tear up the basil leaves and scatter them on top.

14. Place the pan in the middle of the table with a bowl of yoghurt and let everyone tuck in!

By the autumn of 2009, technology had moved on to such an extent that a chef, speaking to you from a device in the palm of your hand, could tell you how to steam a fillet of salmon and serve it on a bed of couscous scented with the fresh flavors of basil and tomato. The chef in this instance was Jamie Oliver and while it was by no means the first food application that you could download onto an iPhone, it quickly became one of the most popular.

The website epicurious.com (see p. 316) boasted a repertoire of thousands, as did the likes of BigOven and Allrecipes. But Oliver's app was different. It offered just sixty recipes with step-by-step photography and video guides and, unlike many, it wasn't free; in fact at £4.99 or $7.99 it was very expensive. But it promised to deliver. "Hi guys," said the man in the hand, familiar to millions from his TV shows and books. "All of this stuff is going to give you the confidence to rattle off brilliant, brilliant meals in around twenty minutes. Really, you can do it. So good luck and have fun."

It had taken six months of development and in the face of considerable skepticism—many had cautioned against investing large sums in a market that showed little promise of financial return. Yet within days of its October launch, the Jamie Oliver "20 Minute Meals" app became Apple's biggest-grossing application. And there soon followed a busy succession of other celebrity chefs eager to exploit the market, sourcing software companies to build their own apps.

"I'm a bit of a geek," Oliver said at the launch of "20 Minute Meals." "I love technology and new ways of doing things. So when I first saw the iPhone I was thinking: 'Recipes.'" The chef approached east London software house Zolmo and together they worked on the project. "There were around thirty people involved as absolutely everything was purpose-built," recalled Zolmo co-founder Tristan Celder. "The contextual nature of the device, the inherent mobility and convenience, meant that [with the recipe app] we could put a tool in your pocket that was always available."

The app came out eighteen months after Apple launched its store for applications to buy or download for free. Commenting on the launch, an editorial in the new-technology magazine *Wired* declared: "Whichever way it goes, we are at the start of an economical and behavioral transformation." Of course this appealed to Oliver who had made a career not just out of presenting cooking shows but campaigning on food-related issues. He was able to present his app as simply another string to his bow of passionate lobbying.

Jamie Oliver.

Born in Essex, the son of a publican, he spent his childhood days helping out in the kitchen. This sparked an interest in cooking and at sixteen he left school and joined a catering college. By the age of twenty-two, he was working at the renowned London restaurant River Café where a TV producer spotted him during the making of a documentary and gave him his own show, *The Naked Chef*. His breezy, laid-back and blokey style proved a massive hit with the public. Books followed and, in between recording cookery shows and opening a chain of Italian restaurants, he devised campaigns, from bringing the unemployed into catering to saving British pig farmers.

So it felt only natural to him that his app should have a campaigning bent. He claimed it was part of his mission to get people interested in healthy eating. "If it's inspired people to cook better then it's succeeded," he said. "I am always on the lookout for new ways to get my message across and I had all these clever little things you could do. All those mad ideas ended up on the app."

With its carefully chosen and small number of recipes, it was designed not to overwhelm the user. "OK guys. Ingredients," he chirped in a video on the app, his head appearing between a box of Maldon salt, a pot of Colman's mustard and a bottle of Heinz tomato ketchup. "If you want to achieve twenty-minute meals, you need your cupboards full of the right gear."

Chefs have always had a passion for communicating their ideas to the world. But none could have imagined quite how, in early twenty-first century, that would develop. It still baffles most people that a small device could be invented that didn't just organize your diary, bring you news and allow you to make telephone calls, but that also held a plethora of recipes by your own culinary hero and that, to choose which one to cook, all you needed to do was shake it and it would decide for you, as well as show you what the dish looked like and exactly how to cook it.

99

Spaghetti alla carbonara

AUTHOR: Mario Batali, FROM: *Molto Gusto*

SERVES 6

Kosher salt

5 ounces sliced pancetta, cut into ½-inch-wide strips

¼ cup extra virgin olive oil

1 tablespoon coarsely ground black pepper

6 fresh large eggs

1 pound spaghetti

½ cup freshly grated Parmigiano-Reggiano, plus extra for serving

¼ cup grated pecorino romano

Bring 6 quarts of water to a boil in a large pot and add 3 tablespoons kosher salt.

Meanwhile, combine the pancetta and oil in another large pot and cook over medium-high heat until the pancetta has rendered some of its fat and is lightly browned, about 7 minutes. Stir in the pepper and remove from the heat.

Separate the eggs, being careful to keep the yolks intact, putting the whites in a small bowl and the yolks in a shallow dish.

Drop the pasta into the boiling water and cook until just al dente. Drain, reserving ⅔ cup of the pasta water.

Add the reserved pasta water to the pancetta and bring to a simmer over medium heat. Add the egg whites and cook, whisking furiously, until they are frothy but not set, about 1 minute. Add the pasta, stirring and tossing well to coat. Stir in the cheeses.

Divide the pasta among six bowls, making a nest in the center of each portion. Gently drop an egg yolk into each nest and serve immediately, advising your guests to stir the yolk into the pasta so it will cook. Pass additional grated Parmigiano on the side.

In the mid-1980s, a few years before he opened Harvey's, Marco Pierre White (see p. 302) landed a job as head chef of the Six Bells pub on the King's Road in London. Given a staff budget of £500 a week, he paid himself £400, leaving £100 for a sous-chef. The man he employed for this role was a young American called Mario Batali. With no cash left for a washer-up, the pair agreed to share the chore and they worked together for a few months.

They may have shared the washing-up duties, but there was nothing else equal about the deal. Marco used the opportunity to hone his uniquely brutal management style, and the young ponytailed American found himself on the receiving end of some particularly harsh treatment. As Marco himself later recalled: "I used to murder Mario every day, physically, mentally and emotionally."

Eventually, in a row over risotto—which Batali deigned to consider perfect, but White less so—their cooking relationship ended. After White threw the pan and its contents at his apprentice, Batali walked out, but not before secretly chucking two large handfuls of salt into every pan of sauce bubbling on the stove.

While White went on to win his three Michelin stars, Mario Batali became one of the most celebrated restaurateurs in New York, with establishments not just across America but abroad in Singapore and Hong Kong.

Some twenty years on, a familiar face on TV—thanks to shows such as *Iron Chef*—and with a seemingly constant presence in newspapers and magazines, Batali reflected on his brief apprenticeship with White: "He was one of the most tenacious, difficult, temper-tantrum-ridden, supertalented, creative artists I've ever met in my life," he said. "And the reason so many people suffered him for so long is because he was a genius in the pan and on the plate."

Batali's own style was very different. For a start, there would be no yelling. "One of the big rules for our kitchens is that if you're not close enough to touch me, you can't talk to me," he explained. "If you're yelling at me, there can be problems understanding the nature of your message."

If a chef is well prepared, Batali argued, then come the inevitable rush midservice, there should be quiet order, not loud chaos. It was a lesson he had learned from his father, a heat-treatment engineer for Boeing, his constant job to find flaws in surface metal. The elder Batali's exacting nature left a mark of fastidiousness on his son that he is deeply proud of: "It's better to start with order and move toward chaos than to start in chaos and move toward order," Batali once explained, "because as a business model, chaos doesn't work."

It's a work ethic that has served him well, a quick scan of his food empire will reveal, but there's also his love of food, Italian food.

Batali was born into a Seattle family of serious food lovers. His father was Italian, his mother French Canadian, and everyone in the family, be it sibling, cousin or grandmother, could cook. Conversations at lunch would center on what would be cooked at dinner; at dinner, the chat was about the following day's lunch. To eat well and interestingly was simply natural. Batali once recalled visiting a friend's house for the first time. He took a peek inside the fridge, spotted a sausage in a packet and said to his friend: "You can buy that? Where'd you get this?" Chez Batali they only ever made their own sausages.

His love of food was entrenched. An attempt to divert his mind by studying for a degree in seventeenth-century Spanish theater gained him a qualification but not a vocation to delve further into the works of monk-playwright Tirso de Molina or the Mexican nun Sor Juana Inés de la Cruz. Instead, with the backing of his parents, he went to London to study at the UK branch of the Cordon Bleu school (see p. 190). Except the lure of working in a real establishment meant he couldn't stick the course, which is why he then found himself having pans of risotto thrown at him by Marco Pierre White.

But having learned how not to run a kitchen he then took a job that finally cemented his family-nurtured love for Italian cuisine. For three years he worked in a trattoria in the tiny northern Italian town of Borgo Capanne.

"I learned how to really capture the essence, which is the simplicity which makes Italian food so good," he later recalled. "It was less about what I learned, but more about what I learned not to do." He remembered tasting a dish of spaghetti with zucchini and asking what was in it, to simply get the reply, "Well, zucchini."

"It's crazy how delicious it can be when there's less of the chef's ego and just perfectly cooked spaghetti, sautéed zucchini and maybe a mint leaf," he said.

Thus armed with his new but deep insights into Italian cooking, he returned to New York and with a partner, Joe Bastianich, opened his first restaurant, Babbo Ristorante e Enoteca, in Manhattan. Babbo, which means "Daddy" in the Bolognese dialect—and both Batali and Bastianich were new daddies—turned out local dishes using Italian techniques. And it did so in an environment that combined smart elegance with extremely loud rock music.

Batali refused to turn down the music and refused to play operatic arias ("We don't take requests," he would say), and he introduced a new concept, which in his own words was that "the customer was not always right." He dressed in shorts with orange clogs and with his hair still tied back in that ponytail. The critics loved him and Babbo, the *New York Times* hailing it with three stars. His restaurant, book and TV empire-building could begin.

But of his many endeavors it was the publication of his eighth book in 2010, based on the food served at his New York establishment (with a Las Vegas offshoot) Otto Enoteca Pizzeria, that encapsulated his Italian culinary spirit.

Molto Gusto was filled with short and simple recipes that would achieve, he wrote in the introduction, "a kind of happy passing sense of content and fullness not associated with the consumption of a huge steak or chop.

"This cookbook," he continued, "is radically different from all of the others I have written in its complete lack of traditional main courses."

He wanted people to eat smaller plates of food, less reliant on a big main course and with protein coming from small portions of cured meat, cheeses or grains. Animal protein was used as flavoring and his own dictate on pasta sauce was that a large part of it should be left behind in the pan. "Italians eat their pasta quite al dente and sauced in a very light and minimal way," he wrote.

Batali published recipes for such dishes as green beans with charred onions, lentils with pancetta, the awesome yet simple spaghetti with butter, as well as pizzas and gelato.

He also made a strong case for salad, stating, "There is no question that, as a category, the most nourishing and healthy things to eat from the entire world of soil and gardens are the edible leafy foliage and greens that lie in the sun above the earth itself."

Batali would have found a soul mate in John Evelyn (see p. 121), who was proselytizing on the merits of salad leaves in 1699.

And it is his recipe for Spaghetti alla carbonara that particularly appeals to the author of this book and is the one that should be marked for posterity. There is no garlic, no cream, there are no onions, no shallots and no wine.

Batali pares down the ingredients and masters the dish by whisking egg whites into the pancetta (with water used to cook the pasta) and serves a raw yolk onto each finished plate. It is the perfect carbonara. Although, as flawless as it is, one can't be sure that Marco Pierre White wouldn't throw it all over his old chum.

100

Meat fruit
(or foie gras & chicken liver parfait)

AUTHORS: Heston Blumenthal and Ashley Palmer-Watts
FROM: The menu at Dinner by Heston Blumenthal, Knightsbridge, London

THIS RECIPE MAKES ONE TERRINE (10 X 4 X 3.5 IN)

100 g finely sliced shallots
3 g minced garlic
15 g sprigs of thyme, tied with string
150 g dry Madeira
150 g ruby port
75 g white port
50 g brandy
250 g foie gras (trimmed weight)
150 g chicken livers (trimmed weight)
18 g table salt
240 g eggs
300 g unsalted butter, melted

Place the shallots, garlic and thyme in a saucepan with the Madeira, ruby port, white port and brandy. Set aside to marinate for 24 hours.

Heat the marinated mixture until nearly all the liquid has evaporated, stirring regularly to prevent the shallots and garlic from burning. Remove from the heat and discard the thyme.

Preheat the oven to 100°C (212°F). Fill a bain-marie with 5 cm water and place in the oven.

Preheat a water bath to 50°C (122°F).

Cut the foie gras into pieces roughly the same size as the chicken livers. Sprinkle the table salt over the livers and mix well.

Put the livers and foie gras in a sous-vide bag. Put the eggs and the alcohol reduction in a second sous-vide bag, and the butter in a third. Seal all the bags under full pressure, then place in the water bath for 20 minutes. Remove the bags from the water bath.

Combine the eggs, alcohol reduction and meats in a Thermomix and blend until smooth at 50°C (122°F). Slowly blitz in the butter and blend until smooth. Pass the mix through a fine sieve using the back of a small ladle.

Pour into a terrine dish and place in the bain-marie and cover the bain-marie with aluminum foil. Cook the parfait until the temperature in the centre reaches 64°C (147°F).

Remove from the oven and allow to cool. Refrigerate for 24 hours before serving.

Eighteen months before the launch of his new restaurant in London, chef Heston Blumenthal hired some office space with a kitchen a couple of miles away from Bray, in Berkshire. There he installed Ashley Palmer-Watts, head chef of his famed restaurant the Fat Duck. The chef's task was to spend the ensuing weeks and months honing recipes for Dinner by Heston Blumenthal, which would open in the heart of the capital's swanky Knightsbridge district, at the chic Mandarin Oriental Hotel.

A very unusual project, it would cost thousands of pounds and was unheard of in the restaurant business. Usually if a chef wanted to devise new recipes, he or she would do it between services. But Blumenthal and Palmer-Watts were developing dishes that hadn't been seen on a menu before—or not for several hundred years.

The last time "rice and flesh," for example, had been eaten in Britain was in the fourteenth century. Indeed a recipe for it appears in *The Forme of Cury* (see p. 49), written in 1390 by the master cook of King Richard II. Such recipes needed a little updating for the modern palate and, as Blumenthal was a perfectionist, to say the least, and the menu had several dozen ancient dishes, it was going to take some time. "It was a lot of money and effort," confirmed Palmer-Watts. "It's very difficult to be creative either side of service as a head chef, but I've never heard of anyone doing quite what we did."

While there were recipes to be explored from across the centuries, all of them celebrating the rich traditions of British food, there was one dish that seemed to encapsulate the spirit of the new restaurant: a dish that drew Blumenthal away from the experimental and whacky cooking at the Fat Duck and into the depths of history. "When I first started looking at historic recipes, particularly from medieval times, there was one dish that really attracted my attention," he said. "Just because it was completely mad: meat fruit."

His attention was captured by the playfulness of medieval chefs. He was especially fascinated by recipes by the likes of Taillevent (see p. 46) from the fourteenth century. Following up this interest with food historians and researchers at Hampton Court Palace, he recalled how "a whole new world opened up to [him]." It was a seam of recipes that was as yet untapped.

He then tracked down food historian Ivan Day who spent his life cooking ancient dishes. "He'd pull out a book worth thousands of pounds from his shelf and start cooking from it," said Blumenthal. "All the hard work I do, everything is worth it for moments like that."

Blumenthal then developed a number of recipes—from beef royale and chocolate wine to lemon salad and lamb in cucumber—for the Fat Duck and his pub the Hinds Head, before realizing that he actually had a concept for an entire restaurant. Unwilling to open a second Fat Duck, in spite of encouragement from people in the restaurants and catering industry, he settled on Dinner in Knightsbridge. Meanwhile, Palmer-Watts had to get the recipes, and that meat fruit dish in particular, to work.

The Tudors were reluctant to eat raw fruit and vegetables, thinking it would make them ill. And so it amused chefs to make meat look like fruit. They made pork balls look like apples, for instance, using parsley and saffron as coloring. And while they were at it, fashioned pretend hedgehogs out of pâté using slivered almonds as spikes. But, as food historian Peter Brears has pointed out, this was nothing compared to their other culinary sleights of hand, such as, for example, sewing the front end of a pig to the back end of a cock to produce a beast that would raise the eyebrows of even the most outré of kings.

While these chefs had ingenious ideas, Blumenthal had the advantage of modern technology to draw upon. His version of meat fruit was achieved using flexible rubber molds, digital probes and liquid nitrogen. But the effect was just as magical. When it finally appeared on the menu at Dinner, to mark the opening of the restaurant in January 2011, it delighted the modern diner as much as its ancient forebear would have entertained the medieval banqueter.

The modern version of the meat fruit recipe, as perfected by Palmer-Watts, consisted of a chicken liver and foie gras parfait, frozen and dipped in a mandarin jelly that dried, by pure chance due to the temperature of the parfait (refrozen speedily by liquid nitrogen before a second dip), with little dimples so that, with the addition of a mandarin leaf, it looked just like the fruit in question. The dish was a triumph—soon every diner wanted one as an appetizer. And the restaurant triumphed too. "When most people open a restaurant they just hope they can fill the place," Palmer-Watts reflected six months after the launch. "We just try and control the number of people that we can let in through the door."

What Blumenthal had planned as an informal bistro that served technically very good food—but that looked simple and tasted delicious—became the new symbol of fine dining. In 2011, the restaurant everyone in London wanted to get a table at didn't have any froths or drizzles or swirls. Instead there was risotto, pork chops and rib of beef. And it was all very different from the Fat Duck where Blumenthal had made his name. There he famously served snail porridge, egg and bacon ice cream and sardine sorbets. His ingenious toying with people's expectations of taste and flavor earned the restaurant three Michelin stars in its first five years.

But it had started as a more simple, French-style bistro. Blumenthal, whose interest in cooking was galvanized during a family trip to a Michelin-starred restaurant in Provence (Oustau de Baumanière)—"I still remember the sounds of chinking glasses, cutlery on crockery, the crunch of the waiters' feet on the gravel. They were carving legs of lamb at the tables, pouring sauces into soufflés," he recalled—was self-taught, except for a brief stint in the kitchens of Raymond Blanc's Le Manoir aux Quat'Saisons.

While working in a variety of jobs from trainee architect to photocopier salesman, Blumenthal spent his evenings wading through French cookbooks and experimenting in the kitchen. To finance the Fat Duck, he sold the cottage he shared with his wife, Susanna, and moved back to his parents' house, spending some nights sleeping at the back of the restaurant on dirty tea towels.

"If I'd known how hard it would be I'd never have started it," he once said. But having successfully produced a menu that replicated his favorite French dishes, he began to experiment. "I'm very inquisitive by nature," he said and his curiosity led him

Through his obsession with the past, Heston Blumenthal has turned old medieval recipes, such as meat fruit, into contemporary dishes using modern technology.

to create what he described as "multi-sensory effects, surprising tastes and a bit of theater at the table."

The Fat Duck influenced a new generation of chefs to think more deeply about the food they cooked—albeit often with disastrous results when they tried it on their own. Dinner then followed. Launched at a time when London was viewed as having the best restaurant scene in the world, it changed the perception of fine dining yet again. "For a chef so thoroughly modern, Heston Blumenthal is surprisingly obsessed with the past," declared the food-industry bible the *Caterer* in January 2011. Yet his warm homage to Britain's culinary past, viewed through deliciously rose-tinted spectacles, sets us on a firm path into the future.

Select bibliography

BOOKS

Accum, F., *Culinary Chemistry* (London: R. Ackermann, 1821).

Adriá, F., *A Day at elBulli* (Phaidon Press, 2008).

Austin, T. (ed.), *Two Fifteenth-Century Cookery-Books* (Oxford: Oxford University Press, 1888).

Batali, M., *Molto Gusto* (New York: Ecco, 2010).

Beeton, I. (ed.), *Beeton's Book of Household Management* (London: S. O. Beeton Publishing, 1861).

Berno, F. R., "Cheese's Revenge: Pantaleone da Confienza and the *Summa Lacticiniorum*" in *Petits Propos Culinaires*, vol. 69 (2002), pp. 21–44.

Black, M. *The Medieval Cook* (London: British Museum Press, 1992).

Blythman, J., *The Food We Eat* (London: Penguin Books, 1996).

——, *Shopped: The Shocking Power of British Supermarkets* (London: Harper, Perennial, 2005).

Bober, P. P., *Art, Culture, and Cuisine: Ancient and Medieval Gastronomy* (Chicago: University of Chicago Press, 1999).

Bottéro, J., *The Oldest Cuisine in the World: Cooking in Mesopotamia*, trans. T. L. Fagan (Chicago: University of Chicago Press, 2004).

Boulestin, M., *Savouries and Hors-d'Oeuvre* (London: William Heinemann, 1932).

Brears, P., *Cooking and Dining in Medieval England* (Totnes: Prospect Books, 2008).

Cassell's Dictionary of Cookery (London, Paris and New York: Cassell, Petter and Galpin, 1896).

Chaney, L., *Elizabeth David* (London: Macmillan, 1998).

Chao, B., *How to Cook and Eat in Chinese* (London: Penguin Books, 1956).

Clarkson, J., *Pie: A Global History* (London: Reaktion Books, 2009).

——, *Soup* (London: Reaktion Books, 2010).

Crocker, B., *Betty Crocker's Dinner Parties* (New York: Golden Press, 1970).

Le Cuisinier gascon (Paris: L'Arche du livre, 1970).

Dalby, A., *Cheese: A Global History* (London: Reaktion Books, 2009).

——, *Siren Feasts: A History of Food and Gastronomy in Greece* (London: Routledge, 1996).

Daves, J., *The Vogue Book of Menus and Recipes for Entertaining at Home* (New York: Harper & Row, 1964).

David, E., *A Book of Mediterranean Food and Other Writings*, 3rd edn (London: Folio Society, 2005).

——, *French Provincial Cooking* (London: Penguin Books, 1960).

Davidson, A. (ed.), *The Oxford Companion to Food*, 2nd edn (Oxford: Oxford University Press, 2006).

Deutsch, T., 2010, *Building a Housewife's Paradise: Gender, Politics, and American Grocery Stores in the Twentieth Century* (Chapel Hill, N.C.: University of North Carolina Press, 2010).

Farmer, F., *The Boston Cooking-School Cook Book* (Boston: Little, Brown & Company, 1929).

Frieda, L., 2003, *Catherine de Medici* (London: Phoenix, 2003).

Gains, T., *A Complete System of Cookery* (London: J. Weston, 1838).

Garrett, T. F. (ed.), *The Encyclopedia of Practical Cookery* (London: L. Upcott Gill, 1892).

Glasse, H., *First Catch Your Hare: The Art of Cookery Made Plain and Easy* (Totnes: Prospect Books, 2004).

Gouffé, J., *The Royal Cookery Book*, trans. A. Gouffé (London: Sampson Low, Son and Marston, 1868).

Greco, G. L., and Rose, C. M. (eds. and trans.), *The Good Wife's Guide (Le Ménagier de Paris)* (Ithaca and London: Cornell University Press, 2009).

Grossman, L., *MasterChef* (London: BBC Books, 1990).

Hartley, D., *Food in England* (London: Macdonald, 1954).

Haywood, J., *Encyclopaedia of the Viking Age* (London: Thames & Hudson, 2000).

Henisch, B. A., *The Medieval Cook,* (Woodbridge: Boydell Press, 2009).
Hieatt, C. B., Hosington, B., and Butler, S., *Pleyn Delit: Medieval Cookery for Modern Cooks* (Toronto: University of Toronto Press, 1976).
Howells, M., *Fondue and Table Top Cookery* (London: Octopus Books, 1977).
Ignotus, *Culina Famulatrix Medicinae: or, Receipts in Modern Cookery* (York: J. Mawman, 1906).
Jaffrey, M., *Climbing the Mango Trees* (London: Ebury Press, 2005).
——, *An Invitation to Indian Cooking* (London: Jonathan Cape, 1976).
Jochens, J., *Women in Old Norse Society* (Ithaca, NY: Cornell University Press, 1995).
Keller, T., *The French Laundry Cookbook* (Artisan, 1999).
———, *Under Pressure: Cooking Sous Vide* (Artisan, 2008).
Kelly, I., *Cooking for Kings: The Life of Antonin Carême, the First Celebrity Chef* (London: Short Books, 2003).
Kiple, K. F., and Kriemhild, C. O. (eds.), *The Cambridge World History of Food* (Cambridge: Cambridge University Press, 2000).
Kitchiner, W., *The Cook's Oracle* (London: Cadell and Co., 1829).
Knight, K., *Spuds, Spam and Eating for Victory: Rationing in the Second World War* (Stroud: Tempus Publishing, 2004).
Kurlansky, M., *Salt: A World History* (New York: Walker, 2002).
Lappé, F. M., *Diet for a Small Planet* (New York: Random House, 1971).
Larousse Gastronomique: The World's Greatest Cookery Encyclopedia (London: Hamlyn, 2001).
Lawrence, F., *Not on the Label* (London: Penguin Books, 2004).
Limpo, B.R., *O Livro de Pantagruel* (1945).
Lin, F., *Florence Lin's Chinese Vegetarian Cookbook* (Boulder, CO: Shambhala, 1983).
Luck, Mrs B., (ed.), *The Belgian Cook Book* (London: William Heinemann, 1915).
Marinetti, F. T., *The Futurist Cook Book, ed. Lesley Chamberlain* (Bedford Arts, 1989).
Mason, C., *The Ladies' Assistant for Regulating and Supplying the Table,* 6th edn (London: J. Walter, 1787).
Mason, L., *Sugar-plums and Sherbet: The Prehistory of Sweets* (Totnes: Prospect Books, 2004).
——, and Brown, C., *The Taste of Britain* (London: Harper Press, 2006).
McNamee, T., *Alice Waters and Chez Panisse: The romantic, impractical, often eccentric, ultimately brilliant making of a food revolution* (Penguin Press, 2007).
Moss, S., and Badenoch, A., *Chocolate* (London: Reaktion Books, 2009).
Norman, C., *Microwave Cookery for the Housewife* (London: Pitman, 1974).
Ó Gráda, C., *Famine: A Short History* (Princeton, NJ: Princeton University Press, 2009).
Patten, M., *Feeding the Nation: Nostalgic Recipes and Facts from 1940–1954* (London: Hamlyn, 2005).
——, *The Victory Cookbook* (London: Hamlyn, 1995).
Peterson, T. S., *The Cookbook that Changed the World: The Origins of Modern Cuisine* (Stroud: Tempus, 2006).
Petrini, C., *The Slow Food Revolution* (New York: Rizzoli, 2005).
van der Post, L. *African Cooking* (Time Life Books, 1970).
Power, E. (trans.), *The Goodman of Paris (Le Ménagier de Paris): A Treatise on Moral and Domestic Economy by a Citizen of Paris* (London: G. Routledge & Sons, 1928).
Quinzio, J., *Of Sugar and Snow: A History of Ice Cream Making* (Berkeley, CA: University of California Press, 2009).
Riddervold, A., and Ropeid, A., *Food Conservation* (London: Prospect Books, 1988).
Ridgway, J., *The Cheese Companion* (London: Apple, 1999).
Rombauer, I., and Becker, M. R., 1999, *Joy of Cooking* (New York: Simon & Schuster, 1999).
Rundell, M., *A New System of Domestic Cookery,* ed. E. Roberts (London: John Murray, 1840).
Saberi, H., *Trifle* (Totnes: Prospect Books, 2001).

Sass, L., *To The King's Taste: Richard II's Book of Feasts and Recipes* (London: John Murray, 1976).
Scully, D. E., and Scully, T., *Early French Cookery: Sources, History, Original Recipes and Modern Adaptations* (Ann Arbor, MI: University of Michigan Press, 1995).
Scully, T. (ed. and trans.), *La Varenne's Cookery: The French Cook; the French Pastry Chef; the French Confectioner* (Totnes: Prospect Books, 2006).
——, *The Opera of Bartolomeo Scappi (1570): L'arte et prudenza d'un maestro cuoco (The Art and Craft of a Master Cook)* (Toronto: University of Toronto Press, 2008).
Serventi, S., and Sabban, F., *Pasta: The Story of a Universal Food* (New York: Columbia University Press, 2002).
Sidorick, D., *Condensed Capitalism: Campbell Soup and the Pursuit of Cheap Production in the Twentieth Century* (Ithaca, NY: Cornell University Press, 2009).
Smith, A. F., *Eating History: 30 Turning Points in the Making of American Cuisine* (New York: Columbia University Press, 2009).
Snodgrass, M. E., *Encyclopedia of Kitchen History* (New York: Fitzroy Dearborn, 2004).
Spencer, C., *British Food: An Extraordinary Thousand Years of History* (London: Grub Street, 2002).
——, *From Microliths to Microwaves* (London: Grub Street, 2011).
——, *Vegetarianism: A History* (London: Grub Street, 2000).
Spurling, H. (ed.), *Elinor Fettiplace's Receipt Book: Elizabethan Country House Cooking* (London: Penguin Books, 1987).
Stapley, C. (ed.), *The Receipt Book of Lady Anne Blencowe* (Basingstoke: Heartsease, 2004).
Stobart, T., *The Cook's Encyclopaedia* (London: B. T. Batsford, 1980).
Tames, R., 2003, *Feeding London: A Taste of History* (London: Historical Publication, 2003).
Toussaint-Samat, Maguelonne, *A History of Food,* trans. A. Bell (Oxford: Wiley-Blackwell, 2009).
Trager, J., *The Food Chronology: A Food Lover's Compendium of Events and Anecdotes from Prehistory to the Present* (London: Aurum Press, 1996).
Vehling, J. D. (ed. and trans.), *Apicius: Cookery and Dining in Imperial Rome* (New York: Dover Publications, 1977).
Waters, A., *Chez Panisse Fruit* (William Morrow Cookbooks, 2003).
White, M. P., *White Slave* (London: Orion, 2006).
Whitley, A., 2006, *Bread Matters* (London: Fourth Estate, 2006).
Willan, A., *Great Cooks and their Recipes: From Taillevent to Escoffier* (London: Pavilion, 2000).
Wilkins, J., Harvey, D. and Dobson, M. (eds.), *Food in Antiquity* (Exeter: University of Exeter Press, 1995).
Wilson, B., *Sandwich: A Global History* (London: Reaktion Books, 2010).
Wilson, C. A., *The Book of Marmalade: Its Antecedents, its History and its Role in the World Today* (London: Constable, 1985).
Yeatman, M., *The Last Food of England* (London: Ebury Press, 2007).
Zaouali, L., *Medieval Cuisine of the Islamic World: A Concise History with 174 Recipes,* trans. M. B. DeBevoise (Berkeley, CA: University of California Press, 2007).

WEBSITES

digital.lib.msu.edu/projects/cookbooks
www.federationoffishfriers.co.uk
www.foodnetwork.com
www.foodreference.com
www.foodtimeline.org
www.gutenberg.org
www.historicfood.com
www.history-magazine.com
www.mrsbeeton.com
www.theoldfoodie.com
www.vegsoc.org

Index

Text credits

The author and publisher would like to thank the following:

"Quick oatmeal cookies" by Irma Rombauer reprinted with the permission of Scribner, a Division of Simon & Schuster, Inc., from *Joy of Cooking* by Irma S. Rombauer and Marion Rombauer Becker. Copyright © 1931, 1936, 1941, 1942, 1943, 1946, 1951, 1952, 1953, 1962, 1963, 1964, 1975 by Simon & Schuster, Inc. copyright 1997 by Simon & Schuster, Inc., The Joy of Cooking Trust and The MRB Revocable Trust. All rights reserved; "Omelette" from *Recipes of Boulestin* reprinted by permission of Peters Fraser and Dunlop (www.petersfraserdunlop.com) on behalf of the Estate of Xavier Marcel Boulestin; Kellogg's® for "Rice Krispies treats"; Kenwood for "Victoria sandwich cake" from *All About Your New Kenwood Chef*; "Cassoulet toulousain" from *A Book of Mediterranean Food* by Elizabeth David. John Lehmann Ltd. London, 1950; "Cheese fondue," recipe courtesy of Betty Crocker; "Mediterranean lemon soup with Middle Eastern tacos" from *Diet for a Small Planet*, by Frances Moore Lappé; "Plum tart" from *The Menu at Chez Panisse* by Alice Waters and Lindsey Shere, 1971, copyright © 2002, used by permission of William Morrow, a division of HarperCollins, Inc., New York, all rights reserved; "Salmon fish cakes" from *How to Cheat at Cooking* by Delia Smith, 1976, reproduced by permission of Hodder and Stoughton Limited; "Lamb korma" from *An Invitation to Indian Cooking*, by Madhur Jaffrey, 1973, used by permission of Alfred A. Knopf, a division of Random House Inc.; "Sweet and sour pork" from Ken Hom's *Chinese Cookery* and *Complete Chinese Cookbook*, by Ken Hom, published by BBC Books; Liliana and Lisetta Burlotto for "Giura (Slow-braised beef)"; Rowley Leigh for "Chicken & goat's cheese mousse with olives"; Marco Pierre White for "Tagliatelle of oyster with caviar"; *Gourmet* for "Individual sausage, tomato & artichoke-heart pizzas"; "Salmon tartare with sweet red onion crème fraîche" from *The French Laundry Cookbook* by Thomas Keller, copyright © 1999, used by permission of Artisan, a division of Workman Publishing Co., Inc., New York, all rights reserved; "Fairy Cakes" from *How to Be a Domestic Goddess*, by Nigella Lawson, 2000; Jane Baxter/Riverford Organic for "Bacon, leek and potato gratin"; "Asian salad with ponzu ginger dressing & wasabi peas" from *Simply Salads* by Jennifer Chandler; "Steamed brioche with rose-scented mozzarella" from *A Day at elBulli* by Ferran Adrià, copyright © 2008, used by permission of Phaidon Press Ltd., London, all rights reserved; Jamie Oliver for "Steamed salmon with tomato basil couscous"; "Spaghetti alla carbonara" from *Molto Gusto: Easy Italian Cooking* by Mario Batali and Mark Ladner, copyright © 2010 by Mario Batali and Mark Ladner, reprinted by permission of HarperCollins Publishers. Heston Blumenthal and Ashley Palmer-Watts for "Meat fruit (or foie gras & chicken liver parfait)."

Note: While every effort has been made to trace the owners of copyright material reproduced herein and secure permissions, the publishers would like to apologize for any omissions and will be pleased to incorporate missing acknowledgments in any future edition of this book.

Picture credits

The author and publisher would like to thank the following:

Werner Forman Archive: 13; Yale Babylonian Collection: 15; Bridgeman Art Library: Biblioteca Estense Universitaria, Modena, Italy 18; Musée de la Tapisserie, Bayeux, France / With special authorisation of the city of Bayeux / Giraudon 38; The McEwan Collection, National Trust Photographic Library / Derrick E. Witty 82; National Portrait Gallery, London, UK 111; CNAM, Conservatoire National des Arts et Métiers, Paris / Giraudon 116; Private Collection / © Charles Plante Fine Arts 131; Getty Images: Photographer's Choice / Thomae Barwick 137; Château Blérancourt, Picardie, France / Giraudon 146; Musée de la Ville de Paris, Musée Carnavalet, Paris, France / Giraudon 158; Bibliothèque des Arts Décoratifs, Paris, France / Archives Charmet 165; Alamy: Mary Evans Picture Library 27; Dinodia Photos 178; Lebrecht Music and Arts Photo Library 183 (l); Mary Evans Picture Library 200; Ancient Art & Architecture Collection Ltd: Uniphoto Japan 34; Topfoto: The Granger Collection, New York 36, 161; The Art Archive: Marc Charmet 43; Bibliothèque de l'Arsenal Paris / Kharbine-Tapabor / Coll. Jean Vigne 57; Templo Mayor Library Mexico / Gianni Dagli Orti 75; Biblioteca Nacional Madrid / Gianni Dagli Orti 79; Private collection 48, 175, 191; The British Library: © The British Library Board (Add. 5016, back of roll, 3rd membrane) 51; (IB.41688, Riii verso) 54; (MS 4016 f.5 verso) 59; (Shelfmark 1037.e.22) 108; (Shelfmark 1037.e.13) 114; (Shelfmark 1570/435) 119; Octavo Corp and The Library of Congress: 67; British Museum: © The Trustees of the British Museum: 71; The Provost and Fellows of Worcester College, Oxford 89; William Bird: © The Estate of William Bird, 2012 98; RMN: © RMN (Château de Versailles) / Gérard Blot 122; Mary Evans Picture Library: 153; Rue des Archives / PVDE 183 (r); © Illustrated London News Ltd 207; Mary Evans Picture Library 218, 227; Scala: Photo Ann Ronan / Heritage Images 171; Getty Images: Museum of the City of New York / Byron Collection 189; Kurt Hutton / Picture Post / Hulton Archive 240; New York Times Co. / Archive Photos 263; Arthur Schatz / Time & Life Pictures 266; Christopher Pillitz 310; Dave Benett 329; Corbis: Bettmann 193; Underwood & Underwood 215; BBC 237; The Salvation Army International Heritage Centre 203; akg-images: 210; The Advertising Archives (Images courtesy of): 223, 247, 268, 289; Royal College of Art / Peter Harrington Books (photograph of book) 259; Superstock: Prisma 274; Scope Features: 281; Rex Features: Denis Jones / Evening Standard 293; Corbis: A day at elBulli 323; Chris Ratcliffe 335; Camera Press: Jason Bell 304; The Guardian: Sarah Lee 351.

Acknowledgments

So many have given encouragement and helped during the course of researching and writing this book that I should really thank everyone that I have come in contact with since Thursday 1 April 2010. For that was the day Iain MacGregor, publishing director at HarperCollins, met with me at a café on Holland Park Avenue in London and very sensibly, and with great wisdom and foresight, kindly—and not as an April Fool—commissioned the book. So thank you all and apologies for boring you to tears about it. Heartfelt thanks also to Michael Sand, executive editor at Little, Brown and Company, NYC, for bringing my book to a whole new audience in the United States.

Huge thanks to my researcher Georgia Machell, without whom I would have floundered around in a muddy pool of food facts. Thanks for your amazing intelligence and knowledge, being a constant and sensible sounding board and for efficiently guiding me through the structure of the book. Georgia introduced me to the wonders of the unique and free resource that is the British Library, whose staff never fail to courteously dig out whatever ancient tome is requested. And apologies to all those who had to suffer my ridiculously loud typing style in the quiet surroundings of the Rare Books and Music Reading Room.

My colleagues at John Brown have supported and encouraged me throughout, so big thanks to everyone, particularly Tabitha, Kerry, Ben, Ollie, James, Dinny, Sam, Daniel (and his wonderful other half, Thea Lenarduzzi, who helped with some translating of ancient Italian texts, as did Anne Jones's buddy James Gherardi and Ciro Gargiulo), Gillian, Jessica, Marina, Eleanor, Emma, Kim, Libby, Dean and Venu (of course!), and especially the saintly Venetia. Thanks also to all those work experience interns—or slaves, as we call them—who thought they were coming in to work on *Waitrose Kitchen* magazine and discovered they were actually researching *A History of Food in 100 Recipes*. Particular thanks to Jason, Hannah, Katherine and Millie. My thanks also to Alison Oakervee and Ollie Rice, compatriots in retail customer publishing. But, above all, heartfelt thanks to the inspirational and wise Andrew Hirsch who has ceaselessly given me support to pursue various foodie projects, but more importantly time to write this book.

There are many I should thank who work for chefs and cooks or who are PRs who assist me in my food writing: Maureen, Jo, Anouschka, Katrina and Andrea, and particularly Monica Brown and Melanie Grocott. Thanks also for the journalistic advice of James Steen, and of Dominic and Rose Prince, who introduced me to Professor Tim Lang, who found my researcher, and to my old, wonderful friend Simon Brown who took my portrait for this book.

At HarperCollins, as well as Iain, I wish to thank Helen Wedgewood for her constant and calming help and guidance. Also to Caroline Hotblack and Anna Gibson and Caroline March in publicity. I also have special gratitude for Kate Parker who expertly and subtly—and with a keen eye for my many typos and howlers—edited the manuscript. Any remaining errors are all mine. Many thanks also to my brilliant agent Caroline Michel and also to Nelle Andrew at PFD.

Finally, thanks to my family and friends but especially to my darling wife, Laura, who coped with me for so many months—with every weekend destroyed—as I sat in my study thumping out words only to come up for air in a stressed and hungry grump now and again. I promise I might start cooking—oh, and shopping for food, even—in 2012. Then much love to my children, Alice and Albert. In answer to Albert's question, "Daddy, are you going to use my fact that pigs kill more people each year than sharks?" well, little man, I have now. Then, to my friends Jasper and Vanessa, you always kept my spirits up, but nothing stopped me complaining about the volume of work and seeing that it was just a walk in the park so much as Toby and Gaby. Thanks for showing us all the real meaning of hope and fighting spirit.

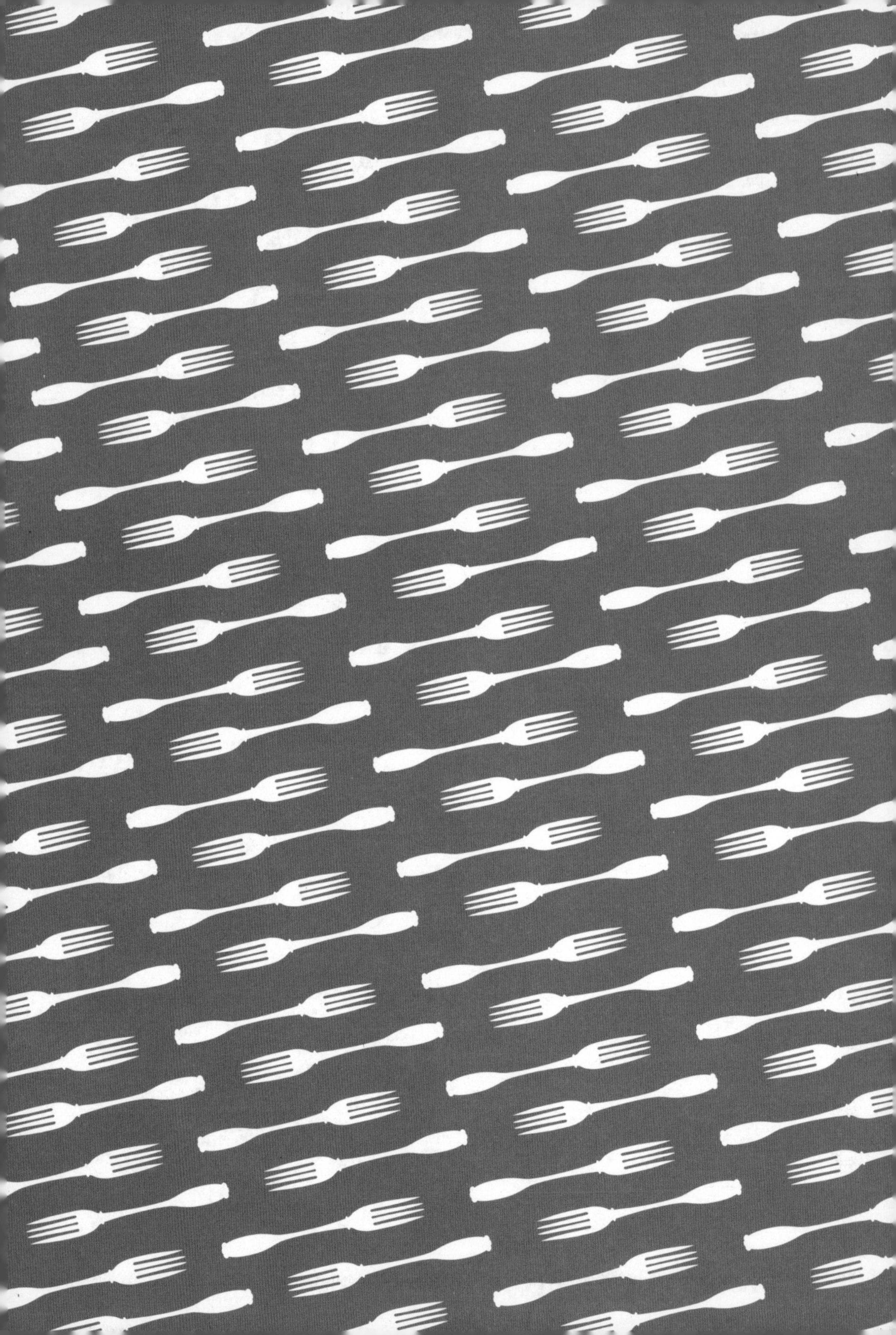